THE AMERICAN READER

The hand and torch of Frédéric-Auguste Bartholdi's Liberty Enlightening the World, now known as the Statue of Liberty, on display in Philadelphia's Fairmount Park during the 1876 Centennial Exposition. It was exhibited to launch a fund-raising drive for the statue and its pedestal. A souvenir stand was set up in the hollow base.

THE AMERICAN READER

WORDS THAT MOVED A NATION

Edited by

Diane Ravitch

HarperCollins*Publishers*

For Mary

If you wou'd not be forgotten
As soon as you are dead and rotten,
Either write things worth reading,
Or do things worth the writing.

Benjamin Franklin
Poor Richard's Almanack

THE AMERICAN READER. Copyright © 1990 by Diane Ravitch.

All rights reserved. Printed in the United States of America. No part of this book may be used or reproduced in any manner whatsoever without written permission except in the case of brief quotations embodied in critical articles and reviews. For information address HarperCollins Publishers, 10 East 53rd Street, New York, N.Y. 10022.

FIRST EDITION

Designed by Joan Greenfield
Photo research by Sabra Moore

Library of Congress Cataloging-in-Publication Data

The American reader : words that moved a nation / edited by
   Diane Ravitch. — 1st ed.
      p.   cm.
   Includes bibliographical references and index.
   ISBN 0-06-016480-8
      1. United States—History—Sources.   I. Ravitch, Diane.
E173.A753   1990
081—dc20   89-46553

90 91 92 93 94   **RRD** 10 9 8 7 6 5 4 3 2 1

CONTENTS

ANTEBELLUM AMERICA: REFORM AND EXPANSION

PRELUDE TO WAR

THE CIVIL WAR

AFTER THE CIVIL WAR

THE PROGRESSIVE AGE

AFTER WORLD WAR II

TROUBLED TIMES

CONTEMPORARY TIMES

INTRODUCTION

The American Reader aims to put its readers into direct contact with the words that inspired, enraged, delighted, chastened, or comforted Americans in days gone by. Gathered here are the classic speeches, poems, arguments, and songs that illuminate—with wit, eloquence, or sharp words—significant aspects of American life.

The imagined audience of *The American Reader* is a group of family or friends, sharing with each other a favorite poem or discovering for the first time a stirring speech. In choosing the contents, I looked for entries that almost everyone once seemed to know, words that resonated in the national consciousness, words that have a timeless quality for the listener and reader. I looked for entries that in their time were widely discussed, that possess literary quality, and that deserve to be remembered. Many of the recent pieces—those that were written since 1970—are not yet established as classics, and perhaps they never will be. But in an anthology of this sort, it is necessary to place bets when dealing with recent work. Not every entry fulfills every criterion, but all, in some manner, speak to the age of which they were part.

A guiding principle for selection of entries was suggested by these questions: What should a reader look like at this time in our history? Who should be added to the pantheon of oft-heard American voices? In my search, I found more material of a very high caliber than I could ever use. I discovered speakers and writers who should be read and heard because of their eloquence and because of the light that they shine on the past and the present. Given the vast number of candidates worthy of inclusion, I could easily have produced several volumes, rather than only one. The number of impassioned speeches, moving poems, and wonderful songs in the American past is far greater than any one volume could encompass.

This collection does not represent every important event in American history; some did not inspire either great oratory or memorable songs. Nor does it represent every major voice; I did not include, for example, those who preached disunion or hatred toward others.

In shaping this collection, I was mindful of the school readers of the nineteenth century, like the *McGuffey's Readers* and the *Sanders' Readers.* Compiled as anthologies, they were the kind of books that families saved and savored. In a similar spirit, this collection offers its readers a respite from the bland and the banal. It contains ample doses of principled rhetoric, angry demands, joyous verse, and uplifting sentiment. Although the longer pieces had to be condensed, the words belong to the original speaker. They have not been homogenized or pasteurized for contemporary consumption. Almost every piece can be read aloud with pleasure. Most of them, at least those written before the mid-twentieth century, were written to be declaimed. Poems and songs, of course, are meant to be recited or sung aloud, not just read silently. Poetry works best when it is spoken and heard. Young people don't read much poetry today; they seldom hear it read out loud or recite it themselves. Most of the poems that they read in school lack the pounding rhythm and the decided rhyme that causes the poem to become a permanent tenant in the brain.

Almost no one memorizes anything anymore, except perhaps baseball statistics or commercial jingles or the comparative prices of consumer goods. But there is something wonderful about having a poem or a song or the rhetorical crest of a speech available for instant recall. When beautiful speeches and poems are memorized, they remain with you as a lifelong resource. Words that are learned "by heart" become one's personal treasure. In some curious way, they are committed to "memory" but stored lovingly in the "heart." Some things are a pleasure to memorize, a pleasure that one may own and enjoy forever.

The range of good material seems to have narrowed in recent years. This is probably due to the fact that we now live in a visual age, where people learn from blinking screens, not from books or political debates. Words don't seem to matter as much as they used to.

In politics, we know this is so. National political candidates seldom bother to deliver carefully crafted speeches. The candidates campaign not for live audiences but for the television camera. Rather than speak eloquently to an audience of thousands, they try to fashion the riveting sentence or pithy comment that will get them a few seconds on television, where they will be seen and heard by millions of viewers.

Some people think that television has made books obsolete and that the use of inter-active technology in schools and offices will make reading obsolete. Some think that it already has. And it is true that many people live utterly in the present, uninterested in anything that happened before today, indifferent to any words except those they hear in the movies, on the radio, or on television.

But reading is not about to disappear. Despite the ease and immediacy of the electronic media, language will continue to be indispensable for intelligent communication. Those who cannot use it will find themselves manipulated and directed by those who can. Those who only listen and watch will be at the mercy of those who write the scripts, program the computers, interpret the news, and extract meaning from the past. No matter how powerful the technology of the future, we will still rely on the power of words and ideas. Those who can command them will be enabled to affect the world. Those who cannot will find themselves excluded not only from jobs and opportunities but from all those experiences that allow us to reflect on the significance of our lives.

The words here collected reveal an integral part of the dynamic of American life. In a democratic society, the power of persuasion is a necessary ingredient of social change. As our society has evolved, articulate men and women have emerged to advocate, argue, debate, demand, and celebrate. Much of what they said and did has relevance for partisans of democratic ideas throughout the world. As we get to know the history of our society and hear the voices of those who created our energetic, complicated, pluralistic, and humane culture, we will understand ourselves and our times better.

In preparing this book, I incurred many personal debts. I owe my deepest gratitude to Eileen Sclan, who worked tirelessly as my assistant. She had the able assistance of Mary Greenfield, Thalassa Curtis, Indira Mehta, Kelly Walsh, and Adam Brightman. I owe special thanks to Nelida Perez of the Center for Puerto Rican Studies at Hunter College, Richard Chabran of the Chicano Studies Research Center of UCLA, Russell Leong of the Asian-

American Studies Center of UCLA, and Nicolás Kanellos of Arte Público Press at the University of Houston.

I wish to express my deep gratitude to Carol Cohen of HarperCollins, who encouraged me to undertake this project, and to Mary Kay Linge of HarperCollins, who labored long and hard to shepherd these many disparate pages to publication.

Diane Ravitch

COLONIAL DAYS AND
THE REVOLUTION

GEORGE   WASHINGTON

PRESIDENT.

1792.

A 1792 commemorative medal showing President George Washington
and an Indian leader passing a peace pipe.

THE MAYFLOWER COMPACT

We whose names are underwriten... doe by these presents solemnly & mutualy in the presence of God, and one of another, covenant & combine our selves togeather into a civill body politick.

The settling of America began with an idea. The idea was that the citizens of a society could join freely and agree to govern themselves by making laws for the common good.

On November 11, 1620, after sixty-six days at sea, the sailing ship *Mayflower* approached land. On board were 102 passengers. Their destination was the area at the mouth of the Hudson River, but because of rough seas they missed their goal and anchored in what is now Provincetown Harbor off Cape Cod. Since it was late autumn, they decided to make their landing there rather than to sail on. And since they were no longer in the territory for which they had a patent, they signed a covenant before they landed in order to establish a basis for self-government by which all of them were bound.

About a third of the passengers were members of an English separatist congregation that had earlier fled to Leyden, the Netherlands, in search of religious freedom. The entire group of English colonists was later called the Pilgrims. The colonists had negotiated an agreement with the Virginia Company of London that gave them the right to locate wherever they chose in that company's vast holdings and to govern themselves.

Forty-one of the male passengers signed the covenant aboard ship. In what was later known as the Mayflower Compact, the signers pledged to create a body politic that would be based on the consent of the governed and ruled by law. And they further agreed to submit to the laws framed by the new body politic.

The compact was signed by every head of a family, every adult bachelor, and most of the hired manservants aboard the *Mayflower*. It was signed both by separatists and non-separatists. Women were not asked to sign, since they did not have political rights.

On the day after Christmas, the 102 settlers disembarked at what is now Plymouth, Massachusetts. Those who had signed the compact became the governing body of the Plymouth colony, with the power to elect officers, pass laws, and admit new voting members. The covenant entered into on that November day on a ship at anchor in a wilderness harbor established the basis for self-government and the rule of law in the new land.

In the name of God Amen. We whose names are underwritcn, the loyall subjects of our dread soveraigne Lord King James by the grace of God, of great Britaine, Franc, & Ireland king, defender of the faith, &c.

Haveing undertaken, for the glorie of God, and advancements of the Christian faith and honour of our king & countrie, a voyage to plant the first colonie in the Northerne parts of Virginia, doe by these presents solemnly & mutualy in the presence of God, and one of another, covenant & combine our selves togeather into a civill body politick; for our better ordering, & preservation & furtherance of the ends aforesaid; and by vertue hearof to enacte, constitute, and frame shuch just & equall lawes, ordinances, Acts, constitutions, & offices, from time to time, as shall be thought most meete & convenient for the generall good of the Colonie: unto which we promise all due submission and obedience.

In witnes whereof we have hereunder sub-scribed our names at Cap-Codd the • 11 • of November, in the year the raigne of our sover-aigne Lord King James of England, France, & Ireland, the eighteenth and of Scotland the fiftie fourth. An°: Dom. 1620.

BENJAMIN FRANKLIN

POOR RICHARD'S ALMANACK

Benjamin Franklin (1706–1790) was one of the most remarkable Americans who ever lived. Author, printer, statesman, diplomat, educator, inventor, philosopher, humorist, entrepreneur, shopkeeper, civic leader, scientist, auto-didact, public servant, national hero, Franklin tried a variety of careers and succeeded brilliantly at all of them. His almanacs, published in Philadelphia as the work of a fictional Richard Saunders (and thus "Poor Richard"), appeared annually from 1733 until 1758. They were immensely popular among the colonists; typically they contained calendars, weather predictions, advice, recipes, and much other useful knowledge. Poor Richard's proverbs, adages, and maxims were sometimes original, sometimes not; they were a popular vehicle for Franklin's pragmatic, tolerant, cheerful wit and philosophy.

Following is a selection from among the hundreds of sayings and commentaries by "Poor Richard."

The poor have little, beggars none, the rich too much, *enough* not one.

He that lies down with Dogs, shall rise up with fleas.

Men and melons are hard to know.

Take this remark from *Richard* poor and lame, Whate'er's begun in anger ends in shame.

No man e'er was glorious, who was not laborious.

All things are easy to Industry,
All things are difficult to *Sloth.*

Would you persuade, speak of Interest, not of Reason.

Teach your child to hold his tongue, he'll learn fast enough to speak.

He that cannot obey, cannot command.

The magistrate should obey the Laws, the People should obey the magistrate.

He that waits upon a Fortune, is never sure of a Dinner.

A learned blockhead is a greater blockhead than an ignorant one.

Keep thy shop, and thy shop will keep thee.

Three may keep a secret if two of them are dead.

Early to bed and early to rise, makes a man healthy wealthy and wise.

To be humble to Superiors is Duty, to Equals Courtesy, to Inferiors Nobleness.

If you know how to spend less than you get, you have the Philosophers-Stone.

Fish & Visitors stink in 3 days.

He that has neither fools, whores nor beggars among his kindred, is the son of a thunder gust.

Diligence is the Mother of Good-Luck.

He that lives upon Hope, dies farting.

Do not do that which you would not have known.

Wealth is not his that has it, but his that enjoys it.

Now I've a sheep and a cow, every body bids me good morrow.

God helps them that help themselves.

Don't throw stones at your neighbours, if your own windows are glass.

Force shites upon Reason's Back.

Creditors have better memories than debtors.

God heals, and the Doctor takes the Fees.

The greatest monarch on the proudest throne, is oblig'd to sit upon his own arse.

The nearest way to come at glory, is to do that for conscience which we do for glory.

The noblest question in the world is, *What Good may I do in it?*

If you wou'd not be forgotten
As soon as you are dead and rotten,
Either write things worth reading,
or do things worth the writing.

Sell not virtue to purchase wealth, nor Liberty to purchase power.

The ancients tell us what is best; but we must learn of the moderns what is fittest.

Drive thy Business, let not that drive thee.

Each year one vicious habit rooted out,
In time might make the worst Man good throughout.

Wink at small faults; remember thou has great ones.

Eat to please thyself, but dress to please others.

He that pays for Work before it's done, has but a pennyworth for twopence.

Historians relate, not so much what is done, as what they would have believed.

This 1754 woodcut by Benjamin Franklin warned the colonies to unite for their common defense. In that year, Franklin proposed the Albany Plan of Union, but the colonies rejected it.

Let thy Child's first lesson be Obedience, and the second may be what thou wilt.

Blessed is he that expects nothing, for he shall never be disappointed.

If thou injurest Conscience, it will have its Revenge on thee.

Hear no ill of a Friend, nor speak any of an Enemy.

Pay what you owe, and you'll know what's your own.

Proclaim not all thou knowest, all thou owest, all thou hast, nor all thou canst.

To bear other Peoples Afflictions, every one has Courage enough, and to spare.

Happy that nation, fortunate that age, whose history is not diverting.

A wolf eats sheep but now and then,
Ten Thousands are devour'd by Men.

Man's tongue is soft, and bone doth lack;
Yet a stroke therewith may break a man's back.

Fear to do ill, and you need fear nought else.

Lend money to an Enemy, and thou'lt gain him, to a Friend and thou'lt lose him.

Learn of the skilful: He that teaches himself, hath a fool for his master.

Let thy discontents be thy Secrets;—if the world knows them, 'twill despise *thee* and increase *them.*

At 20 years of age the Will reigns; at 30 the Wit; at 40 the Judgment.

He that hath a Trade, hath an Estate.

Have you somewhat to do to-morrow; do it to-day.

Men differ daily, about things which are subject to Sense, is it likely then they should agree about things invisible.

Speak with contempt of none, from slave to
  king,
The meanest Bee hath, and will use, a sting.

Tart Words make no Friends: a spoonful of honey will catch more flies than a Gallon of Vinegar.

Make haste slowly.

Beware of little Expences, a small Leak will sink a great ship.

No gains without pains.

Many complain of their Memory, few of their judgment.

When the Well's dry, we know the Worth of Water.

Good Sense is a Thing all need, few have, and none think they want.

There is no Man so bad, but he secretly respects the Good.

A good example is the best sermon.

He that won't be counsell'd, can't be help'd.

A Mob's a Monster; Heads enough, but no Brains.

Life with Fools consists in Drinking;
With the wise Man, Living's Thinking.

Drink does not drown *Care,* but waters it, and makes it grow faster.

Genius without education is like Silver in the Mine.

Little Strokes,
Fell great Oaks

What signifies knowing the Names, if you know not the Nature of Things.

Glass, China, and Reputation, are easily crack'd, and never well mended.

The Golden Age never was the present Age.

Old Boys have their Playthings as well as young Ones; the Difference is only in the Price.

Haste makes Waste.

Love your Neighbour; yet don't pull down your Hedge.

A Child thinks 20 *Shillings* and 20 Years can scarce ever be spent.

Being ignorant is not so much a Shame, as being unwilling to learn.

One *To-day* is worth two *To-Morrows.*

Work as if you were to live 100 years,
Pray as if you were to die To-morrow.

ANDREW HAMILTON
DEFENSE OF FREEDOM OF THE PRESS

The loss of liberty to a generous mind is worse than death.

In 1733, John Peter Zenger began publishing *The New York Weekly Journal*, which criticized the policies of the colonial governor. A year later, Zenger was arrested for seditious libel. He languished in jail for ten months, until his trial in August 1735. His attorney, Andrew Hamilton, argued that the articles in Zenger's journal could not be libelous because they were true; he further insisted, against the settled precedent, that the jury and not the judge should decide the truth of the printed statements. The jurors acquitted Zenger, persuaded by Hamilton that the charges against the royal governor were true. It was a signal victory for freedom of the press in the English colonies.

At the time of Zenger's trial, Andrew Hamilton (c. 1676–1741) was one of the most famous lawyers in the colonies. Born in Scotland, he had migrated to Virginia as an indentured servant shortly before 1700. He taught school, studied for admission to the bar, and served in the Maryland Assembly. After studying law in London, he settled in Philadelphia, where he became a prominent attorney.

May it please your honors, I agree with Mr. Attorney [Richard Bradley] that government is a sacred thing, but I differ very widely from him when he would insinuate that the just complaints of a number of men, who suffer under a bad administration, is libeling that administration. Had I believed that to be law, I should not have given the court the trouble of hearing anything that I could say in this cause. . . .

There is heresy in law as well as in religion, and both have changed very much; and we well know that it is not two centuries ago that a man would have burned as a heretic for owning such opinions in matters of religion as are publicly written and printed at this day. They were fallible men, it seems, and we take the liberty, not only to differ from them in religious opinion, but to condemn them and their opinions too; and I must presume that in taking these freedoms in thinking and speaking about matters of faith or religion, we are in the right; for, though it is said there are very great liberties of this kind taken in New York, yet I have heard of no information preferred by Mr. Attorney for any offenses of this sort. From which I think it is pretty clear that in New York a man may make

very free with his God, but he must take special care what he says of his Governor. It is agreed upon by all men that this is a reign of liberty, and while men keep within the bounds of truth, I hope they may with safety both speak and write their sentiments of the conduct of men of power; I mean of that part of their conduct only which affects the liberty or property of the people under their administration; were this to be denied, then the next step may make them slaves. For what notions can be entertained of slavery beyond that of suffering the greatest injuries and oppressions without the liberty of complaining; or if they do, to be destroyed, body and estate, for so doing?

It is said, and insisted upon by Mr. Attorney, that government is a sacred thing; that it is to be supported and reverenced; it is government that protects our persons and estates; that prevents treasons, murders, robberies, riots, and all the train of evils that overturn kingdoms and states and ruin particular persons; and if those in the administration, especially the supreme magistrates, must have all their conduct censured by private men, government cannot subsist. This is called a licentiousness not to be tolerated. It is said that it brings the rulers of the people into contempt so that their authority is not regarded, and so that in the end the laws cannot be put in execution. These, I say, and such as these, are the general topics insisted upon by men in power and their advocates. But I wish it might be considered at the same time how often it has happened that the abuse of power has been the primary cause of these evils, and that it was the injustice and oppression of these great men which has commonly brought them into contempt with the people. The craft and art of such men are great, and who that is the least acquainted with history or with law can be ignorant of the specious pretenses which have often been made use of by men in power to introduce arbitrary rule and destroy the liberties of a free people. . . .

If a libel is understood in the large and unlimited sense urged by Mr. Attorney, there is scarce a writing I know that may not be called a libel, or scarce any person safe from being called to account as a libeler, for Moses, meek as he was, libeled Cain; and who is it that has not libeled the devil? For, according to Mr. Attorney, it is no justification to say one has a bad name. Eachard has libeled our good King William; Burnet has libeled, among many others, King Charles and King James; and Rapin has libeled them all. How must a man speak or write, or what must he hear, read, or sing? Or when must he laugh, so as to be secure from being taken up as a libeler? I sincerely believe that were some persons to go through the streets of New York nowadays and read a part of the Bible, if it were not known to be such, Mr. Attorney, with the help of his innuendoes, would easily turn it into a libel. As for instance: Isaiah 11:16: "The leaders of the people cause them to err, and they that are led by them are destroyed." But should Mr. Attorney go about to make this a libel, he would read it thus: "The leaders of the people" (*innuendo,* the Governor and council of New York) "cause them" (*innuendo,* the people of this province) "to err, and they" (the Governor and council meaning) "are destroyed" (*innuendo,* are deceived into the loss

of their liberty), "which is the worst kind of destruction." Or if some person should publicly repeat, in a manner not pleasing to his betters, the tenth and the eleventh verses of the fifty-sixth chapter of the same book, there Mr. Attorney would have a large field to display his skill in the artful application of his innuendoes. The words are: "His watchmen are blind, they are ignorant," etc. "Yea, they are greedy dogs, they can never have enough." But to make them a libel, there is, according to Mr. Attorney's doctrine, no more wanting but the aid of his skill in the right adapting his innuendoes. . . .

The loss of liberty to a generous mind is worse than death; and yet we know there have been those in all ages who, for the sakes of preferment or some imaginary honor, have freely lent a helping hand to oppress, nay, to destroy, their country. This brings to my mind that saying of the immortal Brutus, when he looked upon the creatures of Caesar, who were very great men, but by no means good men: "You Romans," said Brutus, "if yet I may call you so, consider what you are doing; remember that you are assisting Caesar to forge those very chains which one day he will make yourselves wear." This is what every man that values freedom ought to consider; he should act by judgment and not by affection or self-interest; for where those prevail, no ties of either country or kindred are regarded; as, upon the other hand, the man who loves his country prefers its liberty to all other considerations, well knowing that without liberty life is a misery. . . .

Power may justly be compared to a great river; while kept within its bounds, it is both beautiful and useful, but when it overflows its banks, it is then too impetuous to be stemmed; it bears down all before it, and brings destruction and desolation wherever it comes. If, then, this be the nature of power, let us at least do our duty, and, like wise men who value freedom, use our utmost care to support liberty, the only bulwark against lawless power, which, in all ages, has sacrificed to its wild lust and boundless ambition the blood of the best men that ever lived.

I hope to be pardoned, sir, for my zeal upon this occasion. It is an old and wise caution that "when our neighbor's house is on fire, we ought to take care of our own." For though, blessed be God, I live in a government where liberty is well understood and freely enjoyed, yet experience has shown us all (I am sure it has to me) that a bad precedent in one government is soon set up for an authority in another; and therefore I cannot but think it mine and every honest man's duty that, while we pay all due obedience to men in authority, we ought, at the same time, to be upon our guard against power wherever we apprehend that it may affect ourselves or our fellow subjects.

I am truly very unequal to such an undertaking, on many accounts. And you see I labor under the weight of many years and am borne down with great infirmities of body; yet old and weak as I am, I should think it my duty, if required, to go to the utmost part of the land, where my service could be of any use in assisting to quench the flame of prosecutions upon informations, set on foot by the government to deprive a people of the right of remonstrating, and complaining too, of the arbitrary attempts of men in power. Men who injure and oppress the people under their administration provoke them to cry out and complain, and then make that very complaint the foundation for new oppressions and prosecutions. I wish I could say there were no instances of this kind. But, to conclude, the question before the court, and you, gentlemen of the jury, is not of small nor private concern; it is not the cause of a poor printer, nor of New York alone, which you are now trying. No! It may, in its consequence, affect every free man that lives under a British government on the main continent of America. It is the best cause; it is the cause of liberty; and I make no doubt but your upright conduct, this day, will not only entitle you to the love and esteem of your fellow citizen, but every man who prefers freedom to a life of slavery will bless and honor you as men who have baffled the attempt of tyranny, and, by an impartial and uncorrupt verdict, have laid a noble foundation for securing to ourselves, our posterity, and our neighbors that to which nature and the laws of our country have given us a right—the liberty of both exposing and opposing arbitrary power (in these parts of the world at least) by speaking and writing truth. . . .

JAMES OTIS

A DEMAND TO LIMIT SEARCH AND SEIZURE

A man's house is his castle; and whilst he is quiet, he is as well guarded as a prince in his castle.

James Otis (1725–1783) began his career as a lawyer in Boston in 1750. Ten years later, he was the king's advocate general of the vice-admiralty court when the British government empowered customs officials to search any house for smuggled goods. Rather than supervise these orders, Otis resigned his position and, in February 1761, argued in court against these "writs of assistance." Since there were no legal grounds on which to oppose the writs, Otis eloquently insisted that they trampled on the people's liberty. John Adams, then a young man of twenty-five, attended the proceedings and later wrote that Otis was "a flame of fire! . . . American independence was there and then born; the seeds of patriots and heroes were then and there sown. Then and there was the first scene of the first act of opposition to the arbitrary claims of Great Britain." Although Otis lost the case, the British government withdrew the writs of assistance.

Otis became a leading political activist after these events. In May 1761, Otis was elected to the legislature of Massachusetts and was chosen as speaker of the house in 1766; however, the royal governor of the province blocked his selection as speaker. For years, his speeches and writings circulated widely throughout the colonies, and he was frequently quoted and frequently denounced in the British Parliament. The phrase "Taxation without representation is tyranny" is usually attributed to him. Otis's career ended suddenly in 1769, when a blow to his head by a British officer left him insane.

May it please your honors, I was desired by one of the court to look into the books, and consider the question now before them concerning writs of assistance. I have, accordingly, considered it, and now appear not only in obedience to your order, but likewise in behalf of the inhabitants of this town, who have presented another petition, and out of regard to the liberties of the subject. And I take this opportunity to declare that, whether under a fee or not (for in such a cause as this I despise a fee), I will to my dying day oppose with all the powers and faculties God has given me all such instruments of slavery, on the one hand, and villainy, on the other, as this writ of assistance is.

It appears to me the worst instrument of arbitrary power, the most destructive of English liberty and the fundamental principles of law, that ever was found in an English lawbook. I must, therefore, beg your honors' patience and attention to the whole range of an argument, that may, perhaps, appear uncommon in many things, as well as to points of learning that are more remote and unusual: that the whole tendency of my design may the more easily be perceived, the conclusions better descend, and the force of them be better felt. I shall not think much of my pains in this cause, as I engaged in it from principle. I was solicited to argue this cause as Advocate General; and because I would not, I have been charged with desertion from my office. To this charge I can give a very sufficient answer. I renounced that office, and I argue this cause from the same principle; and I argue it with the greater pleasure, as it is in favor of British liberty, at a time when we hear the greatest monarch upon earth declaring from his throne that he glories in the name of Briton, and that the privileges of his people are dearer to him than the most valuable prerogatives of his crown; and as it is in opposition to a kind of power the exercise of which, in former periods of history, cost one king of England his head and another his throne. . . .

Your honors will find in the old books concerning the office of a justice of the peace precedents of general warrants to search suspected houses. But in more modern books you will find only special warrants to search such and such houses, specially named, in which the complainant has before sworn that he suspects his goods are concealed; and will find it adjudged that special warrants only are legal. In the same manner I rely on it that the writ prayed for in this petition, being general, is illegal. It is a power that places the liberty of every man in the hands of every petty officer. I say I admit that special writs of assistance, to search special places, may be granted to certain persons on oath; but I deny that the writ now prayed for can be granted, for I beg leave to make some observations on the writ itself, before I proceed to other acts of Parliament. In the first place, the writ is universal, being directed "to all and singular justices, sheriffs, constables, and all other officers and subjects"; so that, in short, it is directed to every subject in the king's dominions. Everyone with this writ may be a tyrant; if this commission be legal, a tyrant in a legal manner, also, may control, imprison, or murder anyone within the realm. In the next place, it is perpetual; there is no return. A man is accountable to no person for his doings. Every man may reign secure in his petty tyranny, and spread terror and desolation around him, until the trump of the archangel shall excite different emotions in his soul.

In the third place, a person with this writ, in the daytime, may enter all houses, shops, etc., at will, and command all to assist him. Fourthly, by this writ, not only deputies, etc., but even their menial servants, are allowed to lord it over us. What is this but to have the curse of Canaan with a witness on us; to be the servant of servants, the most despicable of God's creation? Now, one of the most essential branches of English liberty is the freedom of one's house. A man's house is his castle; and whilst he is quiet, he is as well guarded as a prince in his castle. This writ, if it should be declared legal, would totally annihilate this privilege. Customhouse officers may enter our houses when they please; we are commanded to permit their entry. Their menial servants may enter, may break locks, bars, and everything in their way; and whether they break through malice or revenge, no man, no court, can inquire. Bare suspicion without oath is sufficient. This wanton exercise of this power is not a chimerical suggestion of a heated brain. I will mention some facts. Mr. Pew had one of these writs, and when Mr. Ware succeeded him, he indorsed this writ over to Mr. Ware; so that these writs are negotiable from one officer to another; and so your honors have no opportunity of judging the persons to whom this vast power is delegated. Another instance is this: Mr. Justice Walley had called this same Mr. Ware before him, by a constable, to answer for a breach of the Sabbath Day Acts, or that of profane swearing. As soon as he had finished, Mr. Ware asked him if he had done. He replied: "Yes." "Well, then," said Mr. Ware, "I will show you a little of my power. I command you to permit me to search your house for uncustomed goods"; and went on to search the house from the garret to the cellar, and then served the constable in the same manner! But to show another absurdity in this writ, if it should be established, I insist upon it that every person, by the 14th of Charles II, has this power as well as the customhouse officers. The words are: "It shall be lawful for any person or persons authorized," etc. What a scene does this open! Every man prompted by revenge, ill humor, or wantonness to inspect the inside of his neighbor's house may get a writ of assistance. Others will ask it from self-defense; one arbitrary exertion will provoke another, until society be involved in tumult and in blood. . . .

YANKEE DOODLE

The tune and some stanzas of "Yankee Doodle" were familiar in the British colonies long before the Revolution. Even before the 1770s, British troops sang "Yankee Doodle" to express derision for the colonists; early versions of the lyrics mocked the courage of the colonials and their rude dress and manners. "Yankee" was a pejorative term for a New England bumpkin, and a "doodle" was a simpleton or foolish fellow. However, during the Revolution the American troops adopted "Yankee Doodle" as their own song, a statement of pride in their simple, homespun dress and lack of affectation. There are many different versions of the lyrics. Over the years, the song has served as an unofficial national anthem and a favorite nursery song.

Yankee Doodle went to town,
A-ridin' on a pony,
Stuck a feather in his cap
And called it Macaroni.

CHORUS:
Yankee Doodle, keep it up,
Yankee Doodle Dandy,
Mind the music and the step
And with the girls be handy.

Father and I went down to camp,
Along with Captain Gooding,
And there we saw the men and boys
As thick as hasty pudding.

And there we saw a thousand men,
As rich as Squire David;
And what they wasted every day,
I wish it could be saved.

And there was Captain Washington
Upon a slapping stallion,
A-giving orders to his men;
I guess there was a million.

And there I saw a little keg,
Its head was made of leather;
They knocked upon it with two sticks
To call the men together.

And there I saw a swamping gun,
As big as a log of maple,
Upon a mighty little cart,
A load for father's cattle.

And every time they fired it off
It took a horn of powder,
And made a noise like father's gun,
Only a nation louder.

I can't tell you half I saw,
They kept up such a smother,
So I took my hat off, made a bow
And scampered home to mother.

Yankee Doodle is the tune
Americans delight in,
'Twill do to whistle, sing or play
And just the thing for fightin'.

JOHN ADAMS
LIBERTY AND KNOWLEDGE

Let us dare to read, think, speak, and write. . . . Let every sluice of knowledge be opened and set a-flowing.

Born in Massachusetts, John Adams (1735–1826) graduated from Harvard College, studied law, taught grammar school, and was admitted to the bar. Adams became active in colonial politics in 1765, when he published articles in the *Boston Gazette* denouncing the Stamp Act. These articles, published together as A *Dissertation on the Canon* and *Feudal Law,* are excerpted below.

Although critical of British policies, Adams defended the British soldiers accused of murdering five colonials in the Boston Massacre in 1770; the commanding officer and several soldiers were acquitted. His willingness to defend an unpopular position was not an obstacle to his political career. In 1774, he was a delegate to the First Continental Congress. He was also a member of the committee with Thomas Jefferson that wrote the Declaration of Independence. Adams was the first vice-president of the United States and was then elected president (1797–1801); he was defeated for the presidency in 1800 by Thomas Jefferson. He and Jefferson both died on July 4, 1826, the fiftieth anniversary of the nation's independence.

. . . Wherever a general knowledge and sensibility have prevailed among the people, arbitrary government and every kind of oppression have lessened and disappeared in proportion. Man has certainly an exalted soul; and the same principle in human nature—that aspiring, noble principle founded in benevolence, and cherished by knowledge; I mean the love of power, which has been so often the cause of slavery—has, whenever freedom has existed, been the cause of freedom. If it is this principle that has always prompted the princes and nobles of the earth by every species of fraud and violence to shake off all the limitations of their power, it is the same that has always stimulated the common people to aspire at independency, and to endeavor at confining the power of the great within the limits of equity and reason.

The poor people, it is true, have been much less successful than the great. They have seldom found either leisure or opportunity to form a union and exert their strength; ignorant as they were of arts and letters, they have seldom been able to frame and support a regular opposition. This, however, has been known by the great to be the temper of mankind; and they have accordingly labored, in all ages, to wrest from the populace, as they are contemptuously called, the knowledge of their rights and wrongs, and the power to assert the former or redress the latter. I say RIGHTS, for such they have, undoubtedly, antecedent to all earthly government—*rights* that cannot be repealed or restrained by human laws—*rights* derived from the great Legislator of the universe. . . .

Liberty cannot be preserved without a general knowledge among the people, who have a right, from the frame of their nature, to knowledge, as their great Creator, who does nothing in vain, has given them understandings, and a desire to know; but besides this, they have a right, an indisputable, unalienable, indefeasible, divine right to that most dreaded and envied kind of knowledge; I mean, of the characters and conduct of their rulers. Rulers are no more than attorneys, agents, and trustees, for the people; and if the cause, the interest and trust, is insidiously betrayed, or wantonly trifled away, the people have a right to revoke the authority that they themselves have deputed, and to constitute abler and better agents, attorneys, and trustees. And the preservation of the means of knowledge among the lowest ranks is of more importance to the public than all the property of all the rich men in the country. It is even of more consequence to the rich themselves, and to their pos-

terity. The only question is whether it is a public emolument; and if it is, the rich ought undoubtedly to contribute, in the same proportion as to all other public burdens—that is, in proportion to their wealth, which is secured by public expenses. But none of the means of information are more sacred, or have been cherished with more tenderness and care by the settlers of America, than the press. Care has been taken that the art of printing should be encouraged, and that it should be easy and cheap and safe for any person to communicate his thoughts to the public. . . .

Let us dare to read, think, speak, and write. Let every order and degree among the people rouse their attention and animate their resolution. Let them all become attentive to the grounds and principles of government, ecclesiastical and civil. Let us study the law of nature; search into the spirit of the British Constitution; read the histories of ancient ages; contemplate the great examples of Greece and Rome; set before us the conduct of our own British ancestors, who have defended for us the inherent rights of mankind against foreign and domestic tyrants and usurpers, against arbitrary kings and cruel priests; in short, against the gates of earth and hell. Let us read and recollect and impress upon our souls the views and ends of our own more immediate forefathers in exchanging their native country for a dreary, inhospitable wilderness. Let us examine into the nature of that power, and the cruelty of that oppression, which drove them from their homes. Recollect their amazing fortitude, their bitter sufferings—the hunger, the nakedness, the cold, which they patiently endured—the severe labors of clearing their grounds, building their houses, raising their provisions, amidst dangers from wild beasts and savage men, before they had time or money or materials for commerce. Recollect the civil and religious principles and hopes and expectations which constantly supported and carried them through all hardships with patience and resignation. Let us recollect it was liberty, the hope of liberty for themselves and us and ours, which conquered all the discouragements, dangers, and trials. In such researches as these let us all in our several departments cheerfully engage—but especially the proper patrons and supporters of law, learning, and religion!

Let the pulpit resound with the doctrines and sentiments of religious liberty. Let us hear the danger of thraldom to our consciences from ignorance, extreme poverty, and dependence; in short, from civil and political slavery. Let us see delineated before us the true map of man. Let us hear the dignity of his nature, and the noble rank he holds among the works of God— that consenting to slavery is a sacrilegious breach of trust, as offensive in the sight of God as it is derogatory from our own honor or interest or happiness—and that God Almighty has promulgated from heaven liberty, peace, and goodwill to man!

Let the bar proclaim "the laws, the rights, the generous plan of power" delivered down from remote antiquity—inform the world of the mighty struggles and numberless sacrifices made by our ancestors in defense of freedom. Let it be known that original rights, conditions of original contracts, [are] coequal with prerog-

ative and coeval with government; that many of our rights are inherent and essential, agreed on as maxims and established as preliminaries, even before a parliament existed. Let them search for the foundations of British laws and government in the frame of human nature, in the constitution of the intellectual and moral world. There let us see that truth, liberty, justice, and benevolence are its everlasting basis; and if these could be removed, the superstructure is overthrown of course.

Let the colleges join their harmony in the same delightful concert. Let every declamation turn upon the beauty of liberty and virtue, and the deformity, turpitude, and malignity of slavery and vice. Let the public disputations become researches into the grounds and nature and ends of government, and the means of preserving the good and demolishing the evil. Let the dialogues, and all the exercises, become the instruments of impressing on the tender mind, and of spreading and distributing far and wide, the ideas of right and the sensations of freedom.

In a word, let every sluice of knowledge be opened and set a-flowing.

JOHN DICKINSON
THE LIBERTY SONG

''The Liberty Song'' was the first patriotic American ballad. It was written in 1768 by John Dickinson (1732–1808), who was a prominent Pennsylvania lawyer. He became famous with his *Letters from a Farmer in Pennsylvania,* twelve letters published in 1767–68. The *Letters* helped to turn public opinion against the Townshend Acts, which imposed new taxes on the colonies.

Dickinson was a Pennsylvania delegate to the Continental Congress. He opposed the Declaration of Independence, hoping to avert war, but nonetheless served in the militia. He was also a delegate to the Constitutional Convention, which drafted the Constitution, and he worked for its ratification. Dickinson College in Carlisle, Pennsylvania, was named for him.

''The Liberty Song'' was wildly popular in the colonies. It was sung virtually everywhere—on public occasions and often just to annoy the British and their American friends. People quickly took up the song's credo: ''By uniting we stand, by dividing we fall.''

Come join hand in hand brave Americans all,
And rouse your bold hearts at fair Liberty's call;
No tyrannous acts shall suppress your just
   claim,
Or stain with dishonour America's name.

CHORUS:
In Freedom we're born and in Freedom we'll
   live,
Our purses are ready,
Steady, Friends, Steady.
Not as slaves, but as Freemen our money we'll
   give.

Our worthy Forefathers—Let's give them a
   cheer
To Climates unknown did courageously steer;
Thro' Oceans, to deserts, for freedom they
   came,
And dying bequeath'd us their freedom and
   Fame.

Their generous bosoms all dangers despis'd,
So highly, so wisely, their *Birthrights* they
   priz'd;
We'll keep what they gave, we will piously
   keep,
Nor frustrate their toils on the land and the
   deep.

The Tree their own hands had to Liberty rear'd;
They liv'd to behold growing strong and
   rever'd;
With transport they cry'd, "Now our wishes we
   gain
For our children shall gather the fruits of our
   pain."

Swarms of placemen and pensioners soon will
   appear
Like locusts deforming the charms of the year;
Suns vainly will rise, Showers vainly descend,
If we are to drudge for what others shall spend.

Then join hand in hand brave Americans all,
By uniting we stand, by dividing we fall;
In so Righteous a cause let us hope to succeed,
For Heaven approves of each generous deed.

All ages shall speak with amaze and applause,
Of the courage we'll show in support of our
   laws;
To die we can bear—but to serve we disdain,
For shame is to freedom more dreadful than
   pain.

This bumper I crown for our Sovereign's
   health,
And this for Britannia's glory and wealth;
That wealth and that glory immortal may be,
If she is but just—and if we are but Free.

CHIEF LOGAN'S LAMENT

Who is there to mourn for Logan? Not one.

In 1774, a series of bloody incidents occurred between Indians and whites living in the Ohio River valley. According to an account by Thomas Jefferson in his *Notes on Virginia* (1784–85), white settlers were outraged by robberies committed by Indians. In retaliation, white soldiers killed many innocent Indians, including the family of Logan, chief of the Mingo Indians, who was known as a friend of the whites. Led by Logan, the Indians launched a war against the white settlers, scalping a large number of innocent men, women, and children, but were finally defeated by the Virginia militia in October 1774.

   After the decisive battle, Logan refused to join the other chiefs as a suppliant before the victorious whites. Instead, he sent the following speech to Lord Dunmore, royal governor of Virginia. When Lord Dunmore returned from the expedition against the Indians, he brought the speech with him, and according to Jefferson, "It became the theme of every conversation in Williamsburg." It was printed in the *Virginia Gazette,* reprinted in papers across the continent and even in publications in Great Britain.

Jefferson reprinted the speech in his *Notes on Virginia* to refute those Europeans who "supposed there is something in the soil, climate, and other circumstances of America, which occasions animal nature to degenerate, not excepting even the man, native or adoptive, physical or moral." Jefferson offered Logan's speech as proof "of the talents of the aboriginals of this country, and particularly of their eloquence." He asserted "that Europe had never produced anything superior to this morsel of eloquence."

Logan's speech was a regular feature in school reading books of the nineteenth century, and was familiar to generations of American youngsters.

I appeal to any white man to say, if ever he entered Logan's cabin hungry, and he gave him not meat: if ever he came cold and naked, and he cloathed him not. During the course of the last long and bloody war Logan remained idle in his cabin, an advocate for peace. Such was my love for the whites, that my countrymen pointed as they passed, and said, "Logan is the friend of white man." I had even thought to have lived with you, but for the injuries of one man. Colonel Cresap, the last spring, in cold blood, and unprovoked, murdered all the relations of Logan, not even sparing my women and children. There runs not a drop of my blood in the veins of any living creature. This called on me for revenge. I have sought it: I have killed many: I have fully glutted my vengeance: for my country I rejoice at the beams of peace. But do not harbour a thought that mine is the joy of fear. Logan never felt fear. He will not turn on his heel to save his life. Who is there to mourn for Logan?—Not one.

THE SLAVES' APPEAL TO THE ROYAL GOVERNOR OF MASSACHUSETTS

We are a freeborn Pepel and have never forfeited this Blessing by aney compact or agreement whatever.

A Dutch ship brought twenty Africans to Jamestown, Virginia, in 1619; whether they were slaves or indentured servants is not known. With the rise of the southern plantation system in the late seventeenth century, the importation of Africans increased, as did colonial laws establishing their permanent slave status. During the 350 years of the slave trade, between nine and twelve million Africans were carried to the Americas under brutal conditions; about 400,000 of these were brought to North America.

Some colonists opposed slavery, especially Quakers and Mennonites, and leaders such as Benjamin Franklin, Alexander Hamilton, and John Jay. Revolutionary appeals based on the natural rights of man encouraged some slaves to assert that they, too, had a right to freedom. On May 25, 1774, a group of slaves in Massachusetts addressed the following appeal to Thomas Gage, the royal governor of the colony.

When the revolution began, the American army excluded blacks. But when the British called on slaves to join their side, the revolutionary army reversed its policy. Some 5,000 African Americans, both slave and free, fought in the American army. Many gained their freedom as a result of wartime service, and thousands of others escaped from slavery during the War. Most Africans, however, remained in slavery, a reproach to the ideals of the new nation.

The Petition of a Grate Number of Blacks of this Province who by divine permission are held in a state of Slavery within the bowels of a free and Christian Country

Humbly Shewing

That your Petitioners apprehind we have in common with all other men a naturel right to our freedoms without Being depriv'd of them by our fellow men as we are a freeborn Pepel and have never forfeited this Blessing by ancy compact or agreement whatever. But we were unjustly dragged by the cruel hand of power from our dearest frinds and sum of us stolen from the bosoms of our tender Parents and from a Populous Pleasant and plentiful country and Brought hither to be made slaves for Life in a Christian land. Thus we are deprived of every thing that hath a tendency to make life even tolerable, the endearing ties of husband and wife we are strangers to for we are no longer man and wife than our masters or mistresses thinkes proper marred or onmarred. Our children are also taken from us by force and sent maney miles from us wear we seldom or ever see them again there to be made slaves of for Life which sumtimes is vere short by Reson of Being dragged from their mothers Breest Thus our Lives are imbittered to us on these accounts By our deplorable situation we are rendered incapable of shewing our obedience to Almighty God how can a slave perform the duties of a husband to a wife or parent to his child How can a husband leave master to work and cleave to his wife How can the wife submit themselves to there husbands in all things How can the child obey thear parents in all things. There is a great number of us sencear . . . members of the Church of Christ how can the master and the slave be said to fulfil that command Live in love let Brotherly Love contuner and abound Beare yea onenothers Bordenes How can the master be said to Beare my Borden when he Beares me down whith the Have chanes of slavery and operson against my will and how can we fulfill our parte of duty to him whilst in this condition and as we cannot searve our God as we ought whilst in this situation. Nither can we reap an equal benefet from the laws of the Land which doth not justifi but condemns Slavery or if there had bin aney Law to hold us in Bondage we are Humbely of the Opinion ther never was aney to inslave our children for life when Born in a free Countrey. We therfor Bage your Excellency and Honours will give this its deer weight and consideration and that you will accordingly cause an act of the legislative to be pessed that we may obtain our Natural right our freedoms and our children be set at lebety at the yeare of twenty one for whoues sekes more petequeley your Petitioners is in Duty ever to pray.

PATRICK HENRY

SPEECH TO THE SECOND VIRGINIA CONVENTION

I know not what course others may take; but as for me, give me liberty, or give me death!

Patrick Henry (1736–1799) was a leading patriot in the revolutionary cause. Born in Virginia, he was one of colonial Virginia's most successful lawyers, noted for his quick wit and his oratorical skills. Elected to the Virginia legislature in 1763, he became an outspoken advocate of the rights of the colonies. In 1765, speaking in opposition to the Stamp Act, Henry said, "Caesar had his Brutus, Charles the First his Cromwell, and George III . . ." (he was then interrupted by cries of "Treason! Treason!") *". . . may profit by their example.* If *this* be treason, make the most of it."

Henry played a prominent role in the growing movement for independence. He was a member of the first Virginia Committee of Correspondence and a delegate to the Continental Congresses of 1774 and 1775. His most famous speech, excerpted below, was delivered to the second Virginia Convention on March 23, 1775, at Saint John's Church in Richmond, Virginia. The speech was a powerful argument on behalf of resolutions to equip the Virginia militia to fight against the British.

Henry was the first governor of the state of Virginia, and he served the state and the nation in many other public positions. His lasting fame, however, derives from this fiery speech in 1775, with its world-famous peroration.

. . . It is natural for man to indulge in the illusions of hope. We are apt to shut our eyes against a painful truth, and listen to the song of that siren, till she transforms us into beasts. Is this the part of wise men, engaged in a great and arduous struggle for liberty? Are we disposed to be of the number of those who, having eyes, see not, and having ears, hear not, the things which so nearly concern their temporal salvation? For my part, whatever anguish of spirit it may cost, I am willing to know the whole truth; to know the worst and to provide for it.

I have but one lamp by which my feet are guided; and that is the lamp of experience. I know of no way of judging of the future but by the past. And judging by the past, I wish to know what there has been in the conduct of the British ministry for the last ten years to justify those hopes with which gentlemen have been pleased to solace themselves and the House? Is it that insidious smile with which our petition has been lately received? Trust it not, sir; it will prove a snare to your feet. Suffer not yourselves to be betrayed with a kiss. Ask yourselves how this gracious reception of our petition comports with these warlike preparations which cover our waters and darken our land. Are fleets and armies necessary to a work of love and reconciliation? Have we shown ourselves so unwilling to be reconciled, that force must be called in to win back our love? Let us not deceive ourselves, sir. These are the implements of war and subjugation; the last arguments to which kings resort. I ask gentlemen, sir, what means this martial array, if its purpose be not to force us to submission? Can gentlemen assign any other possible motives for it? Has Great Britain any enemy, in this quarter of the world, to call for all this accumulation of navies and armies? No, sir, she has none. They are meant for us; they can be meant for no other. They are sent over to bind and rivet upon us those chains which the British ministry have been so long forging. And what have we to oppose to them? Shall we try argument? Sir, we have been trying that for the last ten years. Have we anything new to offer on the subject? Nothing. We have held the subject up in every light of which it is capable; but it has been all in vain. Shall we resort to entreaty and humble supplication? What terms shall we find which have not been already exhausted? Let us not, I beseech you, sir, deceive ourselves longer. Sir, we have done everything that could be done to avert the storm which is now coming on. We

Paul Revere's dramatic engraving of the Boston Massacre of 1770, in which five Americans were killed, aroused the colonists' resentment against British troops.

Engrav'd Printed & Sold by PAUL REVERE

have petitioned; we have remonstrated; we have supplicated; we have prostrated ourselves before the tyrannical hands of the ministry and parliament. Our petitions have been slighted; our remonstrances have produced additional violence and insult; our supplications have been disregarded; and we have been spurned, with contempt, from the foot of the throne. In vain, after these things, may we indulge the fond hope of peace and reconciliation. There is no longer any room for hope. If we wish to be free—if we mean to preserve inviolate those inestimable privileges for which we have been so long contending—if we mean not basely to abandon the noble struggle in which we have been so long engaged, and which we have pledged ourselves never to abandon until the glorious object of our contest shall be obtained, we must fight! I repeat it, sir, we must fight! An appeal to arms and to the God of Hosts is all that is left us!

They tell us, sir, that we are weak; unable to cope with so formidable an adversary. But when shall we be stronger? Will it be the next week, or the next year? Will it be when we are totally disarmed, and when a British guard shall be stationed in every house? Shall we gather strength by irresolution and inaction? Shall we acquire the means of effectual resistance by lying supinely on our backs, and hugging the delusive phantom of hope, until our enemies shall have bound us hand and foot? Sir, we are not weak, if we make a proper use of the means which the God of nature hath placed in our power. Three millions of people, armed in the holy cause of liberty, and in such a country as that which we possess, are invincible by any force which our enemy can send against us. Besides, sir, we shall not fight our battles alone. There is a just God who presides over the destinies of nations; and who will raise friends to fight our battles for us. The battle, sir, is not to the strong alone; it is to the vigilant, the active, the brave. Besides, sir, we have no election. If we were base enough to desire it, it is now too late to retire from the contest. There is no retreat but in submission and slavery! Our chains are forged! Their clanking may be heard on the plains of Boston! The war is inevitable—and let it come! I repeat it, sir, let it come!

It is in vain, sir, to extenuate the matter. Gentlemen may cry peace, peace—but there is no peace. The war is actually begun! The next gale that sweeps from the North will bring to our ears the clash of resounding arms! Our brethren are already in the field! Why stand we here idle? What is it that gentlemen wish? What would they have? Is life so dear, or peace so sweet, as to be purchased at the price of chains and slavery? Forbid it, Almighty God! I know not what course others may take; but as for me, give me liberty, or give me death!

THOMAS JEFFERSON

THE DECLARATION OF INDEPENDENCE

We hold these truths to be self-evident, that all men are created equal, that they are endowed by their Creator with certain unalienable Rights, that among these are Life, Liberty and the pursuit of Happiness.

Thomas Jefferson (1743–1826) wrote the first draft of the Declaration of Independence as a member of a committee that included John Adams and Benjamin Franklin. The Continental Congress made significant changes in Jefferson's draft, in particular, removing—at the insistence of delegates from Georgia and South Carolina—his vigorous condemnation of King George III for permitting slavery and the slave trade in the colonies (the deleted material read, in part, "He has waged cruel war against human

nature itself, violating its most sacred rights of life and liberty in the persons of a distant people who never offended him, captivating and carrying them into slavery in another hemisphere, or to incur miserable death in their transportation thither.") On July 4, 1776, the declaration was approved by the Congress.

Thomas Jefferson was born to a wealthy family in Virginia. He attended the College of William and Mary, and was admitted to the Virginia bar in 1767. He was elected to the Virginia House of Burgesses in 1769 and became active in the independence movement representing Virginia at the Continental Congress. He was twice elected governor of Virginia, and served as America's ambassador to France. When he ran for president in 1800, he and Aaron Burr received equal numbers of electoral votes, and the House of Representatives chose Jefferson as president.

Jefferson wrote that the Declaration of Independence was "an appeal to the tribunal of the world." The principles embodied in the declaration have resounded throughout the world in all the years since 1776. American reformers, whatever their cause—whether for abolition of slavery, for barring racial segregation, for advancing the rights of women—have reminded the public that "all men are created equal." Wherever people have fought against undemocratic regimes, they have argued, using Jefferson's words, that governments derive "their just powers from the consent of the governed."

Declaration of Independence

IN CONGRESS, JULY 4, 1776

The unanimous Declaration of the thirteen united States of America

When in the Course of human events, it becomes necessary for one people to dissolve the political bands which have connected them with another, and to assume among the Powers of the earth, the separate and equal station to which the Laws of Nature and of Nature's God entitle them, a decent respect to the opinions of mankind requires that they should declare the causes which impel them to the separation.— We hold these truths to be self-evident, that all men are created equal, that they are endowed by their Creator with certain unalienable Rights, that among these are Life, Liberty and the pursuit of Happiness.—That to secure these rights, Governments are instituted among Men, deriving their just powers from the consent of the governed,—That whenever any Form of Government becomes destructive of these ends, it · is the Right of the People to alter or to abolish it, and to institute new Government, laying its foundation on such principles and organizing its powers in such form, as to them shall seem most

likely to effect their Safety and Happiness. Prudence, indeed, will dictate that Governments long established should not be changed for light and transient causes; and accordingly all experience hath shewn, that mankind are more disposed to suffer, while evils are sufferable, than to right themselves by abolishing the forms to which they are accustomed. But when a long train of abuses and usurpations, pursuing invariably the same Object evinces a design to reduce them under absolute Despotism, it is their right, it is their duty, to throw off such Government, and to provide new Guards for their future security.—Such has been the patient sufferance of these Colonies; and such is now the necessity which constrains them to alter their former Systems of Government. The history of the present King of Great Britain is a history of repeated injuries and usurpations, all having in direct object the establishment of an absolute Tyranny over these States. To prove this, let Facts be submitted to a candid world.—He has refused his Assent to Laws, the most wholesome and necessary for the public good.—He has forbidden his Governors to pass Laws of immediate and pressing importance, unless suspended in their operation till his Assent should be obtained; and when so suspended, he has utterly neglected to attend to them.—He has refused to pass other Laws for the accommodation of large districts of people, unless those people would relinquish the right of Representation in the Legislature, a right inestimable to them and formidable to tyrants only.—He has called together legislative bodies at places unusual, uncomfortable, and distant from the depository of their public Records, for the sole purpose of fatiguing them into compliance with his measures.—He has dissolved Representative Houses repeatedly, for opposing with manly firmness his invasions on the rights of the people.—He has refused for a long time, after such dissolutions, to cause others to be elected; whereby the Legislative powers, incapable of Annihilation, have returned to the People at large for their exercise; the State remaining in the mean time exposed to all the dangers of invasion from without, and convulsions within.—He has endeavoured to prevent the population of these States; for that purpose obstructing the Laws for Naturalization of Foreigners; refusing to pass others to encourage their migrations hither, and raising the conditions of new Appropriations of Lands.—He has obstructed the Administration of Justice, by refusing his Assent to Laws for establishing Judiciary powers.—He has made Judges dependent on his Will alone, for the tenure of their offices, and the amount and payment of their salaries.—He has erected a multitude of New Offices, and sent hither swarms of Officers to harrass our people, and eat out their substance.—He has kept among us, in times of peace, Standing Armies without the Consent of our legislatures.—He has affected to render the Military independent of and superior to the Civil power.—He has combined with others to subject us to a jurisdiction foreign to our constitution, and unacknowledged by our laws; giving his Assent to their Acts of pretended Legislation: —For quartering large bodies of armed troops among us:—For protecting them, by a mock Trial, from punishment for any Murders which they should commit on the Inhabitants of these States:—For cutting off our Trade with all parts of the world:—For imposing Taxes on us without our Consent:—For depriving us in many cases, of the benefits of Trial by Jury:—For transporting us beyond Seas to be tried for pretended offences:—For abolishing the free System of English Laws in a neighbouring Province, establishing therein an Arbitrary government, and enlarging its Boundaries so as to render it at once an example and fit instrument for introducing the same absolute rule into these Colonies:—For taking away our Charters, abolishing our most valuable Laws, and altering fundamentally the Forms of our Governments:—For suspending our own Legislatures, and declaring themselves invested with power to legislate for us in all cases whatsoever.—He has abdicated Government here, by declaring us out of his Protection and waging War against us.—He has plundered our seas, ravaged our Coasts, burnt our towns, and destroyed the Lives of our people.—He is at this time transporting large Armies of foreign Mercenaries to compleat the works of death, desolation and tyranny, already begun with circumstances of Cruelty & perfidy scarcely paralleled in the most barbarous ages, and totally unworthy the Head of a civilized nation.—He has constrained our fellow Citizens taken Captive on the high Seas to bear Arms against their Country, to become the executioners of their friends and Brethren, or to fall themselves by their Hands.—He has excited domestic insurrections amongst us, and has endeavoured to bring on the inhabitants of our frontiers, the merciless Indian Savages, whose known rule of warfare, is an undistinguished destruction of all ages, sexes, and conditions. In every stage of these Oppressions We have Petitioned for Redress in the most humble terms: Our repeated Petitions have been answered only by repeated injury. A Prince, whose character is thus marked by every act which may define a Tyrant, is unfit to be the ruler of a free people. Nor have We been wanting in attentions to our Brittish brethren. We have warned them from time to time of attempts by their legislature to extend an unwarrantable jurisdiction over us. We have reminded them of the circumstances of our emigration and settlement here. We have appealed to their native justice and magnanimity, and we have conjured them by the ties of our common kindred to disavow these usurpations, which, would inevitably interrupt our connections and correspondence. They too have been deaf to the voice of justice and of consanguinity. We must, therefore, acquiesce in the necessity, which denounces our Separation, and hold them, as we hold the rest of mankind, Enemies in War, in Peace Friends.—

We, therefore, the Representatives of the *united States of America,* in General Congress, Assembled, appealing to the Supreme Judge of the world for the rectitude of our intentions, do, in the Name, and by Authority of the good Peo-

ple of these Colonies, solemnly publish and declare, That these United Colonies are, and of Right ought to be *Free and Independent States;* that they are Absolved from all Allegiance to the British Crown, and that all political connection between them and the State of Great Britain, is and ought to be totally dissolved; and that as Free and Independent States, they have full Power to levy War, conclude Peace, contract Alliances, establish Commerce, and to do all other Acts and Things which Independent States may of right do.—And for the support of this Declaration, with a firm reliance on the protection of divine Providence, we mutually pledge to each other our Lives, our Fortunes and our sacred Honor.

THOMAS JEFFERSON

A BILL FOR ESTABLISHING RELIGIOUS FREEDOM IN VIRGINIA

We the General Assembly of Virginia do enact that no man shall be compelled to frequent or support any religious worship, place, or ministry whatsoever, nor shall be enforced, restrained, molested, or burthened in his body or goods, or shall otherwise suffer, on account of his religious opinions or beliefs.

Thomas Jefferson was passionately committed to the principle of the free mind. Toward that end, he unceasingly promoted freedom of speech, freedom of the press, and freedom of religion and education. Like other educated people of his generation, he was well aware of the human costs of religious prejudice, which had been the cause of hatred and bloodshed for centuries. In 1779, Jefferson offered the following landmark bill in the Virginia legislature, but it was not adopted until 1786. Its guarantee of religious liberty was a precursor of the First Amendment to the Constitution, which forbade the Congress from establishing a religion or interfering with the free exercise of religion.

The epitaph that Jefferson wrote for his tombstone reads: "Here was buried Thomas Jefferson, author of the Declaration of American Independence, of the statute of Virginia for religious freedom, and father of the University of Virginia."

Section I. Well aware that the opinions and belief of men depend not on their own will, but follow involuntarily the evidence proposed to their minds; that Almighty God hath created the mind free, and manifested his supreme will that free it shall remain by making it altogether insusceptible of restraint; that all attempts to influence it by temporal punishments, or burthens, or by civil incapacitations, tend only to beget habits of hypocrisy and meanness, and are a departure from the plan of the holy author of our religion, who being lord both of body and mind, yet chose not to propagate it by coercions on either, as was in his almighty power to do, but to exalt it by its influence on reason alone; that the impious presumption of legislature and ruler, civil as well as ecclesiastical, who, being themselves but fallible and uninspired men, have assumed dominion over the faith of others, setting up their own opinions and modes of thinking as the only true and infallible, and as such endeavoring to impose them on others, hath established and maintained false religions over the greatest part of the world and through all time: that to compel a man to furnish contributions of money for the propagation of opinions which he disbelieves and abhors is sinful and tyrannical; that even the forcing him to support this or that teacher of his own religious persuasion is depriving him of the comfortable liberty of giving his contributions to the particular pastor whose morals he would make his pattern and whose powers he feels most persuasive to righteousness, and is withdrawing from the ministry those temporary rewards which, proceeding from an approbation of their personal conduct, are an additional incitement to earnest and unremitting labors for the instruction of mankind; that our civil rights have no dependence on our religious opinions, any more than our opinions in physics or geometry; and therefore the proscribing any citizen as unworthy the public confidence by laying upon him an incapacity of being called to offices of trust or emolument, unless he profess or renounce this or that religious opinion, is depriving him injudiciously of those privileges and advantages to which, in common with his fellow citizens, he has a natural right; that it tends also to corrupt the principles of that very religion it is meant to encourage, by bribing with a monopoly of worldly honors and emoluments those who will externally profess and conform to it; that though indeed these are criminals who do not withstand such temptation, yet neither are those innocent who lay the bait in their way; that the opinions of men are not the object of civil government, nor under its jurisdiction; that to suffer the civil magistrate to intrude his powers into the field of opinion and to restrain the profession or propagation of principles on supposition of their ill tendency is a dangerous fallacy, which at once destroys all religious liberty, because he being of course judge of that tendency will make his opinions the rule of judgment and approve or condemn the sentiments of others only as they shall square with or suffer from his own; that it is time enough for the rightful purposes of civil government for its officers to interfere when principles break out into overt acts against peace and good order; and finally, that the truth is great and will prevail if left to herself; that she is the proper and sufficient antagonist to error, and has nothing to fear from the conflict unless by human interposition disarmed of her natural weapons, free argument and debate; errors ceasing to be dangerous when it is permitted freely to contradict them.

SECTION II. We the General Assembly of Virginia do enact that no man shall be compelled to frequent or support any religious worship, place, or ministry whatsoever, nor shall be enforced, restrained, molested, or burthened in his body or goods, or shall otherwise suffer, on account of his religious opinions or beliefs; but that all men shall be free to profess, and by argument to maintain, their opinions in matters of religion, and that the same shall in no wise diminish, enlarge, or affect their civil capacities.

SECTION III. And though we well know that this Assembly, elected by the people for their ordinary purposes of legislation only, have no power to restrain the acts of succeeding Assemblies, constituted with powers equal to our own, and that therefore to declare this act to be irrevocable would be of no effect in law; yet we are free to declare, and do declare, that the rights hereby asserted are of the natural rights of mankind, and that if any act shall be hereafter passed to repeal the present or to narrow its operations, such act will be an infringement of natural right.

COMMON SENSE

O ye that love mankind! Ye that dare oppose not only the tyranny, but the tyrant, stand forth!

Thomas Paine (1737–1809) was born in England to a poor Quaker father and an Anglican mother and left school at the age of 13 to work with his father as a corset maker. He tried a variety of occupations (including collecting excise duties on liquor and tobacco), none successfully. After meeting Benjamin Franklin in London, he emigrated to the colonies in late 1774 and got a job editing the *Pennsylvania Magazine*. Tensions between England and the colonies were high, and Paine soon leapt into the fray. After the Battle of Lexington and Concord, on April 19, 1775, Paine concluded that the revolt should be aimed not against unjust taxation but in favor of full independence. His arguments were spelled out in *Common Sense*, a fifty-page pamphlet that was published January 10, 1776. It was an immediate sensation. More than 100,000 copies were sold within three months, and possibly as many as 500,000 copies altogether, to a colonial population of but two and a half million people. More than any other single publication, Paine's *Common Sense* persuaded public opinion of the case for independence from Britain.

Volumes have been written on the subject of the struggle between England and America. Men of all ranks have embarked in the controversy, from different motives, and with various designs: but all have been ineffectual, and the period of debate is closed. . . .

I have heard it asserted by some, that as America hath flourished under her former connection with Great Britain, the same connection is necessary towards her future happiness, and will always have the same effect. Nothing can be more fallacious than this kind of argument. We may as well assert that because a child has thriven upon milk, that it is never to have meat, or that the first twenty years of our lives is to become a precedent for the next twenty. But even this is admitting more than is true; for I answer roundly, that America would have flourished as much, and probably much more, had no European power taken any notice of her. The commerce by which she hath enriched herself are the necessaries of life, and will always have a market while eating is the custom of Europe.

But she has protected us, say some. That she

hath engrossed us is true, and defended the continent at our expense as well as her own is admitted; and she would have defended Turkey from the same motive, viz., for the sake of trade and dominion.

Alas! we have been long led away by ancient prejudices, and made large sacrifices to superstition. We have boasted the protection of Great Britain without considering that her motive was *interest*, not *attachment*; and that she did not protect us from *our enemies* on *our account*, but from her enemies on her own account, from those who had no quarrel with us on any *other account*, but who will always be our enemies on the *same account*. Let Britain waive her pretensions to the continent, or the continent throw off the dependence, and we should be at peace with France and Spain were they at war with Britain. . . .

But Britain is the parent country, say some. Then the more shame upon her conduct. Even brutes do not devour their young, nor savages make war upon their families; wherefore, the assertion, if true, turns to her reproach; but it happens not to be true, or only partly so, and the phrase *parent* or *mother country* hath been jesuitically adopted by the king and his parasites, with a low, papistical design of gaining an unfair bias on the credulous weakness of our minds. Europe, and not England, is the parent country of America. This new world hath been the asylum for the persecuted lovers of civil and religious liberty from *every part* of Europe. Hither have they fled, not from the tender embraces of a mother, but from the cruelty of the monster; and it is so far true of England, that the same tyranny which drove the first emigrants from home, pursues their descendants still. . . .

I challenge the warmest advocate for reconciliation to show a single advantage that this continent can reap, by being connected with Great Britain. I repeat the challenge, not a single advantage is derived. Our corn will fetch its price in any market in Europe, and our imported goods must be paid for, buy them where we will.

But the injuries and disadvantages we sustain by that connection are without number; and our duty to mankind at large, as well as to ourselves, instructs us to renounce the alliance: because any submission to, or dependence on, Great Britain, tends directly to involve this continent in European wars and quarrels, and sets us at variance with nations who would otherwise seek our friendship, and against whom we have neither anger nor complaint. As Europe is our market for trade, we ought to form no partial connection with any part of it. 'Tis the true interest of America to steer clear of European contentions, which she never can do while by her dependence on Britain she is made the makeweight in the scale of British politics.

Europe is too thickly planted with kingdoms to be long at peace, and whenever a war breaks out between England and any foreign power, the trade of America goes to ruin, *because of her connection with Britain*. The next war may not turn out like the last, and should it not, the advocates for reconciliation now will be wishing for separation then, because neutrality in that case would be a safer convoy than a man of war. Everything that is right or natural pleads for separation. The blood of the slain, the weeping voice of nature cries, 'TIS TIME TO PART. Even the distance at which the Almighty hath placed England and America is a strong and natural proof that the authority of the one over the other, was never the design of heaven. . . .

It is the good fortune of many to live distant from the scene of present sorrow; the evil is not sufficiently brought to *their* doors to make *them* feel the precariousness with which all American property is possessed. But let our imaginations transport us for a few moments to Boston; that seat of wretchedness will teach us wisdom, and instruct us forever to renounce a power in whom we can have no trust. The inhabitants of that unfortunate city, who but a few months ago were in ease and affluence, have now no other alternative than to stay and starve, or turn out to beg. Endangered by the fire of their friends if they continue within the city, and plundered by the soldiery if they leave it, in their present situation they are prisoners without the hope of redemption, and in a general attack for their relief they would be exposed to the fury of both armies. . . .

But if you say, you can still pass the violations over, then I ask, Hath your house been burnt? Hath your property been destroyed before your face? Are your wife and children destitute of a bed to lie on, or bread to live on? Have you lost a parent or a child by their hands, and yourself the ruined and wretched survivor? If you have not, then you are not a judge of those who have. But if you have, and can still shake hands with the murderers, then you are unworthy the name of husband, father, friend, or lover; and whatever may be your rank or title in life, you have the heart of a coward, and the spirit of a sycophant. . . .

Every quiet method for peace hath been ineffectual. Our prayers have been rejected with disdain; and have tended to convince us that nothing flatters vanity or confirms obstinacy in kings more than repeated petitioning—and nothing hath contributed more than that very measure to make the kings of Europe absolute.

Witness Denmark and Sweden. Wherefore, since nothing but blows will do, for God's sake let us come to a final separation, and not leave the next generation to be cutting throats under the violated unmeaning names of parent and child.

To say they will never attempt it again is idle and visionary; we thought so at the repeal of the stamp act, yet a year or two undeceived us; as well may we suppose that nations which have been once defeated will never renew the quarrel.

As to government matters, it is not in the power of Britain to do this continent justice: the business of it will soon be too weighty and intricate to be managed with any tolerable degree of convenience, by a power so distant from us, and so very ignorant of us; for if they cannot conquer us, they cannot govern us. To be always running three or four thousand miles with a tale or a petition, waiting four or five months for an answer, which, when obtained, requires five or six more to explain it in, will in a few years be looked upon as folly and childishness. There was a time when it was proper, and there is a proper time for it to cease.

Small islands not capable of protecting themselves are the proper objects for kingdoms to take under their care; but there is something very absurd in supposing a continent to be perpetually governed by an island. In no instance hath nature made the satellite larger than its primary planet; and as England and America, with respect to each other, reverse the common order of nature, it is evident that they belong to different systems. England to Europe: America to itself....

But where, say some, is the king of America? I'll tell you, friend, he reigns above, and doth not make havoc of mankind like the Royal Brute of Great Britain. Yet that we may not appear to be defective even in earthly honors, let a day be solemnly set apart for proclaiming the charter; let it be brought forth placed on the divine law, the Word of God; let a crown be placed thereon, by which the world may know, that so far as we approve of monarchy, that in America THE LAW

IS KING. For as in absolute governments the king is law, so in free countries the law *ought* to BE king, and there ought to be no other. But lest any ill use should afterwards arise, let the crown at the conclusion of the ceremony be demolished, and scattered among the people whose right it is.

A government of our own is our natural right; and when a man seriously reflects on the precariousness of human affairs, he will become convinced, that it is infinitely wiser and safer to form a constitition of our own in a cool deliberate manner, while we have it in our power, than to trust such an interesting event to time and chance....

Ye that tell us of harmony and reconciliation, can ye restore to us the time that is passed? Can ye give to prostitution its former innocence? Neither can ye reconcile Britain and America. The last cord now is broken; the people of England are presenting addresses against us. There are injuries which nature cannot forgive; she would cease to be nature if she did. As well can the lover forgive the ravisher of his mistress, as the continent forgive the murders of Britain. The Almighty hath implanted in us these unextinguishable feelings for good and wise purposes. They are the guardians of his image in our hearts. They distinguish us from the herd of common animals. The social compact would dissolve, and justice be extirpated from the earth, or have only a casual existence, were we callous to the touches of affection. The robber and the murderer would often escape unpunished, did not the injuries which our tempers sustain, provoke us into justice.

O ye that love mankind! Ye that dare oppose not only the tyranny but the tyrant, stand forth! Every spot of the old world is overrun with oppression. Freedom hath been hunted round the globe. Asia and Africa have long expelled her. Europe regards her like a stranger, and England hath given her warning to depart. O receive the fugitive, and prepare in time an asylum for mankind.

THOMAS PAINE

THE AMERICAN CRISIS

These are the times that try men's souls.

During the Revolutionary War, Paine wrote a sixteen-pamphlet sequence, *The American Crisis,* published between 1776 and 1783. He signed the pamphlets "Common Sense." The first of these, with its rousing call to fight for freedom, was issued on December 23, 1776; it is excerpted below. This spirited essay was read to General Washington's demoralized troops at Valley Forge, by order of the general.

Although hundreds of thousands of Paine's patriotic works were sold, Paine remained penniless, since he refused to accept any royalties in order that his writings would be widely printed and read. Paine was one of the world's greatest political propagandists. In 1787, he returned to Europe, hoping to promote interest in his plan to build a bridge across the Schuykill River near Philadelphia. However, he soon became fascinated by the French Revolution. In 1791, he published *The Rights of Man,* a defense of the French Revolution and a critique of Edmund Burke's *Reflections of the Revolution in France;* Burke replied, and in 1792, Paine issued *The Rights of Man,* Part II, a critique of monarchy and an advocacy of policies to eradicate poverty, illiteracy, and unemployment. The English government banned Paine's radical proposals and attempted to arrest him, but Paine fled from England to France; there he was elected to the National Convention. Although he had defended the French Revolution, he criticized the Reign of Terror and tried to save the life of the king. For his efforts, the French jailed him for almost a year. Paine's *The Age of Reason* (two parts, 1794 and 1795) earned him the bitter enmity of orthodox religionists everywhere.

Paine returned to the United States in 1802 and died in New York City in 1809.

These are the times that try men's souls. The summer soldier and the sunshine patriot will, in this crisis, shrink from the service of his country; but he that stands it NOW, deserves the love and thanks of man and woman. Tyranny, like hell, is not easily conquered; yet we have this consolation with us, that the harder the conflict, the more glorious the triumph. What we obtain too cheap, we esteem too lightly; 'tis dearness only that gives every thing its value. Heaven knows how to put a proper price upon its goods; and it would be strange indeed, if so celestial an article as FREEDOM should not be highly rated. Britain, with an army to enforce her tyranny, has declared that she has a right (*not only to* TAX) but "to BIND *us in* ALL CASES WHATSOEVER," and if being *bound in that manner,* is not slavery, then is there no such a thing as slavery upon earth. Even the expression is impious, for so unlimited a power can belong only to God. . . .

I have as little superstition in me as any man living, but my secret opinion has ever been, and still is, that God Almighty will not give up a people to military destruction, or leave them unsupportedly to perish, who have so earnestly and so repeatedly sought to avoid the calamities of war, by every decent method which wisdom could invent. Neither have I so much of the infidel in me, as to suppose that He has relinquished the government of the world, and given us up to the care of devils; and as I do not, I cannot see on what grounds the king of Britain can look up to Heaven for help against us: a common murderer, a highwayman, or a housebreaker, has as good a pretence as he.

'Tis surprising to see how rapidly a panic will

sometimes run through a country. All nations and ages have been subject to them: Britain has trembled like an ague at the report of a French fleet of flat bottomed boats; and in the fourteenth century the whole English army, after ravaging the kingdom of France, was driven back like men petrified with fear; and this brave exploit was performed by a few broken forces collected and headed by a woman, Joan of Arc. Would that heaven might inspire some Jersey maid to spirit up her countrymen, and save her fair fellow sufferers from ravage and ravishment! . . .

. . . I call not upon a few, but upon all: not on *this* state or *that* state, but on *every* state; up and help us; lay your shoulders to the wheel; better have too much force than too little, when so great an object is at stake. Let it be told to the future world, that in the depth of winter, when nothing but hope and virtue could survive, that the city and the country, alarmed at one common danger, came forth to meet and to repulse it. Say not that thousands are gone, turn out your tens of thousands; throw not the burden of the day upon Providence, but *"show your faith by your works,"* that God may bless you. It matters not where you live, or what rank of life you hold, the evil or the blessing will reach you all. The far and the near, the home counties and the back, the rich and the poor, will suffer or rejoice alike. The heart that feels not now, is dead: the blood of his children will curse his cowardice, who shrinks back at a time when a little might have saved the whole, and made *them* happy. I love the man that can smile in trouble, that can gather strength from distress, and grow brave by reflection. 'Tis the business of little minds to shrink; but he whose heart is firm, and whose conscience approves his conduct, will pursue his principles unto death. My own line of reasoning is to myself as straight and clear as a ray of light. Not all the treasures of the world, so far as I believe, could have induced me to support an offensive war, for I think it murder; but if a thief breaks into my house, burns and destroys my property, and kills or threatens to kill me, or

those that are in it, and to *"bind me in all cases whatsoever,"* to his absolute will, am I to suffer it? What signifies it to me, whether he who does it is a king or a common man; my countryman or not my countryman: whether it be done by an individual villain, or an army of them? If we reason to the root of things we shall find no difference; neither can any just cause be assigned why we should punish in the one case and pardon in the other. Let them call me rebel, and welcome, I feel no concern from it; but I should suffer the misery of devils, were I to make a whore of my soul by swearing allegiance to one whose character is that of a sottish, stupid, stubborn, worthless, brutish man. I conceive likewise a horrid idea in receiving mercy from a being, who at the last day shall be shrieking to the rocks and mountains to cover him, and fleeing with terror from the orphan, the widow, and the slain of America.

There are cases which cannot be overdone by language, and this is one. There are persons too who see not the full extent of the evil which threatens them, they solace themselves with hopes that the enemy, if they succeed, will be merciful. It is the madness of folly, to expect mercy from those who have refused to do justice; and even mercy, where conquest is the object, is only a trick of war; the cunning of the fox is as murderous as the violence of the wolf; and we ought to guard equally against both. . . .

I thank God that I fear not. I see no real cause for fear. I know our situation well, and can see the way out of it. . . . By perseverance and fortitude we have the prospect of a glorious issue; by cowardice and submission, the sad choice of a variety of evils—a ravaged country—a depopulated city—habitations without safety, and slavery without hope—our homes turned into barracks and bawdy-houses for Hessians, and a future race to provide for, whose fathers we shall doubt of. Look on this picture and weep over it! and if there yet remains one thoughtless wretch who believes it not, let him suffer it unlamented. . . .

THOMAS PAINE
LIBERTY TREE

In addition to writing revolutionary tracts, Thomas Paine wrote "Liberty Tree," a patriotic song that was printed in July 1775, in the *Pennsylvania Magazine: or American Monthly Museum;* the poem was signed "Atlanticus," a pseudonym that Paine often used. The "Liberty Tree" was popular for many years, though it has been forgotten in modern times.

In a chariot of light from the regions of day,
    The Goddess of Liberty came;
Ten thousand celestials directed the way,
    And thither conducted the dame,
This fair budding branch, from the garden
        above,
    Where millions with millions agree;
She bro't in her hand, as a pledge of her love,
    The plant she call'd Liberty Tree.

This celestial exotic struck deep in the ground,
    Like a native it flourish'd and bore;
The fame of its fruit, drew the nations around,
    To seek out its peaceable shore.
Unmindful of names or distinction they came,
    For freemen like brothers agree:
With one spirit endow'd, they one friendship
        pursued,
    And their temple was *Liberty Tree.*

Beneath this fair branch, like the patriarchs of
        old,
    Their bread, in contentment they eat;
Unwearied with trouble, of silver or gold,
    Or the cares of the grand and the great.
With timber and tar, they old England supplied,
    Supported her power on the seas;
Her battles they fought, without having a groat,
    For the honor of *Liberty Tree.*

But hear, O ye swains, ('tis a tale most profane)
    How all the tyrannical powers,
King, Commons, and Lords, are uniting amain,
    To cut down this guardian of ours;
From the east to the west, blow the trumpet to
        arms,
    Thro' the land let the sound of it flee,
Let the far and the near,—all unite with a
        cheer,
    In defense of our *Liberty Tree.*

ABIGAIL ADAMS
CORRESPONDENCE WITH JOHN

Do not put such unlimited power into the hands of the Husbands. Remember all Men would be tyrants if they could.

Abigail Adams (1744–1818) was born in Massachusetts; largely self-educated, she read widely in history. In 1764, she married John Adams, then a young Boston lawyer. During the long years that he was away from home attending to public affairs, the pair maintained a steady correspondence. Over the years—as John Adams attended the Continental Congress, or served abroad in diplomatic assignments or as vice-president and president—Abigail Adams wrote letters to family and friends, describing the life about her. Not only did she defend women's rights, but she opposed slavery.

On March 31, 1776, Abigail Adams wrote to her husband while the Continental Congress was deliberating independence. After describing the arrival of spring in Massachusetts, she admonished him to "Remember the Ladies" when writing the new code of laws. In his reply of April 14, 1776, he treated her "extraordinary Code of Laws" as his dear wife's little joke.

ABIGAIL to JOHN

. . . I long to hear that you have declared an independancy—and by the way in the new Code of Laws which I suppose it will be necessary for you to make I desire you would Remember the Ladies, and be more generous and favourable to them than your ancestors. Do not put such unlimited power into the hands of the Husbands. Remember all Men would be tyrants if they could. If perticuliar care and attention is not paid to the Laidies we are determined to foment a Rebelion, and will not hold ourselves bound by any Laws in which we have no voice, or Representation.

That your Sex are Naturally Tyrannical is a Truth so thoroughly established as to admit of no dispute, but such of you as wish to be happy willingly give up the harsh title of Master for the more tender and endearing one of Friend. Why then, not put it out of the power of the vicious and the Lawless to use us with cruelty and indignity with impunity. Men of Sense in all Ages abhor those customs which treat us only as the vassals of your Sex. Regard us then as Beings placed by providence under your protection and in immitation of the Supreem Being make use of that power only for our happiness.

JOHN to ABIGAIL

. . . As to your extraordinary Code of Laws, I cannot but laugh. We have been told that our Struggle has loosened the bands of Government every where. That Children and Apprentices were disobedient—that schools and Colledges were grown turbulent—that Indians slighted their Guardians and Negroes grew insolent to their Masters. But your Letter was the first Intimation that another Tribe more numerous and powerfull than all the rest were grown discontented.—This is rather too coarse a Compliment but you are so saucy, I wont blot it out.

Depend upon it, We know better than to repeal our Masculine systems. Altho they are in full Force, you know they are little more than Theory. We dare not exert our Power in its full Latitude. We are obliged to go fair, and softly, and in Practice you know We are the subjects. We have only the Name of Masters, and rather than give up this, which would compleatly subject Us to the Despotism of the Peticoat, I hope

Mrs. Elizabeth Freake and Baby Mary, *painted in 1674 by an anonymous artist in Boston.*

General Washington, and all our brave Heroes would fight. I am sure every good Politician would plot, as long as he would against Despotism, Empire, Monarchy, Aristocracy, Oligarchy, or Ochlocracy.—A fine Story indeed. I begin to think the Ministry as deep as they are wicked.

After stirring up Tories, Landjobbers, Trimmers, Bigots, Canadians, Indians, Negroes, Hanoverians, Hessians, Russians, Irish Roman Catholicks, Scotch Renegadoes, at last they have stimulated the [Ladies] to demand new Priviledges and threaten to rebell.

J. HECTOR St. JOHN DE CRÈVECOEUR
LETTERS FROM AN AMERICAN FARMER

Here individuals of all nations are melted into a new race of men, whose labours and posterity will one day cause great changes in the world.

In 1782, a French-American farmer and naturalist published a dozen essays, which he called *Letters from an American Farmer.* This book won fame for its author in the European countries where it was published and won friends for the fledgling country. J. Hector St. John de Crèvecoeur was also known as Michel-Guillaume-Jean de Crèvecoeur (1735–1813), who was born in France and educated in Jesuit schools. Crèvecoeur emigrated to the New World in 1754 and settled on a farm in the colony of New York. During the American Revolution, he had friends and relatives on both sides, and was briefly imprisoned by the English. He sailed for Europe in 1780 and arranged for publication in London of his essays on American life. For several years he served as the French consul in New York, returning to France in 1790, where he lived the rest of his life. For many years, Crèvecoeur's sharp and sympathetic descriptions of the new country made him the most widely read commentator on America. Perhaps the best-known section of his *Letters* is the passage included here, which introduced the concept of America as a melting pot for the people of many nations.

I wish I could be acquainted with the feelings and thoughts which must agitate the heart and present themselves to the mind of an enlightened Englishman, when he first lands on this continent. He must greatly rejoice that he lived at a time to see this fair country discovered and settled; he must necessarily feel a share of national pride, when he views the chain of settlements which embellishes these extended shores. When he says to himself, this is the work of my countrymen, who, when convulsed by factions, afflicted by a variety of miseries and wants, restless and impatient, took refuge here. They brought along with them their national genius, to which they principally owe what liberty they enjoy, and what substance they possess.

Here he sees the industry of his native country displayed in a new manner, and traces in their works the embryos of all the arts, sciences, and ingenuity which flourish in Europe. Here he beholds fair cities, substantial villages, extensive fields, an immense country filled with decent houses, good roads, orchards, meadows, and bridges, where an hundred years ago all was wild, woody, and uncultivated! What a train of pleasing ideas this fair spectacle must suggest; it is a prospect which must inspire a good citizen with the most heartfelt pleasure. The difficulty consists in the manner of viewing so extensive a scene. He is arrived on a new continent; a modern society offers itself to his contemplation, different from what he had hitherto seen.

It is not composed, as in Europe, of great lords who possess everything, and of a herd of people who have nothing. Here are no aristocratical families, no courts, no kings, no bishops, no ecclesiastical dominion, no invisible power giving to a few a very visible one; no great manufacturers employing thousands, no great refinements of luxury. The rich and the poor are not so far removed from each other as they are in Europe. Some few towns excepted, we are all tillers of the earth, from Nova Scotia to West Florida. We are a people of cultivators, scattered over an immense territory, communicating with each other by means of good roads and navigable rivers, united by the silken bands of mild government, all respecting the laws, without dreading their power, because they are equitable. We are all animated with the spirit of an industry which is unfettered and unrestrained, because each person works for himself. If he travels through our rural districts he views not the hostile castle, and the haughty mansion, contrasted with the clay-built hut and miserable cabin, where cattle and men help to keep each other warm, and dwell in meanness, smoke, and indigence. A pleasing uniformity of decent competence appears throughout our habitations. The meanest of our log-houses is a dry and comfortable habitation. Lawyer or merchant are the fairest titles our towns afford; that of a farmer is the only appellation of the rural inhabitants of our country. It must take some time ere he can reconcile himself to our dictionary, which is but short in words of dignity, and names of honour. There, on a Sunday, he sees a congregation of respectable farmers and their wives, all clad in neat homespun, well mounted, or riding in their own humble waggons. There is not among them an esquire, saving the unlettered magistrate. There he sees a parson as simple as his flock, a farmer who does not riot on the labour of others. We have no princes, for whom we toil, starve, and bleed: we are the most perfect society now existing in the world. . . .

The next wish of this traveller will be to know whence came all these people? they are a mixture of English, Scotch, Irish, French, Dutch, Germans, and Swedes. From this promiscuous breed, that race now called Americans have arisen. The eastern provinces must indeed be excepted, as being the unmixed descendants of Englishmen. I have heard many wish that they had been more intermixed also: for my part, I am no wisher, and think it much better as it has happened. They exhibit a most conspicuous figure in this great and variegated picture; they too enter for a great share in the pleasing perspective displayed in these thirteen provinces. I know it is fashionable to reflect on them, but I respect them for what they have done; for the accuracy and wisdom with which they have settled their territory; for the decency of their manners; for their early love of letters; their ancient college, the first in this hemisphere; for their industry; which to me who am but a farmer, is the criterion of everything. There never was a people, situated as they are, who with so ungrateful a soil have done more in so short a time. Do you think that the monarchical ingredients which are more prevalent in other governments, have purged them from all foul stains? Their histories assert the contrary.

In this great American asylum, the poor of Europe have by some means met together, and in consequence of various causes; to what purpose would they ask one another what countrymen they are? Alas, two thirds of them had no country. Can a wretch who wanders about, who works and starves, whose life is a continual scene of sore affliction or pinching penury; can that man call England or any other kingdom his country? A country that had no bread for him, whose fields procured him no harvest, who met with nothing but the frowns of the rich, the severity of the laws, with jails and punishments; who owned not a single foot of the extensive surface of this planet? No! urged by a variety of motives, here they came. Every thing has tended to regenerate them; new laws, a new mode of living, a new social system; here they are become men: in Europe they were as so many useless plants, wanting vegetative mould, and refreshing showers; they withered, and were mowed down by want, hunger, and war: but now by the power of transplantation, like all other plants they have taken root and flourished! Formerly they were not numbered in any civil lists of their country, except in those of the poor; here they rank as citizens. By what invisible power has this surprising metamorphosis been performed? By that of the laws and that of their industry. The laws, the indulgent laws, protect them as they arrive, stamping on them the symbol of adoption; they receive ample rewards for their labours; these accumulated rewards procure them lands; those lands confer on them the title of freemen, and to that title every benefit is affixed which men can possibly require. This is the great operation daily performed by our laws. . . .

What attachment can a poor European emigrant have for a country where he had nothing? The knowledge of the language, the love of a few kindred as poor as himself, were the only cords that tied him: his country is now that which gives him land, bread, protection, and consequence. *Ubi panis ibi patria,* is the motto of all emigrants. What then is the American, this new man? He is either an European, or the descendant of an European, hence that strange mixture of blood, which you will find in no other country. I could point out to you a family whose grandfather was an Englishman, whose wife was Dutch, whose son married a French woman, and whose present four sons have now four wives of different nations. *He* is an American, who, leaving behind him all his ancient prejudices and manners, receives new ones from the new mode of life he has embraced, the new government he obeys, and the new rank he holds. He becomes an American by being received in the broad lap of our great *Alma Mater.* Here individuals of all nations are melted into a new race of men, whose labours and posterity will one day cause great changes in the world. Americans are the western pilgrims, who are carrying along with them the great mass of arts, sciences, vigour, and industry which began long since in the east; they will finish the great circle. The Americans were once scattered all over Europe; here they are incorporated into one of the finest systems of population which has ever appeared, and which will hereafter become distinct by the power of the different climates they inhabit. The American ought therefore to love this country much better than that wherein either he or his forefathers were born. Here the rewards of his industry follow with equal steps the progress of his labour; his labour is founded on the basis of nature, *self-interest;* can it want a stronger allurement? Wives and children, who before in vain demanded of him a morsel of bread, now, fat and frolicsome, gladly help their father to clear those fields whence exuberant crops are to arise to feed and to clothe them all; without any part being claimed, either by a despotic prince, a rich abbot, or a mighty lord. Here religion demands but little of him; a small voluntary salary to the minister, and gratitude to God; can he refuse these? The American is a new man, who acts upon new principles; he must therefore entertain new ideas, and form new opinions. From involuntary idleness, servile dependence, penury, and useless labour, he has passed to toils of a very different nature, rewarded by ample subsistence.—This is an American. . . .

THE NEW NATION

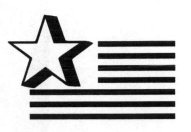

In Liberty & Washington, *painted by an anonymous artist between 1800—1810, Miss Liberty tramples a royal crown while placing the laurel wreath of victory on Washington's head. She is surrounded by icons of liberty and patriotism: the flag, the American eagle, and the liberty tree (which is topped by a Phrygian cap, an ancient symbol of freedom).*

GEORGE WASHINGTON

FAREWELL ADDRESS

The great rule of conduct for us in regard to foreign nations is, in extending our commercial relations, to have with them as little political connection as possible.

After leading the revolutionary army to victory and presiding over the successful Constitutional Convention, George Washington (1732–1799) was chosen without challenge as the first president of the new nation. He accepted a second four-year term with reluctance but refused a third term. In a world still ruled by kings, hereditary chieftains, and petty tyrants, Washington's decision to relinquish power to an elected successor demonstrated that the American democratic experiment was off to a good start.

In his farewell address, delivered to his cabinet on September 17, 1796, Washington counseled, first, against the dangers of sectionalism; second, against the strife of political factions; third, to preserve religion and morality as the "great pillars of human happiness" and to promote "institutions for the general diffusion of knowledge"; and fourth, to maintain neutrality in relations with other nations.

His warning about foreign involvements came to be known as Washington's "Great Rule." Until World War I, the "Great Rule" was one of the keystones of American foreign policy.

The period for a new election of a citizen to administer the executive government of the United States being not far distant, and the time actually arrived when your thoughts must be employed in designating the person who is to be clothed with that important trust, it appears to me proper, especially as it may conduce to a more distinct expression of the public voice, that I should now apprise you of the resolution I have formed to decline being considered among the number of those out of whom a choice is to be made. . . .

The unity of government which constitutes you one people is also now dear to you. It is justly so, for it is a main pillar in the edifice of your real independence, the support of your tranquillity at home, your peace abroad, of your safety, of your prosperity, of that very liberty which you so highly prize. But as it is easy to foresee that from different causes and from different quarters much pains will be taken, many artifices employed, to weaken in your minds the conviction of this truth, as this is the point in your political fortress against which the batter-ies of internal and external enemies will be most constantly and actively (though often covertly and insidiously) directed, it is of infinite moment that you should properly estimate the immense value of your national union to your collective and individual happiness; that you should cherish a cordial, habitual, and immovable attachment to it; accustoming yourselves to think and speak of it as of the palladium of your political safety and prosperity; watching for its preservation with jealous anxiety; discountenancing whatever may suggest even a suspicion that it can in any event be abandoned, and indignantly frowning upon the first dawning of every attempt to alienate any portion of our country from the rest or to enfeeble the sacred ties which now link together the various parts.

For this you have every inducement of sympathy and interest. Citizens by birth or choice of a common country, that country has a right to concentrate your affections. The name of American, which belongs to you in your national capacity, must always exalt the just pride of patriotism more than any appellation derived from local discriminations. With slight shades of difference, you have the same religion, manners, habits, and political principles. You have in a common cause fought and triumphed together. The independence and liberty you possess are the work of joint councils and joint efforts, of common dangers, sufferings, and successes. . . .

In contemplating the causes which may disturb our union it occurs as matter of serious concern that any ground should have been furnished for characterizing parties by *geographical* discriminations—*Northern* and *Southern, Atlantic* and *Western*—whence designing men may endeavor to excite a belief that there is a real difference of local interests and views. One of the expedients of party to acquire influence within particular districts is to misrepresent the opinions and aims of other districts. You can not shield yourselves too much against the jealousies and heartburnings which spring from these misrepresentations; they tend to render alien to each other those who ought to be bound together by fraternal affection. . . .

To the efficacy and permanency of your union a government for the whole is indispensable. No alliances, however strict, between the parts can be an adequate substitute. They must inevitably experience the infractions and interruptions which all alliances in all times have experienced. Sensible of this momentous truth, you have improved upon your first essay by the adoption of a Constitution of government better calculated than your former for an intimate union and for the efficacious management of your common concerns. This government, the offspring of our own choice, uninfluenced and unawed, adopted upon full investigation and mature deliberation, completely free in its principles, in the distribution of its powers, uniting security with energy, and containing within itself a provision for its own amendment, has a just claim to your confidence and your support. Respect for its authority, compliance with its laws, acquiescence in its measures, are duties enjoined by the fundamental maxims of true liberty. The basis of our political systems is the right of the people to make and to alter their constitutions of government. But the constitution which at any time exists till changed by an explicit and authentic act of the whole people is sacredly obligatory upon all. The very idea of the power and the right of the people to establish government presupposes the duty of every individual to obey the established government. . . .

Toward the preservation of your government and the permanency of your present happy state, it is requisite not only that you steadily discountenance irregular oppositions to its acknowledged authority, but also that you resist with care the spirit of innovation upon its principles, however specious the pretexts. One method of assault may be to effect in the forms of the Constitution alterations which will impair the energy of the system, and thus to undermine what can not be directly overthrown. In all the changes to which you may be invited remember that time and habit are at least as necessary to fix the true character of governments as of other human institutions; that experience is the surest standard by which to test the real tendency of the existing constitution of a country; that facility in changes upon the credit of mere hypothesis and opinion exposes to perpetual change, from the endless variety of hypothesis and opinion; and remember especially that for the efficient management of your common interests in a country so extensive as ours a government of as much vigor as is consistent with the perfect security of liberty is indispensable. . . .

I have already intimated to you the danger of parties in the state, with particular reference to the founding of them on geographical discriminations. Let me now take a more comprehensive view, and warn you in the most solemn manner against the baneful effects of the spirit of party generally.

This spirit, unfortunately, is inseparable from our nature, having its root in the strongest passions of the human mind. It exists under different shapes in all governments, more or less stifled, controlled, or repressed; but in those of the popular form it is seen in its greatest rankness and is truly their worst enemy. . . .

It serves always to distract the public councils and enfeeble the public administration. It agitates the community with illfounded jealousies and false alarms; kindles the animosity of one part against another; foments occasionally riot and insurrection. It opens the door to foreign influence and corruption, which find a facilitated access to the government itself through the channels of party passion. Thus the policy and the will of one country are subjected to the policy and will of another....

Of all the dispositions and habits which lead to political prosperity, religion and morality are indispensable supports. In vain would that man claim the tribute of patriotism who should labor to subvert these great pillars of human happiness—these firmest props of the duties of men and citizens. The mere politician, equally with the pious man, ought to respect and to cherish them. A volume could not trace all their connections with private and public felicity. Let it simply be asked, Where is the security for property, for reputation, for life, if the sense of religious obligation *desert* the oaths which are the instruments of investigation in courts of justice? And let us with caution indulge the supposition that morality can be maintained without religion. Whatever may be conceded to the influence of refined education on minds of peculiar structure, reason and experience both forbid us to expect that national morality can prevail in exclusion of religious principle.

It is substantially true that virtue or morality is a necessary spring of popular government. The rule indeed extends with more or less force to every species of free government. Who that is a sincere friend to it can look with indifference upon attempts to shake the foundation of the fabric? Promote, then, as an object of primary importance, institutions for the general diffusion of knowledge. In proportion as the structure of a government gives force to public opinion, it is essential that public opinion should be enlightened.

As a very important source of strength and security, cherish public credit. One method of preserving it is to use it as sparingly as possible, avoiding occasions of expense by cultivating peace, but remembering also that timely disbursements to prepare for danger frequently prevent much greater disbursements to repel it; avoiding likewise the accumulation of debt, not only by shunning occasions of expense, but by vigorous exertions in time of peace to discharge the debts which unavoidable wars have occasioned, not ungenerously throwing upon prosperity the burthen which we ourselves ought to bear....

Against the insidious wiles of foreign influence (I conjure you to believe me, fellow-citizens) the jealousy of a free people ought to be *constantly* awake, since history and experience prove that foreign influence is one of the most baneful foes of republican government. But that jealousy, to be useful, must be impartial, else it becomes the instrument of the very influence to be avoided, instead of a defense against it. Excessive partiality for one foreign nation and excessive dislike of another cause those whom that actuate to see danger only on one side, and serve to veil and even second the arts of influence on the other. Real patriots who may resist the intrigues of the favorite are liable to become suspected and odious, while its tools and dupes usurp the applause and confidence of the people to surrender their interests.

The great rule of conduct for us in regard to foreign nations is, in extending our commercial relations to have with them as little *political* connection as possible. So far as we have already formed engagements let them be fulfilled with perfect good faith. Here let us stop.

Europe has a set of primary interests which to us have none or a very remote relation. Hence she must be engaged in frequent controversies, the causes of which are essentially foreign to our concerns. Hence, therefore, it must be unwise in us to implicate ourselves to artificial ties in the ordinary vicissitudes of her politics or the ordinary combinations and collisions of her friendships or enmities.

Our detached and distant situation invites and enables us to pursue a different course. If we remain one people, under an efficient government, the period is not far off when we may defy material injury from external annoyance; when we may take such an attitude as will cause the neutrality we may at any time resolve upon to be scrupulously respected; when belligerent nations, under the impossibility of making acquisitions upon us, will not lightly hazard the giving us provocation; when we may choose peace or war, as our interest, guided by justice, shall counsel.

Why forego the advantages of so peculiar a situation? Why quit our own to stand upon foreign ground? Why, by interweaving our destiny with that of any part of Europe, entangle our peace and prosperity in the toils of European ambition, rivalship, interest, humor, or caprice? . . .

Though in reviewing the incidents of my ad-

ministration I am unconscious of intentional error, I am nevertheless too sensible of my defects not to think it probable that I may have committed many errors. Whatever they may be, I fervently beseech the Almighty to avert or mitigate the evils to which they may tend. I shall also carry with me the hope that my country will never cease to view them with indulgence, and that, after forty-five years of my life dedicated to its service with an upright zeal, the faults of incompetent abilities will be consigned to oblivion, as myself must soon be to the mansions of rest.

Relying on its kindness in this as in other things, and actuated by that fervent love toward it which is so natural to a man who views in it the native soil of himself and his progenitors for several generations, I anticipate with pleasing

The Residence of David Twining in 1787, *painted by Edward Hicks in the 1840s. One of the finest American folk artists, Hicks portrays himself as a child sitting at the knee of Elizabeth Twining, his guardian, as she reads the Bible.*

expectation that retreat in which I promise myself to realize without alloy the sweet enjoyment of partaking in the midst of my fellow-citizens the benign influence of good laws under a free government—the ever-favorite object of my heart, and the happy reward, as I trust, of our mutual cares, labors, and dangers.

JOSEPH HOPKINSON

HAIL, COLUMBIA

"Hail, Columbia" was introduced at a theater in Philadelphia on April 25, 1798, to wild applause and ovations. It was set to the music of "The President's March," which had been composed for Washington's first inauguration. It was originally titled "The Favorite New Federal Song, Adapted to the President's March," but within a year it was retitled "Hail, Columbia." The fourth stanza began with a direct tribute to the newly elected president John Adams. Adams's portrait was printed on the sheet music, encircled by the phrase "Behold the Chief who now commands." The anti-Federalist press derided the song as a bombastic paean to a party with monarchical pretensions, but the song swept the country, which embraced it with patriotic fervor. For nearly a century, "Hail, Columbia" vied with "The Star-Spangled Banner" as the national anthem; not until 1931 did President Hoover proclaim official status for the latter.

Hail! Columbia happy land
Hail! ye Heroes heav'n born band
 Who fought and bled in freedom's cause
 Who fought and bled in freedom's cause
And when the storm of war was gone
Enjoy'd the peace your valor won
 Let Independence be our boast
 Ever mindful what it cost
 Ever grateful for the prize
 Let its Altar reach the Skies.

CHORUS:
Firm united let us be
Rallying round our Liberty
As a band of Brothers join'd
Peace and safety we shall find.

Immortal Patriots rise once more
Defend your rights—defend your shore
 Let no rude foe with impious hand
 Let no rude foe with impious hand
Invade the shrine where sacred lies
Of toil and blood the well earned prize
 While off'ring peace, sincere and just
 In heav'n we place a manly trust

That truth and justice may prevail
And ev'ry scheme of bondage fail.

Sound sound the trump of fame
Let Washington's great name
 Ring thro the world with loud applause,
 Ring thro the world with loud applause,
Let ev'ry clime to Freedom dear
Listen with a joyful ear—
 With equal skill with godlike pow'r
 He governs in the fearful hour
 Of horrid war or guides with ease
 The happier times of honest peace.

Behold the Chief who now commands
Once more to serve his Country stands
 The rock on which the storm will beat
 The rock on which the storm will beat
But arm'd in virtue firm and true
His hopes are fixed on Heav'n and you—
 When hope was sinking in dismay
 When glooms obscur'd Columbia's day
 His steady mind from changes free
 Resolv'd on Death or Liberty.

THOMAS JEFFERSON

FIRST INAUGURAL ADDRESS

If there be any among us who wish to dissolve this Union or to change its republican form, let them stand undisturbed, as monuments of the safety with which error of opinion may be tolerated where reason is left free to combat it.

Thomas Jefferson (1743–1826) was, like Benjamin Franklin, a man of diverse talents. He was gifted as a writer, statesman, musician, architect, philosopher, inventor, and lawyer. He served in the Virginia legislature and the Continental Congress, where he drafted the Declaration of Independence. Afterward he was governor of Virginia, a diplomat in Europe, and George Washington's secretary of state.

In 1801, he was elected president in a hotly contested election. It was the first time in the United States that control of the government passed from one political party (the Federalists) to another (the Republicans or Democratic-Republicans). There was a tie vote in the electoral college between Jefferson and Aaron Burr, and Jefferson was elected to the presidency by the House of Representatives.

Jefferson's inaugural address was the first to be delivered by a president in Washington, D.C., where the new government had just moved from Philadelphia. Jefferson used his speech to unify the country after the hard-fought campaign and to define the principles that would shape his presidency.

. . . During the contest of opinion through which we have passed the animation of discussions and of exertions has sometimes worn an aspect which might impose on strangers unused to think freely and to speak and to write what they think; but this being now decided by the voice of the nation, announced according to the rules of the Constitution, all will, of course, arrange themselves under the will of the law, and unite in common efforts for the common good. All, too, will bear in mind this sacred principle, that though the will of the majority is in all cases to prevail, that will to be rightful must be reasonable; that the minority possesses their equal rights, which equal law must protect, and to violate would be oppression. Let us, then, fellow-citizens, unite with one heart and one mind. Let us restore to social intercourse that harmony and affection without which liberty and even life itself are but dreary things. And let us reflect that, having banished from our land that religious intolerance under which mankind so long bled and suffered, we have yet gained little if we countenance a political intolerance as despotic, as wicked, and capable of as bitter and bloody persecutions. During the throes and convulsions of the ancient world, during the agonizing spasms of infuriated man, seeking through blood and slaughter his long-lost liberty, it was not wonderful that the agitation of the billows should reach even this distant and peaceful shore; that this should be more felt and feared by some and less by others, and should divide opinions as to measures of safety. But every difference of opinion is not a difference of principle. We have called by different names brethren of the same principle. We are all Republicans, we are all Federalists. If there be any among us who would wish to dissolve this Union or to change its republican form, let them stand undisturbed as monuments of the safety with which error of opinion may be tolerated where reason is left free to combat it. I know, indeed, that some honest men fear that a republican government can not be strong, that this Government is not strong enough; but would the hon-

New Orleans, *painted in 1803 by Boqueto de Woisseri. In that year, President Thomas Jefferson purchased the Louisiana Territory from the French for about fifteen million dollars, less than 3 cents an acre.*

est patriot, in the full tide of successful experiment, abandon a government which has so far kept us free and firm on the theoretic and visionary fear that this Government, the world's best hope, may by possibility want energy to preserve itself? I trust not. I believe this, on the contrary, the strongest Government on earth. I believe it the only one where every man, at the call of the law, would fly to the standard of the law, and would meet invasions of the public order as his own personal concern. Sometimes it is said that man can not be trusted with the government of himself. Can he, then, be trusted with the government of others? Or have we found angels in the forms of kings to govern him? Let history answer this question.

Let us, then, with courage and confidence pursue our own Federal and Republican principles, our attachment to union and representative government. Kindly separated by nature and a wide ocean from the exterminating havoc of one quarter of the globe; too high-minded to endure the degradations of the others; possessing a chosen country, with room enough for our descendants to the thousandth and thousandth generation; entertaining a due sense of our equal right to the use of our own faculties, to the acquisitions of our own industry, to honor and confidence from our fellow-citizens, resulting not from birth, but from our actions and their sense of them; enlightened by a benign religion, professed, indeed, and practiced in various forms, yet all of them inculcating honesty, truth, temperance, gratitude, and the love of man; acknowledging and adoring an overruling Providence, which by all its dispensations proves that it delights in the happiness of man here and his greater happiness hereafter—with all these blessings, what more is necessary to make us a happy and a prosperous people? Still one thing more, fellow-citizens—a wise and frugal Government, which shall restrain men from injuring one another, shall leave them otherwise free to regulate their own pursuits of industry and improvement, and shall not take from the mouth of labor the bread it has earned. This is the sum of good government, and this is necessary to close the circle of our felicities.

About to enter, fellow-citizens, on the exercise of duties which comprehend everything dear and valuable to you, it is proper you should understand what I deem the essential principles of our Government, and consequently those which ought to shape its Administration. I will compress them within the narrowest compass they will bear, stating the general principle, but not all its limitations. Equal and exact justice to all men, of whatever state or persuasion, religious or political; peace, commerce, and honest friendship with all nations, entangling alliances with none; the support of the State governments in all their rights, as the most competent administrations for our domestic concerns and the surest bulwarks against antirepublican tendencies; the preservation of the General Government in its whole constitutional vigor, as the sheet anchor of our peace at home and safety abroad; a jealous care of the right of election by the people—a mild and safe corrective of abuses which are lopped by the sword of revolution where peaceable remedies are unprovided; absolute acquiescence in the decisions of the majority, the vital principle of republics, from which is no appeal but to force, the vital principle and immediate parent of despotism; a well-disciplined militia, our best reliance in peace and for the first moments of war, till regulars may relieve them; the supremacy of the civil over the military authority; economy in the public expense, that labor may be lightly burthened; the honest payment of our debts and sacred preservation of the public faith; encouragement of agriculture, and of commerce as its handmaid; the diffusion of information and arraignment of all abuses at the bar of the public reason; freedom of religion; freedom of the press, and freedom of person under the protection of the habeas corpus, and trial by juries impartially selected. These principles form the bright constellation which has gone before us and guided our steps through an age of revolution and reformation. The wisdom of our sages and blood of our heroes have been devoted to their attainment. They should be the creed of our political faith, the text of civic instruction, the touchstone by which to try the services of those we trust; and should we wander from them in moments of error or of alarm, let us hasten to retrace our steps and to regain the road which alone leads to peace, liberty, and safety. . . .

FRANCIS SCOTT KEY

THE STAR-SPANGLED BANNER

In September 1814, British troops invaded Washington, D.C., and set on fire the Capitol, the president's mansion, the Treasury, and other government buildings. During the British withdrawal from Washington, Dr. William Beanes, an elderly physician, was taken prisoner. Dr. Beanes was a personal friend of Francis Scott Key, a Maryland attorney.

Key (1779–1843) was commissioned to help secure the release of his friend from the British navy. Key and John S. Skinner, a government official who was in charge of prisoner exchanges, sailed to the British fleet under a flag of truce to make their request. On September 7, 1814, their request was granted, but as it happened, the British were

preparing to attack Baltimore and would not release the American visitors. Key and Skinner sailed with the British fleet and watched helplessly as the British first invaded near Baltimore, then bombarded Fort McHenry during the night of September 13–14. Through the smoke and haze, they could dimly see a huge American flag flying over the fort's ramparts. At the end of the bombardment, as dawn arrived, they peered anxiously to see which flag flew over Fort McHenry, and to their relief, the Stars and Stripes were still there! While awaiting their release, Key began making notes for a poem. On the evening of September 16, Key composed the poem in a Baltimore hotel, re-creating the events.

The next day, the poem was printed on a handbill in Baltimore and titled "Defence of Fort McHenry." A month later, the poem had been retitled "The Star-Spangled Banner" and set to the tune "To Anacreon in Heaven," which was well known to Key (and which, according to historians, he may have had in mind while writing the poem). On October 19, 1814, the song was performed at the Baltimore Theatre.

For many years, it was one of many popular patriotic songs, and vied wlth "Hail, Columbia" and "America" as national songs. It gained in favor among federal troops during the Civil War and became ever more popular in the following decades. In 1895, army regulatlons required the playing of "The Star-Spangled Banner" while the flag was lowered; in 1904, the secretary of the navy ordered that it be played at morning and evening colors. Although the song always had its critics (some thought that the tune was too difficult to sing, or that the lyrics were too obscure, or that it was too militaristic), Congress adopted "The Star-Spangled Banner" as the national anthem in 1931.

Oh, say, can you see, by the dawn's early
    light,
  What so proudly we hailed at the twilight's
      last gleaming,
Whose broad stripes and bright stars through
      the perilous fight,
  O'er the ramparts we watched were so
      gallantly streaming?
And the rockets' red glare, the bombs bursting
      in air,
Gave proof thro' the night that our flag was still
      there.
Oh, say, does that star-spangled banner yet
      wave
O'er the land of the free, and the home of the
      brave!

On the shore, dimly seen thro' the mists of the
      deep,
  Where the foe's haughty host in dread
      silence reposes,
What is that which the breeze o'er the
      towering steep,

As it fitfully blows, half conceals, half
      discloses?
Now it catches the gleam of the morning's first
      beam,
In full glory reflected, now shines on the
      stream.
'Tis the star-spangled banner; oh, long may it
      wave
O'er the land of the free, and the home of the
      brave!

And where is that band who so vauntingly
      swore
  That the havoc of war and the battle's
      confusion
A home and a country should leave us no
      more?
  Their blood has washed out their foul
      footsteps' pollution.
No refuge could save the hireling and slave
From the terror of flight, or the gloom of the
      grave:

And the star-spangled banner in triumph doth
    wave
O'er the land of the free, and the home of the
    brave!

Oh, thus be it ever when freemen shall stand
    Between their loved homes and the war's
        desolation;
Blest with victory and peace, may the heaven-
    rescued land

Praise the power that hath made and
    preserved us a nation!
Then conquer we must, when our cause it is
    just,
And this be our motto: "In God is our trust!"
And the star-spangled banner in triumph doth
    wave,
O'er the land of the free, and the home of the
    brave!

SAMUEL WOODWORTH

THE OLD OAKEN BUCKET

Samuel Woodworth (1784–1842) was born in Massachusetts. A poet, playwright, and editor, he wrote only one poem that has survived him, "The Old Oaken Bucket" (1818). This poem well expresses a nostalgia for the country life and rural virtues that were steadily disappearing as industrialism spread and cities grew. It was frequently reproduced in schoolbooks and memorized. When set to music, it became the hit song of 1826 and remained popular for much of the nineteenth century.

How dear to my heart are the scenes of my
    childhood,
    When fond recollection presents them to
        view!
The orchard, the meadow, the deep tangled
    wildwood,
    And every loved spot which my infancy
        knew,
The wide-spreading pond and the mill that
    stood by it,
    The bridge and the rock where the cataract
        fell;
The cot of my father, the dairy house nigh it,
    And e'en the rude bucket that hung in the
        well.

That moss-covered bucket I hailed as a
    treasure,
    For often at noon, when returned from the
        field,
I found it the source of an exquisite pleasure,
    The purest and sweetest that nature can
        yield.

How ardent I seized it, with hands that were
    glowing,
    And quick to the white-pebbled bottom it
        fell.
Then soon, with the emblem of truth
    overflowing,
    And dripping with coolness, it rose from
        the well.

How sweet from the green, mossy brim to
    receive it,
    As, poised on the curb, it inclined to my
        lips!
Not a full, blushing goblet could tempt me to
    leave it,
    Tho' filled with the nectar that Jupiter sips,
And now, far removed from the loved
    habitation,
    The tear of regret will intrusively swell,
As fancy reverts to my father's plantation,
    And sighs for the bucket that hung in the
        well.

HOME, SWEET HOME

John Howard Payne (1791–1852) had an extraordinary career as an actor and writer. He wrote his first play when he was fifteen, attended Union College for a year, and at eighteen made his first appearance on the stage as an actor. He was successful on the European stage, but achieved even greater fame as a playwright. He wrote more than sixty plays, two in collaboration with Washington Irving. His play *Brutus,* first performed in London in 1818, was popular on both sides of the Atlantic for the rest of the nineteenth century. His play *Clari: or The Maid of Milan* (1823) included his famous song "Home, Sweet Home." Despite the popularity of his plays, Payne seldom received royalties and was often penniless and occasionally in debtors' prison. Eventually, Payne's name was forgotten to the public, but "Home, Sweet Home" survived, emblazoned in millions of embroidered stitches; and its best-known phrase, "There's no place like home," served as a talisman for Dorothy in *The Wizard of Oz.* Perhaps Americans were so sentimental about home because of their heritage as immigrants, pioneers, and frontiersmen, a people with shallow roots.

'Mid pleasures and palaces though we may
    roam,
Be it ever so humble, there's no place like
    home;
A charm from the sky seems to hallow us there,
Which, seek through the world, is ne'er met
    with elsewhere.
    Home, home, sweet, sweet home!
There's no place like home, oh, there's no
    place like home!

An exile from home, splendor dazzles in vain;
Oh, give me my lowly thatched cottage again!
The birds singing gayly, that came at my call—
Give me them—and the peace of mind, dearer
    than all!
    Home, home, sweet, sweet home!
There's no place like home, oh, there's no
    place like home!

I gaze on the moon as I tread the drear wild,
And feel that my mother now thinks of her
    child,
As she looks on that moon from our own
    cottage door
Thro' the woodbine, whose fragrance shall
    cheer me no more.

    Home, home, sweet, sweet home!
There's no place like home, oh, there's no
    place like home!

How sweet 'tis to sit 'neath a fond father's
    smile,
And the caress of a mother to soothe and
    beguile!
Let others delight 'mid new pleasure to roam,
But give me, oh, give me, the pleasures of
    home,
    Home, home, sweet, sweet home!
There's no place like home, oh, there's no
    place like home!

To thee I'll return, overburdened with care;
The heart's dearest solace will smile on me
    there;
No more from that cottage again will I roam;
Be it ever so humble, there's no place like
    home.
    Home, home, sweet, sweet home!
There's no place like home, oh, there's no
    place like home!

CLEMENT CLARKE MOORE

A VISIT FROM ST. NICHOLAS

Clement Clarke Moore (1779–1863), professor of biblical learning, published "A Visit from St. Nicholas" anonymously in the *Troy Sentinel* on December 23, 1823. It was widely copied and was eventually printed in Moore's collection of poetry, which appeared in 1844. The one poem that survived to guarantee his fame became known, and loved, as " 'Twas the Night Before Christmas."

'Twas the night before Christmas, when all
    through the house
Not a creature was stirring, not even a mouse;
The stockings were hung by the chimney with
    care,
In hopes that St. Nicholas soon would be there;
The children were nestled all snug in their
    beds,
While visions of sugar-plums danced in their
    heads;
And mamma in her kerchief, and I in my cap,
Had just settled our brains for a long winter's
    nap,—
When out on the lawn there arose such a
    clatter,
I sprang from my bed to see what was the
    matter.
Away to the window I flew like a flash,
Tore open the shutters and threw up the sash.
The moon on the breast of the new-fallen snow
Gave a lustre of midday to objects below;
When what to my wondering eyes should
    appear,
But a miniature sleigh and eight tiny reindeer,
With a little old driver, so lively and quick
I knew in a moment it must be St. Nick.
More rapid than eagles his coursers they came,
And he whistled and shouted, and called them
    by name:
"Now, Dasher! now, Dancer! now, Prancer and
    Vixen!
On, Comet! on, Cupid! on, Donder and Blitzen!
To the top of the porch, to the top of the wall!
Now dash away, dash away, dash away all!"
As dry leaves that before the wild hurricane fly,

When they meet with an obstacle, mount to
    the sky,
So up to the house-top the coursers they flew,
Wtih the sleigh full of toys,—and St. Nicholas
    too.
And then in a twinkling I heard on the roof
The prancing and pawing of each little hoof.
As I drew in my head, and was turning around,
Down the chimney St. Nicholas came with a
    bound.
He was dressed all in fur from his head to his
    foot,
And his clothes were all tarnished with ashes
    and soot;
A bundle of toys he had flung on his back,
And he looked like a pedlar just opening his
    pack.
His eyes, how they twinkled! his dimples, how
    merry!
His cheeks were like roses, his nose like a
    cherry;
His droll little mouth was drawn up like a bow,
And the beard on his chin was as white as the
    snow.
The stump of a pipe he held tight in his teeth,
And the smoke it encircled his head like a
    wreath.
He had a broad face and a little round belly
That shook, when he laughed, like a bowl full
    of jelly.
He was chubby, and plump,—a right jolly old
    elf;
And I laughed, when I saw him, in spite of
    myself.
A wink of his eye and a twist of his head

Soon gave me to know I had nothing to dread.
He spoke not a word, but went straight to his
    work,
And filled all the stockings; then turned with a
    jerk,
And laying his finger aside of his nose,
And giving a nod, up the chimney he rose.

He sprang to his sleigh, to his team gave a
    whistle,
And away they all flew like the down of a
    thistle;
But I heard him exclaim, ere he drove out of
    sight,
"Happy Christmas to all, and to all a good-
    night!"

FRANCES WRIGHT

THE MEANING OF PATRIOTISM IN AMERICA

*Let us rejoice as men, not as children—as human beings rather than as Americans—
as reasoning beings, not as ignorants.*

The Fourth of July oration was an honored custom in the United States for many years
after the American Revolution, and it was usual for esteemed men to voice the sentiments of the community. On July 4, 1828, Frances (Fanny) Wright delivered what was
very likely the first public Independence Day oration by a woman. Wright (1795–1852)
was a tireless social reformer who held advanced views on religion, marriage, birth
control, slavery, and women's rights. Born in Scotland, she first visited the United States
in 1818 and wrote a book about her extensive travels. In 1824, she returned with the
Marquis de Lafayette, the French hero of the American Revolution, and she decided to
settle in the United States.

In 1825, she bought land in Tennessee and created a community for ex-slaves, whom
she bought and emancipated. After her community failed, she moved to New Harmony,
Indiana, to join Robert Dale Owen's experimental socialist community. In 1829, Wright
and Owen settled in New York City, where they established a radical newspaper called
the *Free Enquirer.* She became well known as a lecturer and writer.

. . . Dating, as we justly may, a new era in the history of man from the Fourth of July, 1776, it would be well—that is, it would be useful—if on each anniversary we examined the progress made by our species in just knowledge and just practice. Each Fourth of July would then stand as a tidemark in the flood of time by which to ascertain the advance of the human intellect, by which to note the rise and fall of each successive error, the discovery of each important truth, the gradual melioration in our public institutions, social arrangements, and, above all, in our moral feelings and mental views. . . .

In continental Europe, of late years, the words patriotism and patriot have been used in a more enlarged sense than it is usual here to attribute to them, or than is attached to them in Great Britain. Since the political struggles of France, Italy, Spain, and Greece, the word patriotism has been employed, throughout continental Europe, to express a love of the public good; a preference for the interests of the many to those of the few, a desire for the emancipation of the human race from the thrall of despotism, religious and civil: in short, patriotism there is used rather to express the interest felt in the human race in general than that felt for any country, or inhabitants of a country, in particu-

Joseph Moore and His Family, *painted in 1839 by Erastus Salisbury Field, an itinerant New England artist.*

lar. And patriot, in like manner, is employed to signify a lover of human liberty and human improvement rather than a mere lover of the country in which he lives, or the tribe to which he belongs. Used in this sense, patriotism is a virtue, and a patriot a virtuous man. With such an interpretation, a patriot is a useful member of society, capable of enlarging all minds and bet-

tering all hearts with which he comes in contact; a useful member of the human family, capable of establishing fundamental principles and of merging his own interests, those of his associates, and those of his nation in the interests of the human race. Laurels and statues are vain things, and mischievous as they are childish; but could we imagine them of use, on *such* a patriot alone could they be with any reason bestowed. . . .

If such a patriotism as we have last considered should seem likely to obtain in any country, it should be certainly in this. In this which is truly the home of all nations and in the veins of whose citizens flows the blood of every people on the globe. Patriotism, in the exclusive meaning, is surely not made for America. Mischievous everywhere, it were here both mischievous and absurd. The very origin of the people is opposed to it. The institutions, in their principle, militate against it. The day we are celebrating protests against it. It is for Americans, more especially, to nourish a nobler sentiment; one more consistent with their origin, and more conducive to their future improvement. It is for them more especially to know why they love their country; and to *feel* that they love it, not because it *is* their country, but because it is the palladium of human liberty—the favored scene of human improvement. It is for them, more especially, to examine their institutions; and to *feel* that they honor them because they are based on just principles. It is for them, more especially, to examine their institutions, because they have the means of improving them; to examine their laws, because at will they can alter them. It is for them to lay aside luxury whose wealth is in industry; idle parade whose strength is in knowldge; ambitious distinctions whose principle is equality. It is for them not to rest, satisfied with words, who can seize upon things; and to remember that equality means, not the mere equality of political rights, however valuable, but equality of instruction and equality in virtue; and that liberty means, not the mere voting at elections, but the free and fearless exercise of the mental faculties and that self-possession which springs out of well-reasoned opinions and consistent practice. It is for them to honor principles rather than men—to commemorate events rather than days; when they rejoice, to know for what they rejoice, and to rejoice only for what has brought and what brings peace and happiness to men. The event we commemorate this day has procured much of both, and shall procure in the onward course of human improvement more than we can now conceive of. For this—for the good obtained and yet in store for our race—let us rejoice! But let us rejoice as men, not as children—as human beings rather than as Americans—as reasoning beings, not as ignorants. So shall we rejoice to good purpose and in good feeling; so shall we improve the victory once on this day achieved, until all mankind hold with us the Jubilee of Independence.

DANIEL WEBSTER
AGAINST NULLIFICATION

Liberty and *Union, now and forever, one and inseparable!*

Daniel Webster (1782–1852) was known as the foremost orator of his time. As a senator from Massachusetts, he debated the issue of tariffs with Senator Robert Y. Hayne of South Carolina in 1830. Speaking for the southern states, which opposed the tariff, Hayne cited Vice-President John C. Calhoun's theory of nullification, under which a state could "nullify" a federal law that it believed unconstitutional and, if necessary, secede from the Union rather than accept what was intolerable to its interests. In rebuttal, Webster defended the authority of the federal government and criticized the notion of states' rights. Excerpted below (from an extemporaneous speech that exceeded 100 pages) is the peroration of Webster's reply to Hayne.

. . . If anything be found in the national constitution, either by original provision or subsequent interpretation, which ought not to be in it, the people know how to get rid of it. If any construction be established unacceptable to them, so as to become practically a part of the constitution, they will amend it, at their own sovereign pleasure. But while the people choose to maintain it as it is, while they are satisfied with it, and refuse to change it, who has given, or who can give, to the state legislatures a right to alter it, either by interference, construction, or otherwise? Gentlemen do not seem to recollect that the people have any power to do anything for themselves. They imagine there is no safety for them, any longer than they are under the close guardianship of the state legislatures. Sir, the people have not trusted their safety, in regard to the general constitution, to these hands. They have required other security, and taken other bonds. They have chosen to trust themselves, first, to the plain words of the instrument, and to such construction as the government itself, in doubtful cases, should put on its own powers, and under their oaths of office, and subject to their responsibility to them; just as the people of a state trust their own state government with a similar power. Secondly, they have reposed their trust in the efficacy of frequent elections, and in their own power to remove their own servants and agents whenever they see cause. Thirdly, they have reposed trust in the judicial power, which, in order that it might be trustworthy, they have made as respectable, as disinterested, and as independent as was practicable. Fourthly, they have seen fit to rely, in case of necessity, or high expediency, on their known and admitted power to alter or amend the constitution, peaceably and quietly, whenever experience shall point out defects or imperfections. And, finally, the people of the United States have at no time, in no way, directly or indirectly, authorized any state legislature to construe or interpret *their* high instrument of government; much less, to interfere, by their own power, to arrest its course and operation.

If, sir, the people in these respects had done otherwise than they have done, their constitution could neither have been preserved, nor would it have been worth preserving. And if its plain provisions shall now be disregarded, and these new doctrines interpolated in it, it will become as feeble and helpless a being as its enemies, whether early or more recent, could possibly desire. It will exist in every state but as a poor dependent on state permission. It must borrow leave to be; and will be, no longer than state pleasure, or state discretion, sees fit to grant the indulgence, and prolong its poor existence.

But, sir, although there are fears, there are hopes also. The people have preserved this, their own chosen constitution, for forty years, and have seen their happiness, prosperity, and renown grow with its growth, and strengthen with its strength. They are now, generally, strongly attached to it. Overthrown by direct assault, it cannot be; evaded, undermined, NULLIFIED, it will not be, if we, and those who shall succeed us here, as agents and representatives of the people, shall conscientiously and vigilantly discharge the two great branches of our public trust, faithfully to preserve, and wisely to administer it. . . .

I have not allowed myself, sir, to look beyond the Union, to see what might lie hidden in the dark recess behind. I have not coolly weighed the chances of preserving liberty when the bonds that unite us together shall be broken asunder. I have not accustomed myself to hang over the precipice of disunion, to see whether, with my short sight, I can fathom the depth of the abyss below; nor could I regard him as a safe counselor in the affairs of this government, whose thoughts should be mainly bent on considering, not how the Union should be best preserved, but how tolerable might be the condition of the people when it shall be broken up and destroyed. While the Union lasts, we have high, exciting, gratifying prospects spread out before us, for us and our children. Beyond that I seek not to penetrate the vail. God grant that in my day, at least, that curtain may not rise! God grant that on my vision never may be opened what lies behind! When my eyes shall be turned to behold for the last time the sun in heaven, may I not see him shining on the broken and dishonored fragments of a once glorious Union; on states dissevered, discordant, belligerent; on a land rent with civil feuds, or drenched, it may be, in fraternal blood! Let their last feeble and lingering glance rather behold the gorgeous ensign of the republic, now known and honored throughout the earth, still full high advanced, its arms and trophies streaming in their original luster, not a stripe erased or polluted, nor a single star obscured, bearing for its motto, no such miserable interrogatory as "What is all this worth?" nor those other words of delusion and folly, "Liberty first and Union afterwards;" but everywhere, spread all over in characters of living light, blazing on all its ample folds, as they float over the sea and over the land, and in every wind under the whole heavens, that other sentiment, dear to every true American heart—Liberty *and* Union, now and forever, one and inseparable!

GEORGE PERKINS MORRIS
WOODMAN, SPARE THAT TREE

The poem "Woodman, Spare That Tree" has been popular since its first publication in 1830. George Perkins Morris (1802–1864) was a journalist, poet, and dramatist. He was an editor of the *New York Mirror* in the 1820s, but he is best known for his sentimental poems, chiefly "Woodman, Spare That Tree." As industrialism and urban sprawl replaced bucolic scenes, the poem was treasured both as a nostalgic evocation of the past and as a genteel protest against "progress." Even people who had never read the poem knew the title and used it as a shorthand way of expressing an environmentalist stance before environmentalism became a political movement.

Woodman, spare that tree!
   Touch not a single bough!
In youth it sheltered me,
   And I'll protect it now.
'Twas my forefather's hand
   That placed it near his cot;
There, woodman, let it stand,
   Thy axe shall harm it not!

That old familiar tree,
   Whose glory and renown
Are spread o'er land and sea,
   And wouldst thou hew it down?
Woodman, forbear thy stroke!
   Cut not its earth-bound ties;
O, spare that aged oak,
   Now towering to the skies!

When but an idle boy
   I sought its grateful shade;
In all their gushing joy
   Here too my sisters played.
My mother kissed me here;
   My father pressed my hand—
Forgive this foolish tear,
   But let that old oak stand!

My heart-strings round thee cling,
   Close as thy bark, old friend!
Here shall the wild-bird sing,
   And still thy branches bend.
Old tree! the storm still brave!
   And, woodman, leave the spot;
While I've a hand to save,
   Thy axe shall hurt it not.

OLIVER WENDELL HOLMES

THE HEIGHT OF THE RIDICULOUS and OLD IRONSIDES

Oliver Wendell Holmes (1809–1894) was a man of prodigious gifts. He was noted as a poet, humorist, essayist, physician, and medical researcher. He studied law at Harvard but switched to medicine and received his degree in 1836. He practiced medicine for ten years, then became a professor of anatomy, first at Dartmouth, then at Harvard; for many years he was dean of the Harvard Medical School.

His greatest fame, however, came from his writings. The publication of "Old Ironsides" brought him national acclaim when he was only twenty-one. Holmes had read in a newspaper that the Navy Department planned to scrap the frigate *Constitution*, which was old and no longer seaworthy. He dashed off the poem on a scrap of paper, submitted it to a Boston paper, and set off a national furor. An amazed secretary of the navy withdrew his order to condemn the old ship, and Holmes was launched as a budding poet.

Both "Old Ironsides" and "The Height of the Ridiculous" were published in 1830.

The Height of the Ridiculous

I wrote some lines once on a time
    In wondrous merry mood,
And thought, as usual, men would say
    They were exceeding good.

They were so queer, so very queer,
    I laughed as I would die;
Albeit, in the general way,
    A sober man am I.

I called my servant, and he came;
    How kind it was of him
To mind a slender man like me,
    He of the mighty limb!

"These to the printer," I exclaimed,
    And, in my humorous way,
I added (as a trifling jest),
    "There'll be the devil to pay."

He took the paper, and I watched,
    And saw him peep within;
At the first line he read, his face
    Was all upon the grin.

He read the next; the grin grew broad,
    And shot from ear to ear;

He read the third; a chuckling noise
    I now began to hear.

The fourth; he broke into a roar;
    The fifth; his waistband split;
The sixth; he burst five buttons off,
    And tumbled in a fit.

Ten days and nights, with sleepless eye
    I watched that wretched man,
And since, I never dare to write
    As funny as I can.

Old Ironsides

Ay, tear her tattered ensign down!
    Long has it waved on high,
And many an eye has danced to see
    That banner in the sky;
Beneath it rung the battle shout,
    And burst the cannon's roar;—
The meteor of the ocean air
    Shall sweep the clouds no more.

Her deck, once red with heroes' blood,
    Where knelt the vanquished foe,
When winds were hurrying o'er the flood,
    And waves were white below,

No more shall feel the victor's tread,
    Or know the conquered knee;—
The harpies of the shore shall pluck
    The eagle of the sea!

Oh, better that her shattered hulk
    Should sink beneath the wave;

Her thunders shook the mighty deep,
    And there should be her grave;
Nail to the mast her holy flag,
    Set every threadbare sail,
And give her to the god of storms,
    The lightning and the gale!

SAMUEL F. SMITH

AMERICA

The lyrics for "America" (or "My Country 'Tis of Thee") were written by Reverend Samuel F. Smith (1808–1895) to the music of the English national anthem ("God Save the King"). Smith wrote the lyrics in Amherst, Massachusetts, in February 1832, and the song was first sung at a patriotic celebration on July 4, 1832, at the Park Street Church in Boston. He later wrote that it was "a dismal winter afternoon" when he wrote new words for the well-known tune in a single sitting. Reverend Smith was often asked to autograph copies of the song and to reminisce about his authorship; in 1889, he wrote, "I did not design it for a national hymn, nor did I think it would gain such notoriety."

The tune "God Save the King" was well known to Americans, for it had served as their national anthem until 1776. It was often appropriated to serve for such patriotic airs as "God Save America," "God Save George Washington," and "God Save the Thirteen States." It was even put to use by one of America's earliest feminists, who published a poem titled "Rights of Woman" to the tune of "God Save the King" in the *Philadelphia Minerva* of October 17, 1795, which began:

**God save each Female's right
Show to her ravish'd sight
    Woman is free.**

My country 'tis of thee
Sweet land of liberty;
    Of thee I sing.
Land where my fathers died
Land of the pilgrims' pride
From every mountainside
    Let freedom ring.

My native country—thee
Land of the noble free
    Thy name I love;
I love thy rocks and rills
Thy woods and templed hills
My heart with rapture thrills
    Like that above.

Let music swell the breeze
And ring from all the trees
    Sweet freedom's song
Let all that breathe partake
Let mortal tongues awake
Let rocks their silence break
    The sound prolong.

Our fathers' God to thee
Author of liberty
    To thee we sing
Long may our land be bright
With freedom's holy light
Protect us by thy might
    Great God, our King.

ANTEBELLUM AMERICA: REFORM AND EXPANSION

*A political banner by Terence J. Kennedy, painted about 1840, portrays
the young nation's progress on land and sea, in commerce and industry.*

RALPH WALDO EMERSON
CONCORD HYMN

Ralph Waldo Emerson (1803–1882) achieved renown in his lifetime as a philosopher, lecturer, poet, and essayist. Born in Boston and educated at Harvard, he was briefly a Unitarian minister but resigned his position because he could not accept the confines of religious doctrine. The poem "Concord Hymn" was written in tribute to the heroes of the Battle of Concord. It was sung as a hymn at a ceremony in 1837 to mark the completion of a monument in honor of the Revolutionary patriots of Concord. It was there, on April 19, 1775, that the American Minutemen resisted British troops at the North Bridge. Emerson's poem immortalized the Battle of Concord, and "the shot heard round the world" became a popular metaphor for the worldwide influence of the American Revolution. The poem was a favorite entry in American schoolbooks until the 1930s. Although Emerson is better known for his essays and lectures, generations of America's schoolchildren knew him primarily through this poem.

By the rude bridge that arched the flood,
   Their flag to April's breeze unfurled,
Here once the embattled farmers stood
   And fired the shot heard round the world.

The foe long since in silence slept;
   Alike the conqueror silent sleeps;
And Time the ruined bridge has swept
   Down the dark stream which seaward
     creeps.

On this green bank, by this soft stream,
   We set to-day a votive stone;
That memory may their deed redeem,
   When, like our sires, our sons are gone.

Spirit, that made those heroes dare
   To die, and leave their children free,
Bid Time and Nature gently spare
   The shaft we raise to them and thee.

RALPH WALDO EMERSON
SELF-RELIANCE

A foolish consistency is the hobgoblin of little minds.

With the growth of the lyceum movement, Emerson became a popular lecturer. Started in the 1820s, this movement was an early form of organized adult education which brought lectures, debates, and discussions about public issues and learned topics to communities throughout the northeastern and middle western states. The movement was named for the Athenian school where Aristotle lectured to his students. The lyceums provided a platform and income for speakers like Emerson, Henry David Thoreau, Susan B. Anthony, Frederick Douglass, and Nathaniel Hawthorne.

    Emerson's natural philosophy attracted wide attention and large audiences. His appeal to the inner self, to intuition and to nature as guides to life and reality, challenged those who relied on tradition, authority, and dogma. Emerson's words have enduring appeal to those who would be individualists and nonconformists, who would rebel against received wisdom to find inner truth. Every generation of young Americans rediscovers Emerson. This essay is quintessentially Emersonian, with its epigrammatic sentences and its buoyant individualism. It originally appeared in his first volume of essays, in 1841.

I read the other day some verses written by an eminent painter which were original and not conventional. Always the soul hears an admonition in such lines, let the subject be what it may. The sentiment they instil is of more value than any thought they may contain. To believe your own thought, to believe that what is true for you in your private heart is true for all men,—that is genius. Speak your latent conviction, and it shall be universal sense; for always the inmost becomes the outmost—and our first thought is rendered back to us by the trumpets of the Last Judgment. Familiar as the voice of the mind is to each, the highest merit we ascribe to Moses, Plato and Milton is that they set at naught books and traditions, and spoke not what men, but what they thought. A man should learn to detect and watch that gleam of light which flashes across his mind from within, more than the lustre of the firmament of bards and sages. Yet he dismisses without notice his thought, because it is his. In every work of genius we recognize our own rejected thoughts; they come back to us with a certain alienated majesty. Great works of art have no more affecting lesson for us than this. They teach us to abide by our spontaneous impression with good-humored inflexibility then most when the whole cry of voices is on the other side. Else to-morrow a stranger will say with masterly good sense precisely what we have thought and felt all the time, and we shall be forced to take with shame our own opinion from another.

There is a time in every man's education when he arrives at the conviction that envy is ignorance; that imitation is suicide; that he must take himself for better for worse as his portion; that though the wide universe is full of good, no kernel of nourishing corn can come to him but through his toil bestowed on that plot of ground which is given to him to till. The power which resides in him is new in nature, and none but he knows what that is which he can do, nor does he know until he has tried. Not for nothing one face, one character, one fact, makes much impression on him, and another none. It is not without preëstablished harmony, this sculpture in the memory. The eye was placed where one ray should fall, that it might testify of that particular ray. Bravely let him speak the utmost syllable of his confession. We but half express ourselves, and are ashamed of that divine idea which each of us represents. It may be safely trusted as proportionate and of good issues, so it be faithfully imparted, but God will not have his work made manifest by cowards. It needs a divine man to exhibit anything divine. A man is relieved and gay when he has put his heart into his work and done his best; but what he has said or done otherwise shall give him no peace. It is a deliverance which does not deliver. In the attempt his genius deserts him; no muse befriends; no invention, no hope.

Trust thyself: every heart vibrates to that iron string. Accept the place the divine providence has found for you, the society of your contemporaries, the connexion of events. Great men have always done so, and confided themselves childlike to the genius of their age, betraying their perception that the Eternal was stirring at their heart, working through their hands, predominating in all their being. And we are now men, and must accept in the highest mind the same transcendent destiny; and not pinched in a corner, not cowards fleeing before a revolution, but redeemers and benefactors, pious aspirants to be noble clay under the Almighty effort let us advance on Chaos and the Dark. . . .

These are the voices which we hear in solitude, but they grow faint and inaudible as we enter into the world. Society everywhere is in conspiracy against the manhood of every one of its members. Society is a joint-stock company, in which the members agree, for the better securing of his bread to each shareholder, to surrender the liberty and culture of the eater. The virtue in most request is conformity. Self-reliance is its aversion. It loves not realities and creators, but names and customs.

Whoso would be a man, must be a noncon-formist. He who would gather immortal palms must not be hindered by the name of goodness, but must explore if it be goodness. Nothing is at last sacred but the integrity of our own mind. Absolve you to yourself, and you shall have the suffrage of the world. I remember an answer which when quite young I was prompted to make to a valued adviser who was wont to importune me with the dear old doctrines of the church. On my saying, What have I to do with the sacredness of traditions, if I live wholly from within? My friend suggested,—"But these impulses may be from below, not from above." I replied, "They do not seem to me to be such; but if I am the devil's child, I will live then from the devil." No law can be sacred to me but that of my nature. Good and bad are but names very readily transferable to that or this; the only right is what is after my constitution; the only wrong what is against it. A man is to carry himself in the presence of all opposition as if every thing were titular and ephemeral but he. I am ashamed to think how easily we capitulate to badges and names, to large societies and dead institutions. Every decent and well-spoken individual affects and sways me more than is right. I ought to go upright and vital, and speak the rude truth in all ways. . . .

What I must do is all that concerns me, not what the people think. This rule, equally arduous in actual and in intellectual life, may serve for the whole distinction between greatness and meanness. It is the harder because you will always find those who think they know what is your duty better than you know it. It is easy in the world to live after the world's opinion; it is easy in solitude to live after our own; but the great man is he who in the midst of the crowd keeps with perfect sweetness the independence of solitude.

The objection to conforming to usages that have become dead to you is that it scatters your force. It loses your time and blurs the impression of your character. If you maintain a dead church, contribute to a dead Bible Society, vote with a great party either for the Government or against it, spread your table like base house-keepers,—under all these screens I have difficulty to detect the precise man you are. And of course so much force is withdrawn from your proper life. But do your thing, and I shall know you. Do your work, and you shall reinforce yourself. A man must consider what a blind-man's-buff is this game of conformity. If I know your sect I anticipate your argument. I hear a preacher announce for his text and topic the expediency of one of the institutions of his church. Do I not know beforehand that not possibly can he say a new and spontaneous word? . . . Well, most men have bound their eyes with one or another handkerchief, and attached themselves to some one of these communities of opinion. This conformity makes them not false in a few particulars, authors of a few lies, but false in all particulars. Their every truth is not quite true. Their two is not the real two, their four not the real four: so that every word they say chagrins us and we know not where to begin to set them right. Meantime nature is not slow to equip us in the prison-uniform of the party to which we adhere. We come to wear one cut of face and figure, and acquire by degrees the gentlest asinine expression. There is a mortifying experience in particular, which does not fail to wreak itself also in the general history; I mean "the foolish face of praise," the forced smile which we put on in company where we do not feel at ease, in answer to conversation which does not interest us. The muscles, not spontaneously moved but moved by a low usurping wilfulness, grow tight about the outline of the face, and make the most disagreeable sensation; a sensation of rebuke and warning which no brave young man will suffer twice.

For nonconformity the world whips you

with its displeasure. . . . It is easy enough for a firm man who knows the world to brook the rage of the cultivated classes. Their rage is decorous and prudent, for they are timid, as being very vulnerable themselves. But when to their feminine rage the indignation of the people is added, when the ignorant and the poor are aroused, when the unintelligent brute force that lies at the bottom of society is made to growl and mow, it needs the habit of magnanimity and religion to treat it godlike as a trifle of no concernment.

The other terror that scares us from self-trust is our consistency; a reverence for our past act or word because the eyes of others have no other data for computing our orbit than our past acts, and we are loath to disappoint them.

But why should you keep your head over your shoulder? Why drag about this monstrous corpse of your memory, lest you contradict somewhat you have stated in this or that public place? Suppose you should contradict yourself; what then? . . .

A foolish consistency is the hobgoblin of little minds, adored by little statesmen and philosophers and divines. With consistency a great soul has simply nothing to do. He may as well concern himself with his shadow on the wall. Out upon your guarded lips! Sew them up with packthread, do. Else if you would be a man speak what you think to-day in words as hard as cannon balls, and to-morrow speak what to-morrow thinks in hard words again, though it contradict everything you said to-day. Ah, then, exclaim the aged ladies, you shall be sure to be misunderstood! Misunderstood! It is a right fool's word. Is it so bad then to be misunderstood? Pythagoras was misunderstood, and Socrates, and Jesus, and Luther, and Copernicus, and Galileo, and Newton, and every pure and wise spirit that ever took flesh. To be great is to be misunderstood. . . .

ON TOP OF OLD SMOKY

"On Top of Old Smoky" is a folksong that was first popular in the 1840s among the immigrants of English, Scottish, and Irish heritage who settled in the southern Appalachians. Old Smoky is one of the peaks of the Blue Ridge Mountains; it is not far from Asheville, North Carolina. As the westward movement picked up momentum, pioneers sang this song, and it became one of the most popular on the frontier, far from the Blue Ridge Mountains. It has continued over the years to be one of the nation's best-loved folksongs.

On top of Old Smoky,
All covered with snow,
I lost my true lover
For courtin' too slow.

Now courtin's a pleasure
But partin' is grief,
A false-hearted lover
Is worse than a thief.

A thief will just rob you
And take what you have,

But a false-hearted lover
Will send you to the grave.

They'll hug you and kiss you
And tell you more lies
Than cross-ties on the railroad
Or stars in the skies.

On top of Old Smoky,
All covered with snow,
I lost my true lover
For courtin' too slow.

COLUMBIA, THE GEM OF THE OCEAN

This patriotic song was first published in 1843 as "Columbia, the Land of the Brave," but the following year it was reprinted and given its present title. Its authorship is disputed. In the first edition, credit went to David T. Shaw, an actor and singer who first performed the song in Philadelphia, at the Chestnut Street Theater in 1843. However, credit for the lyrics was also claimed by its arranger, Thomas à Becket. Shaw and Becket were both English born. In England, the same song was called "Britannia, the Pride of the Ocean," and no one knows for sure in which country it was introduced. Possibly Shaw and Becket played both sides of the Atlantic and varied the words to fit the audience.

O Columbia! the gem of the ocean,
The home of the brave and the free,
The shrine of each patriot's devotion,
A world offers homage to thee!
Thy mandates make heroes assemble,
When Liberty's form stands in view;
Thy banners make tyranny tremble,
When borne by the red, white, and blue!
When borne by the red, white, and blue,
When borne by the red, white, and blue,
Thy banners make tyranny tremble,
When borne by the red, white, and blue!

When war wing'd its wide desolation,
And threaten'd the land to deform,
The ark then of freedom's foundation,
Columbia rode safe thro' the storm;
With her garlands of vict'ry around her,
When so proudly she bore her brave crew,

With her flag proudly floating before her,
The boast of the red, white, and blue!
The boast of the red, white, and blue,
The boast of the red, white, and blue,
With her flag proudly floating before her,
The boast of the red, white, and blue!

The Star-Spangled Banner bring hither,
O'er Columbia's true sons let it wave;
May the wreaths they have won never wither,
Nor its stars cease to shine on the brave.
May thy service united ne'er sever,
But hold to their colors so true;
The Army and Navy forever!
Three cheers for the red, white, and blue!
Three cheers for the red, white, and blue,
Three cheers for the red, white, and blue,
The Army and Navy forever,
Three cheers for the red, white, and blue!

HENRY WADSWORTH LONGFELLOW
A PSALM OF LIFE, THE VILLAGE BLACKSMITH, and PAUL REVERE'S RIDE

Henry Wadsworth Longfellow (1807–1820) was born in Maine, graduated from Bowdoin College, and spent most of his adult life in Cambridge, Massachusetts. As a poet, he was immensely popular, on a scale unknown to twentieth-century poets. His poems were frequently printed in school readers. For generations, many schoolchildren could recite from memory large sections of "The Wreck of the Hesperus," "Paul Revere's Ride," *Evangeline*, *The Song of Hiawatha*, and other Longfellow poems. And any schoolchild who heard a friend make a rhyme might quickly state: "You're a poet and you don't know it, but your big feet show it: They're Longfellows!"

"A Psalm of Life" and "The Village Blacksmith" were published in 1839; "Paul Revere's Ride" first appeared in 1863 as part of *Tales of a Wayside Inn*. All three poems have been widely reprinted in schoolbooks and anthologies.

A Psalm of Life

WHAT THE HEART OF THE YOUNG
MAN SAID TO THE PSALMIST

Tell me not, in mournful numbers,
    "Life is but an empty dream!"
For the soul is dead that slumbers,
    And things are not what they seem.

Life is real! Life is earnest!
    And the grave is not its goal;
"Dust thou art, to dust returnest,"
    Was not spoken of the soul.

Not enjoyment, and not sorrow,
    Is our destined end or way;
But to act, that each to-morrow
    Finds us farther than to-day

Art is long, and Time is fleeting,
    And our hearts, though stout and brave,
Still, like muffled drums, are beating
    Funeral marches to the grave.

In the world's broad field of battle,
    In the bivouac of Life,
Be not like dumb, driven cattle!
    Be a hero in the strife!

Trust no Future, howe'er pleasant!
    Let the dead Past bury its dead!
Act,—act in the living Present!
    Heart within, and God o'erhead!

Lives of great men all remind us
    We can make our lives sublime,
And, departing, leave behind us
    Footprints on the sands of time;

Footprints, that perhaps another,
    Sailing o'er life's solemn main,
A forlorn and shipwrecked brother,
    Seeing, shall take heart again.

Let us, then, be up and doing,
    With a heart for any fate;
Still achieving, still pursuing,
    Learn to labour and to wait.

The Village Blacksmith

Under a spreading chestnut tree
    The village smithy stands;
The smith, a mighty man is he,
    With large and sinewy hands;
And the muscles of his brawny arms
    Are strong as iron bands.

His hair is crisp, and black, and long,
    His face is like the tan;
His brow is wet with honest sweat,
    He earns whate'er he can,
And looks the whole world in the face,
    For he owes not any man.

Week in, week out, from morn till night,
    You can hear his bellows blow;
You can hear him swing his heavy sledge,
    With measured beat and slow,
Like a sexton ringing the village bell,
    When the evening sun is low.

And children coming home from school
    Look in at the open door;
They love to see the flaming forge,
    And hear the bellows roar,
And catch the burning sparks that fly
    Like chaff from a threshing floor.

He goes on Sunday to the church,
    And sits among his boys;
He hears the parson pray and preach,
    He hears his daughter's voice,
Singing in the village choir,
    And it makes his heart rejoice.

"The Country Election," painted by George Caleb Bingham in 1851. At election time, men gathered to talk politics and cast their ballot. Bingham, a self-taught frontier artist, was elected to the Missouri legislature in 1846.

It sounds to him like her mother's voice,
    Singing in Paradise!
He needs must think of her once more,
    How in the grave she lies;
And with his hard, rough hand he wipes
    A tear out of his eyes.

Toiling,—rejoicing,—sorrowing
    Onward through life he goes;
Each morning sees some task begin,
    Each evening sees it close;
Something attempted, something done,
    Has earned a night's repose.

Thanks, thanks to thee, my worthy friend,
    For the lesson thou hast taught!
Thus at the flaming forge of life

Our fortunes must be wrought;
Thus on its sounding anvil shaped
    Each burning deed and thought!

Paul Revere's Ride

Listen, my children, and you shall hear
Of the midnight ride of Paul Revere,
On the eighteenth of April, in Seventy-five;
Hardly a man is now alive
Who remembers that famous day and year.

He said to his friend, "If the British march
By land or sea from the town tonight,
Hang a lantern aloft in the belfry arch
Of the North Church tower as a signal light,—

One, if by land, and two, if by sea;
And I on the opposite shore will be,
Ready to ride and spread the alarm
Through every Middlesex village and farm,
For the country folk to be up and to arm."

Then he said, "Good night!" and with muffled
      oar
Silently rowed to the Charlestown shore,
Just as the moon rose over the bay,
Where swinging wide at her moorings lay
The Somerset, British man-of-war;
A phantom ship, with each mast and spar
Across the moon like a prison bar,
And a huge black hulk, that was magnified
By its own reflection in the tide.

Meanwhile, his friend, through alley and street,
Wanders and watches with eager ears,
Till in the silence around him he hears
The muster of men at the barrack door,
The sound of arms, and the tramp of feet,
And the measured tread of the grenadiers,
Marching down to their boats on the shore.

Then he climbed the tower of the Old North
      Church,
By the wooden stairs, with stealthy tread,
To the belfry-chamber overhead,
And startled the pigeons from their perch
On the somber rafters, that round him made
Masses and moving shapes of shade,—
By the trembling ladder, steep and tall,
To the highest window in the wall,
Where he paused to listen and look down
A moment on the roofs of the town,
And the moonlight flowing over all.

Beneath, in the churchyard, lay the dead,
In their night-encampment on the hill,
Wrapped in silence so deep and still
That he could hear, like a sentinel's tread,
The watchful night-wind, as it went
Creeping along from tent to tent,
And seeming to whisper, "All is well!"
A moment only he feels the spell
Of the place and the hour, and the secret dread
Of the lonely belfry and the dead;
For suddenly all his thoughts are bent

On a shadowy something far away,
Where the river widens to meet the bay,—
A line of black that bends and floats
On the rising tide, like a bridge of boats.

Meanwhile, impatient to mount and ride,
Booted and spurred, with a heavy stride
On the opposite shore walked Paul Revere.
Now he patted his horse's side,
Now gazed at the landscape far and near,
Then, impetuous, stamped the earth,
And turned and tightened his saddle-girth;
But mostly he watched with eager search
The belfry-tower of the Old North Church,
As it rose above the graves on the hill,
Lonely and spectral and somber and still.
And lo! as he looks, on the belfry's height
A glimmer, and then a gleam of light!
He springs to the saddle, the bridle he turns,
But lingers and gazes, till full on his sight
A second lamp in the belfry burns!

A hurry of hoofs in a village street,
A shape in the moonlight, a bulk in the dark,
And beneath, from the pebbles, in passing, a
      spark
Struck out by a steed flying fearless and fleet;
That was all! And yet, through the gloom and
      the light
The fate of a nation was riding that night;
And the spark struck out by that steed in his
      flight,
Kindled the land into flame with its heat.

He has left the village and mounted the steep,
And beneath him, tranquil and broad and deep,
Is the Mystic, meeting the ocean tides;
And under the alders, that skirt its edge,
Now soft on the sand, now loud on the ledge,
Is heard the tramp of his steed as he rides.

It was twelve by the village clock
When he crossed the bridge into Medford
      town.
He heard the crowing of the cock,
And the barking of the farmer's dog,
And felt the damp of the river fog,
That rises after the sun goes down.

It was one by the village clock,
When he galloped into Lexington.
He saw the gilded weathercock
Swim in the moonlight as he passed,
And the meeting-house windows, blank and
        bare,
Gaze at him with a spectral glare,
As if they already stood aghast
At the bloody work they would look upon.

It was two by the village clock,
When he came to the bridge in Concord town.
He heard the bleating of the flock,
And the twitter of birds among the trees,
And felt the breath of the morning breeze
Blowing over the meadows brown.
And one was safe and asleep in his bed
Who at the bridge would be first to fall,
Who that day would be lying dead,
Pierced by a British musket-ball.

You know the rest. In the books you have read,
How the British Regulars fired and fled,—
How the farmers gave them ball for ball,
From behind each fence and farmyard wall,
Chasing the redcoats down the lane,
Then crossing the fields to emerge again
Under the trees at the turn of the road.
And only pausing to fire and load.
So through the night rode Paul Revere;
And so through the night went his cry of alarm
To every Middlesex village and farm,—
A cry of defiance, and not of fear,
A voice in the darkness, a knock at the door,
And a word that shall echo forevermore!
For, borne on the night-wind of the Past,
Through all our history, to the last,
In the hour of darkness and peril and need,
The people will waken and listen to hear
The hurrying hoofbeats of that steed,
And the midnight message of Paul Revere.

HENRY DAVID THOREAU
CIVIL DISOBEDIENCE

Under a government which imprisons any unjustly, the true place for a just man is also in prison.

Henry David Thoreau (1817–1862)—essayist, poet, naturalist, reformer, and philosopher—was born in Concord, Massachusetts, and he graduated from Harvard College. After a few years as a schoolmaster, Thoreau determined to make his life's work poetry and nature writing. He was a disciple of Ralph Waldo Emerson and a leading figure in the transcendentalist movement. Transcendentalism blended romanticism and reform; it elevated the senses and intuition over reason; it celebrated individualism and the inner voice—the voice of wholeness and integrity.

Thoreau's sporadic attempts at making a living were seldom remunerative; his published works did not sell well, and from time to time he worked in his family's small pencil-making business. In 1845, at the age of twenty-eight, he determined to free himself from such mundane concerns, and, with Emerson's permission, built a small cabin on land Emerson owned on Walden Pond, two miles from Concord.

In July 1846, while Thoreau was living at Walden Pond, the local constable approached him about paying his poll tax, which he had neglected to do for several years. He refused to pay, and the constable locked him up for the night in the Concord jail. The next day, an unidentified person—probably Thoreau's aunt—paid the tax, and he was released. But he made his point: he could not pay taxes to a government that permitted slavery and that waged an imperialist war against Mexico. He prepared a lecture to explain his actions, and it was published in 1849. At the time, the essay attracted little attention, but by the end of the nineteenth century it had become a classic, with an international following. Leo Tolstoy read it about 1900 and admired it. Mohandas K. Gandhi read it while he was working as a lawyer in South Africa, defending the Indians there who had violated discriminatory laws. Gandhi was deeply impressed by Thoreau and became a lifelong exemplar of civil disobedience and passive resistance to unjust authority. Through Gandhi, Thoreau's ideas became a powerful instrument of political action. Later in the twentieth century, young Martin Luther King, Jr., was influenced by Gandhi, and Thoreau's ideas found new life as the basic ideology of the American civil rights movement.

I heartily accept the motto—"That government is best which governs least;" and I should like to see it acted up to more rapidly and systematically. Carried out, it finally amounts to this, which also I believe,—"That government is best which governs not at all;" and when men are prepared for it, that will be the kind of government which they will have. Government is at best but an expedient; but most governments are usually, and all governments are sometimes, inexpedient. The objections which have been brought against a standing army, and they are many and weighty, and deserve to prevail, may also at last be brought against a standing government. The standing army is only an arm of the standing government. The government itself, which is only the mode which the people have chosen to execute their will, is equally liable to be abused and perverted before the people can act through it. Witness the present Mexican war, the work of comparatively a few individuals using the standing government as their tool; for, in the outset, the people would not have consented to this measure.

This American government,—what is it but a tradition, though a recent one, endeavoring to transmit itself unimpaired to posterity, but each instant losing some of its integrity? It has not the vitality and force of a single living man; for a single man can bend it to his will. It is a sort of wooden gun to the people themselves; and, if ever they should use it in earnest as a real one against each other, it will surely split. But it is not the less necessary for this; for the people must have some complicated machinery or

other, and hear its din, to satisfy that idea of government which they have. Governments show thus how successfully men can be imposed on, even impose on themselves, for their own advantage. It is excellent, we must all allow; yet this government never of itself furthered any enterprise, but by the alacrity with which it got out of its way. *It* does not keep the country free. *It* does not settle the West. *It* does not educate. The character inherent in the American people has done all that has been accomplished; and it would have done somewhat more, if the government had not sometimes got in its way. For government is an expedient by which men would fain succeed in letting one another alone; and, as has been said, when it is most expedient, the governed are most let alone by it. Trade and commerce, if they were not made of india rubber, would never manage to bounce over the obstacles which legislators are continually putting in their way; and, if one were to judge these men wholly by the effects of their actions, and not partly by their intentions, they would deserve to be classed and punished with those mischievous persons who put obstructions on the railroads.

But, to speak practically and as a citizen, unlike those who call themselves no-government men, I ask for, not at once no government, but *at once* a better government. Let every man make known what kind of government would command his respect, and that will be one step toward obtaining it.

After all, the practical reason why, when the power is once in the hands of the people, a majority are permitted, and for a long period continue, to rule, is not because they are most likely to be in the right, nor because this seems fairest to the minority, but because they are physically the strongest. But a government in which the majority rule in all cases cannot be based on justice, even as far as men understand it. Can there not be a government in which majorities do not virtually decide right and wrong, but conscience?—in which majorities decide only those questions to which the rule of expediency is applicable? Must the citizen ever for a moment, or in the least degree, resign his conscience to the legislator? Why has every man a conscience, then? I think that we should be men first, and subjects afterward. It is not desirable to cultivate a respect for the law, so much as for the right. The only obligation which I have a right to assume, is to do at any time what I think right. . . .

How does it become a man to behave toward this American government to-day? I answer that he cannot without disgrace be associated with it. I cannot for an instant recognize that political organization as *my* government which is the *slave's* government also.

All men recognize the right of revolution; that is, the right to refuse allegiance to and to resist the government, when its tyranny or its inefficiency are great and unendurable. But almost all say that such is not the case now. But such was the case, they think, in the Revolution of '75. If one were to tell me that this was a bad government because it taxed certain foreign commodities brought to its ports, it is most probable that I should not make an ado about it, for I can do without them; all machines have their friction; and possibly this does enough good to counterbalance the evil. At any rate, it is a great evil to make a stir about it. But when the friction comes to have its machine, and oppression and robbery are organized, I say, let us not have such a machine any longer. In other words, when a sixth of the population of a nation which has undertaken to be the refuge of liberty are slaves, and a whole country is unjustly overrun and conquered by a foreign army,

and subject to military law, I think that it is not too soon for honest men to rebel and revolutionize. What makes this duty the more urgent is the fact, that the country so overrun is not our own, but ours is the invading army. . . .

Practically speaking, the opponents to a reform in Massachusetts are not a hundred thousand politicians at the South, but a hundred thousand merchants and farmers here, who are more interested in commerce and agriculture than they are in humanity, and are not prepared to do justice to the slave and to Mexico, *cost what it may.* I quarrel not with far-off foes, but with those who, near at home, co-operate with, and do the bidding of those far away, and without whom the latter would be harmless. We are accustomed to say, that the mass of men are unprepared; but improvement is slow, because the few are not materially wiser or better than the many. It is not so important that many should be as good as you, as that there be some absolute goodness somewhere; for that will leaven the whole lump. There are thousands who are *in opinion* opposed to slavery and to the war, who yet in effect do nothing to put an end to them; who, esteeming themselves children of Washington and Franklin, sit down with their hands in their pockets, and say that they know not what to do, and do nothing; who even postpone the question of freedom to the question of free-trade, and quietly read the prices-current along with the latest advices from Mexico, after dinner, and, it may be, fall asleep over them both. . . .

The American has dwindled into an Odd Fellow,—one who may be known by the development of his organ of gregariousness, and a manifest lack of intellect and cheerful self-reliance; whose first and chief concern, on coming into the world, is to see that the alms-houses are in good repair; and, before yet he has lawfully donned the virile garb, to collect a fund for the support of the widows and orphans that may be; who, in short, ventures to live only by the aid of the mutual insurance company, which has promised to bury him decently. . . .

Unjust laws exist: shall we be content to

obey them, or shall we endeavor to amend them, and obey them until we have succeeded, or shall we transgress them at once? Men generally, under such a government as this, think that they ought to wait until they have persuaded the majority to alter them. They think that, if they should resist, the remedy would be worse than the evil. But it is the fault of the government itself that the remedy *is* worse than the evil. *It* makes it worse. Why is it not more apt to anticipate and provide for reform? Why does it not cherish its wise minority? Why does it cry and resist before it is hurt? Why does it not encourage its citizens to be on the alert to point out its faults, and *do* better than it would have them? Why does it always crucify Christ, and excommunicate Copernicus and Luther, and pronounce Washington and Franklin rebels? . . .

If the injustice is part of the necessary friction of the machine of government, let it go, let it go: perchance it will wear smooth,—certainly the machine will wear out. If the injustice has a spring, or a pulley, or a rope, or a crank, exclusively for itself, then perhaps you may consider whether the remedy will not be worse than the evil; but if it is of such a nature that it requires you to be the agent of injustice to another, then, I say, break the law. Let your life be a counter friction to stop the machine. What I have to do is to see, at any rate, that I do not lend myself to the wrong which I condemn.

As for adopting the ways which the State has provided for remedying the evil, I know not of such ways. They take too much time, and a man's life will be gone. I have other affairs to attend to. I came into this world, not chiefly to make this a good place to life, but to live in it, be it good or bad. A man has not everything to do, but something; and because he cannot do *every thing,* it is not necessary that he should do *something* wrong. It is not my business to be petitioning the governor or the legislature any more than it is theirs to petition me; and if they should not hear my petition, what should I do then? But in this case the State has provided no way: its very Constitution is the evil. This may

seem to be harsh and stubborn and unconciliatory; but it is to treat with the utmost kindness and consideration the only spirit that can appreciate or deserves it. So is all change for the better, like birth and death which convulse the body.

I do not hesitate to say, that those who call themselves abolitionists should at once effectually withdraw their support, both in person and property, from the government of Massachusetts, and not wait till they constitute a majority of one, before they suffer the right to prevail through them, I think that it is enough if they have God on their side, without waiting for that other one. Moreover, any man more right than his neighbors constitutes a majority of one already. . . .

Under a government which imprisons any unjustly, the true place for a just man is also in prison. The proper place to-day, the only place which Massachusetts has provided for her freer and less desponding spirits, is in her prisons, to be put out and locked out of the State by her own act, as they have already put themselves out by their principles. It is there that the fugitive slave, and the Mexican prisoner on parole, and the Indian come to plead the wrongs of his race, should find them; on that separate, but more free and honorable ground, where the State places those who are not *with* her, but *against* her,—the only house in a slave-state in which a free man can abide with honor. If any think that their influence would be lost there, and their voices no longer afflict the ear of the State, that they would not be as an enemy within its walls, they do not know by how much truth is stronger than error, nor how much more eloquently and effectively he can combat injustice who has experienced a little in his own person. Cast your whole vote, not a strip of paper merely, but your whole influence. A minority is powerless while it conforms to the majority; it is not even a minority then; but it is irresistible when it clogs by its whole weight. If the alternative is to keep all just men in prison, or give up war and slavery, the State will not hesitate which to choose. If a thousand men were not to pay their tax-bills this year, that would not be a violent and bloody measure, as it would be to pay them, and enable the State to commit violence and shed innocent blood. This is, in fact, the definition of a peaceable revolution, if any such is possible. If the tax-gatherer, or any other public officer, asks me, as one has done, "But what shall I do?" my answer is, "If you really wish to do anything, resign our office." When the subject has refused allegiance, and the officer has resigned his office, then the revolution is accomplished. But even suppose blood should flow. Is there not a sort of blood shed when the conscience is wounded? Through this wound a man's real manhood and immortality flow out, and he bleeds to an everlasting death. I see this blood flowing now. . . .

I have paid no poll-tax for six years. I was put into a jail once on this account, for one night; and, as I stood considering the walls of solid stone, two or three feet thick, the door of wood and iron, a foot thick, and the iron grating which strained the light, I could not help being struck with the foolishness of that institution which treated me as if I were mere flesh and blood and bones, to be locked up. I wondered that it should have concluded at length that this was the best use it could put me to, and had never thought to avail itself of my services in some way. I saw that, if there was a wall of stone between me and my townsmen, there was a still more difficult one to climb or break through, before they could get to be as free as I was. I did not for a moment feel confined, and the walls seemed a great waste of stone and mortar. I felt as if I alone of all my townsmen had paid my tax. They plainly did not know how to treat me, but behaved like persons who are underbred. In every threat and in every compliment there was a blunder; for they thought that my chief desire was to stand the other side of that stone wall. I could not but smile to see how industriously they locked the door on my meditations, which followed them out again without let or hinderance, and *they* were really all that was dangerous. As they could not reach me, they had resolved to punish my body; just as boys, if they

cannot come at some person against whom they have a spite, will abuse his dog. I saw that the State was half-witted, that it was timid as a lone woman with her silver spoons, and that it did not know its friends from its foes, and I lost all my remaining respect for it, and pitied it.

Thus the State never intentionally confronts a man's sense, intellectual or moral, but only his body, his senses, It is not armed with superior wit or honesty, but with superior physical strength. I was not born to be forced. I will breathe after my own fashion. Let us see who is the strongest. What force has a multitude? They only can force me who obey a higher law than I. They force me to become like themselves. I do not hear of *men* being *forced* to live this way or that by masses of men. What sort of life were that to live? When I meet a government which says to me, "Your money or your life," why should I be in haste to give it my money? It may be in a great strait, and not know what to do: I cannot help that. It must help itself; do as I do. It is not worth the while to snivel about it. I am not responsible for the successful working of the machinery of society. I am not the son of the engineer. I perceive that, when an acorn and a chestnut fall side by side, the one does not remain inert to make way for the other, but both obey their own laws, and spring and grow and flourish as best they can, till one, perchance, overshadows and destroys the other. If a plant cannot live according to its nature, it dies; and so a man. . . .

I do not wish to quarrel with any man or nation. I do not wish to split hairs, to make fine distinctions, or set myself up as better than my neighbors. I seek rather, I may say, even an excuse for conforming to the laws of the land. I am but too ready to conform to them. Indeed I have reason to suspect myself on this head; and each year, as the tax-gatherer comes round, I find myself disposed to review the acts and position of the general and state governments, and the spirit of the people, to discover a pretext for conformity. I believe that the State will soon be able to take all my work of this sort out of my hands, and then I shall be no better a patriot than my fellow-countrymen. Seen from a lower point of view, the Constitution, with all its faults, is very good; the law and the courts are very respectable; even this State and this American government are, in many respects, very admirable and rare things, to be thankful for, such as a great many have described them; but seen from a point of view a little higher, they are what I have described them; seen from a higher still, and the highest, who shall say what they are, or that they are worth looking at or thinking of at all?

However, the government does not concern me much, and I shall bestow the fewest possible thoughts on it. It is not many moments that I live under a government, even in this world. If a man is thought-free, fancy-free, imagination-free, that which *is not* never for a long time appearing *to be* to him, unwise rulers or reformers cannot fatally interrupt him. . . .

The authority of government, even such as I am willing to submit to,—for I will cheerfully obey those who know and can do better than I, and in many things even those who neither know nor can do so well,—is still an impure one: to be strictly just, it must have the sanction and consent of the governed. It can have no pure right over my person and property but what I concede to it. The progress from an absolute to a limited monarchy, from a limited monarchy to a democracy, is a progress toward a true respect for the individual. Is a democracy, such as we know it, the last improvement possible in government? Is it not possible to take a step further towards recognizing and organizing the rights of man? There will never be a really free and enlightened State, until the State comes to recognize the individual as a higher and independent power, from which all its own power and authority are derived, and treats him accordingly. I please myself with imagining a State at last which can afford to be just to all men, and to treat the individual with respect as a neighbor, which even would not think it inconsistent with its own repose, if a few were to live aloof from it, not meddling with it, nor embraced by it, who fulfilled all the duties of neighbors and fellowmen. A State which bore this kind of fruit, and suffered it to drop off as fast as it ripened, would prepare the way for a still more perfect and glorious State, which also I have imagined, but not yet anywhere seen.

HENRY DAVID THOREAU
WALDEN

I went to the woods because I wished to live deliberately, to front only the essential facts of life, and see if I could not learn what it had to teach, and not, when I came to die, discover that I had not lived.

Thoreau lived for two years at Walden Pond. There, removed from everyday concerns and social pressures, he had time to think about what was important in life and time to write. He was not, as popular tradition has it, a hermit during this period, but a man who lived on the edge of society—near enough to have visitors but distant enough to strip life down to its essentials.

In the 1850s, Thoreau became deeply committed to the abolition of slavery, and he abandoned a life of reflection and detachment for one of political activism. He lectured and wrote against slavery and helped fugitive slaves fleeing north on the Underground Railroad. In poor health, Thoreau died in 1862, not yet forty-five years old.

Walden, excerpted below, was not a commercial success when first published in

1854; it sold only two thousand copies in five years. Since then, however, it has become a classic of American literature, for it is a beautifully written journal of a man's attempt to find truth and meaning in simple living and an ode of praise to living in harmony with nature and one's conscience.

. . . The mass of men lead lives of quiet desperation. What is called resignation is confirmed desperation. From the desperate city you go into the desperate country, and have to console yourself with the bravery of minks and muskrats. A stereotyped but unconscious despair is concealed even under what are called the games and amusements of mankind. There is no play in them, for this comes after work. But it is a characteristic of wisdom not to do desperate things.

When we consider what, to use the words of the catechism, is the chief end of man, and what are the true necessaries and means of life, it appears as if men had deliberately chosen the common mode of living because they preferred it to any other. Yet they honestly think there is no choice left. But alert and healthy natures remember that the sun rose clear. It is never too late to give up our prejudices. No way of thinking or doing, however ancient, can be trusted without proof. What everybody echoes or in silence passes by as true to-day may turn out to be falsehood to-morrow, mere smoke of opinion, which some had trusted for a cloud that would sprinkle fertilizing rain on their fields. What old people say you cannot do, you try and find that you can. Old deeds for old people, and new deeds for new. Old people did not know enough once, perchance, to fetch fresh fuel to keep the fire a-going; new people put a little dry wood under a pot, and are whirled round the globe with the speed of birds, in a way to kill old people, as the phrase is. Age is no better, hardly so well, qualified for an instructor as youth, for it has not profited so much as it has lost. One may almost doubt if the wisest man has learned anything of absolute value by living. Practically, the old have no very important advice to give the young, their own experience has been so partial, and their lives have been such miserable failures, for private reasons, as

they must believe; and it may be that they have some faith left which belies that experience, and they are only less young than they were. I have lived some thirty years on this planet, and I have yet to hear the first syllable of valuable or even earnest advice from my seniors. They have told me nothing, and probably cannot tell me anything to the purpose. Here is life, an experiment to a great extent untried by me; but it does not avail me that they have tried it. If I have any experience which I think valuable, I am sure to reflect that this my Mentors said nothing about. . . .

When first I took up my abode in the woods, that is, began to spend my nights as well as days there, which, by accident, was on Independence Day, or the Fourth of July, 1845, my house was not finished for winter, but was merely a defence against the rain, without plastering or chimney, the walls being of rough, weather-stained boards, with wide chinks, which made it cool at night. The upright white hewn studs and freshly planed door and window casings gave it a clean and airy look, especially in the morning, when its timbers were saturated with dew, so that I fancied that by noon some sweet gum would exude from them. To my imagination it retained throughout the day more or less of this auroral character, reminding me of a certain house on a mountain which I had visited a year before. This was an airy and unplastered cabin, fit to entertain a traveling god, and where a goddess might trail her garments. The winds which passed over my dwelling were such as sweep over the ridges of mountains, bearing the broken strains, or celestial parts only, of terrestrial music. The morning wind forever blows, the poem of creation is uninterrupted; but few are the ears that hear it. Olympus is but the outside of the earth everywhere. . . .

I went to the woods because I wished to live

deliberately, to front only the essential facts of life, and see if I could not learn what it had to teach, and not, when I came to die, discover that I had not lived. I did not wish to live what was not life, living is so dear; nor did I wish to practise resignation, unless it was quite necessary. I wanted to live deep and suck out all the marrow of life, to live so sturdily and Spartan-like as to put to rout all that was not life, to cut a broad swath and shave close, to drive life into a corner, and reduce it to its lowest terms, and, if it proved to be mean, why then to get the whole and genuine meanness of it, and publish its meanness to the world; or if it were sublime, to know it by experience, and be able to give a true account of it in my next excursion. For most men, it appears to me, are in a strange uncertainty about it, whether it is of the devil or of God, and have *somewhat hastily* concluded that it is the chief end of man here to "glorify God and enjoy him forever."

Still we live meanly, like ants; though the fable tells us that we were long ago changed into men; like pygmies we fight with cranes; it is error upon error, and clout upon clout, and our best virtue has for its occasion a superfluous and evitable wretchedness. Our life is frittered away by detail. An honest man has hardly need to count more than his ten fingers, or in extreme cases he may add his ten toes, and lump the rest. Simplicity, simplicity, simplicity! I say, let your affairs be as two or three, and not a hundred or a thousand; instead of a million count half a dozen, and keep your accounts on your thumb-nail. In the midst of this chopping sea of civilized life, such are the clouds and storms and quicksands and thousand-and-one items to be allowed for, that a man has to live, if he would not founder and go to the bottom and not make his port at all, by dead reckoning, and he must be a great calculator indeed who succeeds. Simplify, simplify. Instead of three meals a day, if it be necessary eat but one; instead of a hundred dishes, five; and reduce other things in proportion. Our life is like a German Confederacy, made up of petty states, with its boundary for-

ever fluctuating, so that even a German cannot tell you how it is bounded at any moment. The nation itself, with all its so-called internal improvements, which, by the way, are all external and superficial, is just such an unwieldy and overgrown establishment, cluttered with furniture and tripped up by its own traps, ruined by luxury and heedless expense, by want of calculation and a worthy aim, as the million households in the land; and the only cure for it, as for them, is in a rigid economy, a stern and more than Spartan simplicity of life and elevation of purpose. It lives too fast. Men think that it is essential that the *Nation* have commerce, and export ice, and talk through a telegraph, and ride thirty miles an hour, without a doubt, whether *they* do or not; but whether we should live like baboons or like men, is a little uncertain. . . .

Why should we live with such hurry and waste of life? We are determined to be starved before we are hungry. Men say that a stitch in time saves nine, and so they take a thousand stitches to-day to save nine to-morrow. As for *work,* we haven't any of any consequence. We have the Saint Vitus' dance, and cannot possibly keep our heads still. . . . Hardly a man takes a half-hour's nap after dinner, but when he wakes he holds up his head and asks, "What's the news?" as if the rest of mankind had stood his sentinels. Some give directions to be waked every half-hour, doubtless for no other purpose; and then, to pay for it, they tell what they have dreamed. After a night's sleep the news is as indispensable as the breakfast. "Pray tell me anything new that has happened to a man anywhere on this globe,"—and he reads it over his coffee and rolls, that a man has had his eyes gouged out this morning on the Wachito River; never dreaming the while that he lives in the dark unfathomed mammoth cave of this world, and has but the rudiment of an eye himself.

For my part, I could easily do without the post-office. I think that there are very few important communications made through it. To speak critically, I never received more than one or two letters in my life—I wrote this some years ago—that were worth the postage. The penny-post is, commonly, an institution through which you seriously offer a man that penny for his thoughts which is so often safely offered in jest. And I am sure that I never read any memorable news in a newspaper. If we read of one man robbed, or murdered, or killed by accident, or one house burned, or one vessel wrecked, or one steamboat blown up, or one cow run over on the Western Railroad, or one mad dog killed, or one lot of grasshoppers in the winter,—we never need read of another. One is enough. If you are acquainted with the principle, what do you care for a myriad instances and applications? To a philosopher all *news,* as it is called, is gossip, and they who edit and read it are old women over their tea. . . .

Let us spend one day as deliberately as Nature, and not be thrown off the track by every nutshell and mosquito's wing that falls on the rails. Let us rise early and fast, or break fast, gently and without perturbation; let company come and let company go, let the bells ring and the children cry,—determined to make a day of it. Why should we knock under and go with the stream? Let us not be upset and overwhelmed in that terrible rapid and whirlpool called a dinner, situated in the meridian shallows. Weather this danger and you are safe, for the rest of the way is down hill. With unrelaxed nerves, with morning vigor, sail by it, looking another way, tied to the mast like Ulysses. If the engine whistles, let it whistle till it is hoarse for its pains. If the bell rings, why should we run? We will con-

sider what kind of music they are like. Let us settle ourselves, and work and wedge our feet downward through the mud and slush of opinion, and prejudice, and tradition, and delusion, and appearance, that alluvion which covers the globe, through Paris and London, through New York and Boston and Concord, through Church and State, through poetry and philosophy and religion, till we come to a hard bottom and rocks in place, which we can call *reality,* and say, This is, and no mistake. . . . Be it life or death, we crave only reality. If we are really dying, let us hear the rattle in our throats and feel cold in the extremities; if we are alive, let us go about our business.

Time is but the stream I go a-fishing in. I drink at it; but while I drink I see the sandy bottom and detect how shallow it is. Its thin current slides away, but eternity remains. I would drink deeper; fish in the sky, whose bottom is pebbly with stars. I cannot count one. I know not the first letter of the alphabet. I have always been regretting that I was not as wise as the day I was born. The intellect is a cleaver; it discerns and rifts its way into the secret of things. I do not wish to be any more busy with my hands than is necessary. My head is hands and feet. I feel all my best faculties concentrated in it. My instinct tells me that my head is an organ for burrowing, as some creatures use their snout and fore paws, and with it I would mine and burrow my way through these hills. I think that the richest vein is somewhere hereabouts; so by the divining-rod and thin rising vapors I judge; and here I will begin to mine.

JOHN GREENLEAF WHITTIER
THE BAREFOOT BOY

Editor, poet, and essayist, John Greenleaf Whittier (1807–1892) was a Quaker who was passionately committed to social reform, and especially to the abolition of slavery. Raised on the family farm at Haverhill, Massachusetts, he also came to be known as the poet of New England rural life. His poem "Maud Muller" contained this famous couplet:

"Of all sad words of tongue and pen / The saddest are these: It might have been." His poem "The Barefoot Boy" was well loved for its evocation of the simple joys of country life. It was written in 1855.

Blessings on thee, little man,
Barefoot boy, with cheek of tan!
With thy turned-up pantaloons,
And thy merry whistled tunes;
With thy red lip, redder still
Kissed by strawberries on the hill;
With the sunshine on thy face,
Through thy torn brim's jaunty grace;
From my heart I give thee joy,—
I was once a barefoot boy!
Prince thou art,—the grown-up man
Only is republican.
Let the million-dollared ride!
Barefoot, trudging at his side,
Thou hast more than he can buy
In the reach of ear and eye,—
Outward sunshine, inward joy:
Blessings on thee, barefoot boy!

Oh for boyhood's painless play,
Sleep that wakes in laughing day,
Health that mocks the doctor's rules,
Knowledge never learned of schools,
Of the wild bee's morning chase,
Of the wild flower's time and place,
Flight of fowl and habitude
Of the tenants of the wood;
How the tortoise bears his shell,
How the woodchuck digs his cell,
And the ground mole sinks his well
How the robin feeds her young,
How the oriole's nest is hung;
Where the whitest lilies blow,
Where the freshest berries grow,
Where the groundnut trails its vine,
Where the wood grape's clusters shine;
Of the black wasp's cunning way,
Mason of his walls of clay,
And the architectural plans
Of gray hornet artisans!—
For, eschewing books and tasks,
Nature answers all he asks;

Hand in hand with her he walks,
Face to face with her he talks,
Part and parcel of her joy,—
Blessings on thee, barefoot boy!

Oh for boyhood's time of June,
Crowding years in one brief moon,
When all things I heard or saw
Me, their master, waited for.
I was rich in flowers and trees,
Humming birds and honeybees;
For my sport the squirrel played,
Plied the snouted mole his spade;
For my taste the blackberry cone
Purpled over hedge and stone;
Laughed the brook for my delight
Through the day and through the night,
Whispering at the garden wall,
Talked with me from fall to fall;
Mine the sand-rimmed pickerel pond,
Mine the walnut slopes beyond,
Mine, on bending orchard trees,
Apples of Hesperides!
Still, as my horizon grew,
Larger grew my riches too;
All the world I saw or knew
Seemed a complex Chinese toy,
Fashioned for a barefoot boy!

Oh for festal dainties spread,
Like my bowl of milk and bread,—
Pewter spoon and bowl of wood,
On the doorstone, gray and rude!
O'er me, like a regal tent,
Cloudy-ribbed, the sunset bent,
Purple-curtained, fringed with gold;
Looped in many a wind-swung fold;
While for music came the play
Of the pied frog's orchestra;
And to light the noisy choir,
Lit the fly his lamp of fire.
I was monarch: pomp and joy
Waited on the barefoot boy!

Cheerily, then, my little man,	Lose the freedom of the sod,
Live and laugh, as boyhood can!	Like a colt's for work be shod,
Though the flinty slopes be hard,	Made to tread the mills of toil,
Stubble-speared the new-mown sward,	Up and down in ceaseless moil:
Every morn shall lead thee through	Happy if their track be found
Fresh baptisms of the dew;	Never on forbidden ground;
Every evening from thy feet	Happy if they sink not in
Shall the cool wind kiss the heat:	Quick and treacherous sands of sin.
All too soon these feet must hide	Ah! that thou shouldst know thy joy
In the prison cells of pride,	Ere it passes, barefoot boy!

THOMAS CORWIN

AGAINST THE MEXICAN WAR

If I were a Mexican I would tell you, "Have you not room enough in your own country to bury your dead?"

As America expanded westward, its borders grew at the expense of Mexico. American settlers in Texas rebelled against Mexican authorities and proclaimed an independent republic in 1836. In the summer of 1845, as Congress debated whether to annex Texas, John L. O'Sullivan, editor of the *Democratic Review,* urged annexation because nothing should interfere with America's "manifest destiny to overspread the continent allotted by Providence for the free development of our yearly multiplying millions." Later that year, the Republic of Texas became a state. Meanwhile, American settlers led by John C. Fremont marched into California and proclaimed the Bear Flag Republic in 1846.

Since Mexico and the United States did not agree on their border, President James K. Polk sent a representative to Mexico and a military force to the disputed border area. When negotiations broke down, war broke out. The war had popular support, since the public embraced the idea of "manifest destiny." But some courageous voices —such as Daniel Webster, Frederick Douglass, and a young Illinois congressman named Abraham Lincoln—condemned the war.

The most eloquent opponent of the Mexican War was Thomas Corwin (1794–1865), a Whig Senator from Ohio. A self-taught lawyer and a former governor of Ohio, Corwin was in his first term in the Senate when he denounced the war on February 11, 1847. Corwin predicted that the war in Mexico would aggravate tensions between the pro-slavery and anti-slavery forces and would lead to civil war in the United States.

Corwin lost the debate, and America won the war. In February 1848, the United States and Mexico signed the Treaty of Guadalupe Hidalgo, which ceded to the United States the vast territory that consists of the present states of California, Nevada, and Utah, plus parts of Arizona, Wyoming, Colorado, and New Mexico. Five years later, the United States purchased a strip of land from Mexico in what is now New Mexico and Arizona, thus completing the present southwestern border.

What is the territory, Mr. President, which you propose to wrest from Mexico? It is consecrated to the heart of the Mexican by many a well-fought battle with his old Castilian master. His Bunker Hills, and Saratogas, and Yorktowns are there! The Mexican can say, "There I bled for liberty! and shall I surrender that consecrated home of my affections to the Anglo-Saxon invaders? What do they want with it? They have Texas already. They have possessed themselves of the territory between the Nueces and the Rio Grande. What else do they want? To what shall I point my children as memorials of that independence which I bequeath to them, when those battlefields shall have passed from my possession?"

Sir, had one come and demanded Bunker Hill of the people of Massachusetts, had England's lion ever showed himself there, is there a man over thirteen and under ninety who would not have been ready to meet him? Is there a river on this continent that would not have run red with blood? Is there a field but would have been piled high with unburied bones of slaughtered Americans before these consecrated battlefields of liberty should have been wrested from us? But this same American goes into a sister republic, and says to poor, weak Mexico, "Give up your territory, you are unworthy to possess it; I have got one half already, and all I ask of you is to give up the other!" England might as well, in the circumstances I have described, have come and demanded of us, "Give up the Atlantic slope—give up this trifling territory from the Allegheny Mountains to the sea; it is only from Maine to St. Mary's—only about one third of your Republic, and the least interesting portion of it." What would be the response? They would say we must give this up to John Bull. Why? "He wants room." The Senator from Michigan says he must have this. Why, my worthy Christian brother; on what principle of justice? "I want room!"

Sir, look at this pretense of want of room. With twenty millions of people, you have about one thousand millions of acres of land, inviting settlement by every conceivable argument,

bringing them down to a quarter of a dollar an acre, and allowing every man to squat where he pleases. But the Senator from Michigan says we will be two hundred millions in a few years, and we want room. If I were a Mexican I would tell you, "Have you not room enough in your own country to bury your dead? If you come into mine, we will greet you with bloody hands, and welcome you to hospitable graves." . . .

I was somewhat amazed the other day to hear the Senator from Michigan declare that Europe had quite forgotten us, till these battles waked them up. I suppose the Senator feels grateful to the President for "waking up" Europe. Does the President, who is, I hope, read in civic as well as military lore, remember the saying of one who had pondered upon history long; long, too, upon man, his nature, and true destiny. Montesquieu did not think highly of this way of "waking up." "Happy," says he, "is that nation whose annals are tiresome."

The Senator from Michigan has a different view. He thinks that a nation is not distinguished until it is distinguished in war. He fears that the slumbering faculties of Europe have not been able to ascertain that there are twenty millions of Anglo-Saxons here, making railroads and canals, and speeding all the arts of peace to the utmost accomplishment of the refined civilization! They do not know it! And what is the wonderful expedient which this democratic method of making history would adopt in order to make us known? Storming cities, desolating peaceful, happy homes; shooting men—ay, sir, such is war—and shooting women, too. . . .

There is one topic connected with this subject which I tremble when I approach, and yet I cannot forbear to notice it. It meets you in every step you take; it threatens you which way soever you go in the prosecution of this war. I allude to the question of slavery. Opposition to its further extension, it must be obvious to everyone, is a deeply rooted determination with men of all parties in what we call the nonslaveholding states. New York, Pennsylvania, and Ohio, three of the most powerful, have already sent their legislative instructions here. So it will be, I doubt not, in all the rest. It is vain now to speculate about the reasons for this. Gentlemen of the South may call it prejudice, passion, hypocrisy, fanaticism. I shall not dispute with them now on that point. The great fact that it is so, and not otherwise, is what it concerns us to know. You and I cannot alter or change this opinion, if we would. These people only say we will not, cannot consent that you shall carry slavery where it does not already exist. They do not seek to disturb you in that institution as it exists in your states. Enjoy it if you will and as you will. This is their language; this their determination. How is it in the South? Can it be expected that they should expend in common their blood and their treasure in the acquisition of immense territory, and then willingly forgo the right to carry thither their slaves, and inhabit the conquered country if they please to do so? Sir, I know the feelings and opinions of the South too well to calculate on this. Nay, I believe they would even contend to any extremity for the mere right, had they no wish to exert it. I believe (and I confess I tremble when the conviction presses upon me) that there is equal obstinacy on both sides of this fearful question.

If, then, we persist in war, which, if it terminates in anything short of a mere wanton waste of blood as well as money, must end (as this bill proposes) in the acquisition of territory, to which at once this controversy must attach— this bill would seem to be nothing less than a bill to produce internal commotion. Should we prosecute this war another moment, or expend one dollar in the purchase or conquest of a single acre of Mexican land, the North and the South are brought into collision on a point where neither will yield. Who can foresee or foretell the result! Who so bold or reckless as to look such a conflict in the face unmoved! I do not envy the heart of him who can realize the possibility of such a conflict without emotions too painful to be endured. Why, then, shall we, the representatives of the sovereign states of the Union—the chosen guardians of this confederated Republic, why should we precipitate this fearful struggle, by continuing a war the result

of which must be to force us at once upon a civil conflict? Sir, rightly considered, this is treason, treason to the Union, treason to the dearest interests, the loftiest aspirations, the most cherished hopes of our constituents. It is a crime to risk the possibility of such a contest. It is a crime of such infernal hue that every other in the catalogue of iniquity, when compared with it, whitens into virtue. Oh, Mr. President, it does seem to me, if hell itself could yawn and vomit up the fiends that inhabit its penal abodes, commissioned to disturb the harmony of this world, and dash the fairest prospect of happiness that ever allured the hopes of men, the first step in the consummation of this diabolical purpose would be to light up the fires of internal war and plunge the sister states of this Union into the bottomless gulf of civil strife. We stand this day on the crumbling brink of that gulf—we see its bloody eddies wheeling and boiling before us— shall we not pause before it be too late? How plain again is here the path, I may add the only way, of duty, of prudence, of true patriotism. Let us abandon all idea of acquiring further territory and by consequence cease at once to prosecute this war. Let us call home our armies, and bring them at once within our own acknowledged limits. Show Mexico that you are sincere when you say you desire nothing by conquest. She has learned that she cannot encounter you in war, and if she had not, she is too weak to disturb you here. Tender her peace, and, my life on it, she will then accept it. But whether she shall or not, you will have peace without her consent. It is your invasion that has made war; your retreat will restore peace. Let us then close forever the approaches of internal feud, and so return to the ancient concord and the old ways of national prosperity and permanent glory. Let us here, in this temple consecrated to the Union, perform a solemn lustration; let us wash Mexican blood from our hands, and on these altars, and in the presence of that image of the Father of his Country that looks down upon us, swear to preserve honorable peace with all the world and eternal brotherhood with each other.

HORACE MANN

THE CASE FOR PUBLIC SCHOOLS

Education, then, beyond all other devices of human origin, is the great equalizer of the conditions of men—the balance-wheel of the social machinery.

As the young nation grew, each community was responsible for deciding how much or how little schooling to provide for its children. In many districts, the quality of schooling was meager: teachers were poorly trained, and corporal punishment was common.

The Massachusetts legislature responded to reformers' demands in 1837 by creating a state board of education, which hired Horace Mann (1796–1859) as its secretary. In his eleven years as secretary, Mann led a crusade for better education. In 1848, Mann resigned to go to Congress, where he championed abolitionism. He later served as president of Antioch College in Ohio. Two months before his death, Mann advised the senior class: "I beseech you to treasure up in your hearts these my parting words: Be ashamed to die until you have won some victory for humanity."

The following excerpt is drawn from Mann's last report to the Massachusetts Board of Education, in 1848. It was the credo of a man whose name became synonymous with the struggle to make popular education in America free, secular, humane, and universal.

. . . According to the European theory, men are divided into classes,—some to toil and earn, others to seize and enjoy. According to the Massachusetts theory, all are to have an equal chance for earning, and equal security in the enjoyment of what they earn. The latter tends to equality of condition; the former to the grossest inequalities. . . .

I suppose it to be the universal sentiment of all those who mingle any ingredient of benevolence with their notions on Political Economy, that vast and overshadowing private fortunes are among the greatest dangers to which the happiness of the people in a republic can be subjected. Such fortunes would create a feudalism of a new kind; but one more oppressive and unrelenting than that of the Middle Ages. The feudal lords in England, and on the continent, never held their retainers in a more abject condition of servitude, than the great majority of foreign manufacturers and capitalists hold their operatives and laborers at the present day. The means employed are different, but the similarity in results is striking. What force did then, money does now. . . .

Now, surely, nothing but Universal Education can counter-work this tendency to the domination of capital and the servility of labor. If one class possesses all the wealth and the education, while the residue of society is ignorant and poor, it matters not by what name the relation between them may be called; the latter, in fact and in truth, will be the servile dependants and subjects of the former. But if education be equally diffused, it will draw property after it, by the strongest of all attractions; for such a thing never did happen, and never can happen, as that an intelligent and practical body of men should be permanently poor. Property and labor, in different classes, are essentially antagonistic; but property and labor, in the same class, are essentially fraternal. The people of Massachusetts have, in some degree, appreciated the truth, that the unexampled prosperity of the State,—its comfort, its competence, its general intelligence and virtue,—is attributable to the education, more or less perfect, which all its people have received; but are they sensible of a fact equally important?—namely, that it is to this same education that two thirds of the people are indebted for not being, to-day, the vassals of as severe a tyranny, in the form of capital, as the lower classes of Europe are bound to in the form of brute force.

Education, then, beyond all other devices of human origin, is the great equalizer of the conditions of men—the balance-wheel of the social machinery. I do not here mean that it so elevates the moral nature as to make men disdain and abhor the oppression of their fellow-men. This idea pertains to another of its attributes. But I mean that it gives each man the independence and the means, by which he can resist the selfishness of other men. It does better than to disarm the poor of their hostility towards the rich; it prevents being poor. . . . The spread of education, by enlarging the cultivated class or caste, will open a wider area over which the social feelings will expand; and, if this education should be universal and complete, it would do more than all things else to obliterate factitious distinctions in society.

The main idea set forth in the creeds of some political reformers, or revolutionizers, is, that some people are poor *because* others are rich. This idea supposes a fixed amount of property in the community, which, by fraud or force, or arbitrary law, is unequally divided among men; and the problem presented for solution is, how to transfer a portion of this property from those who are supposed to have too much, to those who feel and know that they have too little. At this point, both their theory and their expectation is of reform stop. But the beneficent power of education would not be exhausted, even though it should peaceably abolish all the miseries that spring from the coëxistence, side by side, of enormous wealth and squalid want. It has a higher function. Beyond the power of diffusing old wealth, it has the prerogative of creating new. It is a thousand times more lucrative than fraud; and adds a thousand fold more to a nation's resources than the most successful conquests. Knaves and robbers can obtain only

Illustration of a schoolroom, probably an academy (or private high school) for boys and girls, from The Bentley Pictorial Reader, *1849.*

what was before possessed by others. But education creates or develops new treasures,—treasures not before possessed or dreamed of by any one. . . .

If a savage will learn how to swim, he can fasten a dozen pounds' weight to his back, and transport it across a narrow river, or other body of water of moderate width. If he will invent an axe, or other instrument, by which to cut down a tree, he can use the tree for a float, and one of its limbs for a paddle, and can thus transport many times the former weight, many times the former distance. Hollowing out his log, he will increase, what may be called, its tonnage,—or, rather, its *poundage,*—and, by sharpening its ends, it will cleave the water both more easily and more swiftly. Fastening several trees together, he makes a raft, and thus increases the buoyant power of his embryo water-craft. Turning up the ends of small poles, or using knees of timber instead of straight pieces, and grooving them together, or filling up the interstices between them, in some way, so as to make them water-tight, he brings his rude raft literally into *ship-shape.* Improving upon hull below and rigging above, he makes a proud merchantman, to be wafted by the winds from continent to continent. But, even this does not content the adventurous naval architect. He frames iron arms for his ship; and, for oars, affixes iron wheels, capable of swift revolution, and stronger than the strong sea. Into iron-walled cavities in her bosom, he puts iron organs of massive structure and strength, and of cohesion insoluble by fire. Within these, he kindles a small volcano; and then, like a sentient and rational existence, this wonderful creation of his hands cleaves oceans, breasts tides, defies tempests, and bears its living and jubilant freight around the globe. Now, take away intelligence from the ship-builder, and the steamship,—that miracle of human art,—falls back into a floating log; the log itself is lost; and the savage swimmer, bearing his dozen pounds on his back, alone remains.

And so it is, not in one department only, but in the whole circle of human labors. The annihilation of the sun would no more certainly be followed by darkness, than the extinction of human intelligence would plunge the race at once into the weakness and helplessness of barbarism. To have created such beings as we are, and to have placed them in this world, without the light of the sun, would be no more cruel than for a government to suffer its laboring classes to grow up without knowledge. . . .

For the creation of wealth, then,—for the existence of a wealthy people and a wealthy nation,—intelligence is the grand condition. The number of improvers will increase, as the intellectual constituency, if I may so call it, increases. In former times, and in most parts of the world even at the present day, not one man in a million has ever had such a development of mind, as made it possible for him to become a contributor to art or science. Let this development precede, and contributions, numberless, and of inestimable value, will be sure to follow. That Political Economy, therefore, which busies itself about capital and labor, supply and demand, interest and rents, favorable and unfavorable balances of trade; but leaves out of account the element of a wide-spread mental development, is nought but stupendous folly. The greatest of all the arts in political economy is, to change a consumer into a producer; and the next greatest is to increase the producer's producing power; —an end to be directly attained, by increasing his intelligence.

SENECA FALLS DECLARATION OF SENTIMENTS AND RESOLUTIONS

The history of mankind is a history of repeated injuries and usurpations on the part of man toward woman.

In the mid-nineteenth century, women had few legal or political rights, even though increasing numbers of women worked in the nation's offices, shops, factories, fields, and classrooms. Women's dissatisfaction with their lot was fed by American democratic ideology. Women knew how to read, and they, too, read the Declaration of Independence; they, too, heard the rhetoric of natural rights, egalitarianism, and freedom used by abolitionists and other reformers. It was inevitable, then, in a country that prized individual conscience, that some women would loudly ask why women were treated as legal and political inferiors.

Elizabeth Cady Stanton (1815–1902) and four other women planned a convention on July 19 and 20, 1848, "to discuss the social, civil, and religious conditions and rights of women." Led by Stanton, the group drafted a Declaration of Sentiments modeled on the Declaration of Independence. About one hundred women and men met in Seneca Falls, New York, where they discussed, amended, and adopted their Declaration. They were far in advance of popular opinion, which spurned women's rights, and especially women's suffrage.

The first state to permit women to vote was Wyoming in 1869. The first nations to adopt women's suffrage were New Zealand (1893), Finland (1906), and Norway (1913). American women won the vote in 1920, when the Nineteenth Amendment to the Constitution was ratified.

W hen, in the course of human events, it becomes necessary for one portion of the family of man to assume among the people of the earth a position different from that which they have hitherto occupied, but one to which the laws of nature and of nature's God entitle them, a decent respect to the opinions of mankind requires that they should declare the causes that impel them to such a course.

We hold these truths to be self-evident: that all men and women are created equal; that they are endowed by their Creator with certain inalienable rights; that among these are life, liberty, and the pursuit of happiness; that to secure these rights governments are instituted, deriving their just powers from the consent of the governed.—Whenever any form of Government becomes destructive of these ends, it is the right of those who suffer from it to refuse allegiance to it, and to insist upon the institution of a new government, laying its foundation on such principles, and organizing its powers in such form as to them shall seem most likely to effect their safety and happiness. Prudence, indeed, will dictate that governments long established should not be changed for light and transient causes; and accordingly, all experience hath shown that mankind are more disposed to suffer, while evils are sufferable, than to right themselves by abolishing the forms to which they are accustomed. But when a long train of abuses and usurpations, pursuing invariably the same object, evinces a design to reduce them under absolute despotism, it is their duty to throw off such government, and to provide new guards for their future security. Such has been the patient sufferance of the women under this government, and such is now the necessity which constrains them to demand the equal station to which they are entitled.

The history of mankind is a history of repeated injuries and usurpations on the part of man toward woman, having in direct object the establishment of an absolute tyranny over her. To prove this, let facts be submitted to a candid world.

He has never permitted her to exercise her inalienable right to the elective franchise.

He has compelled her to submit to laws, in the formation of which she had no voice.

He has withheld from her rights which are given to the most ignorant and degraded men—both natives and foreigners.

Having deprived her of this first right of a citizen, the elective franchise, thereby leaving her without representation in the halls of legislation, he has oppressed her on all sides.

He has made her, if married, in the eye of the law, civilly dead.

He has taken from her all right in property, even to the wages she earns.

He has made her, morally, an irresponsible being, as she can commit many crimes with impunity, provided they be done in the presence of her husband. In the covenant of marriage, she is compelled to promise obedience to her husband, he becoming, to all intents and purposes, her master—the law giving him power to deprive her of her liberty, and to administer chastisement.

He has so framed the laws of divorce, as to what shall be the proper causes of divorce; in case of separation, to whom the guardianship of the children shall be given; as to be wholly regardless of the happiness of women—the law, in all cases, going upon the false supposition of the supremacy of man, and giving all power into his hands.

After depriving her of all rights as a married woman, if single and the owner of property, he has taxed her to support a government which recognizes her only when her property can be made profitable to it.

He has monopolized nearly all the profitable employments, and from those she is permitted to follow, she receives but a scanty remuneration.

He closes against her all avenues to wealth and distinction, which he considers most honorable to himself. As a teacher of theology, medicine, or law, she is not known.

He has denied her the facilities for obtaining a thorough education—all colleges being closed against her.

He allows her in Church as well as State, but a subordinate position, claiming Apostolic authority for her exclusion from the ministry, and, with some exceptions, from any public participation in the affairs of the Church.

He has created a false public sentiment, by giving to the world a different code of morals for men and women, by which moral delinquencies which exclude women from society, are not only tolerated but deemed of little account in man.

He has usurped the prerogative of Jehovah himself, claiming it as his right to assign for her a sphere of action, when that belongs to her conscience and her God.

He has endeavored, in every way that he could to destroy her confidence in her own powers, to lessen her self-respect, and to make her willing to lead a dependant and abject life.

Now, in view of this entire disfranchisement of one-half the people of this country, their social and religious degradation,—in view of the unjust laws above mentioned, and because women do feel themselves aggrieved, oppressed, and fraudulently deprived of their most sacred rights, we insist that they have immediate admission to all the rights and privileges which belong to them as citizens of these United States.

In entering upon the great work before us, we anticipate no small amount of misconception, misrepresentation, and ridicule; but we shall use every instrumentality within our power to effect our object. We shall employ agents, circulate tracts, petition the State and national Legislatures, and endeavor to enlist the pulpit and the press in our behalf. We hope this Convention will be followed by a series of Conventions, embracing every part of the country.

Firmly relying upon the final triumph of the Right and the True, we do this day affix our signatures to this declaration.

Resolutions

Whereas, the great precept of nature is conceded to be, "that man shall pursue his own true and substantial happiness." Blackstone, in his Commentaries, remarks, that this law of Nature being coeval with mankind, and dictated by God himself, is of course superior in obligation to any other. It is binding over all the globe, in all countries, and at all times; no human laws are of any validity if contrary to this, and such of them as are valid, derive all their force, and all their validity, and all their authority, mediately and immediately, from this origin; Therefore,

Resolved, That such laws as conflict, in any way, with the true and substantial happiness of woman, are contrary to the great precept of nature, and of no validity; for this is "superior in obligation to any other."

Resolved, That all laws which prevent women from occupying such a station in society as her conscience shall dictate, or which place her in a position inferior to that of man, are contrary to the great precept of nature, and therefore of no force or authority.

Resolved, That woman is man's equal—was intended to be so by the Creator, and the highest good of the race demands that she should be recognized as such.

Resolved, That the women of this country ought to be enlightened in regard to the laws under which they live, that they may no longer publish their degradation, by declaring themselves satisfied with their present position, nor their ignorance, by asserting that they have all the rights they want.

Resolved, That inasmuch as man, while claiming for himself intellectual superiority, does accord to woman moral superiority, it is pre-eminently his duty to encourage her to speak, and teach, as she has an opportunity, in all religious assemblies.

Resolved, That the same amount of virtue, delicacy, and refinement of behavior, that is required of woman in the social state, should also be required of man, and the same transgressions should be visited with equal severity on both man and woman.

Resolved, That the objection of indelicacy and impropriety, which is so often brought against woman when she addresses a public audience, comes with a very ill grace from those who encourage, by their attendance, her appearance on the stage, in the concert, or in the feats of the circus.

Resolved, That woman has too long rested satisfied in the circumscribed limits which corrupt customs and a perverted application of the Scriptures have marked out for her, and that it is time she should move in the enlarged sphere which her great Creator has assigned her.

Resolved, That it is the duty of the women of this country to secure to themselves their sacred right to the elective franchise.

Resolved, That the equality of human rights results necessarily from the fact of the identity of the race in capabilities and responsibilities.

Resolved, therefore, That, being invested by the Creator with the same capabilities, and the same consciousness of responsibility for their exercise, it is demonstrably the right and duty of woman, equally with man, to promote every righteous cause, by every righteous means; and especially in regard to the great subjects of morals and religion, it is self-evidently her right to participate with her brother in teaching them, both in private and in public, by writing and by speaking, by any instrumentalities proper to be used, and in any assemblies proper to be held; and this being a self-evident truth, growing out of the divinely implanted principles of human nature, any custom or authority adverse to it, whether modern or wearing the hoary sanction of antiquity, is to be regarded as self-evident falsehood, and at war with the interests of mankind.

Resolved, That the speedy success of our cause depends upon the zealous and untiring efforts of both men and women, for the overthrow of the monopoly of the pulpit, and for the securing to woman an equal participation with men in the various trades, professions and commerce.

ADDRESS TO THE OHIO WOMEN'S RIGHTS CONVENTION

And ain't I a woman?

Sojourner Truth (c. 1797–1883) was born into slavery in Ulster County in New York state and named Isabella. Before slavery was abolished in New York in 1827, she was sold to a master named Van Wagenen, who set her free. She moved to New York City, where she worked as a domestic and became involved in evangelical activities.

In 1843, she renamed herself Sojourner Truth and began to travel across the country as a religious missionary. A riveting speaker, she preached and sang and called on people to accept the word of God and the brotherhood of man. Her message was a mixture of religion and abolitionism, and after she discovered the women's rights movement, of feminism as well. During the Civil War, she worked on behalf of the Union cause, gathering supplies for black regiments. In 1864, she visited Washington, D.C., where she helped integrate the streetcars and was received at the White House by President Abraham Lincoln.

In 1850, Sojourner Truth attended the first National Woman's Rights Convention in Worcester, Massachusetts, where she was the only black woman. The following year, Sojourner Truth attended the Ohio Women's Rights Convention in Akron; many participants objected to her presence, fearing that the feminist cause would get mixed up with the unpopular abolitionist cause. As Sojourner Truth rose to speak, there was a hiss of disapproval. But when she finished, there were "roars of applause" from the audience.

Well, children, where there is so much racket there must be something out of kilter. I think that 'twixt the Negroes of the South and the women at the North, all talking about rights, the white men will be in a fix pretty soon. But what's all this here talking about?

That man over there says that women need to be helped into carriages, and lifted over ditches, and to have the best place everywhere. Nobody ever helps me into carriages, or over mud-puddles, or gives me any best place! And ain't I a woman? Look at me! Look at my arm. I have ploughed and planted, and gathered into barns, and no man could head me! And ain't I a woman? I could work as much and eat as much as a man—when I could get it—and bear the lash as well! And ain't I a woman? I have borne thirteen children, and seen them most all sold off to slavery, and when I cried out with my mother's grief, none but Jesus heard me! And ain't I a woman?

Then they talk about this thing in the head; what's this they call it? [Intellect, someone whispers.] That's it, honey. What's that got to do with women's rights or Negro's rights? If my cup won't hold but a pint, and yours holds a quart, wouldn't you be mean not to let me have my little half-measure full?

Then that little man in black there, he says women can't have as much rights as men, 'cause Christ wasn't a woman! Where did your Christ come from? Where did your Christ come from?

From God and a woman! Man had nothing to do with Him.

If the first woman God ever made was strong enough to turn the world upside down all alone, these women together ought to be able to turn it back, and get it right side up again! And now they is asking to do it, the men better let them.

Obliged to you for hearing me, and now old Sojourner ain't got nothing more to say.

William Sidney Mount was one of the first American artists to depict blacks empathetically, but he was best known for his scenes of country life. He painted The Power of Music *in 1847.*

STEPHEN FOSTER

OH! SUSANNA and OLD FOLKS AT HOME

Stephen Collins Foster (1826–1864) was born in Pennsylvania on July 4, 1826. His family tried to discourage his interest in music, and for a few years he was a bookkeeper in his brother's business in Cincinnati. But Foster's musical gifts could not be repressed, and he wrote about two hundred songs. Influenced by the minstrel shows that were in vogue and by black folksongs, Foster produced a remarkable body of work. Among his best-known songs are "Oh! Susanna," "Old Folks at Home," "My Old Kentucky Home," "Jeannie with the Light Brown Hair," "Camptown Races," "Old Black Joe," and "Beautiful Dreamer." Even though many of Foster's songs were instantly popular, Foster was a poor businessman and made disadvantageous financial arrangements with song publishers. Perhaps if he had listened to his parents, he would have been able to negotiate better royalties and protect his rights to his work. Impoverished and alcoholic, he died at the age of thirty-seven.

"Oh! Susanna" was one of Foster's earliest songs; he sold the rights to a music publisher for $100 in 1848. Like so many of Foster's songs, it was written for the minstrel shows. It became an overnight sensation—an instant "folksong," a special favorite of the pioneers heading west in the Gold Rush of 1849.

"Old Folks at Home," written in 1851, was long popular because of its sentimentality and nostalgia for a long-lost family home. Foster never longed to go back to the Swanee River or the old plantation, because when he wrote the song, he had never been in the South, and he never saw the Swanee River. When writing the lyrics, he considered "way down upon the Yazoo River," discarded that, tried the "Pedee River," discarded that, then turned to an atlas and picked the Swanee River in Florida as the place he longed to see once more. His only trip to the South was in 1852, a year after this song was published.

Oh! Susanna

I come from Alabama with a banjo on my knee;
I'm gone to Lou'siana
My true love for to see.
It rained all night the day I left,
The weather it was dry.
The sun so hot I froze to death,
Susanna, don't you cry.

CHORUS:
Oh! Susanna, don't you cry for me;
I come from Alabama with a banjo on my knee.

I had a dream the other night,
When everything was still;
I thought I saw Susanna dear,
a'coming down the hill.
The buckwheat cake was in her mouth,
The tear was in her eye.
Says I, I'm coming from the South,
Susanna, don't you cry.

I soon will be in New Orleans,
And then I'll look all 'round,
And when I find Susanna,

I'll fall upon the ground.
But if I do not find her,
This darkey'll surely die,
And when I'm dead and buried,
Susanna, don't you cry.

Old Folks at Home

'Way down upon the Swanee River,
        Far far away,
There's where my heart is turning ever,
There's where the old folks stay.
All up and down the whole creation,
        Sadly I roam,
Still longing for the old plantation,
And for the old folks at home.

CHORUS:
All the world is sad and dreary
Everywhere I roam,
Oh, darkies, how my heart grows weary,
Far from the old folks at home.

All 'round the little farm I wandered
When I was young,
Then many happy days I squandered,
Many the songs I sung.
When I was playing with my brother
Happy was I.
Oh! take me to my kind old mother,
There let me live and die.

One little hut among the bushes,
One that I love,
Still sadly to my mem'ry rushes,
No matter where I rove.
When will I see the bees a-humming
All 'round the comb?
When will I hear the banjo strumming
Down in my good old home?

ELIZABETH CADY STANTON

ADDRESS TO THE LEGISLATURE OF NEW YORK ON WOMEN'S RIGHTS

We ask no better laws than those you have made for yourselves . . . simply on the ground that the rights of every human being are the same and identical.

Elizabeth Cady Stanton (1815–1902) was the leading strategist, orator, philosopher, and publicist of the movement for women's equality in the United States. The daughter of a wealthy, conservative family in upstate New York, she married Henry B. Stanton, an abolitionist and lawyer, and had seven children (the last was born in 1859). She worked to pass landmark legislation in New York in 1848 that gave property rights to married women, and she was the prime mover behind the Seneca Falls convention for women's rights in the same year. In 1851, she joined forces with Susan B. Anthony, and the two directed the course of the women's rights movement for the rest of the century.

In February 1854, Stanton appeared before the New York State legislature in Albany on behalf of a state convention of women's rights advocates. Stanton and Anthony put a copy of the speech on every legislator's desk and printed 50,000 copies for distribution as tracts. Before giving the speech, Stanton (then thirty-eight) read it to her father, a respected jurist, who threatened to disinherit her but ended by assisting her with the legal analysis.

. . . Gentlemen, in republican America, in the nineteenth century, we, the daughters of the revolutionary heroes of '76, demand at your hands the redress of our grievances—a revision of your State Constitution—a new code of laws. Permit us then, as briefly as possible, to call your attention to the legal disabilities under which we labor.

1st. Look at the position of woman as woman. It is not enough for us that by your laws we are permitted to live and breathe, to claim the necessaries of life from our legal protectors —to pay the penalty of our crimes; we demand the full recognition of all our rights as citizens of the Empire State. We are persons; native, free-born citizens; property-holders, tax-payers; yet are we denied the exercise of our right to the elective franchise. We support ourselves, and, in part, your schools, colleges, churches, your poor-houses, jails, prisons, the army, the navy, the whole machinery of government, and yet we have no voice in your councils. We have every qualification required by the Constitution, necessary to the legal voter, but the one of sex. We are moral, virtuous, and intelligent, and in all respects quite equal to the proud white man himself, and yet by your laws we are classed with idiots, lunatics, and negroes; and though we do not feel honored by the place assigned us, yet, in fact, our legal position is lower than that of either; for the negro can be raised to the dignity of a voter if he possess himself of $250; the lunatic can vote in his moments of sanity, and the idiot, too, if he be a male one, and not more than nine-tenths a fool; but we, who have guided great movements of charity, established missions, edited journals, published works on history, economy, and statistics; who have governed nations, led armies, filled the professor's chair, taught philosophy and mathematics to the savants of our age, discovered planets, piloted ships across the sea, are denied the most sacred rights of citizens, because, forsooth, we came not into this republic crowned with the dignity of manhood! . . . Can it be that here, where we acknowledge no royal blood, no apostolic descent, that you, who have declared that all men were created equal—that governments derive their just powers from the consent of the governed, would willingly build up an aristocracy that places the ignorant and vulgar above the educated and refined—the alien and the ditch-digger above the authors and poets of the day— an aristocracy that would raise the sons above the mothers that bore them? . . .

2d. Look at the position of woman as wife. Your laws relating to marriage—founded as they are on the old common law of England, a compound of barbarous usages, but partially modified by progressive civilization—are in open violation of our enlightened ideas of justice, and of the holiest feelings of our nature. If you take the highest view of marriage, as a Divine relation, which love alone can constitute and sanctify, then of course human legislation can only recognize it. Men can neither bind nor loose its ties, for that prerogative belongs to God alone, who makes man and woman, and the laws of attraction by which they are united. But if you regard marriage as a civil contract, then let it be subject to the same laws which control

all other contracts. Do not make it a kind of half-human, half-divine institution, which you may build up, but can not regulate. Do not, by your special legislation for this one kind of contract, involve yourselves in the grossest absurdities and contradictions.

So long as by your laws no man can make a contract for a horse or piece of land until he is twenty-one years of age, and by which contract he is not bound if any deception has been practiced, or if the party contracting has not fulfilled his part of the agreement—so long as the parties in all mere civil contracts retain their identity and all the power and independence they had before contracting, with the full right to dissolve all partnerships and contracts for any reason, at the will and option of the parties themselves, upon what principle of civil jurisprudence do you permit the boy of fourteen and the girl of twelve, in violation of every natural law, to make a contract more momentous in importance than any other, and then hold them to it come what may, the whole of their natural lives, in spite of disappointment, deception, and misery? Then, too, the signing of this contract is instant civil death to one of the parties. The woman who but yesterday was sued on bended knee, who stood so high in the scale of being as to make an agreement on equal terms with a proud Saxon man, to-day has no civil existence, no social freedom. The wife who inherits no property holds about the same legal position that does the slave of the Southern plantation. She can own nothing, sell nothing. She has no right even to the wages she earns; her person, her time, her services are the property of another. . . .

3d. Look at the position of woman as widow. Whenever we attempt to point out the wrongs of the wife, those who would have us believe that the laws can not be improved, point us to the privileges, powers, and claims of the widow. Let us look into these a little. . . . Behold the magnanimity of the law in allowing the widow to retain a life interest in one-third the landed estate, and one-half the personal property of her husband, and taking the lion's share to itself! Had she died first, the house and land would all have been the husband's still. No one would have dared to intrude upon the privacy of his home, or to molest him in his sacred retreat of sorrow. How, I ask you, can that be called justice, which makes such a distinction as this between man and woman? . . .

Many times and oft it has been asked us, with unaffected seriousness, "What do you women want? What are you aiming at?" Many have manifested a laudable curiosity to know what the wives and daughters could complain of in republican America, where their sires and sons have so bravely fought for freedom and gloriously secured their independence, trampling all tyranny, bigotry, and caste in the dust, and declaring to a waiting world the divine truth that all men are created equal. What can woman want under such a government? Admit a radical difference in sex, and you demand different spheres—water for fish, and air for birds.

It is impossible to make the Southern planter believe that his slave feels and reasons just as he does—that injustice and subjection are as galling as to him—that the degradation of living by the will of another, the mere dependent on his caprice, at the mercy of his passions, is as keenly felt by him as his master. If you can force on his unwilling vision a vivid picture of the negro's wrongs, and for a moment touch his soul, his logic brings him instant consolation. He says, the slave does not feel this as I would. Here, gentlemen, is our difficulty: When we plead our cause before the law-makers and savants of the republic, they can not take in the idea that men and women are alike; and so long as the mass rest in this delusion, the public mind will not be so much startled by the revelations made of the injustice and degradation of woman's position as by the fact that she should at length wake up to a sense of it. . . .

But if, gentlemen, you take the ground that the sexes are alike, and, therefore, you are our faithful representatives—then why all these special laws for woman? Would not one code answer for all of like needs and wants? Christ's golden rule is better than all the special legislation that the ingenuity of man can devise: "Do

unto others as you would have others do unto you." This, men and brethren, is all we ask at your hands. We ask no better laws than those you have made for yourselves. We need no other protection than that which your present laws secure to you.

In conclusion, then, let us say, in behalf of the women of this State, we ask for all that you have asked for yourselves in the progress of your development, since the *Mayflower* cast anchor beside Plymouth rock; and simply on the ground that the rights of every human being are the same and identical. You may say that the mass of the women of this State do not make the demand; it comes from a few sour, disappointed old maids and childless women.

You are mistaken; the mass speak through us. A very large majority of the women of this State support themselves and their children, and many their husbands too. . . .

Now, do you candidly think these wives do not wish to control the wages they earn—to own the land they buy—the houses they build? to have at their disposal their own children, without being subject to the constant interference and tyranny of an idle, worthless profligate? Do you suppose that any woman is such a pattern of devotion and submission that she willingly stitches all day for the small sum of fifty cents, that she may enjoy the unspeakable privilege, in obedience to your laws, of paying for her husband's tobacco and rum? Think you the wife of the confirmed, beastly drunkard would consent to share with him her home and bed, if law and public sentiment would release her from such gross companionship? Verily, no! . . .

For all these, then, we speak. If to this long list you add the laboring women who are loudly demanding remuneration for their unending toil; those women who teach in our seminaries, academies, and public schools for a miserable pittance; the widows who are taxed without mercy; the unfortunate ones in our workhouses, poor-houses, and prisons; who are they that we do not now represent? But a small class of the fashionable butterflies, who, through the short summer days, seek the sunshine and the flowers; but the cool breezes of autumn and the hoary frosts of winter will soon chase all these away; then they too, will need and seek protection, and through other lips demand in their turn justice and equity at your hands.

CHIEF SEATTLE'S ORATION

Every part of this soil is sacred in the estimation of my people. Every hillside, every valley, every plain and grove, has been hallowed by some sad or happy event in days long vanished.

Chief Seattle was the leader of six Indian tribes in the Pacific Northwest. In December 1854, he spoke to an assemblage that included the territorial governor, white settlers, and about one thousand Indians. His speech was directed to Governor Isaac I. Stevens, who had just returned from Washington, D.C., with instructions to buy the Indians' lands and to establish Indian reservations. Speaking on the site of what would become the city of Seattle, the chief gave what has been called the "funeral oration" or "swan song" of his people as he described his decision to accept the federal government's offer instead of joining what was sure to be a disastrous war against the overwhelming strength of the government. Early histories frequently reprinted terrifying accounts of the warfare between settlers and Indians, with particular emphasis on the cruelty of the Indians. But by the mid-nineteenth century, when most Indian tribes had been driven west, domesticated, or destroyed, the Indian had become an object of sympathy or sentimentality, an inevitable victim of "progress" or Manifest Destiny. Chief Seattle's speech has been often reprinted, not to sentimentalize the people for whom he spoke but because of his moving description of the contrast between the Red Man's way and the White Man's way. The following account of Chief Seattle's speech was written by Dr. Henry A. Smith, who served as the translator for Chief Seattle on the historic occasion in 1854.

. . . Yonder sky that has wept tears of compassion upon my people for centuries untold, and which to us appears changeless and eternal, may change. Today is fair. Tomorrow it may be overcast with clouds. My words are like the stars that never change. Whatever Seattle says the great chief at Washington can rely upon with as much certainty as he can upon the return of the sun or the seasons. The White Chief says that Big Chief at Washington sends us greetings of friendship and goodwill. This is kind of him for we know he has little need of our friendship in return. His people are many. They are like the grass that covers vast prairies. My people are few. They resemble the scattering trees of a storm-swept plain. The great, and I presume—good White Chief sends us word that he wishes to buy our lands but is willing to allow us enough to live comfortably. This indeed appears just, even generous, for the Red Man no longer has rights that he need respect, and the offer may be wise also, as we are no longer in need of an extensive country.

There was a time when our people covered the land as the waves of a wind-ruffled sea cover its shell paved floor, but that time long since passed away with the greatness of tribes that are now but a mournful memory. I will not dwell on, nor mourn over, our untimely decay, nor reproach my paleface brothers with hastening it as we too may have been somewhat to blame.

Youth is impulsive. When our young men grow angry at some real or imaginary wrong, and disfigure their faces with black paint, it denotes that their hearts are black, and that they are often cruel and relentless, and our old men and old women are unable to restrain them. Thus it has ever been. Thus it was when the white men first began to push our forefathers further westward. But let us hope that the hostilities between us may never return. We would have everything to lose and nothing to gain. Revenge by young men is considered gain, even at the cost of their own lives, but old men who stay at home in times of war, and mothers who have sons to lose, know better.

Our good father at Washington—for I presume he is now our father as well as yours, since King George has moved his boundaries further north—our great and good father, I say, sends us word that if we do as he desires he will protect us. His brave warriors will be to us a bristling wall of strength, and his wonderful ships of war will fill our harbors so that our ancient enemies far to the northward—the Hydas and Tsimpsians, will cease to frighten our women, children and old men. Then in reality will he be our father and we his children. But can that ever be? Your God is not our God! Your God loves your people and hates mine. He folds his strong protecting arms lovingly about the pale face and leads him by the hand as a father leads his infant son—but He has forsaken His red children—if they really are his. Our God, the Great Spirit, seems also to have forsaken us. Your God makes your people wax strong every day. Soon they will fill all the land. Our people are ebbing away like a rapidly receding tide that will never return. The white man's God cannot love our people or He would protect them. They seem to be orphans who can look nowhere for help. How then can we be brothers? How can your God become our God and renew our prosperity and awaken in us dreams of returning greatness. If we have a common heavenly father He must be partial—for He came to His paleface children. We never saw him. He gave you laws but had no word for his red children whose teeming multitudes once filled this vast continent as stars fill the firmament. No; we are two distinct races with separate origins and separate destinies. There is little in common between us.

To us the ashes of our ancestors are sacred and their resting place is hallowed ground. You wander far from the graves of your ancestors and seemingly without regret. Your religion was written upon tables of stone by the iron finger of your God so that you could not forget. The Red Man could never comprehend nor remember it. Our religion is the traditions of our ancestors—the dreams of our old men, given them in solemn hours of night by the Great Spirit; and the visions of our sachems, and is written in the hearts of our people.

Your dead cease to love you and the land of their nativity as soon as they pass the portals of the tomb and wander away beyond the stars. They are soon forgotten and never return. Our dead never forget the beautiful world that gave them being. They still love its verdant valleys, its murmuring rivers, its magnificent mountains, sequestered vales and verdant lined lakes and bays, and ever yearn in tender, fond affection over the lonely hearted living, and often return from the Happy Hunting Ground to visit, guide, console and comfort them.

Day and night cannot dwell together. The Red Man has ever fled the approach of the White Man, as the morning mist flees before the morning sun.

However, your proposition seems fair and I think that my people will accept it and will retire to the reservation you offer them. Then we will dwell apart in peace, for the words of the Great White Chief seem to be the words of nature speaking to my people out of dense darkness.

It matters little where we pass the remnant of our days. They will not be many. The Indians' night promises to be dark. Not a single star of hope hovers above his horizon. Sad-voiced winds moan in the distance. Grim fate seems to be on the Red Man's Trail, and wherever he goes he will hear the approaching footsteps of his fell destroyer and prepare stolidly to meet his doom, as does the wounded doe that hears the approaching footsteps of the hunter.

A few more moons. A few more winters—and not one of the descendants of the mighty hosts that once moved over this broad land or lived in happy homes, protected by the Great Spirit, will remain to mourn over the graves of a people—once more powerful and hopeful than yours. But why should I mourn at the untimely fate of my people? Tribe follows tribe, and nation follows nation, like the waves of the sea. It is the order of nature, and regret is useless. Your time of decay may be distant, but it will surely come, for even the White Man whose God walked and talked with him as friend with friend, cannot be exempt from the common destiny. We may be brothers after all. We will see.

We will ponder your proposition and when we decide we will let you know. But should we accept it, I here and now make this condition that we will not be denied the privilege without molestation of visiting at any time the tombs of our ancestors, friends and children. Every part of this soil is sacred in the estimation of my people. Every hillside, every valley, every plain and grove, has been hallowed by some sad or happy event in days long vanished. Even the rocks, which seem to be dumb and dead as they swelter in the sun along the silent shore, thrill with memories of stirring events connected with the lives of my people, and the very dust upon which you now stand responds more lovingly to their footsteps than to yours, because it is rich with the blood of our ancestors and our bare feet are conscious of the sympathetic touch. Our departed braves, fond mothers, glad, happy-hearted maidens, and even the little children who lived here and rejoiced here for brief season, will love these somber solitudes and at eventide they greet shadowy returning spirits. And when the last Red Man shall have perished, and the memory of my tribe shall have become a myth among the White Men, these shores will swarm with the invisible dead of my tribe, and when your children's children think themselves alone in the field, the store, the shop, upon the highway, or in the silence of the pathless woods, they will not be alone. In all the earth there is no place dedicated to solitude. At night when the streets of your cities and villages are silent and you think them deserted, they will throng with the returning hosts that once filled them and still love this beautiful land. The White Man will never be alone.

Let him be just and deal kindly with my people, for the dead are not powerless. Dead, did I say? There is no death, only a change of worlds.

LUCY STONE

A DISAPPOINTED WOMAN

In education, in marriage, in religion, in everything, disappointment is the lot of woman.

Lucy Stone (1818–1893) was born in Massachusetts, the eighth of nine children. When her family refused to help her attend college, she taught school and saved enough to enter Oberlin College, the first in the United States to admit women. An abolitionist and feminist, Stone became a prominent orator. When she married the reformer Henry Blackwell in 1855, they devised a new marriage contract to protest the laws that subjected the wife to her husband. To symbolize her separate identity, Stone kept her maiden name, a remarkable step in that era. For many years, the Lucy Stone League encouraged women to maintain their maiden names after marriage.

Lucy Stone and Henry Blackwell helped establish the National American Woman Suffrage Association in 1869 and founded the *Woman's Journal,* a major suffrage journal.

The following excerpt is from a speech she delivered extemporaneously at a national women's rights convention in Cincinnati, Ohio, in October 1855.

The last speaker alluded to this movement as being that of a few disappointed women. From the first years to which my memory stretches, I have been a disappointed woman. When, with my brothers, I reached forth after the sources of knowledge, I was reproved with "It isn't fit for you; it doesn't belong to women." Then there was but one college in the world where women were admitted, and that was in Brazil. I would have found my way there, but by the time I was prepared to go, one was opened in the young State of Ohio—the first in the United States where women and Negroes could enjoy opportunities with white men. I was disappointed when I came to seek a profession worthy an immortal being—every employment was closed to me, except those of the teacher, the seamstress, and the housekeeper. In education, in marriage, in religion, in everything, disappointment is the lot of woman. It shall be the business of my life to deepen this disappointment in every woman's heart until she bows down to it no longer. I wish that women, instead of being walking show-cases, instead of begging of their fathers and brothers the latest and gayest new bonnet, would ask of them their rights.

The question of Woman's Rights is a practical one. The notion has prevailed that it was only an ephemeral idea; that it was but women claiming the right to smoke cigars in the streets, and to frequent bar-rooms. Others have supposed it a question of comparative intellect; others still, of sphere. Too much has already been said and written about woman's sphere. Trace all the doctrines to their source and they will be found to have no basis except in the usages and prejudices of the age. This is seen in the fact that what is tolerated in woman in one country is not tolerated in another. In this country women may hold prayer-meetings, etc., but in Mohammedan countries it is written upon their mosques, "Women and dogs, and other impure animals, are not permitted to enter." Wendell Phillips says, "The best and greatest thing one is capable of doing, that is his sphere." I have confidence in the Father to believe that when He gives us the capacity to do anything He does not make a blunder. Leave women, then, to find their sphere. And do not tell us before we are born even, that our province is to cook dinners, darn stockings, and sew on buttons. . . .

EMILY DICKINSON
SUCCESS

Emily Dickinson (1830–1886) is now recognized as one of America's finest poets, but few of her poems were published during her lifetime. She led a secluded life in Amherst, Massachusetts, and was educated at Amherst Academy (a local private secondary school) and Mount Holyoke Female Seminary. She seldom ventured away from Amherst, or even from the family home, in which she was born and died. Despite her paucity of worldly experience, Emily Dickinson developed an intense internal universe, focusing on eternal themes like love, death, and nature. In the century since her death, her poems have won the admiration of people of all ages. She is today one of the few American poets who is regularly anthologized in schoolbooks. In part, this is because her poems are short, but also because they do not require interpretation by experts. They speak directly to the reader.

Success is counted sweetest
By those who ne'er succeed.
To comprehend a nectar
Requires sorest need.

Not one of all the purple host
Who took the flag to-day

Can tell the definition
So clear, of victory,

As he, defeated, dying,
On whose forbidden ear
The distant strains of triumph
Break, agonized and clear.

PRELUDE TO WAR

THE

LIBERTY

ALMANAC,

FOR

1847.

New York:

WILLIAM HARNED, 5 SPRUCE STREET.

The cover of the Liberty Almanac, *an abolitionist publication.*

DAVID WALKER

WALKER'S APPEAL

We (coloured people of these United States) are the most degraded, wretched, and abject set of beings that ever lived since the world began.

One of the most notorious essays in American history was written by David Walker (1785–1830), the son of a slave father and a free mother. Born in Wilmington, North Carolina, Walker settled in Boston, where he became active in the abolitionist movement. He contributed articles to *Freedom's Journal,* the first black newspaper in the country, and owned a second-hand clothing store on the waterfront. In 1829, he wrote *Walker's Appeal in Four Articles, Together with a Preamble to the Coloured Citizens of the World, but in Particular and very Expressly to Those of the United States of America.*

The *Appeal* condemned slavery and predicted that it would cause the destruction of the United States. Walker rejected schemes to create a black colony in Liberia and denounced the indifference of white clergymen. Through Walker's contacts with sailors, his *Appeal* was smuggled into the South, to the fury of slave owners. In reaction, southern states prohibited the circulation of abolitionist literature and made it illegal to teach slaves to read and write. Although a price was put on his head, Walker refused to flee. He is reported to have said, "I will stand my ground. Somebody must die in this cause." In June 1830, he was found dead near his shop, and it is believed that he was poisoned.

The *Appeal,* excerpted below, was frequently reprinted by abolitionists during the next thirty years.

Having travelled over a considerable portion of these United States, and having, in the course of my travels, taken the most accurate observations of things as they exist, the result of my observations has warranted the full and unshaken conviction, that we (coloured people of these United States) are the most degraded, wretched, and abject set of beings that ever lived since the world began; and I pray God that none like us ever may live again until time shall be no more. They tell us of the Israelites in Egypt, the Helots in Sparta, and of the Roman Slaves, which last were made up from almost every nation under heaven, whose sufferings under those ancient and heathen nations, were, in comparison with ours, under this enlightened and Christian nation, no more than a cypher— or, in other words, those heathen nations of antiquity, had but little more among them than the name and form of slavery; while wretchedness

and endless miseries were reserved, apparently in a phial, to be poured out upon our fathers, ourselves and our children, by *Christian* Americans. . . .

I am fully aware, in making this appeal to my much afflicted and suffering brethren, that I shall not only be assailed by those whose greatest earthly desires are to keep us in abject ignorance and wretchedness, and who are of the firm conviction that Heaven has designed us and our children to be slaves and *beasts of burden* to them and their children. I say, I do not only expect to be held up to the public as an ignorant, impudent and restless disturber of the public peace, by such avaricious creatures, as well as a mover of insubordination—and perhaps put in prison or to death, for giving a superficial exposition of our miseries, and exposing tyrants. But I am persuaded, that many of my brethren, particularly those who are ignorantly in league with slave-holders or tyrants, who acquire their daily bread by the blood and sweat of their more ignorant brethren—and not a few of those too, who are too ignorant to see an inch beyond their noses, will rise up and call me cursed— Yea, the jealous ones among us will perhaps use more abject subtlety, by affirming that this work is not worth perusing, that we are well situated, and there is no use in trying to better our condition, for we cannot. I will ask one question here.—Can our condition be any worse?—Can it be more mean and abject? If there are any changes, will they not be for the better, though they may appear for the worse at first? Can they get us any lower? Where can they get us? They are afraid to treat us worse, for they know well, the day they do it they are gone. But against all accusations which may or can be preferred against me, I appeal to Heaven for my motive in writing—who knows what my object is, if possible, to awaken in the breasts of my afflicted, degraded and slumbering brethren, a spirit of inquiry and investigation respecting our miseries and wretchedness in this *Republican Land of Liberty!!!!!* . . .

I saw a paragraph, a few years since, in a South Carolina paper, which, speaking of the barbarity of the Turks, said: "The Turks are the most barbarous people in the world—they treat the Greeks more like *brutes* than human beings." And in the same paper was an advertisement, which said: "Eight well built Virginia and Maryland *Negro fellows* and four *wenches* will positively be *sold* this day, to the highest bidder!" And what astonished me still more was, to see in this same *humane* paper!! the cuts of three men, with clubs and budgets on their backs, and an advertisement offering a considerable sum of money for their apprehension and delivery. I declare, it is really amusing to hear the Southerners and Westerners of this country talk about *barbarity,* that it is positively enough to make a man *smile*. . . .

Men of colour, who are also of sense, for you particularly is my *Appeal* designed. Our more ignorant brethren are not able to penetrate its value. I call upon you therefore to cast your eyes upon the wretchedness of your brethren, and to do your utmost to enlighten them—*go to work and enlighten your brethren!*—Let the Lord see you doing what you can to rescue them and yourselves from degradation. There is a great work for you to do, as trifling as some of you may think of it. You have to prove to the Americans and the world, that we are *Men,* and not *brutes,* as we have been represented, and by millions treated. Remember, to let the aim of your labours among your brethren, and particularly the youths, be the dissemination of education and religion. . . .

What the American preachers can think of us, I aver this day before my God, I have never been able to define. They have newspapers and monthly periodicals, which they receive in continual succession, but on the pages of which, you will scarcely ever find a paragraph respecting slavery, which is ten thousand times more injurious to this country than all the other evils put together; and which will be the final overthrow of its government, unless something is very speedily done; for their cup is nearly full. —Perhaps they will laugh at or make light of this; but I tell you Americans! that unless you speedily alter your course, *you* and your Country are gone!!!!! For God Almighty will tear up the very face of the earth!!! Will not that very remarkable passage of Scripture be fulfilled on Christian Americans? Hear it Americans!! "He that is unjust, let him be unjust still:—and he which is filthy, let him be filthy still: and he that is righteous, let him be righteous still: and he that is holy, let him be holy still." I hope that the Americans may hear, but I am afraid that they have done us so much injury, and are so firm in the belief that our Creator made us to be an inheritance to them forever, that their hearts will be hardened, so that their destruction may be sure. This language, perhaps, is too harsh for the American's delicate ears. But O Americans! Americans!! I warn you in the name of the Lord (whether you will hear, or forbear,) to repent and reform, or you are ruined!!! Do you think that our blood is hiding from the Lord, because you can hide it from the rest of the world, by sending out missionaries, and by your charitable deeds to the Greeks, Irish, etc.? Will he not publish your secret crimes on the house top? Even here in Boston, pride and prejudice have got to such a pitch, that in the very houses erected to the Lord, they have built little places for the reception of coloured people, where they must sit during meeting, or keep away from the house of God, and the preachers say nothing about it —much less go into the hedges and highways seeking the lost sheep of the house of Israel, and try to bring them in to their Lord and Master.

There are not a more wretched, ignorant, miserable and abject set of beings in all the world than the blacks in the southern and western sections of this country, under tyrants and devils. The preachers of America can not see them, but they can send out missionaries to convert the heathens, notwithstanding. . . . O Americans! Americans!! I call God—I call angels—I call men, to witness, that your *destruction* is at hand, and will be speedily consummated unless you *repent.*

WILLIAM LLOYD GARRISON
PROSPECTUS FOR *THE LIBERATOR*

I do not wish to think, or speak, or write, with moderation. . . . I am in earnest—I will not equivocate—I will not excuse—I will not retreat a single inch—AND I WILL BE HEARD.

William Lloyd Garrison (1805–1879), born in Massachusetts, became a journalist and professional reformer, championing not only abolitionism but women's rights, pacifism, and temperance. In 1829, he joined with a Quaker friend to edit *The Genius of Universal Emancipation,* an abolitionist newspaper in Baltimore. In 1830, he spent seven weeks in jail for libel, after writing an editorial in which he denounced a Newburyport merchant who was engaged in the slave trade. A year later, he moved to Boston to found *The Liberator* and advance the abolitionist cause. Garrison condemned slavery as sinful and demanded immediate emancipation. In 1832, he founded the New England Anti-Slavery Society and a year later, the American Anti-Slavery Society. Garrison was a brilliant polemicist, who minced no words in denouncing evil. His contemporaries considered him an extremist and a fanatic, but his contemporaries were prepared to live with slavery indefinitely. Garrison was not. His searing rhetoric roused moral indignation and made increasing numbers of Americans realize that slavery was neither natural nor right nor defensible.

The prospectus appeared in the first issue of *The Liberator* in 1831.

. . . During my recent tour for the purpose of exciting the minds of the people by a series of discourses on the subject of slavery, every place that I visited gave fresh evidence of the fact, that a greater revolution in public sentiment was to be effected in the free states—*and particularly in New-England*—than at the south. I found contempt more bitter, opposition more active, detraction more relentless, prejudice more stubborn, and apathy more frozen, than among the slave owners themselves. Of course, there were individual exceptions to the contrary. This state of things afflicted, but did not dishearten me. I determined, at every hazard, to lift up the standard of emancipation in the eyes of the nation, *within sight of Bunker Hill and in the birth place of liberty.* That standard is now unfurled; and long may it float, unhurt by the spoliations of time or the missiles of a desperate foe—yea, till every chain be broken, and every bondman set free! Let southern oppressors tremble—let their secret abettors tremble—let their northern apologists tremble —let all the enemies of the persecuted blacks tremble.

I deem the publication of my original Prospectus unnecessary, as it has obtained a wide circulation. The principles therein inculcated will be steadily pursued in this paper, excepting that I shall not array myself as the political partisan of any man. In defending the great cause of human rights, I wish to derive the assistance of all religions and of all parties.

Assenting to the "self-evident truth" maintained in the American Declaration of Independence, "that all men are created equal and endowed by their Creator with certain inalienable rights—among which are life, liberty and the pursuit of happiness," I shall strenuously contend for the immediate enfranchisement of our slave population. In Park-street Church, on the Fourth of July, 1829, in an address on slavery, I unreflectingly assented to the popular but pernicious doctrine of *gradual* abolition. I seize this opportunity to make a full and unequivocal recantation, and thus publicly to ask pardon of my God, of my country, and of my brethren the poor slaves, for having uttered a sentiment so full of timidity, injustice and absurdity. A similar

recantation, from my pen, was published in the *Genius of Universal Emancipation* at Baltimore, in September, 1829. My conscience is now satisfied.

I am aware that many object to the severity of my language; but is there not cause for severity? I *will be* as harsh as truth, and as uncompromising as justice. On this subject, I do not wish to think, or speak, or write, with moderation. No! no! Tell a man whose house is on fire, to give a moderate alarm; tell him to moderately rescue his wife from the hands of the ravisher; tell the mother to gradually extricate her babe from the fire into which it has fallen;—but urge me not to use moderation in a cause like the present. I am in earnest—I will not equivocate —I will not excuse—I will not retreat a single inch—AND I WILL BE HEARD. The apathy of the people is enough to make every statue leap from its pedestal, and to hasten the resurrection of the dead.

It is pretended, that I am retarding the cause of emancipation, by the coarseness of my invective, and the precipitancy of my measures. *The charge is not true.* On this question my influence,—humble as it is,—is felt at this moment to a considerable extent, and shall be felt in coming years—not perniciously, but beneficially—not as a curse, but as a blessing; and posterity will bear testimony that I was right. I desire to thank God, that he enables me to disregard "the fear of man which bringeth a snare," and to speak his truth in its simplicity and power. . . .

JOHN GREENLEAF WHITTIER
STANZAS FOR THE TIMES

In the generation before the Civil War, Whittier was known as the leading poet of the abolitionist movement. His passionate attacks on slavery offended some sensibilities, so anthologies preferred his bucolic poems like "The Barefoot Boy" and "Snowbound," and the patriotic "Barbara Frietchie." Whittier's first poem was published in 1826 in the *Newburyport Free Press*, whose editor was the fiery abolitionist William Lloyd Garrison.

Garrison visited Whittier and discovered a Quaker farmboy with little education and a stern father who was not pleased by his versifying. Garrison adopted him as his protégé and introduced him to the abolitionist movement. Whittier edited abolitionist journals and spoke at public meetings, occasionally to angry crowds. Whittier was a founder of the Republican Party, but after the Civil War, his dislike for the radical Republicans led him to withdraw from political life and to devote his time to poetry.

"Stanzas for the Times" was written in 1835 in reaction to a pro-slavery meeting at Faneuil Hall in Boston, where speakers proposed restrictions on free speech in order to curb the abolitionists.

Is this the land our fathers loved,
  The freedom which they toiled to win?
Is this the soil whereon they moved?
  Are these the graves they slumber in?
Are we the sons by whom are borne
The mantles which the dead have worn?

And shall we crouch above these graves,
  With craven soul and fettered lip?
Yoke in with marked and branded slaves,
  And tremble at the driver's whip?
Bend to the earth our pliant knees,
And speak but as our masters please?

Shall outraged Nature cease to feel?
  Shall Mercy's tears no longer flow?
Shall ruffian threats of cord and steel,
  The dungeon's gloom, the assassin's blow,
Turn back the spirit roused to save
The Truth, our Country, and the slave?

Of human skulls that shrine was made,
  Round which the priests of Mexico
Before their loathsome idol prayed;
  Is Freedom's altar fashioned so?
And must we yield to Freedom's God,
As offering meet, the negro's blood?

Shall tongue be mute, when deeds are wrought
  Which well might shame extremest hell?
Shall freemen lock the indignant thought?
  Shall Pity's bosom cease to swell?
Shall Honor bleed?—shall Truth succumb?
Shall pen, and press, and soul be dumb?

No; by each spot of haunted ground,
  Where Freedom weeps her children's fall;
By Plymouth's rock, and Bunker's mound;
  By Griswold's stained and shattered wall;

By Warren's ghost, by Langdon's shade;
By all the memories of our dead!

By their enlarging souls, which burst
  The bands and fetters round them set;
By the free Pilgrim spirit nursed
  Within our inmost bosoms, yet,
By all above, around, below,
Be ours the indignant answer,—No!

No; guided by our country's laws,
  For truth, and right, and suffering man,
Be ours to strive in Freedom's cause,
  As Christians may, as freemen can!
Still pouring on unwilling ears
That truth oppression only fears.

What! shall we guard our neighbor still,
  While woman shrieks beneath his rod,
And while he tramples down at will
  The image of a common God?
Shall watch and ward be round him set,
Of Northern nerve and bayonet?

And shall we know and share with him
  The danger and the growing shame?
And see our Freedom's light grow dim,
  Which should have filled the world with
      flame?
And, writhing, feel, where'er we turn,
A world's reproach around us burn?

Is't not enough that this is borne?
  And asks our haughty neighbor more?
Must fetters which his slaves have worn
  Clank round the Yankee farmer's door?
Must he be told, beside his plough,
What he must speak, and when, and how?

Must he be told his freedom stands
    On Slavery's dark foundations strong;
On breaking hearts and fettered hands,
    On robbery, and crime, and wrong?
That all his fathers taught is vain,—
That Freedom's emblem is the chain?

Its life, its soul, from slavery drawn!
    False, foul, profane! Go, teach as well
Of holy Truth from Falsehood born!

Of Heaven refreshed by airs from Hell!
Of Virtue in the arms of Vice!
Of Demons planting Paradise!

Rail on, then, brethren of the South,
    Ye shall not hear the truth the less;
No seal is on the Yankee's mouth,
    No fetter on the Yankee's press!
From our Green Mountains to the sea,
One voice shall thunder, We are free!

THEODORE S. WRIGHT

PREJUDICE AGAINST THE COLORED MAN

None can feel the lash but those who have it upon them . . . none know where the chain galls but those who wear it.

Theodore S. Wright (1797–1847) was a prominent clergyman and abolitionist. Born in New Jersey, he was educated at Princeton Theological Seminary, becoming the first black to graduate from an American theological seminary. He was pastor of the First Colored Presbyterian Church in New York City. He was a founder of the American Anti-Slavery Society, and he agitated for temperance, education, black suffrage, and land reform.

The following speech was delivered at a meeting of the New York Anti-Slavery Society in Utica on September 20, 1837. Wright spoke on the following resolution: "Resolved, that the prejudice peculiar to our country, which subjects our colored brethren to a degrading distinction in our worship, assemblies, and schools, which withholds from them that kind and courteous treatment to which as well as other citizens, they have a right, at public houses, on board steamboats, in stages, and in places of public concourse, is the spirit of slavery, is nefarious and wicked and should be practically reprobated and discountenanced."

Mr. President, with much feeling do I rise to address the society on this resolution, and I should hardly have been induced to have done it had I not been requested. I confess I am personally interested in this resolution. But were it not for the fact that none can feel the lash but those who have it upon them, that none know where the chain galls but those who wear it, I would not address you.

This is a serious business, sir. The prejudice which exists against the colored man, the free man is like the atmosphere, everywhere felt by him. It is true that in these United States and in this State, there are men, like myself, colored with the skin like my own, who are not subjected to the lash, who are not liable to have their wives and their infants torn from them; from whose hand the Bible is not taken. It is true that we may walk abroad; we may enjoy our domestic comforts, our families; retire to the closet; visit the sanctuary, and may be permitted to urge on our children and our neighbors in well doing. But sir, still we are slaves—everywhere we feel the chain galling us. It is by that prejudice which the resolution condemns, the spirit of slavery, the law which has been enacted here, by a corrupt public sentiment, through the influence of slavery which treats moral agents different from the rule of God, which treats them irrespective of their morals or intellectual cultivation. This spirit is withering all our hopes, and ofttimes causes the colored parent as he looks upon his child, to wish he had never been born. Often is the heart of the colored mother, as she presses her child to her bosom, filled with sorrow to think that, by reason of this prejudice, it is cut off from all hopes of usefulness in this land. Sir, this prejudice is wicked.

If the nation and church understood this matter, I would not speak a word about that killing influence that destroys the colored man's reputation. This influence cuts us off from everything; it follows us up from childhood to manhood; it excludes us from all stations of profit, usefulness and honor; takes away from us all motive for pressing forward in enterprises, useful and important to the world and to ourselves.

In the first place, it cuts us off from the advantages of the mechanic arts almost entirely. A colored man can hardly learn a trade, and if he does it is difficult for him to find any one who will employ him to work at that trade, in any part of the State. In most of our large cities there are associations of mechanics who legislate out of their society colored men. And in many cases where our young men have learned trades, they have had to come to low employments for want of encouragement in those trades.

It must be a matter of rejoicing to know that in this vicinity colored fathers and mothers have the privileges of education. It must be a matter of rejoicing that in this vicinity colored parents can have their children trained up in schools.—At present, we find the colleges barred against them.

I will say nothing about the inconvenience which I have experienced myself, and which every man of color experiences, though made in the image of God. I will say nothing about the inconvenience of traveling; how we are frowned upon and despised. No matter how we may demean ourselves, we find embarrassments everywhere.

But sir, this prejudice goes farther. It debars men from heaven. While sir, slavery cuts off the colored portion of the community from religious privileges men are made infidels. What, they demand, is your Christianity? How do you regard your brethren? How do you treat them at the Lord's table? Where is your consistency in talking about the heathen, traversing the ocean to circulate the Bible everywhere, while you frown upon them at the door? These things meet us and weigh down our spirits. . . .

Thanks be to God, there is a buoyant principle which elevates the poor down-trodden colored man above all this:—It is that there is society which regards man according to his worth; it is the fact, that when he looks up to Heaven he knows that God treats him like a moral agent, irrespective of caste or the circumstances in which he may be placed. Amid the embarrassments which he has to meet, and the scorn and contempt that is heaped upon him, he is cheered by the hope that he will be disenthralled, and soon, like a bird set forth from its cage, wing his flight to Jesus, where he can be happy, and look down with pity on the man who despises the poor slave for being what God made him, and who despises him because he is identified with the poor slave. Blessed be God for the principles of the Gospel. Were it not for these, and for the fact that a better day is dawning, I would not wish to live.—Blessed be God for the anti-slavery movement. Blessed be God that there is a war waging with slavery, that the granite rock is about to be rolled from its base. But as long as the colored man is to be looked upon as an inferior caste, so long will they disregard his cries, his groans, his shrieks.

I rejoice, sir, in this Society; and I deem the day when I joined this Society as one of the proudest days of my life. And I know I can die better, in more peace to-day, to know there are men who will plead the cause of my children.

Let me, through you, sir, request this delegation to take hold of this subject. This will silence the slaveholder, when he says where is your love for the slave? Where is your love for the colored man who is crushed at your feet? Talking to us about emancipating our slaves when you are enslaving them by your feelings, and doing more violence to them by your prejudice, than we are to our slaves by our treatment. They call on us to evince our love for the slave, by treating man as man, the colored man as a man, according to his worth.

ANGELINA GRIMKÉ
BEARING WITNESS AGAINST SLAVERY

As a Southerner, I feel that it is my duty to stand up here to-night and bear testimony against slavery. I have seen it! I have seen it!

Angelina Grimké (1805–1879) and her older sister, Sarah, were daughters of a wealthy, aristocratic slaveholding judge in Charleston, South Carolina. As young women, they detested slavery. They moved to Philadelphia, where they became Quakers and active in the abolitionist movement. In 1836, Angelina Grimké wrote ''An Appeal to the Christian Women of the South,'' calling on the women of the South to join the fight against slavery. The pamphlets were burned in South Carolina, and the sisters were warned that they would be arrested if they ever returned to their native state.

Angelina Grimké delivered the address below at the National Anti-Slavery Convention in Philadelphia on May 16, 1838. Only two days earlier, she had married the prominent abolitionist Theodore Weld. Before the meeting, notices had been posted around the city warning that the building in which it was held, Pennsylvania Hall, would be destroyed by foes of abolition. During the three days that the convention met, an angry mob gathered outside the hall, including many southern visitors and southern students at the local medical college. While Grimké spoke, the crowd outside kept up a constant uproar and pelted stones against the windows. At the end of the third day, the mob entered the hall, set fire to it, and demolished the building.

Do you ask, "What has the North to do with slavery?" Hear it, hear it! Those voices without tell us that the spirit of slavery is *here,* and has been roused to wrath by our Conventions; for surely liberty would not foam and tear herself with rage, because her friends are multiplied daily, and meetings are held in quick succession to set forth her virtues and extend her peaceful kingdom. This opposition shows that slavery has done its deadliest work in the hearts of our citizens. Do you ask, then, "What has the North to do?" I answer, cast out first the spirit of slavery from your own hearts, and then lend your aid to convert the South. Each one present has a work to do, be his or her situation what it may, however limited their means or insignificant their supposed influence. The great men of this country will not do this work; the Church will never do it. A desire to please the world, to keep the favor of all parties and of all conditions, makes them dumb on this and every other unpopular subject.

As a Southerner, I feel that it is my duty to stand up here to-night and bear testimony against slavery. I have seen it! I have seen it! I know it has horrors that can never be described.

I was brought up under its wing. I witnessed for many years its demoralizing influences and its destructiveness to human happiness. I have never seen a happy slave. I have seen him dance in his chains, it is true, but he was not happy. There is a wide difference between happiness and mirth. Man can not enjoy happiness while his manhood is destroyed. Slaves, however, may be, and sometimes are mirthful. When hope is extinguished, they say, "Let us eat and drink, for to-morrow we die." [Here stones were thrown at the windows—a great noise without and commotion within.]

What is a mob? what would the breaking of every window be? What would the levelling of this hall be? Any evidence that we are wrong, or that slavery is a good and wholesome institution? What if the mob should now burst in upon us, break up our meeting, and commit violence upon our persons, would that be anything compared with what the slaves endure? No, no; and we do not remember them, "as bound with them," if we shrink in the time of peril, or feel unwilling to sacrifice ourselves, if need be, for their sake. [Great noise.] I thank the Lord that there is yet life enough left to feel the truth, even though it rages at it; that conscience is not so completely seared as to be unmoved by the truth of the living God. [Another outbreak of the mob and confusion in the house.]

How wonderfully constituted is the human mind! How it resists, as long as it can, all efforts to reclaim it from error! I feel that all this disturbance is but an evidence that our efforts are the best that could have been adopted, or else the friends of slavery would not care for what we say and do. The South know what we do. I am thankful that they are reached by our efforts. Many times have I wept in the land of my birth over the system of slavery. I knew of none who sympathized in my feelings; I was unaware that any efforts were made to deliver the oppressed; no voice in the wilderness was heard calling on the people to repent and do works meet for repentance, and my heart sickened within me. Oh, how should I have rejoiced to know that such efforts as these were being made. I only

wonder that I had such feelings. But in the midst of temptation I was preserved, and my sympathy grew warmer, and my hatred of slavery more inveterate, until at last I have exiled myself from my native land, because I could no longer endure to hear the wailing of the slave.

I fled to the land of Penn; for here, thought I, sympathy for the slave will surely be found. But I found it not. The people were kind and hospitable, but the slave had no place in their thoughts. I therefore shut up my grief in my own heart. I remembered that I was a Carolinian, from a State which framed this iniquity by law. Every Southern breeze wafted to me the discordant tones of weeping and wailing, shrieks and groans, mingled with prayers and blasphemous curses. My heart sank within me at the abominations in the midst of which I had been born and educated. What will it avail, cried I, in bitterness of spirit, to expose to the gaze of strangers the horrors and pollutions of slavery, when there is no ear to hear nor heart to feel and pray for the slave? But how different do I feel now! Animated with hope, nay, with an assurance of the triumph of liberty and good-will to man, I will lift up my voice like a trumpet, and show this people what they can do to influence the Southern mind and overthrow slavery. [Shouting, and stones against the windows.]

We often hear the question asked, "What shall we do?" Here is an opportunity. Every man and every woman present may do something, by showing that we fear not a mob, and in the midst of revilings and threatenings, pleading the cause of those who are ready to perish. Let me urge every one to buy the books written on this subject; read them, and lend them to your neighbors. Give your money no longer for things which pander to pride and lust, but aid in scattering "the living coals of truth upon the naked heart of the nation"; in circulating appeals to the sympathies of Christians in behalf of the outraged slave.

But it is said by some, our "books and papers do not speak the truth"; why, then, do they not contradict what we say? They can not. Moreover, the South has entreated, nay, commanded us, to be silent; and what greater evidence of the truth of our publications could be desired?

Women of Philadelphia! allow me as a Southern woman, with much attachment to the land of my birth, to entreat you to come up to this work. Especially, let me urge you to petition. Men may settle this and other questions at the ballot-box, but you have no such right. It is only through petitions that you can reach the Legislature. It is, therefore, peculiarly your duty to petition. Do you say, "It does no good!" The South already turns pale at the number sent. They have read the reports of the proceedings of Congress, and there have seen that among other petitions were very many from the women of the North on the subject of slavery. Men who hold the rod over slaves rule in the councils of the nation; and they deny our right to petition and remonstrate against abuses of our sex and our kind. We have these rights, however, from our God. Only let us exercise them, and, though often turned away unanswered, let us remember the influence of importunity upon the unjust judge, and act accordingly. The fact that the South looks jealously upon our measures shows that they are effectual. There is, therefore, no cause for doubting or despair.

It was remarked in England that women did much to abolish slavery in her colonies. Nor are they now idle. Numerous petitions from them have recently been presented to the Queen to abolish apprenticeship, with its cruelties, nearly equal to those of the system whose place it supplies. One petition, two miles and a quarter long, has been presented. And do you think these labors will be in vain? Let the history of the past answer. When the women of these States send up to Congress such a petition our legislators will arise, as did those of England, and say: "When all the maids and matrons of the land are knocking at our doors we must legislate." Let the zeal and love, the faith and works of our English sisters quicken ours; that while the slaves continue to suffer, and when they shout for deliverance, we may feel the satisfaction of "having done what we could."

HENRY HIGHLAND GARNET

AN ADDRESS TO THE SLAVES OF THE UNITED STATES OF AMERICA

Let your motto be resistance! resistance! *RESISTANCE!*

Henry Highland Garnet (1815–1882) was born on a slave plantation in Maryland. When he was nine, his father and he escaped to New York City, aided by Quakers. He prepared for the ministry at Oneida Theological Institute near Utica, New York. One of the nation's best-known abolitionists, he lectured in England and Scotland.

His most famous speech, known as the "Call to Rebellion," was delivered to the National Negro Convention held in 1843 in Buffalo, New York. He urged African Americans, both slave and free, to make a motto of resistance to slavery, including armed rebellion, if necessary. The speech shocked conservative black leaders of the day, and the convention failed by one vote to endorse Garnet's appeal as its official resolution. Black militancy grew, however, and only four years later another national convention, in Troy, New York, did endorse a similar appeal by Garnet.

In 1865, Garnet became the first black clergyman to deliver a sermon to the House of Representatives. He served as minister to Liberia, where he died.

Your brethren of the North, East, and West have been accustomed to meet together in National Conventions, to sympathize with each other, and to weep over your unhappy condition. In these meetings we have addressed all classes of the free, but we have never, until this time, sent a word of consolation and advice to you. We have been contented in sitting still and mourning over your sorrows, earnestly hoping that before this day your sacred liberties would have been restored. But, we have hoped in vain. Years have rolled on, and tens of thousands have been borne on streams of blood and tears to the shores of eternity. While you have been oppressed, we have also been partakers with you; nor can we be free while you are enslaved. We, therefore, write to you as being bound with you.

Many of you are bound to us, not only by the ties of a common humanity, but we are connected by the more tender relations of parents, wives, husbands, and sisters, and friends. As such we most affectionately address you.

Slavery has fixed a deep gulf between you and us, and while it shuts out from you the relief and consolation which your friends would willingly render, it afflicts and persecutes you with a fierceness which we might not expect to see in fiends of hell. But still the Almighty Father of mercies has left to us a glimmering ray of hope, which shines out like a lone star in a cloudy sky. Mankind are becoming wiser, and better—the oppressor's power is fading, and you, every day, are becoming better informed, and more numerous. Your grievances, brethren, are many. We shall not attempt, in this short address, to present to the world all the dark catalogue of the nation's sins, which have been committed upon an innocent people. Nor is it indeed necessary, for you feel them from day to day, and all the civilized world looks upon them with amazement.

Two hundred and twenty-seven years ago the first of our injured race were brought to the shores of America. They came not with glad spirits to select their homes in the New World. They came not with their own consent, to find an unmolested enjoyment of the blessings of this fruitful soil. The first dealings they had with men calling themselves Christians exhibited to them the worst features of corrupt and sordid hearts: and convinced them that no cruelty is too great, no villainy and no robbery too abhorrent for even enlightened men to perform, when influenced by avarice and lust. Neither did they come flying upon the wings of Liberty to a land of freedom. But they came with broken hearts, from their beloved native land, and were doomed to unrequited toil and deep degradation. Nor did the evil of their bondage end at their emancipation by death. Succeeding generations inherited their chains, and millions have come from eternity into time, and have returned again to the world of spirits, cursed and ruined by American slavery.

The propagators of the system, or their immediate successors, very soon discovered its growing evil, and its tremendous wickedness, and secret promises were made to destroy it. The gross inconsistency of a people holding slaves, who had themselves "ferried o'er the wave" for freedom's sake, was too apparent to be entirely overlooked. The voice of Freedom cried, "Emancipate your slaves." Humanity supplicated with tears for the deliverance of the children of Africa. Wisdom urged her solemn plea. The bleeding captive plead his innocence, and pointed to Christianity who stood weeping at the cross. Jehovah frowned upon the nefarious institution, and thunderbolts, red with vengeance, struggled to leap forth to blast the guilty wretches who maintained it. But all was vain. Slavery had stretched its dark wings of death over the land, the Church stood silently by— the priests prophesied falsely, and the people loved to have it so. Its throne is established, and now it reigns triumphant.

Nearly three millions of your fellow-citizens are prohibited by law and public opinion (which in this country is stronger than law) from reading the Book of Life. Your intellect has been destroyed as much as possible, and every ray of light they have attempted to shut out from your minds. The oppressors themselves have become involved in the ruin. They have become weak, sensual, and rapacious—they have cursed you—they have cursed themselves—they have cursed the earth which they have trod....

SLAVERY! How much misery is comprehended in that single word. What mind is there that does not shrink from its direful effects? Unless the image of God be obliterated from the soul, all men cherish the love of liberty. The nice discerning political economist does not regard the sacred right more than the untutored African who roams in the wilds of Congo. Nor has the one more right to the full enjoyment of his freedom than the other. In every man's mind the good seeds of liberty are planted, and he who brings his fellow down so low, as to make him contented with a condition of slavery, commits the highest crime against God and man....

Brethren, the time has come when you must act for yourselves. It is an old and true saying that, "if hereditary bondmen would be free, they must themselves strike the blow." You can plead your own cause, and do the work of emancipation better than any others.... Think of the undying glory that hangs around the ancient name of Africa—and forget not that you are native-born American citizens, and as such you are justly entitled to all the rights that are granted to the freest. Think how many tears you have poured out upon the soil which you have cultivated with unrequited toil and enriched with your blood; and then go to your lordly enslavers and tell them plainly, that you *are determined to be free.* Appeal to their sense of justice, and tell them that they have no more right to oppress you than you have to enslave them. Entreat them to remove the grievous burdens which they have imposed upon you, and to remunerate you for your labor. Promise them renewed diligence in the cultivation of the soil, if they will render to you an equivalent for your services. Point them to the increase of happiness and prosperity in the British West Indies since the Act of Emancipation. Tell them in language which they cannot misunderstand of the exceeding sinfulness of slavery, and of a future

judgment, and of the righteous retributions of an indignant God. Inform them that all you desire is FREEDOM, and that nothing else will suffice. Do this, and forever after cease to toil for the heartless tyrants, who give you no other reward but stripes and abuse. If they then commence work of death, they, and not you, will be responsible for the consequences. You had far better all die—*die immediately,* than live slaves, and entail your wretchedness upon your posterity....

Fellowmen! patient sufferers! behold your dearest rights crushed to the earth! See your sons murdered, and your wives, mothers and sisters doomed to prostitution. In the name of the merciful God, and by all that life is worth, let it no longer be a debatable question, whether it is better to choose *liberty* or *death.*

In 1822, Denmark Veazie, of South Carolina, formed a plan for the liberation of his fellowmen. In the whole history of human efforts to overthrow slavery, a more complicated and tremendous plan was never formed. He was betrayed by the treachery of his own people, and died a martyr to freedom. Many a brave hero fell, but history, faithful to her high trust, will transcribe his name on the same monument with Moses, Hampden, Tell, Bruce, and Wallace, Toussaint L'Ouverture, Lafayette, and Washington....

The patriotic Nathaniel Turner followed Denmark Veazie. He was goaded to desperation by wrong and injustice. By despotism, his name has been recorded on the list of infamy, and future generations will remember him among the noble and brave.

Next arose the immortal Joseph Cinque, the hero of the Amistad. He was a native African, and by the help of God he emancipated a whole ship-load of his fellowmen on the high seas. And he now sings of liberty on the sunny hills of Africa and beneath his native palm-trees, where he hears the lion roar and feels himself as free as the king of the forest.

Next arose Madison Washington, that bright star of freedom, and took his station in the constellation of true heroism. He was a slave on

Harriet Tubman (far left) with some of the 300 slaves that she led to freedom. Born into slavery, she escaped in 1849 and returned to the South nineteen times to guide others to freedom on the Underground Railroad.

board the brig *Creole,* of Richmond, bound to New Orleans, that great slave mart, with a hundred and four others. Nineteen struck for liberty or death. But one life was taken, and the whole were emancipated, and the vessel was carried into Nassau, New Providence.

Noble men! Those who have fallen in freedom's conflict, their memories will be cherished by the true-hearted and the God-fearing in all future generations; those who are living, their names are surrounded by a halo of glory.

Brethren, arise, arise! Strike for your lives and liberties. Now is the day and the hour. Let every slave throughout the land do this, and the

days of slavery are numbered. You cannot be more oppressed than you have been—you cannot suffer greater cruelties than you have already. *Rather die freemen than live to be slaves.* Remember that you are FOUR MILLIONS! . . .

Let your motto be resistance! *resistance!* RE- SISTANCE! No oppressed people have ever se- cured their liberty without resistance. What kind of resistance you had better make you must decide by the circumstances that surround you, and according to the suggestion of expediency. Brethren, adieu! Trust in the living God. Labor for the peace of the human race, and remember that you are FOUR MILLIONS!

THE PRESENT CRISIS

James Russell Lowell (1819–1891) was born in Cambridge, Massachusetts, into a distinguished New England family. After graduating from Harvard and earning a law degree, he devoted himself to writing poetry and essays, and he became a major literary figure. In 1855, he succeeded Henry Wadsworth Longfellow as professor of belles lettres at Harvard. He also served as editor of two major journals, *The Atlantic Monthly* and then the *North American Review.* He also served as minister to Spain and then minister to Britain.

Lowell's poem "The Present Crisis," written in 1844, provided inspiration for the leaders of the National Association for the Advancement of Colored People. Mary White Ovington, one of the original founders, recalled the day in 1910 that the organizers sat around a table trying to think of a name for their magazine. Suddenly she thought of Lowell's poem, and the group agreed that the magazine should be called *The Crisis.* Ovington wrote, "If we had a creed to which our members, black and white, our branches North and South and East and West, our college societies, our children's circles, should all subscribe, it should be the lines of Lowell's noble verse, lines that are as true to-day as when they were written seventy years ago," and she cited the fifth and the eleventh stanzas of the poem.

When a deed is done for Freedom, through
    the broad earth's aching breast
Runs a thrill of joy prophetic, trembling on
    from east to west,
And the slave, where'er he cowers, feels the
    soul within him climb
To the awful verge of manhood, as the energy
    sublime
Of a century bursts full-blossomed on the
    thorny stem of Time.

Through the walls of hut and palace shoots the
    instantaneous throe,
When the travail of the Ages wrings earth's
    systems to and fro;
At the birth of each new Era, with a
    recognizing start,
Nation wildly looks at nation, standing with
    mute lips apart,
And glad Truth's yet mightier man-child leaps
    beneath the Future's heart.

So the Evil's triumph sendeth, with a terror and
    a chill,

Under continent to continent, the sense of
    coming ill,
And the slave, where'er he cowers, feels his
    sympathies with God
In hot tear-drops ebbing earthward, to be
    drunk up by the sod,
Till a corpse crawls round unburied, delving in
    the nobler clod.

For mankind are one in spirit, and an instinct
    bears along,
Round the earth's electric circle, the swift flash
    of right or wrong;
Whether conscious or unconscious, yet
    Humanity's vast frame
Through its ocean-sundered fibres feels the
    gush of joy or shame;—
In the gain or loss of one race all the rest have
    equal claim.

Once to every man and nation comes the
    moment to decide,
In the strife of Truth with Falsehood, for the
    good or evil side;

Some great cause, God's new Messiah, offering
each the bloom or blight,
Parts the goats upon the left hand, and the
sheep upon the right,
And the choice goes by forever 'twixt that
darkness and that light.

Hast thou chosen, O my people, on whose
party thou shalt stand,
Ere the Doom from its worn sandals shakes the
dust against our land?
Though the cause of Evil prosper, yet 't is
Truth alone is strong,
And, albeit she wander outcast now, I see
around her throng
Troops of beautiful, tall angels, to enshield her
from all wrong.

Backward look across the ages and the beacon-
moments see,
That, like peaks of some sunk continent, jut
through Oblivion's sea;
Not an ear in court or market for the low
foreboding cry
Of those Crises, God's stern winnowers, from
whose feet earth's chaff must fly;
Never shows the choice momentous till the
judgment hath passed by.

Careless seems the great Avenger; history's
pages but record
One death-grapple in the darkness 'twixt old
systems and the Word;
Truth forever on the scaffold, Wrong forever
on the throne,—
Yet that scaffold sways the future, and, behind
the dim unknown,
Standeth God within the shadow, keeping
watch above his own.

We see dimly in the Present what is small and
what is great,
Slow of faith how weak an arm may turn this
iron helm of fate,
But the soul is still oracular; amid the market's
din,
List the ominous stern whisper from the
Delphic cave within,—

"They enslave their children's children who
make compromise with sin."

Slavery, the earth-born Cyclops, fellest of the
giant brood,
Sons of brutish Force and Darkness, who have
drenched the earth with blood,
Famished in his self-made desert, blinded by
our purer day,
Gropes in yet unblasted regions for his
miserable prey;—
Shall we guide his gory fingers where our
helpless children play?

Then to side with Truth is noble when we
share her wretched crust,
Ere her cause bring fame and profit, and 't is
prosperous to be just;
Then it is the brave man chooses, while the
coward stands aside,
Doubting in his abject spirit, till his Lord is
crucified,
And the multitude make virtue of the faith they
had denied.

Count me o'er the earth's chosen heroes,—
they were souls that stood alone,
While the men they agonized for hurled the
contumelious stone,
Stood serene, and down the future saw the
golden beam incline
To the side of perfect justice, mastered by their
faith divine,
By one man's plain truth to manhood and to
God's supreme design.

By the light of burning heretics Christ's
bleeding feet I track,
Toiling up new Calvaries ever with the cross
that turns not back,
And these mounts of anguish number how each
generation learned
One new word of that grand *Credo* which in
prophet-hearts hath burned
Since the first man stood God-conquered with
his face to heaven upturned.

For Humanity sweeps onward: where to-day
the martyr stands,

On the morrow, crouches Judas with the silver
    in his hands;
Far in front the cross stands ready and the
    crackling fagots burn,
While the hooting mob of yesterday in silent
    awe return
To glean up the scattered ashes into History's
    golden urn.

'Tis as easy to be heroes as to sit the idle slaves
Of a legendary virtue carved upon our father's
    graves,
Worshippers of light ancestral make the
    present light a crime;—
Was the Mayflower launched by cowards,
    steered by men behind their time?
Turn those tracks toward Past or Future, that
    make Plymouth Rock sublime?

They were men of present valor, stalwart old
    iconoclasts,
Unconvinced by axe or gibbet that all virtue
    was the Past's;
But we make their truth our falsehood,
    thinking that hath made us free,
Hoarding it in mouldy parchments, while our
    tender spirits flee

The rude grasp of that great Impulse which
    drove them across the sea.

They have rights who dare maintain them; we
    are traitors to our sires,
Smothering in their holy ashes Freedom's new-
    lit altar-fires;
Shall we make their creed our jailer? Shall we,
    in our haste to slay,
From the tombs of the old prophets steal the
    funeral lamps away
To light up the martyr-fagots round the
    prophets of to-day?

New occasions teach new duties; Time makes
    ancient good uncouth;
They must upward still, and onward, who
    would keep abreast of Truth;
Lo, before us gleam her camp-fires! we
    ourselves must Pilgrims be,
Launch our Mayflower, and steer boldly
    through the desperate winter sea,
Nor attempt the Future's portal with the Past's
    blood-rusted key.

FREDERICK DOUGLASS

INDEPENDENCE DAY SPEECH AT ROCHESTER

Fellow-citizens, pardon me, allow me to ask, why am I called upon to speak here today? What have I, or those I represent, to do with your national independence? . . . What, to the American slave, is your Fourth of July?

Frederick Douglass (1817–1895) was a brilliant speaker, writer, humanitarian, and political activist. He was a towering figure in the movement to abolish slavery. Born a slave, he never knew his mother or father. He was raised by his grandmother on a plantation in Maryland, then sent to work as a house slave in Baltimore at the age of eight. In Baltimore, his mistress taught him to read, an act forbidden by law. Later he was returned to work on the plantation as a field hand. At the age of twenty-one, he escaped to New York City and New Bedford, Massachusetts, where he changed his last name to Douglass (it was originally Bailey).

Invited to speak to an anti-slavery gathering in Nantucket in 1841, Douglass spoke so eloquently that he was engaged as an agent for the Massachusetts Anti-Slavery

Society. He became a leading speaker, and in response to critics who doubted his authenticity, he wrote his autobiography in 1845. But fearing that he might be identified and recaptured, Douglass spent two years abroad on a lecture tour. He returned with enough money to buy his freedom and to launch his own abolitionist paper, the *North Star,* in Rochester, New York, in 1847.

From 1841 on, Douglass was the most prominent black abolitionist in the country. In 1852, he was invited to speak in Rochester on the occasion of Independence Day. He opened with conventional praise for the well-known accomplishments of the founding fathers. But midway through his speech, he suddenly shifted course and stunned his listeners by reminding them of the nation's hypocrisy, since blacks in America did not enjoy independence.

Fellow citizens, pardon me, allow me to ask, why am I called upon to speak here today? What have I, or those I represent, to do with your national independence? Are the great principles of political freedom and of natural justice, embodied in that Declaration of Independence, extended to us? and am I, therefore, called upon to bring our humble offering to the national altar, and to confess the benefits and express devout gratitude for the blessings resulting from your independence to us?

Would to God, both for your sakes and ours, that an affirmative answer could be truthfully returned to these questions! Then would my task be light, and my burden easy and delightful. For who is there so cold that a nation's sympathy could not warm him? Who so obdurate and dead to the claims of gratitude that would not thankfully acknowledge such priceless benefits? Who so stolid and selfish that would not give his voice to swell the hallelujahs of a nation's jubilee, when the chains of servitude had been torn from his limbs? I am not that man. In a case like that the dumb might eloquently speak and the "lame man leap as an hart."

But such is not the state of the case. I say it with a sad sense of the disparity between us. I am not included within the pale of this glorious anniversary! Your high independence only reveals the immeasurable distance between us. The blessings in which you, this day, rejoice are not enjoyed in common. The rich inheritance of justice, liberty, prosperity, and independence bequeathed by your fathers is shared by you, not

by me. The sunlight that brought light and healing to you has brought stripes and death to me. This Fourth of July is yours, not mine. You may rejoice, I must mourn. To drag a man in fetters into the grand illuminated temple of liberty, and call upon him to join you in joyous anthems, were inhuman mockery and sacrilegious irony. Do you mean, citizens, to mock me by asking me to speak today? If so, there is a parallel to your conduct. And let me warn you that it is dangerous to copy the example of a nation whose crimes, towering up to heaven, were thrown down by the breath of the Almighty, burying that nation in irrevocable ruin! I can today take up the plaintive lament of a peeled and woe-smitten people!

"By the rivers of Babylon, there we sat down. Yea! we wept when we remembered Zion. We hanged our harps upon the willows in the midst thereof. For there, they that carried us away captive, required of us a song; and they who wasted us required of us mirth, saying, Sing us one of the songs of Zion. How can we sing the Lord's song in a strange land? If I forget thee, O Jerusalem, let my right hand forget her cunning. If I do not remember thee, let my tongue cleave to the roof of my mouth."

Fellow citizens, above your national, tumultuous joy, I hear the mournful wail of millions! whose chains, heavy and grievous yesterday, are, today, rendered more intolerable by the jubilee shouts that reach them. If I do forget, if I do not faithfully remember those bleeding children of sorrow this day, "may my right hand

Executive Committee of the Philadelphia Anti-Slavery Society, 1851. Back row, from left: Mary Grew, E. M. Davis, Haworth Wetherald, Abby Kimber, J. Miller McKim, Sarah Pugh. Front row, from left: Oliver Johnson, Mrs. Margaret James Burleigh, Benjamin C. Bacon, Robert Purvis, Lucretia Mott, James Mott.

forget her cunning, and may my tongue cleave to the roof of my mouth"! To forget them, to pass lightly over their wrongs, and to chime in with the popular theme would be treason most scandalous and shocking, and would make me a reproach before God and the world. My subject, then, fellow citizens, is *American slavery.* I shall see this day and its popular characteristics from the slave's point of view. Standing there identified with the American bondman, making his wrongs mine. I do not hesitate to declare with all my soul that the character and conduct of this nation never looked blacker to me than on this Fourth of July! Whether we turn to the declarations of the past or to the professions of the present, the conduct of the nation seems equally hideous and revolting. America is false to the past, false to the present, and solemnly binds herself to be false to the future. Standing with God and the crushed and bleeding slave on this occasion, I will, in the name of humanity which is outraged, in the name of liberty which is fettered, in the name of the Constitution and the Bible which are disregarded and trampled upon, dare to call in question and to denounce, with all the emphasis I can command, everything that serves to perpetuate slavery—the great sin and shame of America! "I will not equivocate, I will not excuse"; I will use the severest language I can command; and yet not one word shall escape me that any man, whose judgment is not blinded by prejudice, or who is not at heart a slaveholder, shall not confess to be right and just.

But I fancy I hear someone of my audience say, "It is just in this circumstance that you and your brother abolitionists fail to make a favorable impression on the public mind. Would you argue more and denounce less, would you persuade more and rebuke less, your cause would be much more likely to succeed." But, I submit, where all is plain, there is nothing to be argued. What point in the antislavery creed would you have me argue? On what branch of the subject do the people of this country need light? Must I undertake to prove that the slave is a man? That point is conceded already. Nobody doubts it. The slaveholders themselves acknowledge it in the enactment of laws for their government. They acknowledge it when they punish disobedience on the part of the slave. There are seventy-two crimes in the state of Virginia which, if committed by a black man (no matter how ignorant he be), subject him to the punishment of death; while only two of the same crimes will subject a white man to the like punishment. What is this but the acknowledgment that the slave is a moral, intellectual, and responsible being? The manhood of the slave is conceded. It is admitted in the fact that the Southern statute books are covered with enactments forbidding, under severe fines and penalties, the teaching of the slave to read or to write. When you can point to any such laws in reference to the beasts of the field, then I may consent to argue the manhood of the slave. When the dogs in your streets, when the fowls of the air, when the cattle on your hills, when the fish of the sea and the reptiles that crawl shall be unable to distinguish the slave from a brute, then will I argue with you that the slave is a man!

For the present, it is enough to affirm the equal manhood of the Negro race. Is it not astonishing that, while we are plowing, planting, and reaping, using all kinds of mechanical tools, erecting houses, constructing bridges, building ships, working in metals of brass, iron, copper, silver, and gold; that, while we are reading, writing, and ciphering, acting as clerks, merchants, and secretaries, having among us lawyers, doctors, ministers, poets, authors, editors, orators, and teachers; that, while we are engaged in all manner of enterprises common to other men, digging gold in California, capturing the whale in the Pacific, feeding sheep and cattle on the hillside, living, moving, acting, thinking, planning, living in families as husbands, wives, and children, and, above all, confessing and worshiping the Christian's God, and looking hopefully for life and immortality beyond the grave, we are called upon to prove that we are men!

Would you have me argue that man is entitled to liberty? That he is the rightful owner of his own body? You have already declared it. Must I argue the wrongfulness of slavery? Is that a question for republicans? Is it to be settled by the rules of logic and argumentation, as a matter beset with great difficulty, involving a doubtful application of the principle of justice, hard to be understood? How should I look today, in the presence of Americans, dividing and subdividing a discourse, to show that men have a natural right to freedom? speaking of it relatively and positively, negatively and affirmatively? To do so would be to make myself ridiculous and to offer an insult to your understanding. There is not a man beneath the canopy of heaven that does not know that slavery is wrong for him.

What, am I to argue that it is wrong to make men brutes, to rob them of their liberty, to work them without wages, to keep them ignorant of their relations to their fellow men, to beat them with sticks, to flay their flesh with the lash, to load their limbs with irons, to hunt them with dogs, to sell them at auction, to sunder their families, to knock out their teeth, to burn their flesh, to starve them into obedience and submission to their masters? Must I argue that a system thus marked with blood, and stained with pollution, is wrong? No! I will not. I have better employment for my time and strength than such arguments would imply.

What, then, remains to be argued? Is it that slavery is not divine; that God did not establish it; that our doctors of divinity are mistaken? There is blasphemy in the thought. That which is inhuman cannot be divine! Who can reason on such a proposition? They that can may; I cannot. The time for such argument is past.

At a time like this, scorching iron, not convincing argument, is needed. O! had I the ability, and could I reach the nation's ear, I would today pour out a fiery stream of biting ridicule, blasting reproach, withering sarcasm, and stern rebuke. For it is not light that is needed, but fire; it is not the gentle shower, but thunder. We need the storm, the whirlwind, and the earthquake. The feeling of the nation must be quickened; the conscience of the nation must be roused; the propriety of the nation must be startled; the hypocrisy of the nation must be exposed; and its crimes against God and man must be proclaimed and denounced.

What, to the American slave, is your Fourth of July? I answer: a day that reveals to him, more than all other days in the year, the gross injustice and cruelty to which he is the constant victim. To him, your celebration is a sham; your boasted liberty, an unholy license; your national greatness, swelling vanity; your sounds of rejoicing are empty and heartless; your denunciation of tyrants, brass-fronted impudence; your shouts of liberty and equality, hollow mockery; your prayers and hymns, your sermons and thanksgivings, with all your religious parade and solemnity, are, to Him, mere bombast, fraud, deception, impiety, and hypocrisy—a thin veil to cover up crimes which would disgrace a nation of savages. There is not a nation of savages. There is not a nation on the earth guilty of practices more shocking and bloody than are the people of the United States at this very hour.

Go where you may, search where you will, roam through all the monarchies and despotisms of the Old World, travel through South America, search out every abuse, and when you have found the last, lay your facts by the side of the everyday practices of this nation, and you will say with me that, for revolting barbarity and shameless hypocrisy, America reigns without a rival.

ABRAHAM LINCOLN

THE HOUSE DIVIDED SPEECH

I believe this Government can not endure permanently half slave and half free.

Abraham Lincoln (1809–1865) was born near Hodgenville, Kentucky. Self-educated, he tried his hand at a variety of occupations—flatboatman, storekeeper, postmaster, surveyor, blacksmith—before studying law. He became one of the most successful lawyers in Illinois, noted for his wit, common sense, and honesty. After serving in the state legislature and in Congress, he challenged Stephen A. Douglas for the Senate in 1858. On June 16, 1858, in Springfield, Illinois, Lincoln accepted the Republican party's nomination with a speech that dissected the great issues confronting the nation. "A house divided against itself can not stand," said Lincoln, paraphrasing the New Testament.

Lincoln used this speech to accuse the Democratic party of abetting the expansion of slavery and to analyze three recent, critical events. One event was the passing of the Kansas–Nebraska Bill by Congress in 1854, which allowed the voters in the new western territories to decide whether they wanted to allow slavery; this act repealed the Missouri Compromise, which had prohibited slavery in these territories. Lincoln reminded his listeners that Senator Stephen Douglas had sponsored the "Nebraska bill." Lincoln frequently alluded to Douglas' statement that he "cares not whether slavery be voted down or voted up." A second event was the Supreme Court's Dred Scott decision of 1857, which held that blacks were not (and could not be) citizens of the United States, and that Congress had no authority to prohibit slavery in free states or territories because it would deprive a slaveowner of his property. A third event was the bitter controversy in Kansas over the legitimacy of the Lecompton Constitution, a state constitution written by pro-slavery settlers who attempted to avoid a popular referendum; when submitted to the voters, however, it was overwhelmingly rejected.

Lincoln described these events as "a piece of machinery" constructed by "Stephen, Franklin, Roger, and James"—Senator Douglas, ex-President Franklin Pierce, Chief Justice Roger B. Taney, and President James Buchanan—all Democrats.

If we could first know where we are, and whither we are tending, we could better judge what to do, and how to do it. We are now far into the fifth year since a policy was initiated with the avowed object and confident promise of putting an end to slavery agitation. Under the operation of that policy that agitation has not only not ceased, but has constantly augmented. In my opinion, it will not cease until a crisis shall have been reached and passed. "A house divided against itself can not stand." I believe this Government can not endure permanently half slave and half free. I do not expect the Union to be dissolved—I do not expect the house to fall—but I do expect it will cease to be divided. It will become all one thing, or all the other. Either the opponents of slavery will arrest the further spread of it, and place it where the public mind shall rest in the belief that it is in course of ultimate extinction; or its advocates will push it forward till it shall become alike lawful in all the States, old as well as new, North as well as South.

Have we no tendency to the latter condition? Let any one who doubts carefully contemplate that now almost complete legal combination—piece of machinery, so to speak —compounded of the Nebraska doctrine and the Dred Scott decision. Let him consider not only what work the machinery is adapted to do, and how well adapted; but also let him study the history of its construction, and trace, if he can, or rather fail, if he can, to trace the evidences of design and concert of action among its chief master-workers from the beginning.

The new year of 1854 found slavery excluded from more than half the States by State Constitutions, and from most of the national territory by Congressional prohibition. Four days later commenced the struggle which ended in repealing that Congressional prohibition. This opened all the national territory to slavery, and was the first point gained.

But, so far, Congress only had acted; and an indorsement by the people, real or apparent, was indispensable to save the point already gained and give chance for more. This necessity had not been overlooked, but had been provided for, as well as might be, in the notable argument of "squatter sovereignty," otherwise called "sacred right of self-government," which latter phrase, though expressive of the only rightful basis of any government, was so perverted in this attempted use of it as to amount to just this: that if any one man choose to enslave another, no third man shall be allowed to object. That argument was incorporated into the Nebraska Bill itself, in the language which follows: "It being the true intent and meaning of this act not to legislate slavery into any Territory or State, nor to exclude it therefrom; but to leave the people thereof perfectly free to form and regulate their domestic institutions in their own way, subject only to the Constitution of the United States."

Then opened the roar of loose declamation in favor of "squatter sovereignty" and "sacred right of self-government."

"But," said opposition members, "let us

amend the bill so as to expressly declare that the people of the territory may exclude slavery." "Not we," said the friends of the measure; and down they voted the amendment.

While the Nebraska Bill was passing through Congress, a law case involving the question of a Negro's freedom, by reason of his owner having voluntarily taken him first into a free State and then a territory covered by the Congressional prohibition, and held him as a slave for a long time in each, was passing through the U.S. Circuit Court for the District of Missouri and both the Nebraska Bill and law suit were brought to a decision in the same month of May, 1854. The Negro's name was "Dred Scott," which name now designates the decision finally made in the case.

Before the then next Presidential election, the law case came to and was argued in the Supreme Court of the United States; but the decision of it was deferred until after the election. Still, before the election, Senator Trumbull, on the floor of the Senate, requested the leading advocate of the Nebraska Bill to state his opinion whether the people of a territory can constitutionally exclude slavery from their limits; and the latter answered, "That is a question for the Supreme Court."

The election came. Mr. Buchanan was elected, and the indorsement, such as it was, secured. That was the second point gained. The indorsement, however, fell short of a clear popular majority by nearly four hundred thousand votes, and so, perhaps, was not overwhelmingly reliable and satisfactory. The outgoing President, in his last annual message, as impressively as possible echoed back upon the people the weight and authority of the indorsement.

The Supreme Court met again; did not announce their decision, but ordered a re-argument. The Presidential inauguration came, and still no decision of the court; but the incoming President in his Inaugural Address fervently exhorted the people to abide by the forthcoming decision, whatever it might be. Then, in a few days came the decision.

This was the third point gained.

The reputed author of the Nebraska Bill finds an early occasion to make a speech at this capitol indorsing the Dred Scott decision, and vehemently denouncing all opposition to it. The new President, too, seizes an early occasion to indorse and strongly construe that decision, and to express his astonishment that any different view had ever been entertained!

At length a squabble springs up between the President and the author of the Nebraska Bill, on the mere question of fact, whether the Lecompton Constitution was or was not, in any just sense, made by the people of Kansas; and in that quarrel the latter declares that all he wants is a fair vote for the people, and that he cares not whether slavery be voted down or voted up. I do not understand his declaration that he cares not whether slavery be voted down or voted up to be intended by him other than as an apt definition of the policy he would impress upon the public mind—the principle for which he declares he has suffered much, and is ready to suffer to the end.

And well may he cling to that principle. If he has any parental feeling, well may he cling to it. That principle is the only shred left of his original Nebraska doctrine. Under the Dred Scott decision "squatter sovereignty" squatted out of existence, tumbled down like temporary scaffolding,—like the mould at the foundry, served through one blast and fell back into loose sand, —helped to carry an election, and then was kicked to the winds. His late joint struggle with the Republicans against the Lecompton Constitution involves nothing of the original Nebraska doctrine. That struggle was made on a point— the right of a people to make their own Constitution—upon which he and the Republicans have never differed.

The several points of the Dred Scott decision, in connection with Senator Douglas's "care not" policy, constitute the piece of machinery in its present state of advancement. The working points of that machinery are:

(1) That no Negro slave, imported as such from Africa, and no descendant of such slave, can ever be a citizen of any State, in the sense of

that term as used in the Constitution of the United States.

This point is made in order to deprive the Negro in every possible event of the benefit of this provision of the United States Constitution which declares that, "The citizens of each State shall be entitled to all the privileges and immunities of citizens in the several States."

(2) That, "subject to the Constitution of the United States," neither Congress nor a Territorial Legislature can exclude slavery from any United States Territory.

This point is made in order that individual men may fill up the Territories with slaves, without danger of losing them as property, and thus enhance the chances of permanency to the institution through all the future.

(3) That whether the holding a Negro in actual slavery in a free State makes him free as against the holder, the United States courts will not decide, but will leave it to be decided by the courts of any slave State the Negro may be forced into by the master.

This point is made not to be pressed immediately, but, if acquiesced in for a while, and apparently indorsed by the people at an election, then to sustain the logical conclusion that what Dred Scott's master might lawfully do with Dred Scott in the free State of Illinois, every other master may lawfully do with any other one or one thousand slaves in Illinois or in any other free State.

Auxiliary to all this, and working hand in hand with it, the Nebraska doctrine, or what is left of it, is to educate and mould public opinion, at least Northern public opinion, not to care whether slavery is voted down or voted up. This shows exactly where we now are, and partially, also, whither we are tending.

It will throw additional light on the latter, to go back and run the mind over the string of historical facts already stated. Several things will now appear less dark and mysterious than they did when they were transpiring. The people were to be left "perfectly free," "subject only to the Constitution." What the Constitution had to do with it outsiders could not then see. Plainly enough now, it was an exactly fitted niche for the Dred Scott decision afterward to come in, and declare that perfect freedom of the people to be just no freedom at all. Why was the amendment expressly declaring the right of the people to exclude slavery voted down? Plainly enough now, the adoption of it would have spoiled the niche for the Dred Scott decision. Why was the court decision held up? Why even a Senator's individual opinion withheld till after the Presidential election? Plainly enough now, the speaking out then would have damaged the "perfectly free" argument upon which the election was to be carried. Why the outgoing President's felicitation on the indorsement? Why the delay of a re-argument? Why the incoming President's advance exhortation in favor of the decision? These things look like the cautious patting and petting of a spirited horse preparatory to mounting him, when it is dreaded that he may give the rider a fall. And why the hasty after-indorsement of the decision, by the President and others?

We cannot absolutely know that all these exact adaptations are the result of pre-concert. But when we see a lot of framed timbers, different portions of which we know have been gotten out at different times and places and by different workmen,—Stephen, Franklin, Roger, and James, for instance,—and when we see these timbers joined together, and see they exactly make the frame of a house or a mill, all the tenons and mortices exactly fitting, and all the lengths and proportions of the different pieces exactly adapted to their respective places, and not a piece too many or too few, not omitting even scaffolding—or, if a single piece be lacking, we see the place in the frame exactly fitted and prepared to yet bring such piece in—in such a case we find it impossible not to believe that Stephen and Franklin and Roger and James all understood one another from the beginning, and all worked upon a common plan or draft drawn up before the first blow was struck. . . .

While the opinion of the court, by Chief Justice Taney, in the Dred Scott case, and the separate opinions of all the concurring judges, expressly declare that the Constitution of the

United States neither permits Congress nor a Territorial Legislature to exclude slavery from any United States Territory, they all omit to declare whether or not the same Constitution permits a State, or the people of a State, to exclude it. Possibly, this was a mere omission; but who can be quite sure . . . Put this and that together, and we have another nice little niche, which we may, ere long, see filled with another Supreme Court decision, declaring that the Constitution of the United States does not permit a State to exclude slavery from its limits. And this may especially be expected if the doctrine of "care not whether slavery be voted down or voted up" shall gain upon the public mind sufficiently to give promise that such a decision can be maintained when made.

Such a decision is all that slavery now lacks of being alike lawful in all the States. Welcome, or unwelcome, such decision is probably coming, and will soon be upon us, unless the power of the present political dynasty shall be met and overthrown. We shall lie down pleasantly dreaming that the people of Missouri are on the verge of making their State free, and we shall awake to the reality instead that the Supreme Court has made Illinois a slave State. To meet and overthrow the power of that dynasty is the work now before all those who would prevent that consummation. That is what we have to do. How can we best do it?

There are those who denounce us openly to their own friends, and yet whisper us softly that Senator Douglas is the aptest instrument there is with which to effect that object. They do not tell us, nor has he told us, that he wishes any such object to be effected. They wish us to infer all from the facts that he now has a little quarrel with the present head of the dynasty; and that he has regularly voted with us on a single point upon which he and we have never differed. They remind us that he is a very great man, and that the largest of us are very small ones. Let this be granted. But "a living dog is better than a dead lion." Judge Douglas, if not a dead lion for this work, is at least a caged and toothless one. How can he oppose the advances of slavery? He don't care anything about it. His avowed mission is impressing the "public heart" to care nothing about it. . . .

Our cause, then, must be intrusted to, and conducted by, its own undoubted friends—those whose hands are free, whose hearts are in the work, who do care for the result. Two years ago the Republicans of the nation mustered over thirteen hundred thousand strong. We did this under the single impulse of resistance to a common danger, with every external circumstance against us. Of strange, discordant, and even hostile elements, we gathered from the four winds, and formed and fought the battle through, under the constant hot fire of a disciplined, proud, and pampered enemy. Did we brave all then to falter now?—now, when that same enemy is wavering, dissevered, and belligerent? The result is not doubtful. We shall not fail—if we stand firm, we shall not fail. Wise counsels may accelerate or mistakes delay it, but, sooner or later, the victory is sure to come.

THE LINCOLN–DOUGLAS DEBATES

Stephen A. Douglas: *This Union was established on the right of each State to do as it pleased on the question of slavery.*

Abraham Lincoln: *The real issue in this controversy . . . is the sentiment on the part of one class that looks upon the institution of slavery* as a wrong, *and of another class that* does not *look upon it as a wrong.*

In 1858, when Lincoln ran against Senator Stephen A. Douglas for the Senate seat from Illinois, he challenged Douglas to a series of debates across the state. Douglas was a national figure in the Democratic Party, and Lincoln was little known outside the state. Thousands of people—farmers, workers, clerks, and others—came to listen, ask questions, and cheer for their favorite. The debates focused on one question only: slavery.

Douglas (1813–1861), born in Vermont, moved to Illinois when he was twenty and was elected to Congress at the age of thirty. A gifted orator, small in stature, Douglas was known as "The Little Giant." Elected to the Senate in 1846, Douglas avidly supported national expansion. Since westward expansion involved bitter controversy over whether slavery should be permitted in the new territories, Douglas championed the Kansas–Nebraska Act of 1854, which repealed the Missouri Compromise and allowed local option.

Douglas believed that the voters in each state or territory should decide whether to permit slavery, but Lincoln argued that slavery should not be allowed to spread beyond the existing slave states. Lincoln insisted that slavery was wrong. Douglas was equally insistent that the survival of the Union required respect for popular sovereignty, even if it led to the spread of slavery.

Lincoln won the popular vote, but lost the election (senators were at that time chosen by the legislature, not by popular vote). The debates made him a national leader of the Republican Party and a contender for the presidential campaign in 1860.

The following exchange took place at Alton, Illinois, on October 15, 1858.

Douglas' Opening Speech

It is now nearly four months since the canvass between Mr. Lincoln and myself commenced. On the sixteenth of June the Republican Convention assembled at Springfield and nominated Mr. Lincoln as their candidate for the United States Senate, and he, on that occasion, delivered a speech in which he laid down what he understood to be the Republican creed, and the platform on which he proposed to stand during the contest.

The principal points in that speech of Mr. Lincoln's were: First, that this government could not endure permanently divided into free and slave States, as our fathers made it; that they must all become free or all become slave; all become one thing or all become the other,—otherwise this Union could not continue to exist. I give you his opinions almost in the identical language he used. His second proposition was a crusade against the Supreme Court of the United States because of the Dred Scott decision, urging as an especial reason for his opposition to that decision that it deprived the Negroes of the rights and benefits of that clause in the Constitution of the United States which guarantees to the citizens of each State all the rights, privileges, and immunities of the citizens of the several States.

On the tenth of July I returned home, and delivered a speech to the people of Chicago, in which I announced it to be my purpose to appeal to the people of Illinois to sustain the course I had pursued in Congress. In that speech I joined issue with Mr. Lincoln on the points which he had presented. Thus there was an issue clear and distinct made up between us on these two propositions laid down in the speech of Mr. Lincoln at Springfield, and controverted by me in my reply to him at Chicago. On the next day, the eleventh of July, Mr. Lincoln replied to me at Chicago, explaining at some length, and reaffirming the positions which he had taken in his Springfield speech. In that Chicago speech he even went further than he had before, and uttered sentiments in regard to the negro being on an equality with the white man. He adopted in support of this position the argument which Lovejoy and Codding and other Abolition lecturers had made familiar in the northern and central portions of the State: to wit, that the Declaration of Independence having declared all men free and equal, by divine law, also that negro equality was an inalienable right, of which they could not be deprived. He insisted, in that speech, that the Declaration of Independence included the negro in the clause asserting that all men were created equal, and went so far as to say that if one man was allowed to take the position that it did not include the negro, others might take the position that it did not include other men. He said that all these distinctions between this man and that man, this race and the other race, must be discarded, and we must all stand by the Declaration of Independence, declaring that all men were created equal.

The issue thus being made up between Mr. Lincoln and myself on three points, we went before the people of the State. During the following seven weeks, between the Chicago speeches and our first meeting at Ottawa, he and I addressed large assemblages of the people in many of the central counties. In my speeches I confined myself closely to those three positions which he had taken, controverting his proposition that this Union could not exist as our fathers made it, divided into free and slave States, controverting his proposition of a crusade against the Supreme Court because of the Dred Scott decision, and controverting his proposition that the Declaration of Independence included and meant the negroes as well as the white men, when it declared all men to be created equal. . . . I took up Mr. Lincoln's three propositions in my several speeches, analyzed them, and pointed out what I believed to be the radical errors contained in them. First, in regard to his doctrine that this government was in violation of the law of God, which says that a house divided against itself cannot stand, I repudiated it as slander upon the immortal framers of our Constitution. I then said, I have often repeated, and now again assert, that in my opinion our government can endure forever, divided into free and slave States as our fathers made it,— each State having the right to prohibit, abolish, or sustain slavery, just as it pleases. This government was made upon the great basis of the sovereignty of the States, the right of each State to regulate its own domestic institutions to suit itself; and that right was conferred with the understanding and expectation that, inasmuch as each locality had separate interests, each locality must have different and distinct local and domestic institutions, corresponding to its wants and interests. Our fathers knew when they made the government that the laws and institutions which were well adapted to the Green Mountains of Vermont were unsuited to the rice plantations of South Carolina. They knew then, as well as we know now, that the laws and institutions which would be well adapted to the beautiful prairies of Illinois would not be suited to the mining regions of California. They knew that in a republic as broad as this, having such a variety of soil, climate, and interest, there must necessarily be a corresponding variety of local laws,—the policy and institutions of each State adapted to its condition and wants. For this reason this Union was established on the right of each State to do as it pleased on the question of slavery, and every other question; and the various states were not allowed to complain of, much less interfere with, the policy of their neighbors.

Lincoln's Reply

It is not true that our fathers, as Judge Douglas assumes, made this government part slave and part free. Understand the sense in which he puts it. He assumes that slavery is a rightful thing within itself,—was introduced by the framers of the Constitution. The exact truth is, that they found the institution existing among us, and they left it as they found it. But in making the government they left this institution with many clear marks of disapprobation upon it. They found slavery among them, and they left it among them because of the difficulty—the absolute impossibility—of its immediate removal. And when Judge Douglas asks me why we cannot let it remain part slave and part free, as the fathers of the government made it, he asks a question based upon an assumption which is itself a falsehood; and I turn upon him and ask him the question, when the policy that the fathers of the government had adopted in relation to this element among us was the best policy in the world, the only wise policy, the only policy that we can ever safely continue upon, that will ever give us peace, unless this dangerous element masters us all and becomes a national institution,—*I turn upon him and ask him why he could not leave it alone.* I turn and ask him

An 1860 election cartoon shows a boxing match between Abraham Lincoln and Stephen Douglas.

THE UNDECIDED POLITICAL PRIZE FIGHT.

why he was driven to the necessity of introducing a *new policy* in regard to it. He has himself said he introduced a new policy. . . .

Now, irrespective of the moral aspect of this question as to whether there is a right or wrong in enslaving a Negro, I am still in favor of our new Territories being in such a condition that white men may find a home,—may find some spot where they can better their condition; where they can settle upon new soil and better their condition in life. I am in favor of this, not merely (I must say it here as I have elsewhere) for our own people who are born amongst us, but as an outlet for *free white people everywhere*—the world over—in which Hans, and Baptiste, and Patrick, and all other men from all the world, may find new homes and better their conditions in life.

I have stated upon former occasions, and I may as well state again, what I understand to be the real issue in this controversy between Judge Douglas and myself. On the point of my wanting to make war between the free and the slave States, there has been no issue between us. So, too, when he assumes that I am in favor of introducing a perfect social and political equality between the white and black races. These are false issues, upon which Judge Douglas has tried to force the controversy. There is no foundation in truth for the charge that I maintain either of these propositions. The real issue in this controversy—the one pressing upon every mind—is the sentiment on the part of one class that looks upon the institution of slavery *as a wrong,* and of another class that *does not* look upon it as a wrong. The sentiment that contemplates the institution of slavery in this country as a wrong is the sentiment of the Republican party. It is the sentiment around which all their actions, all their arguments, circle, from which all their propositions radiate. They look upon it as being a moral, social, and political wrong; and, while they contemplate it as such, they nevertheless have due regard for its actual existence among us, and the difficulties of getting rid of it in any satisfactory way, and to all the constitutional obligations thrown about it. Yet, having a due re-

gard for these, they desire a policy in regard to it that looks to its not creating any more danger. They insist that it should, as far as may be, *be treated* as a wrong; and one of the methods of treating it as a wrong is to *make provision that it shall grow no larger.* They also desire a policy that looks to a peaceful end of slavery at sometime, as being wrong. These are the views they entertain in regard to it as I understand them; and all their sentiments, all their arguments and propositions, are brought within this range. I have said, and I repeat it here, that if there be a man amongst us who does not think that the institution of slavery is wrong in any one of the aspects of which I have spoken, he is misplaced and ought not to be with us. And if there be a man amongst us who is so impatient of it as a wrong as to disregard its actual presence among us and the difficulty of getting rid of it suddenly in a satisfactory way, and to disregard the constitutional obligations thrown about it, that man is misplaced if he is on our platform. We disclaim sympathy with him in practical action. He is not placed properly with us.

On this subject of treating it as a wrong, and limiting its spread, let me say a word. Has anything ever threatened the existence of this Union save and except this very institution of slavery? What is it that we hold most dear amongst us? Our own liberty and prosperity. What has ever threatened our liberty and prosperity, save and except this institution of slavery? If this is true, how do you propose to improve the condition of things by enlarging slavery—by spreading it out and making it bigger? You may have a wen or cancer upon your person, and not be able to cut it out, lest you bleed to death; but surely it is no way to cure it, to engraft it and spread it over your whole body. That is no proper way of treating what you regard a wrong. You see this peaceful way of dealing with it as a wrong,—restricting the spread of it, and not allowing it to go into new countries where it has not already existed. That is the peaceful way, the old-fashioned way, the way in which the fathers themselves set us the example.

On the other hand, I have said there is a sentiment which treats it as *not* being wrong. This is the Democratic sentiment of this day. I do not mean to say that every man who stands within that range positively asserts that it is right. That class will include all who positively assert that it is right, and all who, like Judge Douglas, treat it as indifferent and do not say it is either right or wrong. These two classes of men fall within the general class of those who do not look upon it as a wrong. . . .

The Democratic policy in regard to that institution will not tolerate the merest breath, the slightest hint, of the least degree of wrong about it. Try it by some of Judge Douglas' arguments. He says he "don't care whether it is voted up or voted down" in the Territories. I do not care myself, in dealing with that expression, whether it is intended to be expressive of his individual sentiments on the subject or only of the national policy he desires to have established. It is alike valuable for my purpose. Any man can say that who does not see anything wrong in slavery; but no man can logically say it who does see a wrong in it, because no man can logically say he does not care whether a wrong is voted up or voted down. He may say he does not care whether an indifferent thing is voted up or down, but he must logically have a choice between a right thing and a wrong thing. He contends that whatever community wants slaves has a right to have them. So they have, if it is not a wrong. But if it is a wrong, he cannot say people have a right to do wrong. He says that upon the score of equality slaves should be allowed to go in a new Territory, like other property. This is strictly logical if there is no difference between it and other property. If it and other property are equal, this argument is entirely logical. But if you insist that one is wrong and the other right, there is no use to institute a comparison between right and wrong. You may turn over everything in the Democratic policy from beginning to end, whether in the shape it takes on the statute book, in the shape it takes in the Dred Scott decision, in the shape it takes in conversation, or the shape it takes in short maxim-like arguments,—it everywhere carefully excludes the idea that there is anything wrong in it.

That is the real issue. That is the issue that will continue in this country when these poor tongues of Judge Douglas and myself shall be silent. It is the eternal struggle between these two principles—right and wrong—throughout the world. They are the two principles that have stood face to face from the beginning of time and will ever continue to struggle. The one is the common right of humanity, and the other the divine right of kings. It is the same principle in whatever shape it develops itself. It is the same spirit that says, "You work and toil and earn bread, and I'll eat it." No matter in what shape it comes, whether from the mouth of a king who seeks to bestride the people of his own nation and live by the fruit of their labor, or from one race of men as an apology for enslaving another race, it is the same tyrannical principle. . . .

JOHN BROWN
LAST STATEMENT TO THE COURT

I believe that to have interfered as I have done . . . in behalf of His despised poor, I did no wrong, but right.

John Brown (1800–1859) was a zealous abolitionist who believed that God had chosen him to destroy the evil institution of slavery. Born in Torrington, Connecticut, Brown and his large family (he fathered twenty children) moved from place to place, in Ohio,

Massachusetts, New York, and Pennsylvania, as he sought a vocation. At various times, he was a farmer, wool merchant, tanner, and land speculator. But the abiding passion of his life was his hatred of slavery. Brown migrated to Kansas in 1855, joining several of his sons, who had staked claims in the strife-torn territory. Kansas was then a hotbed of controversy over whether it would enter the Union as a free state or a slave state. Armed conflict between "free-staters" and "border ruffians" (as the pro-slavery gangs were called) gave rise to the term "Bleeding Kansas."

In 1856, Brown became outraged when he learned that pro-slavery men had sacked the town of Lawrence, Kansas. In retaliation, Brown and his men dragged five pro-slavery settlers from their homes and hacked them to death. This event, known as the Pottawatomie massacre, led to more violence, in which more than two hundred people lost their lives. Two years later, Brown led another raid, in Missouri, where he killed a slaveowner, liberated eleven slaves, and fled with the slaves to Canada.

In October 1859, John Brown seized the U.S. arsenal at Harpers Ferry, Virginia (now West Virginia). Brown's raiding party consisted of five blacks and seventeen whites, including three of his sons. Brown expected to arm the local slaves, who would then join his rebellion, but none did. The raiders were captured in a bloody battle with state and federal troops. The raid was a tactical failure but, in terms of Brown's larger purposes, a brilliant success. It captured the nation's attention, and it heightened the sectional tensions leading toward the ultiimate conflict—war.

Brown was convicted of treason, murder, and fomenting insurrection; five of his compatriots escaped, but the rest were either killed during the raid or hanged. Brown was convicted on November 2 and hanged on December 2, 1859. His statement to the court, delivered when his sentence was pronounced, was reprinted the next day in the *New York Herald*. On the day of his execution, he was hailed as a saint and a hero throughout the North.

I have, may it please the Court, a few words to say.

In the first place, I deny everything but what I have all along admitted: of a design on my part to free slaves. I intended certainly to have made a clean thing of that matter, as I did last winter, when I went into Missouri and there took slaves without the snapping of a gun on either side, moving them through the country, and finally leaving them in Canada. I designed to have done the same thing again on a larger scale. That was all I intended. I never did intend murder, or treason, or the destruction of property, or to exercise or incite slaves to rebellion, or to make insurrection.

I have another objection, and that is that it is unjust that I should suffer such a penalty. Had I interfered in the manner which I admit, and which I admit has been fairly proved—for I ad-mire the truthfulness and candor of the greater portion of the witnesses who have testified in this case—Had I so interfered in behalf of the rich, the powerful, the intelligent, the so-called great, or in behalf of any of their friends, either father, mother, brother, sister, wife or children, or any of that class, and suffered and sacrificed what I have in this interference, it would have been all right. Every man in this Court would have deemed it an act worthy of reward rather than punishment.

This Court acknowledges, too, as I suppose, the validity of the law of God. I see a book kissed, which I suppose to be the Bible, or at least the New Testament, which teaches me that all things whatsoever I would that men should do to me, I should do even so to them. It teaches me, further, to remember them that are in bonds as bound with them. I endeavored to act up to that instruction. I say I am yet too young to understand that God is any respecter of persons. I believe that to have interfered as I have done, as I have always freely admitted I have done, in behalf of His despised poor, I did no wrong, but right. Now, if it is deemed necessary that I should forfeit my life for the furtherance of the ends of justice, and mingle my blood further with the blood of my children and with the blood of millions in this slave country whose rights are disregarded by wicked, cruel, and unjust enactments, I say, let it be done.

Let me say one word further. I feel entirely satisfied with the treatment I have received on my trial. Considering all the circumstances, it has been more generous than I expected. But I feel no consciousness of guilt. I have stated from the first what was my intention, and what was not. I never had any design against the liberty of any person, nor any disposition to commit treason or incite slaves to rebel or make any general insurrection. I never encouraged any man to do so, but always discouraged any idea of that kind.

Let me say, also, in regard to the statements made by some of those who were connected with me, I hear it has been stated by some of them that I have induced them to join me. But the contrary is true. I do not say this to injure them, but as regretting their weakness. Not one but joined me of his own accord, and the greater part at their own expense. A number of them I never saw, and never had a word of conversation with, till the day they came to me, and that was for the purpose I have stated.

Now, I have done.

ABRAHAM LINCOLN

THE COOPER UNION SPEECH

Let us have faith that right makes might, and in that faith let us to the end dare to do our duty as we understand it.

Abraham Lincoln was a dark-horse candidate for the Republican nomination for president in 1860. Outside Illinois, he was scarcely known at all. The debates with Douglas brought him some attention; then in 1859, he gave speeches in other midwestern states, and on February 27, 1860, he spoke to a large audience at the Cooper Union in New York City. This brought him into the home territory of William H. Seward, the former governor of New York and the leading candidate for Republican nomination. Lincoln followed his triumphant reception in New York with a speaking tour of New England, which helped bring him to the attention of crucial delegates in the Northeast. At the Republican convention in Chicago in May 1860, Lincoln won the nomination on the third ballot. Sixty years later, H. L. Mencken maintained that the Cooper Union speech "got him the Presidency."

In the Cooper Union speech, Lincoln challenged the assertion by Senator Stephen A. Douglas (soon to be the Democratic nominee for president and Lincoln's opponent in the general election) that the founding fathers knowingly preserved slavery. In this widely noted speech, Lincoln carefully analyzed the intentions of those who wrote the Constitution with regard to slavery. The point is of more than antiquarian interest: more than a century later, legal scholars continue to debate whether the framers of the Constitution intended to end slavery.

... In his speech last autumn at Columbus, Ohio, as reported in the New York *Times,* Senator Douglas said:

"Our fathers, when they framed the Government under which we live, understood this question just as well, and even better, than we do now."

I fully indorse this, and I adopt it as a text for this discourse. I so adopt it because it furnishes a precise and an agreed starting point for the discussion between Republicans and that wing of the Democracy headed by Senator Douglas....

Who were our fathers that framed the Constitution? I suppose the "thirty-nine" who signed the original instrument may be fairly called our fathers who framed that part of the present Government....

What is the question which, according to the text, those fathers understood just as well, and even better, than we do now?

It is this: Does the proper division of local from federal authority, or anything in the Constitution, forbid our Federal Government control as to slavery in our Federal Territories?

Upon this, Douglas holds the affirmative, and Republicans the negative. This affirmative and denial form an issue; and this issue—this question—is precisely what the text declares our fathers understood better than we.

Let us now inquire whether the "thirty-nine," or any of them, ever acted upon this question; and if they did, how they acted upon it—how they expressed that better understanding.

In 1784, three years before the Constitution, the United States then owning the Northwestern Territory, and no other, the Congress of the Confederation had before them the question of prohibiting slavery in that Territory; and four of the "thirty-nine" who afterward framed the Constitution were in that Congress, and voted on that question. Of these, Roger Sherman, Thomas Mifflin, and Hugh Williamson voted for the prohibition, thus showing that, in their understanding, no line dividing local from federal authority, nor anything else, properly forbade the Federal Government control as to slavery in federal territory. The other of the four, James McHenry, voted against the prohibition, showing that for some cause he thought it improper to vote for it.

In 1787, still before the Constitution, but while the Convention was in session framing it, and while the Northwestern Territory still was the only territory owned by the United States, the same question of prohibiting slavery in the territory again came before the Congress of the Confederation; and two more of the "thirty-nine," who afterward signed the Constitution, were in that Congress, and voted on the question. They were William Blount and William Few; and they both voted for the prohibition ...

In 1789, by the first Congress which sat under the Constitution, an act was passed to enforce the Ordinance of '87, including the prohibition of slavery in the Northwestern Territory. The bill for this act was reported by one of the "thirty-nine"—Thomas Fitzsimmons, then a member of the House of Representatives from Pennsylvania. It went through all its stages without a word of opposition, and finally passed both branches without yeas and nays, which is equivalent to a unanimous passage. In this Congress there were sixteen of the "thirty-nine" fathers who framed the original Constitution. They were John Langdon, Nicholas Gilman, Wm. S. Johnson, Roger Sherman, Robert Morris, Thos. Fitzsimmons, William Few, Abraham Baldwin, Rufus King, William Patterson, George Clymer, Richard Bassett, George Read, Pierce Butler, Daniel Carrol, James Madison....

Again, George Washington, another of the "thirty-nine," was then President of the United States, and as such approved and signed the bill, thus completing its validity as a law, and thus showing that, in his understanding, no line dividing local from federal authority, nor anything in the Constitution, forbade the Federal Government control as to slavery in federal territory.

No great while after the adoption of the original Constitution, North Carolina ceded to the Federal Government the country now constituting the State of Tennessee; and a few years later Georgia ceded that which now constitutes the States of Mississippi and Alabama. In both deeds of cession it was made a condition by the ceding States that the Federal Government should not prohibit slavery in the ceded country. Besides this, slavery was then actually in the ceded country. Under these circumstances, Congress, on taking charge of these countries, did not absolutely prohibit slavery within them. But they did interfere with it—take control of it—even there, to a certain extent. In 1798 Congress organized the Territory of Mississippi. In the act of organization they prohibited the bringing of slaves into the Territory from any place without the United States by fine and giving freedom to slaves so brought. This act passed both branches of Congress without yeas and nays. In that Congress were three of the "thirty-nine" who framed the original Constitution. They were John Langdon, George Read, and Abraham Baldwin. . . .

In 1803 the Federal Government purchased the Louisiana country. Our former territorial acquisitions came from certain of our own States; but this Louisiana country was acquired from a foreign nation. In 1804 Congress gave a territorial organization to that part of it which now constitutes the State of Louisiana. New Orleans, lying within that part, was an old and comparatively large city. There were other considerable towns and settlements, and slavery was extensively and thoroughly intermingled with the people. Congress did not, in the Territorial Act, prohibit slavery; but they did interfere with it—take control of it—in a more marked and extensive way than they did in the case of Mississippi. The substance of the provision therein made in relation to slaves was:

(1) That no slave should be imported into the territory from foreign parts.

(2) That no slave should be carried into it who had been imported into the United States since the first day of May, 1798.

(3) That no slave should be carried into it, except by the owner, and for his own use as a settler; the penalty in all the cases being a fine

upon the violator of the law, and freedom to the slave.

This act also was passed without yeas and nays. In the Congress which passed it there were two of the "thirty-nine." They were Abraham Baldwin and Jonathan Dayton. . . .

In 1819–20 came and passed the Missouri question. Many votes were taken, by yeas and nays, in both branches of Congress, upon the various phases of the general question. Two of the "thirty-nine"—Rufus King and Charles Pinckney—were members of that Congress. Mr. King steadily voted for slavery prohibition and against all compromises, while Mr. Pinckney as steadily voted against slavery prohibition and against all compromises. . . .

The cases I have mentioned are the only acts of the "thirty-nine," or of any of them, upon the direct issue, which I have been able to discover. . . .

Here, then, we have twenty-three out of our "thirty-nine" fathers who framed the Government under which we live, who have, upon their official responsibility and their corporal oaths, acted upon the very question which the text affirms they "understood just as well, and even better, than we do now"; and twenty-one of them—a clear majority of the whole "thirty-nine"—so acting upon it as to make them guilty of gross political impropriety and willful perjury if, in their understanding, any proper division between local and federal authority, or anything in the Constitution they had made themselves, and sworn to support, forbade the Federal Government control as to slavery in the federal territories. Thus the twenty-one acted; and, as actions speak louder than words, so actions under such responsibility speak still louder. . . .

The remaining sixteen of the "thirty-nine," so far as I have discovered, have left no record of their understanding upon the direct question of federal control of slavery in the Federal Territories. But there is much reason to believe that their understanding upon that question would not have appeared different from that of their twenty-three compeers, had it been manifested at all.

For the purpose of adhering rigidly to the text, I have purposely omitted whatever understanding may have been manifested by any person, however distinguished, other than the "thirty-nine" fathers who framed the original Constitution; and, for the same reason, I have also omitted whatever understanding may have been manifested by any of the "thirty-nine" even on any other phase of the general question of slavery. If we should look into their acts and declarations on those other phases, as the foreign slave-trade, and the morality and policy of slavery generally, it would appear to us that on the direct question of federal control of slavery in Federal Territories, the sixteen, if they had acted at all, would probably have acted just as the twenty-three did. Among that sixteen were several of the most noted anti-slavery men of those times,—as Dr. Franklin, Alexander Hamilton, and Gouverneur Morris,—while there was not one now known to have been otherwise, unless it may be John Rutledge, of South Carolina.

The sum of the whole is, that of our "thirty-nine" fathers who framed the original Constitution, twenty-one—a clear majority of the whole —certainly understood that no proper division of local from federal authority, nor any part of the Constitution, forbade the Federal Government to control slavery in the Federal Territories; while all the rest probably had the same understanding. Such, unquestionably, was the understanding of our fathers who framed the original Constitution; and the text affirms that they understood the question "better than we."...

It is surely safe to assume that the "thirty-nine" framers of the original Constitution, and the seventy-six members of the Congress which framed the amendments thereto, taken together, do certainly include those who may be fairly called "our fathers who framed the Government under which we live." And so assuming, I defy any man to show that any one of them ever, in his whole life, declared that, in his understanding, any proper division of local from federal authority, or any part of the Constitution, forbade the Federal Government control as to slavery in the Federal Territories. I go a step further. I defy any one to show that any living man in the whole world ever did, prior to the beginning of the present century (and I might almost say prior to the beginning of the last half of the present century), declare that, in his understanding, any proper division of local from federal authority, or any part of the Constitution, forbade the Federal Government control as to slavery in the Federal Territories. To those who now so declare I give not only "our fathers who framed the Government under which we live," but with them all other living men within the century in which it was framed, among whom to search, and they shall not be able to find the evidence of a single man agreeing with them.

Now, and here, let me guard a little against being misunderstood. I do not mean to say we are bound to follow implicitly in whatever our fathers did. To do so would be to discard all the lights of current experience, to reject all progress, all improvement. What I do say is that if we would supplant the opinions and policy of our fathers in any case, we should do so upon evidence so conclusive, and argument so clear, that even their great authority, fairly considered and weighed, cannot stand; and most surely not in a case whereof we ourselves declare they understood the question better than we....

And now, if they would listen,—as I suppose they will not,—I would address a few words to the Southern people.

I would say to them: You consider yourselves a reasonable and a just people; and I consider that in the general qualities of reason and justice you are not inferior to any other people. Still, when you speak of us Republicans, you do so only to denounce us as reptiles, or, at the best, as no better than outlaws....

You say we are sectional. We deny it. That makes an issue; and the burden of proof is upon you. You produce your proof; and what is it? Why, that our party has no existence in your section—gets no votes in your section. The fact is substantially true; but does it prove the issue? If it does, then in case we should, without change of principle, begin to get votes in your section, we should thereby cease to be sectional. You cannot escape this conclusion; and yet, are you willing to abide by it? If you are, you will probably soon find that we have ceased to be sectional, for we shall get votes in your section this very year. You will then begin to discover, as the truth plainly is, that your proof does not touch the issue. . . .

Some of you delight to flaunt in our faces the warning against sectional parties given by Washington in his Farewell Address. Less than eight years before Washington gave that warning, he had, as President of the United States, approved and signed an act of Congress enforcing the prohibition of slavery in the Northwestern Territory, which act embodied the policy of the government upon that subject up to and at the very moment he penned that warning; and about one year after he penned it he wrote Lafayette that he considered that prohibition a wise measure, expressing in the same connection his hope that we should some time have a confederacy of free States.

Bearing this in mind, and seeing that sectionalism has since arisen upon this same subject, is that warning a weapon in your hands against us, or in our hands against you? Could Washington himself speak, would he cast the blame of that sectionalism upon us, who sustain his policy, or upon you, who repudiate it? . . .

And how much would it avail you, if you could . . . break up the Republican organization? Human action can be modified to some extent, but human nature cannot be changed. There is a judgment and a feeling against slavery in this nation, which cast at least a million and a half of votes. You cannot destroy that judgment and feeling—that sentiment—by breaking up the political organization which rallies around it. You can scarcely scatter and disperse an army which has been formed into order in the face of your heaviest fire; but if you could, how much would you gain by forcing the sentiment which

created it out of the peaceful channel of the ballot box into some other channel? What would that other channel probably be? Would the number of John Browns be lessened or enlarged by the operation?

But you will break up the Union rather than submit to a denial of your Constitutional rights.

That has a somewhat reckless sound; but it would be palliated, if not fully justified, were we proposing, by the mere force of numbers, to deprive you of some right plainly written down in the Constitution. But we are proposing no such thing.

When you make these declarations, you have a specific and well-understood allusion to an assumed Constitutional right of yours to take slaves into the Federal Territories and hold them there as property. But no such right is specifically written in the Constitution. That instrument is literally silent about any such right. We, on the contrary, deny that such a right has any existence in the Constitution, even by implication.

Your purpose, then, plainly stated, is that you will destroy the Government, unless you be allowed to construe and enforce the Constitution as you please, on all points in dispute between you and us. You will rule or ruin in all events.

This, plainly stated, is your language to us. Perhaps you will say the Supreme Court has decided the disputed Constitutional question in your favor. Not quite so. But waiving the lawyer's distinction between dictum and decision, the Court has decided the question for you in a sort of way. The Court has substantially said, it is your Constitutional right to take slaves into the Federal Territories, and to hold them there as property.

When I say the decision was made in a sort of way, I mean it was made in a divided Court, by a bare majority of the Judges, and they not quite agreeing with one another in the reasons for making it; that it is so made as that its avowed supporters disagree with one another about its meaning, and that it was mainly based upon a mistaken statement of fact—the statement in the opinion that "the right of property in a slave is distinctly and expressly affirmed in the Constitution."

An inspection of the Constitution will show that the right of property in a slave is not distinctly and expressly affirmed in it. . . .

If they had only pledged their judicial opinion that such right is affirmed in the instrument by implication, it would be open to others to show that neither the word "slave" nor "slavery" is to be found in the Constitution, nor the word "property" even, in any connection with language alluding to the things slave, or slavery; and that wherever in that instrument the slave is alluded to, he is called a "person"; and wherever his master's legal right in relation to him is alluded to, it is spoken of as "service or labor which may be due," as a "debt" payable in service or labor. Also it would be open to show, by contemporaneous history, that this mode of alluding to slaves and slavery, instead of speaking of them, was employed on purpose to exclude from the Constitution the idea that there could be property in man. . . .

Under all these circumstances, do you really feel yourselves justified to break up this Government unless such a court decision as yours is shall be at once submitted to as a conclusive and final rule of political action? But you will not abide the election of a Republican President! In that supposed event, you say, you will destroy the Union; and then, you say, the great crime of having destroyed it will be upon us! That is cool. A highwayman holds a pistol to my ear, and mutters through his teeth, "Stand and deliver, or I shall kill you, and then you will be a murderer!" . . .

A few words now to Republicans. It is exceedingly desirable that all parts of this great Confederacy shall be at peace, and in harmony one with another. Let us Republicans do our part to have it so. Even though much provoked, let us do nothing through passion and ill-temper. Even though the southern people will not so much as listen to us, let us calmly consider their demands, and yield to them if in our delib-erate view of our duty, we possibly can. Judging by all they say and do, and by the subject and nature of their controversy with us, let us determine, if we can, what will satisfy them.

Will they be satisfied if the Territories be unconditionally surrendered to them? We know they will not. In all their present complaints against us, the Territories are scarcely mentioned. Invasions and insurrections are the rage now. Will it satisfy them if, in the future, we have nothing to do with invasions and insurrections? We know it will not. We so know, because we know we never had anything to do with invasions and insurrections; and yet this total abstaining does not exempt us from the charge and the denunciation.

The question recurs, what will satisfy them? . . . This, and this only: Cease to call slavery wrong, and join them in calling it right. And this must be done thoroughly—done in acts as well as in words. Silence will not be tolerated—we must place ourselves avowedly with them. Senator Douglas's new sedition law must be enacted and enforced, suppressing all declarations that slavery is wrong, whether made in politics, in presses, in pulpits, or in private. We must arrest and return their fugitive slaves with greedy pleasure. We must pull down our Free-State Constitutions. The whole atmosphere must be disinfected from all taint of opposition to slavery, before they will cease to believe that all their troubles proceed from us. . . .

Holding, as they do, that slavery is morally right and socially elevating, they cannot cease to demand a full national recognition of it as a legal right and a social blessing.

Nor can we justifiably withhold this on any ground save our conviction that slavery is wrong. If slavery is right, all words, acts, laws, and constitutions against it are themselves wrong, and should be silenced and swept away. If it is right, we cannot justly object to its nationality—its universality; if it is wrong, they cannot justly insist upon its extension—its enlargement. All they ask we could readily grant, if we thought slavery right; all we ask they could as readily grant if they thought it wrong. Their thinking it right and our thinking it wrong is the precise fact upon which depends the whole controversy. Thinking it right, as they do, they are not to blame for desiring its full recognition as being right; but thinking it wrong, as we do, can we yield to them? Can we cast our votes with their view, and against our own? In view of our moral, social, and political responsibilities, can we do this?

Wrong as we think slavery is, we can yet afford to let it alone where it is, because that much is due to the necessity arising from its actual presence in the nation; but can we, while our votes will prevent it, allow it to spread into the National Territories, and to overrun us here in these Free States?

If our sense of duty forbids this, then let us stand by our duty fearlessly and effectively. Let us be diverted by none of those sophistical contrivances wherewith we are so industriously plied and belabored—contrivances such as groping for some middle ground between the right and the wrong; vain as the search for a man who should be neither a living man nor a dead man; such as a policy of "don't care" on a question about which all true men do care; such as Union appeals beseeching true Union men to yield to Disunionists, reversing the Divine rule, and calling, not the sinners, but the righteous to repentance; such as invocations to Washington, imploring men to unsay what Washington said, and undo what Washington did.

Neither let us be slandered from our duty by false accusations against us, nor frightened from it by menaces of destruction to the Government, nor of dungeons to ourselves. Let us have faith that right makes might, and in that faith let us to the end dare to do our duty as we understand it.

GO DOWN, MOSES

The songs of the slaves, working in the fields and on the plantation, form a distinct element in American literature. Negro spirituals were composed, as the black poet James Weldon Johnson put it, by "black and unknown bards." These beautiful and poignant songs spread far beyond the physical confines where they were created and entered the American consciousness as a fundamental part of the national culture. James Weldon Johnson held in 1925 that the spirituals were "America's only folk music and, up to this time, the finest distinctive artistic contribution she has to offer the world." With more than a touch of irony, he observed, "It is strange!"

The spirituals fused characteristics of African music with elements of the Old Testament to become dignified and rhythmic expressions of faith. Most were written for group or choral singing. Immediately after emancipation, educated blacks discouraged the singing of spirituals as a reminder of slavery; but the old songs nonetheless remained popular in black churches and in time received wide public recognition. The spirituals were introduced to a large popular audience by the Fisk University Jubilee Singers, who toured the country in 1871. In time, songs like "Swing Low, Sweet Chariot," "Gimme Dat Ol'-Time Religion," and "Nobody Knows de Trouble I Seen" became American standards.

In his collection *The Book of American Negro Spirituals*, Johnson says of "Go Down, Moses," "There is not a nobler theme in the whole musical literature of the world. If the Negro had voiced himself in only that one song, it would have been evidence of his nobility of soul."

Go down, Moses,
Way down in Egyptland
Tell old Pharaoh
To let my people go.

When Israel was in Egyptland
Let my people go
Oppressed so hard they could not stand
Let my people go.

Go down, Moses,
Way down in Egyptland

Tell old Pharaoh
"Let my people go."

"Thus saith the Lord," bold Moses said,
"Let my people go;
If not I'll smite your first-born dead
Let my people go."

Go down, Moses,
Way down in Egyptland,
Tell old Pharaoh,
"Let my people go!"

THE CIVIL WAR

*A political cartoon from 1861 comments on the
secession of Southern states from the Union.*

DANIEL DECATUR EMMETT
DIXIE

Daniel Decatur Emmett (1815–1904) hurriedly dashed off the words and music of "Dixie" in the spring of 1859. Emmett, an Ohio-born performer, wrote it for Bryant's Minstrel Show in New York as a "walk-around," a musical number sung and danced by a few featured soloists in the foreground while the company remained in the background. Its original title was "I Wish I Was in Dixie's Land." A quick hit, "Dixie" entered the repertoire of many minstrel companies and became known throughout the country. As war fervor grew in the South, southerners adopted the song as their own, seeing their region as Dixie Land. The original lyrics of "Dixie" were apolitical, but militaristic versions were soon substituted on both sides of the Mason-Dixon line. The North was unwilling to cede "Dixie" to the South, however, and it was one of the tunes played at Abraham Lincoln's inauguration. But southerners saw it as a tribute to the South, and "Dixie" became the battle hymn of the Confederacy. It was played at Jefferson Davis's inauguration as president of the Confederacy. Emmett also wrote "Old Dan Tucker," the hit song of 1843.

I wish I was in de land ob cotton,
Old times dar am not forgotten,
Look away! Look away! Look away! Dixie land.
In Dixie Land where I was born in
Early on one frosty mornin'
Look away! Look away! Look away! Dixie land.

CHORUS:
Den I wish I was in Dixie, Hooray! Hooray!
In Dixie Land I'll take my stand,
To lib and die in Dixie,
Away, Away, Away down south in Dixie.
Away, Away, Away down south in Dixie.

Old Missus marry "Will-de-weaber,"
Willyum was a gay deceber,
Look away! Look away! Look away! Dixie land.
But when he put his arm around her,
He smiled as fierce as a forty-pounder.
Look away! Look away! Look away! Dixie land.

His face was sharp as a butcher's cleaber,
But dat did not seem to grieb 'er,
Look away! Look away! Look away! Dixie land.
Old Missus acted de foolish part,
And died for a man dat broke her heart.
Look away! Look away! Look away! Dixie land.

Now here's a health to de next old Missus,
An' all de gals dat want to kiss us;
Look away! Look away! Look away! Dixie land.
But if you want to drive 'way sorrow,
Come and hear dis song tomorrow.
Look away! Look away! Look away! Dixie land.

Dar's buckwheat cakes an' Injun batter,
Makes you fat or a little fatter,
Look away! Look away! Look away! Dixie land.
Den hoe it down and scratch your grabble,
To Dixie's land I'm bound to trabble.
Look away! Look away! Look away! Dixie land.

ABRAHAM LINCOLN

FIRST INAUGURAL ADDRESS

The mystic chords of memory, stretching from every battlefield and patriot grave to every living heart and hearthstone all over this broad land, will yet swell the chorus of the Union, when again touched, as surely they will be, by the better angels of our nature.

In the 1860 election, a split in the Democratic Party between southerners and northerners cleared the way for a victory by Lincoln and the Republican Party. Although Lincoln had been selected in part because of his reputation as a moderate, southerners warned that a Lincoln victory would be cause for secession. His election was widely viewed, in the North and the South, as a rejection of slavery and the political power of the slave owners. Seven states (South Carolina, Mississippi, Florida, Alabama, Georgia, Louisiana, and Texas) seceded from the Union following Lincoln's election and formed the Confederate States of America, in Montgomery, Alabama, on February 4, 1861. A few weeks later, a constitutional amendment was introduced in Congress to prohibit slavery in the United States (it was ratified in 1865 and became the Thirteenth Amendment).

When Lincoln took the oath of office on the Capitol steps in Washington, D.C., on March 4, 1861, he addressed a nation that was on the verge of dissolution and civil war. He appealed for reason and calm. His speech was a last-ditch effort to preserve the Union and to avert war. Lincoln made clear, however, that the Union would defend itself, that secession from the Union was not lawful, and that violence against the federal government would be considered revolutionary.

Lincoln's plea fell on deaf ears. The Civil War began on April 12, 1861, when Confederate forces bombarded Fort Sumter at Charleston, South Carolina. Following the fall of Fort Sumter, Virginia, Arkansas, North Carolina, and Tennessee joined the Confederate States of America.

. . . Apprehension seems to exist among the people of the Southern States that by the accession of a Republican Administration their property and their peace and personal security are to be endangered. There has never been any reasonable cause for such apprehension. Indeed, the most ample evidence to the contrary has all the while existed and been open to their inspection. It is found in nearly all the published speeches of him who now addresses you. I do but quote from one of those speeches when I declare that—

I have no purpose, directly or indirectly, to interfere with the institution of slavery in the States where it exists. I believe I have no lawful right to do so, and I have no inclination to do so. . . .

It is seventy-two years since the first inauguration of a President under our National Constitution. During that period fifteen different and greatly distinguished citizens have in succession administered the executive branch of the Government. They have conducted it through many perils, and generally with great success. Yet, with all this scope of precedent, I now enter upon the same task for the brief constitutional term of four years under great and peculiar difficulty. A disruption of the Federal Union, heretofore only menaced, is now formidably attempted.

I hold that in contemplation of universal law and of the Constitution the Union of these States is perpetual. Perpetuity is implied, if not expressed, in the fundamental law of all national governments. It is safe to assert that no government proper ever had a provision in its organic law for its own termination. Continue to execute all the express provisions of our National Constitution, and the Union will endure forever, it being impossible to destroy it except by some action not provided for in the instrument itself.

Again: If the United States be not a government proper, but an association of States in the nature of contract merely, can it, as a contract, be peaceably unmade by less than all the parties who made it? One party to a contract may violate it—break it, so to speak—but does it not require all to lawfully rescind it? . . .

It follows from these views that no State upon its own mere motion can lawfully get out of the Union; that *resolves* and *ordinances* to that effect are legally void, and that acts of violence within any State or States against the authority of the United States are insurrectionary or revolutionary, according to circumstances.

I therefore consider that in view of the Constitution and the laws the Union is unbroken, and to the extent of my ability, I shall take care, as the Constitution itself expressly enjoins upon me, that the laws of the Union be faithfully executed in all the States. Doing this I deem to be only a simple duty on my part, and I shall perform it so far as practicable unless my rightful masters, the American people, shall withhold the requisite means or in some authoritative manner direct the contrary. I trust this will not be regarded as a menace, but only as the declared purpose of the Union that it *will* constitutionally defend and maintain itself.

In doing this there needs to be no bloodshed or violence, and there shall be none unless it be forced upon the national authority. The power confided to me will be used to hold, occupy, and possess the property and places belonging to the Government and to collect the duties and imposts; but beyond what may be necessary for these objects, there will be no invasion, no using of force against or among the people anywhere. . . .

That there are persons in one section or another who seek to destroy the Union at all events and are glad of any pretext to do it I will neither affirm nor deny; but if there be such, I need address no word to them. To those, however, who really love the Union may I not speak?

Before entering upon so grave a matter as the destruction of our national fabric, with all its benefits, its memories, and its hopes, would it not be wise to ascertain precisely why we do it? Will you hazard so desperate a step while there is any possibility that any portion of the ills you fly from have no real existence? Will you, while the certain ills you fly to are greater than all the real ones you fly from, will you risk the commission of so fearful a mistake?

All profess to be content in the Union if all constitutional rights can be maintained. Is it true, then, that any right plainly written in the Constitution has been denied? I think not. . . .

No organic law can ever be framed with a provision specifically applicable to every question which may occur in practical administration. No foresight can anticipate nor any document of reasonable length contain express provisions for all possible questions. Shall fugitives from labor be surrendered by national or by State authority? The Constitution does not expressly say. *May* Congress prohibit slavery in the Territories? The Constitution does not expressly say. *Must* Congress protect slavery in the Territories? The Constitution does not expressly say.

From questions of this class spring all our constitutional controversies, and we divide upon them into majorities and minorities. If the minority will not acquiesce, the majority must, or the Government must cease. There is no other alternative, for continuing the Government is acquiescence on one side or the other. If a minority in such case will secede rather than acquiesce, they make a precedent which in turn will divide and ruin them, for a minority of their own will secede from them whenever a majority refuses to be controlled by such minority. For instance, why may not any portion of a new confederacy a year or two hence arbitrarily secede again, precisely as portions of the present Union now claim to secede from it? All who cherish disunion sentiments are now being educated to the exact temper of doing this.

Is there such perfect identity of interests among the States to compose a new union as to produce harmony only and prevent renewed secession?

Plainly the central idea of secession is the essence of anarchy. A majority held in restraint by constitutional checks and limitations, and always changing easily with deliberate changes of popular opinions and sentiments, is the only true sovereign of a free people. Whoever rejects it does of necessity fly to anarchy or to despotism. Unanimity is impossible. The rule of a minority, as a permanent arrangement, is wholly inadmissible; so that, rejecting the majority principle, anarchy or despotism in some form is all that is left. . . .

One section of our country believes slavery is *right* and ought to be extended, while the other believes it is *wrong* and ought not to be extended. This is the only substantial dispute. . . .

Physically speaking, we can not separate. We can not remove our respective sections from each other nor build an impassable wall between them. A husband and wife may be divorced and go out of the presence and beyond the reach of each other, but the different parts of our country can not do this. They can not but remain face to face, and intercourse, either amicable or hostile, must continue between them. Is it possible, then, to make that intercourse more advantageous or more satisfactory *after* separation than *before?* Can aliens make treaties easier than friends can make laws? Can treaties be more faithfully enforced between aliens than laws can among friends? Suppose you go to war, you can not fight always; and when, after much loss on both sides and no gain on either, you cease fighting, the identical old questions, as to terms of intercourse, are again upon you. . . .

Why should there not be a patient confidence in the ultimate justice of the people? Is there any better or equal hope in the world? In our present differences, is either party without faith of being in the right? If the Almighty Ruler of Nations, with His eternal truth and justice, be on your side of the North, or on yours of the South, that truth and that justice will surely prevail by the judgment of this great tribunal of the American people.

By the frame of the Government under which we live this same people have wisely given their public servants but little power for mischief, and have with equal wisdom provided for the return of that little to their own hands at very short intervals. While the people retain their virtue and vigilance no Administration by any extreme of wickedness or folly can very seriously injure the Government in the short space of four years.

My countrymen, one and all, think calmly and *well* upon this whole subject. Nothing valuable can be lost by taking time. If there be an object to *hurry* any of you in hot haste to a step which you would never take *deliberately,* that object will be frustrated by taking time; but no good object can be frustrated by it. Such of you as are now dissatisfied still have the old Constitution unimpaired, and, on the sensitive point, the laws of your own framing under it; while the new Administration will have no immediate power, if it would, to change either. If it were admitted that you who are dissatisfied hold the right side in the dispute, there still is no single good reason for precipitate action. Intelligence, patriotism, Christianity, and a firm reliance on Him who has never yet forsaken this favored land are still competent to adjust in the best way all our present difficulty.

In *your* hands, my dissatisfied fellow-countrymen, and not in *mine,* is the momentous issue of civil war. The Government will not assail *you.* You can have no conflict without being yourselves the aggressors. *You* have no oath registered in heaven to destroy the Government, while *I* shall have the most solemn one to "preserve, protect, and defend it."

I am loath to close. We are not enemies, but friends. We must not be enemies. Though passion may have strained it must not break our bonds of affection. The mystic chords of memory, stretching from every battlefield and patriot grave to every living heart and hearthstone all over this broad land, will yet swell the chorus of the Union, when again touched, as surely they will be, by the better angels of our nature.

HARRY MACARTHY
THE BONNIE BLUE FLAG

When South Carolina seceded from the Union on December 20, 1860, its flag was blue with a single star in the center. Five weeks later, the state adopted a new flag to represent its status as a member of the Confederacy, a blue flag with a palmetto tree and a crescent in the upper left corner. But during that five-week period, a song appeared about the first South Carolina flag that swept the South and became the national anthem of the Confederacy.

Harry Macarthy, an Arkansas-born comedian and vaudevillian, wrote "The Bonnie Blue Flag," set to the tune of a well-known Irish air, "The Irish Jaunting Car." Macarthy's "The Bonnie Blue Flag" was sung at the Mississippi Convention in Jackson where the act of secession was passed on January 9, 1861. The first, second, and last stanzas printed here were original; the others were quickly added as new states joined the Confederacy.

We are a band of brothers, and native to the
    soil,
Fighting for the property we gained by honest
    toil;
And when our rights were threatened, the cry
    rose near and far:
Hurrah! for the bonnie blue flag that bears a
    single star.

CHORUS:
Hurrah! hurrah! for Southern rights! hurrah!
Hurrah! for the bonnie blue flag that bears a
    single star

As long as the Union was faithful to her trust,
Like friends and like brothers, kind were we
    and just;
But now, when Northern treachery attempts
    our rights to mar,
We hoist, on high, the bonnie blue flag that
    bears a single star.

First gallant South Carolina nobly made the
    stand,
Then came Alabama who took her by the hand;
Next, quickly Mississippi, Georgia and Florida,
All raised, on high, the bonnie blue flag that
    bears a single star.

Ye men of valor, gather 'round the banner of
    the right,
Texas and fair Louisianna join us in the fight;
Davis, our loved President, and Stevens,
    statesman rare,
Now rally 'round the bonnie blue flag that
    bears a single star.

And here's to brave Virginia, the old Dominion
    State,
With the young Confederacy, at length, has
    linked her fate;
Impelled by her example now other States
    prepare
To hoist, on high, the bonnie blue flag that
    bears a single star.

Then cheer, boys, cheer, raise the joyous
    shout—
For Arkansas and North Carolina now have
    both gone out;
And let another rousing cheer for Tennessee be
    given—
The single star of the bonnie blue flag has
    grown to be eleven.

Then here's to our Confederacy—strong we
    are and brave,
Like patriots of old, we'll fight our heritage to
    save;
And rather than submit to shame, to die we
    would prefer—
So cheer for the bonnie blue flag that bears a
    single star.

JAMES RYDER RANDALL

MARYLAND, MY MARYLAND

"Maryland, My Maryland" was written by James Ryder Randall, a professor of English at a Louisiana college. Randall, a native of Baltimore, read about fighting in Baltimore on April 19, 1861, when a Massachusetts regiment passing through the city had been attacked by angry local residents. Both soldiers and civilians were killed in the fighting. This incident inspired him to write a hymn to southern resistance, and an appeal to Maryland to join the Confederacy (which never happened).

The poem was published first in a newspaper, the New Orleans *Delta,* where it gave a great boost to southern morale. When the poem was introduced in Baltimore, it was set to the music of "Tannenbaum, O Tannenbaum" and printed by a pro-Confederate music publisher with the Maryland state coat of arms on the cover. As happened to many popular songs of the period, "Maryland, My Maryland" promptly circulated in several versions, including some written to favor the Union cause. One Union song began "The rebel horde is on thy shore/Maryland! my Maryland!/Arise and drive him from thy door . . ."

Maryland voted overwhelmingly to remain in the Union. However, the city of Baltimore, occupied by Union forces, was staunchly pro-Confederate.

The despot's heel is on thy shore,
Maryland, my Maryland!
His torch is at thy temple door,
Maryland, my Maryland!
Avenge the patriotic gore
That flecked the streets of Baltimore,
And be the battle queen of yore,
Maryland, my Maryland!

Hark to an exiled son's appeal,
Maryland, my Maryland!
My mother state, to thee I kneel,
Maryland, my Maryland!
For life or death, for woe or weal,
Thy peerless chivalry reveal,

And gird thy beauteous limbs with steel,
Maryland, my Maryland!

Thou wilt not cower in the dust,
Maryland, my Maryland!
Thy beaming sword shall never rust,
Maryland, my Maryland!
Remember Carroll's sacred trust,
Remember Howard's warlike thrust,
And all thy slumberers with the just,
Maryland, my Maryland!

Come! 'Tis the red dawn of the day,
Maryland, my Maryland!
Come with thy panoplied array,
Maryland, my Maryland!

With Ringgold's spirit for the fray,
With Watson's blood at Monterey,
With fearless Lowe and dashing May,
Maryland, my Maryland!

Dear mother, burst the tyrant's chain,
Maryland, my Maryland!
Virginia should not call in vain,
Maryland, my Maryland!
She meets her sisters on the plain,
"Sic temper," 'tis the proud refrain
That baffles minion's back amain,
Maryland, my Maryland!

Come! for thy shield is bright and strong,
Maryland, my Maryland!
Come! for thy dalliance does thee wrong,
Maryland, my Maryland!
Come to thine own heroic throng,
Stalking with liberty along,
And chant thy dauntless slogan-song,
Maryland, my Maryland!

I see the blush upon thy cheek,
Maryland, my Maryland!

But thou wast ever bravely meek,
Maryland, my Maryland!
But lo! there surges forth a shriek,
From hill to hill, from creek to creek,
Potomac calls to Chesapeake,
Maryland, my Maryland!

Thou wilt not yield the vandal toll,
Maryland, my Maryland!
Thou wilt not crook to his control,
Maryland, my Maryland!
Better the fire upon the roll,
Better the shot, the blade, the bowl,
Than crucifixion of the soul,
Maryland, my Maryland!

I hear the distant thunder-hum,
Maryland, my Maryland!
The "Old Line's" bugle, fife and drum,
Maryland, my Maryland!
She is not dead, nor deaf nor dumb,
Huzza! she spurns the Northern scum—
She breathes! She burns! She'll come! She'll
    come!
Maryland, my Maryland!

President Abraham Lincoln inspects the headquarters of the Army of the Potomac on October 1, 1862.

GEORGE F. ROOT

BATTLE CRY OF FREEDOM

"Battle Cry of Freedom," also known as "Rally Round the Flag, Boys," was written by George F. Root in 1861. It is sung to a rousing patriotic tune and was probably the best loved of Union songs. Root composed two different versions, one a "rallying" song for civilians, the other a "battle" song for soldiers. The first version was sung at patriotic gatherings, at conscription meetings, and in camp; the second was a marching song.

Root (1820–1895) wrote the popular Union marching song "Tramp! Tramp! Tramp!" and other songs of the period, including "Just Before the Battle, Mother" and "There's Music in the Air, Boys." He later wrote hymns and cantatas. His most successful sentimental ballad was "Rosalie, the Prairie Flower." He published his autobiography, *The Story of a Musical Life*, in 1891.

Rallying Song

Yes, we'll rally 'round the flag, boys, we'll rally
    once again,
  Shouting the battle-cry of freedom;
We will rally from the hillside, we'll gather
    from the plain,
  Shouting the battle-cry of freedom.

CHORUS:
The Union forever, Hurrah! boys, hurrah!
Down with the traitor and up with the star;
While we rally 'round the flag, boys, rally once
    again,
Shouting the battle-cry of freedom.

We are springing to the call of our Brothers
    gone before,
And we'll fill the vacant ranks with a million
    freemen more.

We will welcome to our numbers the loyal,
    true and brave,
And altho' they may be poor, not a man shall be
    a slave.

So we're springing to the call from the East and
    from the West,
And we'll hurl the rebel crew from the land we
    love the best.

Battle Song

We are marching to the field, boys, we're going
    to the fight,
  Shouting the battle-cry of freedom;
And we bear the glorious stars for the Union
    and the right,
  Shouting the battle-cry of freedom.

CHORUS:
The Union forever, Hurrah! boys, hurrah!
Down with the traitor, up with the star;
For we're marching to the field, boys, going to
    the fight
  Shouting the battle-cry of freedom.

We will meet the rebel host, boys, with fearless
    hearts and true,
And we'll show what Uncle Sam has for loyal
    boys to do.

If we fall amid the fray, boys, we'll face them to
    the last,
And our comrades brave shall hear us, as they
    go rushing past.

Yes, for Liberty and Union we're springing to
    the fight,
And the vict'ry shall be ours, for we're rising in
    our might.

THE JOHN BROWN SONG

Although this song is sung about John Brown, the zealous martyr of Harpers Ferry, it was not originally written about him. Apparently, it was written by members of the "Tiger" battalion of the Twelfth Massachusetts Regiment, stationed at Fort Warren in Boston, as a spoof of their own Sergeant John Brown. The music was borrowed from a popular camp song written by William Steffe of South Carolina, whose original refrain was "Say, brothers, will you meet us on Canaan's happy shore?" Published in Boston in the summer of 1861 with the title "Glory Hallelujah!" the song was an immediate hit and a popular marching song. As the abolition of slavery came to be one of the war's goals, the song became a staple among soldiers and civilians alike. It came to be known as "John Brown's Body" or "The John Brown Song."

John Brown's body lies a-mouldering in the
    grave [Repeat 3 times],
His soul is marching on.

CHORUS:
Glory, glory, Hallelujah! Glory, glory,
    Hallelujah!
Glory, glory, Hallelujah! His soul is marching
    on.

The stars of heaven are looking kindly down
On the grave of old John Brown.

He's gone to be a soldier in the army of the
    Lord
His soul is marching on.

John Brown's knapsack is strapped upon his
    back
His soul is marching on.

His pet lambs will meet him on the way
And they'll go marching on.

They will hang Jeff Davis to a sour apple tree
As they go marching on.

JULIA WARD HOWE
BATTLE HYMN OF THE REPUBLIC

Julia Ward Howe (1819–1910) wrote "The Battle Hymn of the Republic" in the early morning hours of November 18, 1861. A well-known abolitionist, poet, suffragist, and humanitarian, she was visiting Washington, D.C., with her husband, Dr. Samuel Gridley Howe, a prominent Massachusetts reformer. On the previous day, the Howes had observed army maneuvers south of the Potomac and had joined the soldiers in singing the popular "John Brown's Body." A companion suggested that she write new lyrics for the marching song. According to her account, she rose before dawn, found pen and paper, and wrote "Battle Hymn of the Republic" while her infant daughter slept nearby. It was published (without her name) in *The Atlantic Monthly* in February 1862. The song won great praise from eminent literary figures like Ralph Waldo Emerson, William Cullen Bryant, and Henry Wadsworth Longfellow, but, more importantly, it was immediately embraced by the Union army as its marching song. It was the only Civil War song that eventually rose above sectionalism to become a truly national song; it was sung by American troops in the Spanish-American War, World War I, and World

War II. Its durability as a national song can be attributed not merely to its spirited music, but to the fact that the lyrics are simultaneously patriotic, religious, and a celebration of freedom.

Mine eyes have seen the glory of the coming
   of the Lord;
He is trampling out the vintage where the
   grapes of wrath are stored;
He hath loosed the fateful lightning of His
   terrible swift sword:
           His truth is marching on.

I have seen Him in the watch-fires of a hundred
   circling camps;
They have builded Him an altar in the evening
   dews and damps;
I can read His righteous sentence by the dim
   and flaring lamps:
           His day is marching on.

I have read a fiery gospel writ in burnished
   rows of steel:
"As ye deal with my contemners, so with you
   my grace shall deal;

Let the Hero, born of woman, crush the
   serpent with his heel,
           Since God is marching on."

He has sounded forth the trumpet that shall
   never call retreat;
He is sifting out the hearts of men before His
   judgment-seat:
Oh, be swift, my soul, to answer Him! be
   jubilent, my feet!
           Our God is marching on.

In the beauty of the lilies Christ was born
   across the sea,
With a glory in his bosom that transfigures you
   and me:
As he died to make men holy, let us die to
   make men free,
           While God is marching on.

JOHN GREENLEAF WHITTIER
BARBARA FRIETCHIE

Written in 1863, "Barbara Frietchie" became a well-known patriotic poem, often anthologized and lovingly memorized. For a century or so, the line " 'Shoot, if you must, this old gray head,/But spare your country's flag,' she said" maintained a special niche in the nation's cultural vocabulary. Whittier insisted that the story was true, that it was well known in Washington and Maryland, and that he had no reason to doubt its accuracy. True or not, the poem has delighted several generations of Americans.

Up from the meadows rich with corn,
Clear in the cool September morn,

The clustered spires of Frederick stand
Green-walled by the hills of Maryland.

Round about them orchards sweep,
Apple and peach tree fruited deep,

Fair as the garden of the Lord
To the eyes of the famished rebel horde,

On that pleasant morn of the early fall
When Lee marched over the mountain-wall;

Over the mountains winding down,
Horse and foot, into Frederick town.

Forty flags with their silver stars,
Forty flags with their crimson bars,

Flapped in the morning wind: the sun
Of noon looked down, and saw not one.

Up rose old Barbara Frietchie then,
Bowed with her fourscore years and ten;

Bravest of all in Frederick town,
She took up the flag the men hauled down;

In her attic window the staff she set,
To show that one heart was loyal yet.

Up the street came the rebel tread,
Stonewall Jackson riding ahead.

Under his slouched hat left and right
He glanced; the old flag met his sight.

"Halt!"—the dust-brown ranks stood fast.
"Fire!"—out blazed the rifle-blast.

It shivered the window, pane and sash;
It rent the banner with seam and gash.

Quick, as it fell, from the broken staff
Dame Barbara snatched the silken scarf.

She leaned far out on the window-sill,
And shook it forth with a royal will.

"Shoot, if you must, this old gray head,
But spare your country's flag," she said.

A shade of sadness, a blush of shame,
Over the face of the leader came;

The nobler nature within him stirred
To life at that woman's deed and word;

"Who touches a hair on yon gray head
Dies like a dog! March on!" he said.

All day long through Frederick street
Sounded the tread of marching feet:

All day long that free flag tost
Over the heads of the rebel host.

Ever its torn folds rose and fell
On the loyal winds that loved it well;

And through the hill-gaps sunset light
Shone over it with a warm good-night.

Barbara Frietchie's work is o'er,
And the Rebel rides on his raids no more.

Honor to her! and let a tear
Fall, for her sake, on Stonewall's bier.

Over Barbara Frietchie's grave
Flag of Freedom and Union, wave!

Peace and order and beauty draw
Round thy symbol of light and law;

And ever the stars above look down
On thy stars below in Frederick town!

ABRAHAM LINCOLN

THE GETTYSBURG ADDRESS

Four score and seven years ago our fathers brought forth on this continent, a new nation, conceived in liberty, and dedicated to the proposition that all men are created equal.

The victory of Union troops at Gettysburg, Pennsylvania, on July 3, 1863, marked a crucial turning point in the Civil War. General Robert E. Lee had invaded Pennsylvania in hopes of dividing and demoralizing the North and bringing a quick end to the war. The Battle of Gettysburg was the bloodiest of the war. The Union suffered 23,000 casualties, while 28,000 Confederate soldiers were killed, wounded, or missing. The North reacted joyously to the triumph at Gettysburg. Four months later, President

The charge at Fort Wagner, South Carolina, in July 1863 by the 54th Massachusetts Volunteers, an all-black regiment led by Colonel Robert Gould Shaw, who was white. This lithograph, by Kurz and Allison, was printed in 1890.

Abraham Lincoln visited the battlefield to dedicate a cemetery for the victims of the great battle. The speech was delivered on November 19, 1863.

Lincoln's Gettysburg Address is one of the most beautiful and poetic statements in American literature. Though it celebrated a military victory, it is not martial in spirit; rather, it is a moving tribute to those who made the ultimate sacrifice and to the ideals for which they died.

Four score and seven years ago our fathers brought forth on this continent, a new nation, conceived in liberty, and dedicated to the proposition that all men are created equal.

Now we are engaged in a great civil war, testing whether that nation or any nation so conceived and so dedicated, can long endure.

We are met on a great battle-field of that war. We have come to dedicate a portion of that field, as a final resting place for those who here gave their lives that that nation might live. It is altogether fitting and proper that we should do this.

But, in a larger sense, we can not dedicate— we can not consecrate—we can not hallow—

this ground. The brave men, living and dead, who struggled here, have consecrated it, far above our poor power to add or detract. The world will little note, nor long remember what we say here, but it can never forget what they did here. It is for us the living, rather, to be dedicated here to the unfinished work which they who fought here have thus far so nobly advanced. It is rather for us to be here dedicated to the great task remaining before us—that from these honored dead we take increased devotion to that cause for which they gave the last full measure of devotion—that we here highly resolve that these dead shall not have died in vain —that this nation, under God, shall have a new birth of freedom—and that government of the people, by the people, for the people, shall not perish from the earth.

ABRAHAM LINCOLN

SECOND INAUGURAL ADDRESS

With malice toward none, with charity for all, with firmness in the right as God gives us to see the right, let us strive on to finish the work we are in, to bind up the nation's wounds, to care for him who shall have borne the battle and for his widow and his orphan, to do all which may achieve and cherish a just and lasting peace among ourselves and with all nations.

Until late in the summer of 1864, Lincoln did not expect to win the presidential election. He believed that the Democratic candidate, General George B. McClellan, would carry the victory. The Democratic Party wanted an end to the war and was prepared to negotiate away Lincoln's commitment to emancipation in exchange for peace. However, victories by Union troops in the autumn of 1864, particularly the fall of Atlanta, turned the tide, both on the field and at the ballot box.

Lincoln delivered his second inaugural address in Washington on March 4, 1865. It is Lincoln at his best: honest, simple, and eloquent. He knew that the war was all but over. He knew that the time had come to reflect on the nation's ordeal and to look to the future.

At this second appearing to take the oath of the Presidential office there is less occasion for an extended address than there was at the first. Then a statement somewhat in detail of a course to be pursued seemed fitting and proper. Now, at the expiration of four years, during which public declarations have been constantly called forth on every point and phase of the great contest which still absorbs the attention and engrosses the energies of the nation, little that is new could be presented. The progress of our arms, upon which all else chiefly depends, is as well known to the public as to myself, and it is, I trust, reasonably satisfactory and encouraging to all. With high hope for the future, no prediction in regard to it is ventured.

On the occasion corresponding to this four years ago all thoughts were anxiously directed to an impending civil war. All dreaded it, all sought to avert it. While the inaugural address was being delivered from this place, devoted altogether to *saving* the Union without war, insurgent agents were in the city seeking to *destroy* it without war—seeking to dissolve the

Union and divide effects by negotiation. Both parties deprecated war, but one of them would *make* war rather than let the nation survive, and the other would *accept* war rather than let it perish, and the war came.

One-eighth of the whole population were colored slaves, not distributed generally over the Union, but localized in the southern part of it. These slaves constituted a peculiar and powerful interest. All knew that this interest was somehow the cause of war. To strengthen, perpetuate, and extend this interest was the object for which the insurgents would rend the Union even by war, while the Government claimed no right to do more than to restrict the territorial enlargement of it. Neither party expected for the war the magnitude or the duration which it has already attained. Neither anticipated that the

cause of the conflict might cease with or even before the conflict itself should cease. Each looked for an easier triumph, and a result less fundamental and astounding. Both read the same Bible and pray to the same God, and each invokes His aid against the other. It may seem strange that any men should dare to ask a just God's assistance in wringing their bread from the sweat of other men's faces, but let us judge not, that we be not judged. The prayers of both could not be answered. That of neither has been answered fully. The Almighty has His own purposes. "Woe unto the world because of offenses; for it must needs be that offenses come, but woe to that man by whom the offense cometh." If we shall suppose that American slavery is one of those offenses which, in the providence of God, must needs come, but which, having continued

The young boys who joined the Confederate and Union armies to serve as drummer boys sometimes fought and died in battle. The Union soldier shown here is David Wood, age ten; the Confederate soldier is unidentified.

through His appointed time, He now wills to remove, and that He gives to both North and South this terrible war as the woe due to those by whom the offense came, shall we discern therein any departure from those divine attributes which the believers in a living God always ascribe to Him? Fondly do we hope, fervently do we pray, that this mighty scourge of war may speedily pass away. Yet, if God wills that it continue until all the wealth piled by the bondsman's two hundred and fifty years of unrequited toil shall be sunk, and until every drop of blood drawn with the lash shall be paid by another drawn with the sword, as was said three thousand years ago, so still it must be said "the judgments of the Lord are true and righteous altogether."

With malice toward none, with charity for all, with firmness in the right as God gives us to see the right, let us strive on to finish the work we are in, to bind up the nation's wounds, to care for him who shall have borne the battle and for his widow and his orphan, to do all which may achieve and cherish a just and lasting peace among ourselves and with all nations.

He Returns No More *was painted by Paul Schnitzler in 1868. With 618,000 deaths, the Civil War had the highest death toll of any war in American history.*

WALT WHITMAN

I HEAR AMERICA SINGING and O CAPTAIN! MY CAPTAIN!

Walt Whitman (1819–1892) was born on Long Island, New York, and grew up in Brooklyn, New York. Printer, journalist, teacher, and government clerk, Whitman edited several newspapers, including the Brooklyn *Daily Eagle*.

Whitman first published *Leaves of Grass*, in 1855, at his own expense. Only about nine hundred copies were printed, most of which he gave to friends. A slender volume, consisting of twelve untitled poems and a preface, it initially attracted little attention. In time, however, it influenced generations of American poets. Whitman's innovative free verse—without rhyme or meter—and his realistic imagery and personal tone represented an abrupt departure from conventional poetry. *Leaves of Grass* was expanded and revised periodically by Whitman throughout his life.

"I Hear America Singing" was published in 1860. "O Captain! My Captain!" was written soon after Lincoln's assassination and was published in Whitman's *Sequel to Drum-Taps* (1865–66).

I Hear America Singing

I hear America singing, the varied carols I hear,
Those of mechanics, each one singing his as it
    should be blithe and strong,
The carpenter singing his as he measures his
    plank or beam,
The mason singing his as he makes ready for
    work, or leaves off work,
The boatman singing what belongs to him in
    his boat, the deckhand singing on the
    steamboat deck,
The shoemaker singing as he sits on his bench,
    the hatter singing as he stands,
The wood-cutter's song, the ploughboy's on his
    way in the morning, or at noon
    intermission or at sundown,
The delicious singing of the mother, or of the
    young wife at work, or of the girl sewing
    or washing,
Each singing what belongs to him or her and to
    none else,
The day what belongs to the day—at night the
    party of young fellows, robust, friendly,
Singing with open mouths their strong
    melodious songs.

O Captain! My Captain!

O Captain! my Captain! our fearful trip is done,
The ship has weather'd every rack, the prize
    we sought is won,

The port is near, the bells I hear, the people all
    exulting,
While follow eyes the steady keel, the vessel
    grim and daring;
    But O heart! heart! heart!
        O the bleeding drops of red,
            Where on the deck my Captain lies,
                Fallen cold and dead.

O Captain! my Captain! rise up and hear the
    bells;
Rise up—for you the flag is flung—for you the
    bugle trills,
For you bouquets and ribbon'd wreaths—for
    you the shores a-crowding,
For you they call, the swaying mass, their eager
    faces turning;
    Here Captain! dear father!
        This arm beneath your head!
            It is some dream that on the deck,
                You've fallen cold and dead.

My Captain does not answer, his lips are pale
    and still,
My father does not feel my arm, he has no
    pulse nor will,
The ship is anchor'd safe and sound, its voyage
    closed and done,
From fearful trip the victor ship comes in with
    object won;
    Exult O shores, and ring O bells!
        But I with mournful tread,
            Walk the deck my Captain lies,
                Fallen cold and dead.

FREDERICK DOUGLASS

SPEECH TO THE AMERICAN ANTI-SLAVERY SOCIETY

Slavery is not abolished until the black man has the ballot.

With the assurance of a northern victory over the South, the fight against slavery appeared to be won. Congress approved the Thirteenth Amendment to the Constitution, prohibiting slavery, on February 1, 1865, and within a week eight states ratified the amendment. It was only a matter of months until it was adopted officially. But what would happen to the newly freed blacks? What legal protections would be available to guarantee their rights? No one could predict what the future held. The American Anti-Slavery Society met in Boston to discuss whether it had reason to exist, now that slavery had become a thing of the past. Frederick Douglass spoke on May 10, 1865, urging the society not to disband but to continue the fight against racial discrimination. With a certainty born of hard experience, he knew that the subordination of blacks, whatever it might be called, would continue until blacks were able to exercise the rights of citizenship without fear and to receive the full protection of the laws.

. . . I do not wish to appear here in any fault-finding spirit, or as an impugner of the motives of those who believe that the time has come for this Society to disband. I am conscious of no suspicion of the purity and excellence of the motives that animate the President of this Society [William Lloyd Garrison], and other gentlemen who are in favor of its disbandment. I take this ground; whether this Constitutional Amendment [the thirteenth] is law or not, whether it has been ratified by a sufficient number of States to make it law or not, I hold that the work of Abolitionists is not done. Even if every State in the Union had ratified that Amendment, while the black man is confronted in the legislation of the South by the word "white," our work as Abolitionists, as I conceive it, is not done. I took the ground, last night, that the South, by unfriendly legislation, could make our liberty, under that provision, a delusion, a mockery, and a snare, and I hold that ground now. What advantage is a provision like this Amendment to the black man, if the Legislature of any State can to-morrow declare that no black man's testimony shall be received in a court of law? Where are we then? Any wretch may enter the house of a black man, and commit any violence he pleases; if he happens to do it only in the presence of black persons, he goes unwhipt of justice. ["Hear, hear."] And don't tell me that those people down there have become so just and honest all at once that they will not pass laws denying to black men the right to testify against white men in the courts of law. Why, our Northern States have done it. Illinois, Indiana and Ohio have done it. Here, in the midst of institutions that have gone forth from old Plymouth Rock, the black man has been excluded from testifying in the courts of law; and if the Legislature of every Southern State to-morrow pass a law, declaring that no Negro shall testify in any courts of law, they will not violate that provision of the Constitution. Such laws exist now at the South, and they might exist under this provision of the Constitution, that there shall be neither slavery not involuntary servitude in any State of the Union. . . .

Slavery is not abolished until the black man has the ballot. While the Legislatures of the South retain the right to pass laws making any discrimination between black and white, slavery still lives there. [Applause.] As Edmund Quincy once said, "While the word 'white' is on the statute-book of Massachusetts, Massachusetts is a slave State. While a black man can be turned out of a car in Massachusetts, Massachusetts is a slave State. While a slave can be taken from old Massachusetts, Massachusetts is a slave State." That is what I heard Edmund Quincy say twenty-three or twenty-four years ago. I never forget such a thing. Now, while the black man can be denied a vote, while the Legislatures of the South can take from him the right to keep and bear arms, as they can—they would not allow a Negro to walk with a cane where I came from, they would not allow five of them to assemble together—the work of the Abolitionists is not finished. Notwithstanding the provision in the Constitution of the United States, that the right to keep and bear arms shall not be abridged, the black man has never had the right either to keep or bear arms; and the Legislatures of the States will still have the power to forbid it, under this Amendment. They can carry on a system of unfriendly legislation, and will they not do it? Have they not got prejudice there to do it with? Think you, that because they are for the moment in the talons and beak of our glorious eagle, instead of the slave being there, as formerly, that they are converted? I hear of the loyalty at Wilmington, the loyalty at South Carolina—what is it worth?

["Not a straw."]

Not a straw. I thank my friend for admitting it. They are loyal while they see 200,000 sable soldiers, with glistening bayonets, walking in their midst. [Applause.] But let the civil power of the South be restored, and the old prejudices and hostility to the Negro will revive. Aye, the very fact that the Negro has been used to defeat this rebellion and strike down the standards of the Confederacy will be a stimulus to all their hatred, to all their malice, and lead them to legislate with greater stringency towards this class than ever before. [Applause.] The American people are bound—bound by their sense of honor (I hope by their sense of honor, at least, by a just sense of honor), to extend the franchise to the Negro; and I was going to say, that the Abolitionists of the American Anti-Slavery Society were bound to "stand still, and see the salvation of God," until that work is done. [Applause.] Where shall the black man look for support, my friends, if the American Anti-Slavery Society fails him? ["Hear, hear."] From whence shall we expect a certain sound from the trumpet of freedom, when the old pioneer, when this Society that has survived mobs, and martyrdom, and the combined efforts of priest-craft and state-craft to suppress it, shall all at once subside, on the mere intimation that the Constitution has been amended, so that neither slavery not involuntary servitude shall hereafter be allowed in this land? What did the slaveholders of Richmond say to those who objected to arming the Negro, on the ground that it would make him a freeman? Why, they said, "The argument is absurd. We may make these Negroes fight for us; but while we retain the political power of the South, we can keep them in their subordinate positions." That was the argument; and they were right. They might have employed the Negro to fight for them, and while they retained in their hands power to exclude him from political rights, they could have reduced him to a condition similar to slavery. They would not call it slavery, but some other name. Slavery has been fruitful in giving itself names. It has been called "the peculiar institution," "the social system," and the "impediment," as it was called by the General conference of the Methodist Episcopal Church. It has been called by a great many names, and it will call itself by yet another name; and you and I and all of us had better wait and see what new form this old monster will assume, in what new skin this old snake will come forth. [Loud applause.]

AFTER THE CIVIL WAR

Photographer William Henry Jackson on Yosemite Ledge in the 1880s. Jackson accompanied government surveying expeditions to the West and was the first to photograph Yellowstone and Pike's Peak.

FRANCIS MILES FINCH

THE BLUE AND THE GRAY

Francis Miles Finch (1827–1907) was a judge of the New York Court of Appeals and later taught law at Cornell University. His poem "The Blue and the Gray," which first appeared in *The Atlantic Monthly* in 1867, was printed in the hugely successful 1879 edition of *McGuffey's Reader*. Consequently, it was known by millions of schoolchildren. The poem was frequently recited at Memorial Day ceremonies and was said to have been inspired by the women of Columbus, Mississippi, who spread flowers over the graves of both the Union and the Confederate dead.

By the flow of the inland river,
   Whence the fleets of iron have fled,
Where the blades of the grave grass quiver,
   Asleep are the ranks of the dead;—
      Under the sod and the dew,
         Waiting the judgment day;—
      Under the one, the Blue;
         Under the other, the Gray.

These in the robings of glory,
   Those in the gloom of defeat,
All with the battle blood gory,
   In the dusk of eternity meet;—
      Under the sod and the dew,
         Waiting the judgment day;—
      Under the laurel, the Blue;
         Under the willow, the Gray.

From the silence of sorrowful hours
   The desolate mourners go,
Lovingly laden with flowers
   Alike for the friend and the foe,—
      Under the sod and the dew,
         Waiting the judgment day;—
      Under the roses, the Blue;
         Under the lilies, the Gray.

So with an equal splendor
   The morning sun rays fall,
With a touch, impartially tender,
   On the blossoms blooming for all;—

      Under the sod and the dew,
         Waiting the judgment day;—
      'Broidered with gold, the Blue;
         Mellowed with gold, the Gray.

So, when the summer calleth,
   On forest and field of grain
With an equal murmur falleth
   The cooling drip of the rain;—
      Under the sod and the dew,
         Waiting the judgment day;—
      Wet with the rain, the Blue;
         Wet with the rain, the Gray.

Sadly, but not with upbraiding,
   The generous deed was done;
In the storm of the years that are fading,
   No braver battle was won;—
      Under the sod and the dew,
         Waiting the judgment day;—
      Under the blossoms, the Blue;
         Under the garlands, the Gray.

No more shall the war cry sever,
   Or the winding rivers be red;
They banish our anger forever
   When they laurel the graves of our dead!
      Under the sod and the dew,
         Waiting the judgment day;—
      Love and tears for the Blue,
         Tears and love for the Gray.

WOMEN'S RIGHT TO VOTE

It was we, the people, not we, the white male citizens, nor we, the male citizens; but we, the whole people, who formed this Union.

Susan B. Anthony (1820–1906) grew up in a liberal Quaker family in Massachusetts. She taught school, and as an unmarried woman she became acutely aware of women's need for economic and personal independence. She worked actively in the temperance and abolition movements in New York. In 1851, she met Elizabeth Cady Stanton, who was then raising her large brood of children. Anthony was free to travel, speak, and organize during a long period when Stanton had to remain at home with her children. They formed a working partnership on behalf of women's rights that lasted for the rest of their lives and shaped the course of American feminism.

In the 1872 presidential election, Anthony led a group of women in Rochester, New York, to the polls to vote. Since women's suffrage was illegal, she was arrested and indicted. Before her trial in June 1873, Anthony traveled widely in upstate New York, giving the following speech about the injustice of denying women the suffrage. She was ultimately convicted and fined, but she refused to pay the fine. No attempt was made to collect. In this speech, she argued that no Constitutional amendment was needed to "give" women the vote, because the Fourteenth Amendment—passed in 1868—said that "all persons born or naturalized in the United States" were citizens and entitled to the rights of citizenship. Since women were persons and citizens, she insisted that they were fully entitled to vote.

I stand before you under indictment for the alleged crime of having voted at the last presidential election, without having a lawful right to vote. It shall be my work this evening to prove to you that in thus doing, I not only committed no crime, but instead simply exercised my citizen's rights, guaranteed to me and all United States citizens by the National Constitution beyond the power of any State to deny.

Our democratic-republican government is based on the idea of the natural right of every individual member thereof to a voice and a vote in making and executing the laws. We assert the province of government to be to secure the people in the enjoyment of their inalienable rights. We throw to the winds the old dogma that government can give rights. No one denies that before governments were organized each individual possessed the right to protect his own life, liberty and property. When 100 to 1,000,000 people enter into a free government, they do not barter away their natural rights; they simply pledge themselves to protect each other in the enjoyment of them through prescribed judicial and legislative tribunals. They agree to abandon the methods of brute force in the adjustment of their differences and adopt those of civilization. . . . The Declaration of Independence, the United States Constitution, the constitutions of the several States and the organic laws of the Territories, all alike propose to *protect* the people in the exercise of their God-given rights. Not one of them pretends to bestow rights.

All men are created equal, and endowed by their Creator with certain inalienable rights. Among these are life, liberty and the pursuit of happiness. To secure these, governments are instituted among men, deriving their just powers from the consent of the governed.

Here is no shadow of government authority over rights, or exclusion of any class from their full and equal enjoyment. Here is pronounced the right of all men, and "consequently," as the Quaker preacher said, "of all women," to a voice in the government. And here, in this first paragraph of the Declaration, is the assertion of the natural right of all to the ballot; for how can "the consent of the governed" be given, if the right to vote be denied? . . . The women, dissatisfied as they are with this form of government, that enforces taxation without representation—that compels them to obey laws to which they never have given their consent—that imprisons and hangs them without a trial by a jury of their peers—that robs them, in marriage, of the custody of their own persons, wages, and children —are this half of the people who are left wholly at the mercy of the other half, in direct violation of the spirit and letter of the declarations of the framers of this government, every one of which was based on the immutable principle of equal rights to all. By these declarations, kings, popes, priests, aristocrats, all were alike dethroned and placed on a common level, politically, with the lowliest born subject or serf. By them, too, men, as such, were deprived of their divine right to rule and placed on a political level with women. By the practice of these declarations all class and caste distinctions would be abolished, and slave, serf, plebeian, wife, woman, all alike rise from their subject position to the broader platform of equality.

The preamble of the Federal Constitution says:

We, the people of the United States, in order to form a more perfect union, establish justice, insure domestic tranquillity, provide for the common defence, promote the general welfare and secure the blessings of liberty to ourselves and our posterity, do ordain and establish this Constitution for the United States of America.

It was we, the people, not we, the white male citizens, nor we, the male citizens; but we, the whole people, who formed this Union. We formed it not to give the blessings of liberty but to secure them; not to the half of ourselves and the half of our posterity, but to the whole people—women as well as men. It is downright mockery to talk to women of their enjoyment of the blessings of liberty while they are denied the only means of securing them provided by this democratic-republican government—the ballot. . . .

When, in 1871, I asked [Senator Charles Sumner] to declare the power of the United States Constitution to protect women in their right to vote—as he had done for black men— he handed me a copy of all his speeches during that reconstruction period, and said:

Put "sex" where I have "race" or "color," and you have here the best and strongest argument I can make for woman. There is not a doubt but women have the constitutional right to vote, and I will never vote for a Sixteenth Amendment to guarantee it to them. I voted for both the Fourteenth and Fifteenth under protest; would never have done it but for the pressing emergency of that hour; would have insisted that the power of the original Constitution to protect all citizens in the equal enjoyment of their rights should have been vindicated through the courts. But the newly-made freedmen had neither the intelligence, wealth nor time to await that slow process. Women do possess all these in an eminent degree, and I insist that they shall appeal to the courts and through them establish the powers of our American magna charta to protect every citizen of the republic.

But, friends, when in accordance with Senator Sumner's counsel I went to the ballot-box, last November, and exercised my citizen's right to vote, the courts did not wait for me to appeal to them—they appealed to me, and indicted me on the charge of having voted illegally. . . .

For any State to make sex a qualification, which must ever result in the disfranchisement of one entire half of the people, is to pass a bill of attainder, an ex post facto law, and is therefore a violation of the supreme law of the land. By it the blessings of liberty are forever withheld from women and their female posterity. For them, this government has no just powers derived from the consent of the governed. For them this government is not a democracy; it is not a republic. It is the most odious aristocracy ever established on the face of the globe. An oligarchy of wealth, where the rich govern the poor; an oligarchy of learning, where the educated govern the ignorant; or even an oligarchy of race, where the Saxon rules the African, might be endured; but this oligarchy of sex which makes father, brothers, husband, sons, the oligarchs over the mother and sisters, the wife and daughters of every household; which ordains all men sovereigns, all women subjects—carries discord and rebellion into every home of the nation....

It is urged that the use of the masculine pronouns *he, his* and *him* in all the constitutions and laws, is proof that only men were meant to be included in their provisions. If you insist on this version of the letter of the law, we shall insist that you be consistent and accept the other horn of the dilemma, which would compel you to exempt women from taxation for the support of the government and from penalties for the violation of laws. There is no *she* or *her* or *hers* in the tax laws, and this is equally true of all the criminal laws.

Take for example, the civil rights law which I am charged with having violated; not only are all the pronouns in it masculine, but everybody knows that it was intended expressly to hinder the rebel men from voting. It reads, "If any person shall knowingly vote without *his* having a lawful right." ... I insist if government officials may thus manipulate the pronouns to tax, fine, imprison and hang women, it is their duty to thus change them in order to protect us in our right to vote....

Though the words persons, people, inhabitants, electors, citizens, are all used indiscriminately in the national and State constitutions, there was always a conflict of opinion, prior to the war, as to whether they were synonymous terms, but whatever room there was for doubt, under the old regime, the adoption of the Four-

teenth Amendment settled that question forever in its first sentence:

All persons born or naturalized in the United States, and subject to the jurisdiction thereof, are citizens of the United States, and of the State wherein they reside.

The second settles the equal status of all citizens:

No State shall make or enforce any law which shall abridge the privileges or immunities of citizens of the United States; nor shall any State deprive any person of life, liberty or property without due process of law, or deny to any person within its jurisdiction the equal protection of the laws.

The only question left to be settled now is: Are women persons? I scarcely believe any of our opponents will have the hardihood to say they are not. Being persons, then, women are citizens, and no State has a right to make any new law, or to enforce any old law, which shall abridge their privileges or immunities. Hence, every discrimination against women in the constitutions and laws of the several States is today null and void, precisely as is every one against negroes.

Is the right to vote one of the privileges or immunities of citizens? I think the disfranchised ex-rebels and ex-State prisoners all will agree that it is not only one of them, but the one without which all the others are nothing. Seek first the kingdom of the ballot and all things else shall be added, is the political injunction....

However much the doctors of the law may disagree as to whether people and citizens, in the original Constitution, were one and the same, or whether the privileges and immunities in the Fourteenth Amendment include the right of suffrage, the question of the citizen's right to vote is forever settled by the Fifteenth Amendment. "The right of citizens of the United States to vote shall not be denied or abridged by the United States, or by any State, on account of race, color or previous condition of servitude." How can the State deny or abridge the right of the citizen, if the citizen does not possess it?

There is no escape from the conclusion that to vote is the citizen's right, and the specifications of race, color or previous condition of servitude can in no way impair the force of that emphatic assertion that the citizen's right to vote shall not be denied or abridged. . . .

If, however, you will insist that the Fifteenth Amendment's emphatic interdiction against robbing United States citizens of their suffrage "on account of race, color or previous condition of servitude," is a recognition of the right of either the United States or any State to deprive them of the ballot for any or all other reasons, I will prove to you that the class of citizens for whom I now plead are, by all the principles of our government and many of the laws of the States, included under the term "previous conditions of servitude."

Consider first married women and their legal status. What is servitude? "The condition of a slave." What is a slave? "A person who is robbed of the proceeds of his labor; a person who is subject to the will of another." By the laws of Georgia, South Carolina and all the States of the South, the negro had no right to the custody and control of his person. He belonged to his master. If he were disobedient, the master had the right to use correction. If the negro did not like the correction and ran away, the master had the right to use coercion to bring him back. By the laws of almost every State in this Union today, North as well as South, the married woman has no right to the custody and control of her person. The wife belongs to the husband; and if she refuse obedience he may use moderate correction, and if she do not like his moderate correction and leave his "bed and board," the husband may use moderate coercion to bring her back. The little word "moderate," you see, is the saving clause for the wife, and would

The Executive Committee that arranged the First International Council for Women in 1888. Susan B. Anthony is second from the left in the first row, and Elizabeth Cady Stanton is fourth from the left in the first row.

doubtless be overstepped should her offended husband administer his correction with the "cat-o'-nine-tails," or accomplish his coercion with blood-hounds.

Again the slave had no right to the earnings of his hands, they belonged to his master; no right to the custody of his children, they belonged to his master; no right to sue or be sued, or to testify in the courts. If he committed a crime, it was the master who must sue or be sued. In many of the States there has been special legislation, giving married women the right to property inherited or received by bequest, or earned by the pursuit of any avocation outside the home; also giving them the right to sue and be sued in matters pertaining to such separate property; but not a single State of this Union has ever secured the wife in the enjoyment of her right to equal ownership of the joint earnings of the marriage copartnership. And since, in the nature of things, the vast majority of married women never earn a dollar by work outside their families, or inherit a dollar from their fathers, it follows that from the day of their marriage to the day of the death of their husbands not one of them ever has a dollar, except it shall please her husband to let her have it. . . .

Is anything further needed to prove woman's condition of servitude sufficient to entitle her to the guarantees of the Fifteenth Amendment? Is there a man who will not agree with me that to talk of freedom without the ballot is mockery to the women of this republic, precisely as New England's orator, Wendell Phillips, at the close of the late war declared it to be to the newly emancipated black man? I admit that, prior to the rebellion, by common consent, the right to enslave, as well as to disfranchise both native and foreign born persons, was conceded to the States. But the one grand principle settled by the war and the reconstruction legislation, is the supremacy of the national government to protect the citizens of the United States in their right to freedom and the elective franchise, against any and every interference on the part of the several States; and again and again have the American people asserted the triumph of

this principle by their overwhelming majorities for Lincoln and Grant.

The one issue of the last two presidential elections was whether the Fourteenth and Fifteenth Amendments should be considered the irrevocable will of the people; and the decision was that they should be, and that it is not only the right, but the duty of the national government to protect all United States citizens in the full enjoyment and free exercise of their privileges and immunities against the attempt of any State to deny or abridge. . . .

It is upon this just interpretation of the United States Constitution that our National Woman Suffrage Association, which celebrates the twenty-fifth anniversary of the woman's rights movement next May in New York City, has based all its arguments and action since the passage of these amendments. We no longer petition legislature or Congress to give us the right to vote, but appeal to women everywhere to exercise their too long neglected "citizen's right." We appeal to the inspectors of election to receive the votes of all United States citizens, as it is their duty to do. We appeal to United States commissioners and marshals to arrest, as is their duty, the inspectors who reject the votes of United States citizens, and leave alone those who perform their duties and accept these votes. We ask the juries to return verdicts of "not guilty" in the cases of law-abiding United States citizens who cast their votes, and inspectors of election who receive and count them.

We ask the judges to render unprejudiced opinions of the law, and wherever there is room for doubt to give the benefit to the side of liberty and equal rights for women, remembering that, as Sumner says, "The true rule of interpretation under our National Constitution, especially since its amendments, is that anything *for* human rights is constitutional, everything *against* human rights unconstitutional." It is on this line that we propose to fight our battle for the ballot—peacably but nevertheless persistently—until we achieve complete triumph and all United States citizens, men and women alike, are recognized as equals in the government.

THE BALLAD OF JOHN HENRY

After the Civil War, the railroads spread across the nation from region to region until they spanned the continent. The railroad gangs produced memorable ballads, rhythmic songs to accompany the backbreaking work of blasting tunnels, laying track, and building bridges. In 1870, the Chesapeake and Ohio Railroad began blasting the Big Bend Tunnel in the Allegheny Mountains in West Virginia. Most of the workers were ex-slaves. The job of the steel driver was to hammer the long steel bits into the rock and make a hole for explosive charges. As the work progressed, the company introduced a mechanical steam drill. According to story and legend, a black steel driver named John Henry matched his strength against the steam drill. He won the contest, but fell dead.

"The Ballad of John Henry" became a fixture in American legend and song, and John Henry entered American folklore as a black Paul Bunyan, a man who would rather die than be bested by a machine. The song achieved enormous popularity as a mythic tribute to the spirit of man against machine. It can be found in many different versions, but the basic story is always the same.

John Henry was a little baby boy
You could hold him in the palm of your hand.
He gave a long and lonesome cry,
"Gonna be a steel-drivin' man, Lawd, Lawd,
Gonna be a steel-drivin' man."

They took John Henry to the tunnel,
Put him in the lead to drive,
The rock was so tall, John Henry so small,
That he laid down his hammer and he cried,
        "Lawd, Lawd,"
Laid down his hammer and he cried.

John Henry started on the right hand,
The steam drill started on the left,
"Fo' I'd let that steamdrill beat me down,
I'd hammer my fool self to death, Lawd, Lawd,
Hammer my fool self to death."

John Henry told his captain,
"A man ain't nothin' but a man,
Fo' I let your steamdrill beat me down
I'll die with this hammer in my hand, Lawd,
        Lawd,
Die with this hammer in my hand."

Now the Captain told John Henry,
"I believe my tunnel's sinkin' in."
"Stand back, Captain, and doncha be afraid,
That's nothin' but my hammer catchin' wind,
        Lawd, Lawd,
That's nothin' but my hammer catchin' wind."

John Henry told his Cap'n,
"Look yonder, boy, what do I see?
Your drill's done broke and your hole's done
        choke,
And you can't drive steel like me, Lawd, Lawd,
You can't drive steel like me."

John Henry hammerin' in the mountain,
Til the handle of his hammer caught on fire,
He drove so hard till he broke his po' heart,
Then he laid down his hammer and he died,
        Lawd, Lawd,
He laid down his hammer and he died.

They took John Henry to the tunnel,
And they buried him in the sand,
An' every locomotive come rollin' by
Say, "There lies a steel-drivin' man, Lawd, Lawd,
There lies a steel-drivin' man."

HOME ON THE RANGE

Depending on which source you choose to believe, "Home on the Range" was either written by Dr. Brewster Higley and Dan Kelley of Kansas or is a cowboy song with no known authors. According to some sources, Dr. Higley, of Hutchinson, Kansas, wrote the words in 1873, and his friend Dan Kelley, who lived at a trading post in Smith County, Kansas, set the words to music. The song was never copyrighted, and many people have claimed authorship without success. After President Franklin D. Roosevelt said that it was one of his favorite songs, it achieved great popularity.

Oh, give me a home,
Where the buffalo roam,
Where the deer and the antelope play;
Where seldom is heard a discouraging word,
And the skies are not cloudy all day.

CHORUS:
Home, home on the range,
Where the deer and the antelope play;
Where seldom is heard a discouraging word,
And the skies are not cloudy all day.

How often at night when the heavens are
     bright
With the lights of the glittering stars,

Have I stood there amazed and asked as I gazed
If their glory exceeds that of ours.

Oh, give me a land where the bright diamond
     sand
Flows leisurely down the stream;
Where the graceful white swan goes gliding
     along
Like a maid in a heavenly dream.

Where the air is so pure, the zephyrs so free,
The breezes so balmy and light,
That I would not exchange my home on the
     range,
For all the cities so bright.

I'VE BEEN WORKING ON THE RAILROAD

"I've Been Working on the Railroad," one of the most popular of American folk songs, is of unknown origin. Apparently it began as "The Levee Song" among black workers building the levees on the southern Mississippi River in Louisiana in the 1830s and 1840s. As levee building gave way to railroad building, new words were fitted to the strong melody of the song, and it became a song identified with the largely Irish work gangs building the rail lines west of the Mississippi. By 1880, almost 100,000 miles of track had been laid by men of all races and national backgrounds, and "I've Been Working on the Railroad" was known in all of the thirty-eight states. Another version of the song ("The Eyes of Texas") was adopted as the official song of the University of Texas, which opened in 1883. The second stanza, beginning "Dinah, won't you blow," was a later addition to the song. Back in the days when colleges printed song books, "I've Been Working on the Railroad" was invariably included. It was a song that everybody seemed to know and that was part of every community sing.

I've been working on the railroad,
All the live-long day,
I've been working on the railroad,
Just to pass the time away.
Don't you hear the whistle blowing,
Rise up so early in the morn;
Don't you hear the captain shouting,
"Dinah, blow your horn!"

Dinah, won't you blow,
Dinah, won't you blow,
Dinah, won't you blow your horn.

Dinah, won't you blow
Dinah, won't you blow,
Dinah, won't you blow your horn.
Someone's in the kitchen with Dinah,
Someone's in the kitchen I know,
Someone's in the kitchen with Dinah,
Strummin' on the old banjo, and singin':
Fee-fi-fidd-lee-i-o,
Fee-fi-fidd-lee-i-o,
Fee-fi-fidd-lee-i-o,
Strummin' on the old banjo.

HELEN HUNT JACKSON

A CENTURY OF DISHONOR

The tale of the wrongs, the oppressions, the murders of the Pacific-slope Indians in the last thirty years . . . is too monstrous to be believed.

Born in Amherst, Massachusetts, Helen (Fiske) Hunt Jackson (1830–1885) was raised to be a conventional wife and mother. Her father taught Latin and philosophy at Amherst College, and she was a neighbor and lifelong friend of Emily Dickinson. As a girl, she attended private schools in Ipswich and New York, and in 1852, she married an army officer, Edward B. Hunt. She dutifully followed him as he was reassigned, and gave birth to two sons, one of whom died in infancy. Eleven years after her marriage, her husband died in an accident; two years later her second son died. Bereft, she began writing poems and articles for magazines. In 1875, she married William S. Jackson, and they settled in Colorado Springs. After hearing a lecture, she became interested in the plight of the Indians and embarked on extensive research to expose the government's mistreatment of the Indians. In 1881, she published *A Century of Dishonor*, which she sent to every member of Congress; an excerpt appears below.

There is not among these three hundred bands of Indians [in the United States] one which has not suffered cruelly at the hands either of the Government or of white settlers. The poorer, the more insignificant, the more helpless the band, the more certain the cruelty and outrage to which they have been subjected. This is especially true of the bands on the Pacific slopes. These Indians found themselves of a sudden surrounded by and caught up in the great influx of gold-seeking settlers, as helpless creatures on a shore are caught up in a tidal wave. There was not time for the Government to make treaties; not even time for communities to make laws. The tale of the wrongs, the oppressions, the murders of the Pacific-slope Indians in the last thirty years would be a volume by itself, and is too monstrous to be believed.

It makes little difference, however, where one opens the record of the history of the Indians; every page and every year has its dark stain. The story of one tribe is the story of all, varied only by differences of time and place; but neither time nor place makes any difference in the main facts. Colorado is as greedy and unjust in 1880 as was Georgia in 1830, and Ohio in 1795; and the United States Government breaks promises now as deftly as then, and with added ingenuity from long practice.

One of its strongest supports in so doing is the wide-spread sentiment among the people of dislike to the Indian, of impatience with his presence as a "barrier to civilization," and distrust of it as a possible danger. The old tales of the frontier life, with its horrors of Indian warfare, have gradually, by two or three generations' telling, produced in the average mind something like an hereditary instinct of unquestioning and unreasoning aversion which it is almost impossible to dislodge or soften.

There are hundreds of pages of unimpeachable testimony on the side of the Indian; but it goes for nothing, is set down as sentimentalism or partisanship, tossed aside and forgotten.

President after president has appointed commission after commission to inquire into and report upon Indian affairs, and to make suggestions as to the best methods of managing them. The reports are filled with eloquent statements of wrongs done to the Indians, of perfidies on the part of the Government; they counsel, as earnestly as words can, a trial of the simple and unperplexing expedients of telling truth, keeping promises, making fair bargains, dealing justly in all ways and all things. These reports are bound up with the Government's Annual Reports, and that is the end of them. It would probably be no exaggeration to say that not one American citizen out of ten thousand ever sees them or knows that they exist, and yet any one of them, circulated throughout the country, read by the right-thinking, right-feeling men and women of this land, would be of itself a "campaign document" that would initiate a revolution which would not subside until the Indians' wrongs were, so far as is now left possible, righted.

In 1869 President Grant appointed a commission of nine men, representing the influence and philanthropy of six leading States, to visit the different Indian reservations, and to "examine all matters appertaining to Indian affairs."

In the report of this commission are such paragraphs as the following: "To assert that 'the Indian will not work' is as true as it would be to say that the white man will not work.

'Why should the Indian be expected to plant corn, fence lands, build houses, or do anything but get food from day to day, when experience has taught him that the product of his labor will be seized by the white man to-morrow? The most industrious white man would become a drone under similar circumstances. Nevertheless, many of the Indians" (the commissioners might more forcibly have said 130,000 of the Indians) "are already at work, and furnish ample refutation of the assertion that 'the Indian will not work.' There is no escape from the inexorable logic of facts.

"The history of the Government connections with the Indians is a shameful record of broken treaties and unfulfilled promises. The history of the border, white man's connection with the Indians is a sickening record of murder, outrage, robbery, and wrongs committed by the former, as the rule, and occasional savage outbreaks and unspeakably barbarous deeds of retaliation by the latter, as the exception.

"Taught by the Government that they had rights entitled to respect, when those rights have been assailed by the rapacity of the white man, the arm which should have been raised to protect them has ever been ready to sustain the aggressor.

"The testimony of some of the highest military officers of the United States is on record to the effect that, in our Indian wars, almost without exception, the first aggressions have been made by the white man, and the assertion is supported by every civilian of reputation who has studied the subject. In addition to the class of robbers and outlaws who find impunity in their nefarious pursuits on the frontiers, there is a large class of professedly reputable men who use every means in their power to bring on Indian wars for the sake of the profit to be realized

Ration day at Pine Ridge Reservation in South Dakota in 1891, as demoralized Sioux Indians wait their turn. Defeated by the nation's westward growth, the tribe resisted their forced transition from nomadic hunters to sedentary farmers.

from the presence of troops and the expenditures of Government funds in their midst. They proclaim death to the Indians at all times in words and publications, making no distinction between the innocent and the guilty. They irate the lowest class of men to the perpetration of the darkest deeds against their victims, and as judges and jurymen shield them from the justice due to their crimes. Every crime committed by a white man against an Indian is concealed or palliated. Every offence committed by an Indian against a white man is borne on the wings of the post or the telegraph to the remotest corner of the land, clothed with all the horrors which the reality or imagination can throw around it. Against such influences as these the people of the United States need to be warned."

To assume that it would be easy, or by any one sudden stroke of legislative policy possible,

to undo the mischief and hurt of the long past, set the Indian policy of the country right for the future, and make the Indians at once safe and happy, is the blunder of a hasty and uninformed judgment. The notion which seems to be growing more prevalent, that simply to make all Indians at once citizens of the United States would be a sovereign and instantaneous panacea for all their ills and all the Government's perplexities, is a very inconsiderate one. To administer complete citizenship of a sudden, all round, to all Indians, barbarous and civilized alike, would be as grotesque a blunder as to dose them all round with any one medicine, irrespective of the symptoms and needs of their diseases. It would kill more than it would cure. Nevertheless, it is true, as was well stated by one of the superintendents of Indian Affairs in 1857, that, "so long as they are not citizens of the United States, their rights of property must remain insecure against invasion. The doors of the federal tribunals being barred against them while wards and dependents, they can only partially exercise the rights of free government, or give to those who make, execute, and construe the few laws they are allowed to enact, dignity sufficient to make them respectable. While they continue individually to gather the crumbs that fall from the table of the United States, idleness, improvidence, and indebtedness will be the rule, and industry, thrift, and freedom from debt the exception. The utter absence of individual title to particular lands deprives every one among them of the chief incentive to labor and exertion—the very mainspring on which the prosperity of a people depends."

All judicious plans and measures for their safety and salvation must embody provisions for their becoming citizens as fast as they are fit, and must protect them till then in every right and particular in which our laws protect other "persons" who are not citizens.

There is a disposition in a certain class of minds to be impatient with any protestation against wrong which is unaccompanied or unprepared with a quick and exact scheme of remedy. This is illogical. When pioneers in a new country find a tract of poisonous and swampy wilderness to be reclaimed, they do not withhold their hands from fire and axe till they see clearly which way roads should run, where good water will spring, and what crops will best grow on the redeemed land. They first clear the swamp. So with this poisonous and baffling part of the domain of our national affairs—let us first "clear the swamp."

However great perplexity and difficulty there may be in the details of any and every plan possible for doing at this late day anything like justice to the Indian, however hard it may be for good statesmen and good men to agree upon the things that ought to be done, there certainly is, or ought to be, no perplexity whatever, no difficulty whatever, in agreeing upon certain things that ought not to be done, and which must cease to be done before the first steps can be taken toward righting the wrongs, curing the ills, and wiping out the disgrace to us of the present condition of our Indians.

Cheating, robbing, breaking promises—these three are clearly things which must cease to be done. One more thing, also, and that is the refusal of the protection of the law to the Indian's rights of property, "of life, liberty, and the pursuit of happiness."

When these four things have ceased to be done, time, statesmanship, philanthropy, and Christianity can slowly and surely do the rest. Till these four things have ceased to be done, statesmanship and philanthropy alike must work in vain, and even Christianity can reap but small harvest.

FREDERICK DOUGLASS

SPEECH AT THE NATIONAL CONVENTION OF COLORED MEN

Liberty given is never so precious as liberty sought for and fought for.

After the Civil War, three constitutional amendments were adopted to secure the rights of blacks: the Thirteenth, which prohibited slavery and involuntary servitude; the Fourteenth, which conferred citizenship on all persons born or naturalized in the United States and forbade states from making laws that deprive citizens of their rights or of their life, liberty, or property without due process of law; and the Fifteenth, which guaranteed the right to vote. Furthermore, in 1875, Congress passed a Civil Rights Act, which banned racial discrimination in public accommodations, such as inns, public vehicles, and theaters. Many whites came to believe that blacks were fully protected by the law and the Constitution. In 1877, federal troops were withdrawn from the South and Reconstruction was ended.

While many whites were satisfied that they had done all that was possible and necessary, blacks continued to be overwhelmingly poor and illiterate and to suffer racial discrimination. Black leaders tried to organize and to develop a political force, but their efforts to create black political organizations were seen as divisive.

On September 24, 1883, the great orator Frederick Douglass addressed the National Convention of Colored Men at Louisville, Kentucky, and explained why blacks needed to fight for their rights. Only three weeks later, on October 15, 1883, the United States Supreme Court struck down the Civil Rights Act of 1875. The court declared that racial discrimination in public accommodations was not contrary to the Constitution. Stripped of judicial support, the post-Civil War constitutional amendments became meaningless in the South, and the way was clear for the adoption of Jim Crow laws, which imposed racial segregation.

W ith apparent surprise, astonishment and impatience we have been asked: "What more can the colored people of this country want than they now have, and what more is possible to them?" It is said they were once slaves, they are now free; they were once subjects, they are now sovereigns; they were once outside of all American institutions, they are now inside of all and are a recognized part of the whole American people. Why, then, do they hold Colored National Conventions and thus insist upon keeping up the color line between themselves and their white fellow countrymen? We do not deny the pertinence and plausibility of these questions, nor do we shrink from a candid answer to the argument which they are supposed to contain. For we do not forget that they are not only put to us by those who have no sympathy with us, but by many who wish us well, and that in any case they deserve an answer. . . .

If liberty, with us, is yet but a name, our citizenship is but a sham, and our suffrage thus far only a cruel mockery, we may yet congratulate ourselves upon the fact, that the laws and institutions of the country are sound, just and liberal. There is hope for a people when their laws are righteous, whether for the moment they conform to their requirements or not. But until this nation shall make its practice accord with its Constitution and its righteous laws, it will not do to reproach the colored people of this country with keeping up the color line— for that people would prove themselves scarcely worthy of even theoretical freedom, to say nothing of practical freedom, if they settled down in silent, servile and cowardly submission to their wrongs, from fear of making their color visible. They are bound by every element of manhood to hold conventions, in their own name, and on their own behalf, to keep their grievances before the people and make every organized protest against the wrongs inflicted upon them within their power. They should scorn the counsels of cowards, and hang their banner on the outer wall.

Who would be free, themselves must strike the blow. We do not believe, as we are often told, that the Negro is the ugly child of the National family, and the more he is kept out of sight the better it will be for him. You know that liberty given is never so precious as liberty sought for and fought for. The man outraged is the man to make the outcry. Depend upon it, men will not care much for people who do not care for themselves. . . .

If the six millions of colored people of this

country, armed with the Constitution of the United States, with a million votes of their own to lean upon, and millions of white men at their back, whose hearts are responsive to the claims of humanity, have not sufficient spirit and wisdom to organize and combine to defend themselves from outrage, discrimination and oppression, it will be idle for them to expect that the Republican party or any other political party will organize and combine for them or care what becomes of them. Men may combine to prevent cruelty to animals, for they are dumb and cannot speak for themselves; but we are men and must speak for ourselves, or we shall not be spoken for at all. We have conventions in America for Ireland, but we should have none if Ireland did not speak for herself. It is because she makes a noise and keeps her cause before the people that other people go to her help. It was the sword of Washington that gave Independence the sword of Lafayette. In conclusion upon this color objection, we have to say that we meet here in open daylight. There is nothing sinister about us. The eyes of the nation are upon us. Ten thousand newspapers may tell if they choose of whatever is said and done here. They may commend our wisdom or condemn our folly, precisely as we shall be wise or foolish.

We put ourselves before them as honest men, and ask their judgment upon our work.

Not the least important among the subjects to which we invite your earnest attention is the condition of the laboring class at the South. Their cause is one with the laboring classes all over the world. The labor unions of the country should not throw away this colored element of strength. . . .

What labor everywhere wants, what it ought to have and will some day demand and receive, is an honest day's pay for an honest day's work. As the laborer becomes more intelligent he will develop what capital already possess—that is the power to organize and combine for its own protection. Experience demonstrates that there may be a wages of slavery only a little less galling and crushing in its effects than chattel slav-

ery, and that this slavery of wages must go down with the other. . . .

No more crafty and effective device for defrauding the Southern laborer could be adopted than the one that substitutes orders upon shopkeepers for currency in payment of wages. It has the merit of a show of honesty, while it puts the laborer completely at the mercy of the landowner and the shop-keeper. He is between the upper and the nether millstones and is hence ground to dust. It gives the shop-keeper a customer who can trade with no other storekeeper, and thus leaves the latter no motive for fair dealing except his own moral sense, which is never too strong. While the laborer holding the orders is tempted by their worthlessness as a circulating medium, to get rid of them at any sacrifice, and hence is led into extravagance and consequent destitution.

The merchant puts him off with his poorest commodities at highest prices, and can say to him take those or nothing. Worse still. By this means the laborer is brought into debt, and hence is kept always in the power of the landowner. When this system is not pursued and land is rented to the freedman, he is charged more for the use of an acre of land for a single year than the land would bring in the market if offered for sale. On such a system of fraud and wrong one might well invoke a bolt from heaven—red with uncommon wrath.

It is said if the colored people do not like the conditions upon which their labor is demanded and secured, let them leave and go elsewhere. A more heartless suggestion never emanated from an oppressor. Having for years paid them in shop orders, utterly worthless outside the shop to which they are directed, without a dollar in their pockets, brought by this crafty process into bondage to the land-owners, who can and would arrest them if they should attempt to leave them when they are told to go. . . .

It is everywhere an accepted truth, that in a country governed by the people, like ours, education of the youth of all classes is vital to its welfare, prosperity, and to its existence.

In the light of this unquestioned proposition, the patriot cannot but view with a shudder the widespread and truly alarming illiteracy as revealed by the census of 1880.

The question as to how this evil is to be remedied is an important one. Certain it is that it will not do to trust to the philanthropy of wealthy individuals or benevolent societies to remove it. The States in which this illiteracy prevails either cannot or will not provide adequate systems of education for their own youth. But however this may be, the fact remains that the whole country is directly interested in the education of every child that lives within its borders. The ignorance of any part of the American people so deeply concerns all the rest that there can be no doubt of the right to pass laws compelling the attendance of every child at school. . . .

The National Government, with its immense resources, can carry the benefits of a sound common-school education to the door of every poor man from Maine to Texas, and to withhold this boon is to neglect the greatest assurance it has of its own perpetuity. As a part of the American people we unite most emphatically with others who have already spoken on this subject, in urging Congress to lay the foundation for a great national system of aid to education at its next session. . . .

Flagrant as have been the outrages committed upon colored citizens in respect to their civil rights, more flagrant, shocking and scandalous still have been the outrages committed upon our political rights, by means of bull-dozing and Kukluxing, Mississippi plans, fraudulent counts, tissue ballots and the like devices. Three States in which the colored people outnumber the white population are without colored representation and their political voice suppressed. The colored citizens in those States are virtually disfranchised, the Constitution held in utter contempt and its provisions nullified. This has been done in the face of the Republican party and successive Republican Administrations.

It was once said by the great O'Connell that the history of Ireland might be traced like a

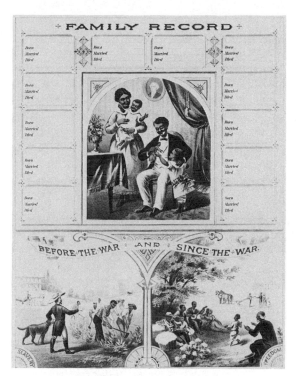

An 1880 lithograph of a black family record book, showing the changes that the Civil War and the abolition of slavery made in the lives of black Americans.

wounded man through a crowd by the blood, and the same may be truly said of the history of the colored voters of the South.

They have marched to the ballot-box in face of gleaming weapons, wounds and death. They have been abandoned by the Government and left to the laws of nature. So far as they are concerned, there is no Government or Constitution of the United States.

They are under control of a foul, haggard and damning conspiracy against reason, law and constitution. How you can be indifferent, how any leading colored men can allow themselves to be silent in presence of this state of things we cannot see. . . .

This is no question of party. It is a question of law and government. It is a question whether men shall be protected by law or be left to the mercy of cyclones of anarchy and bloodshed. It is whether the Government or the mob shall rule this land; whether the promises solemnly made to us in the Constitution be manfully kept or meanly and flagrantly broken. Upon this vital point we ask the whole people of the United States to take notice that whatever of political power we have shall be exerted for no man of any party who will not in advance of election promise to use every power given him by the Government, State or National, to make the black man's path to the ballot-box as straight, smooth and safe as that of any other American citizen. . . .

We hold it to be self-evident that no class or color should be the exclusive rulers of this country. If there is such a ruling class, there must of course be a subject class, and when this condition is once established this Government of the people, by the people and for the people, will have perished from the earth.

EMMA LAZARUS
THE NEW COLOSSUS

Emma Lazarus (1849–1887) was born into a well-to-do Jewish family in New York City and was schooled in the classics and foreign languages. Her first book of poetry and translations was published when she was only eighteen years old. In 1883, when a committe of civic leaders was trying to raise money to pay for the pedestal of the Statue of Liberty, then under construction in Paris, a number of artists and writers contributed their work to be auctioned as a fund-raising device. Lazarus wrote "The New Colossus" in honor of the Frédéric-Auguste Bartholdi statue, which was both a symbol of French-American friendship and a tribute to the ideal of liberty. This new colossus, she predicted, unlike the famous Colossus of Rhodes, one of the Seven Wonders of the Ancient World, would be a "Mother of Exiles," welcoming the outcasts of other nations.

At the time she wrote it, "The New Colossus" attracted no attention. When the Statue of Liberty was unveiled in 1886, Lazarus's poem was not mentioned. In 1903, Georgina Schuyler, an admirer of Lazarus, obtained permission to place the poem on a bronze plaque inside the statue. For another thirty years, the poem was little noted. Many Americans did not share the poem's exuberant welcome to "the wretched refuse" of Europe; periodic efforts to restrict immigration finally brought the great European exodus to a halt in 1924.

In the 1930s, as persecution of the Jews in Nazi Germany raised the refugee issue again, Louis Adamic, a Yugoslav-American journalist, helped to popularize the Lazarus poem as a way of calling attention to America's mission as a home and refuge for many peoples. Through his efforts, the poem enriched the national vocabulary with new images, redefining the way people thought of the statue and the nation itself. In 1945, the plaque containing the poem was moved from the interior of the Statue of Liberty to its main entrance.

Not like the brazen giant of Greek fame,
With conquering limbs astride from land to
    land;

Here at our sea-washed, sunset gates shall stand
A mighty woman with a torch, whose flame
Is the imprisoned lightning, and her name

Mother of Exiles. From her beacon-hand
Glows world-wide welcome; her mild eyes command
The air-bridged harbor that twin cities frame.

"Keep, ancient lands, your storied pomp!" cries she

With silent lips. "Give me your tired, your poor,
Your huddled masses yearning to breathe free,
The wretched refuse of your teeming shore.
Send these, the homeless, tempest-tost to me,
I lift my lamp beside the golden door!"

CLEMENTINE

"Clementine" appeared in the 1880s and has been popular ever since. Some sources say it is a traditional folksong of unknown origins, others say that the words and music are by Percy Montross. Since the song bears no copyright, there is no substantiation for anyone's claim as its writer. The odd and comical story of Clementine has been a perennial favorite in schoolrooms, on college campuses, and at community songfests.

In a cavern, in a canyon,
Excavating for a mine,
Lived a miner, forty-niner,
And his daughter Clementine.

CHORUS:
Oh my darling, O my darling, O my darling Clementine!
You are lost and gone forever, Dreadful sorry, Clementine!

Light she was and like a fairy,
And her shoes were number nine,
Herring boxes, without topses,
Sandals were for Clementine.

Drove she ducklings to the water
Every morning just at nine,
Hit her foot against a splinter,
Fell into the foaming brine.

Ruby lips above the water,
Blowing bubbles soft and fine;
Alas, for me! I was no swimmer,
So I lost my Clementine.

In a churchyard, near the cavern,
Where the myrtle doth entwine,
There grow roses and other posies,
Fertilized by Clementine.

Then the miner, forty-niner,
Soon began to peak and pine,
Thought he oughter jine his daughter,
Now he's with his Clementine.

In my dreams she oft doth haunt me,
With her garments soaked in brine,
Though in life I used to hug her,
Now she's dead I draw the line.

ERNEST LAWRENCE THAYER

CASEY AT THE BAT

Ernest Lawrence Thayer (1863–1940) first published "Casey at the Bat" pseudonymously in the *San Francisco Examiner* on June 3, 1888. Louis Untermeyer called the poem "the acknowledged classic of baseball, its anthem and theme song." Americans have loved it not only because of its baseball theme, but because of its anti-heroic twist at the end.

It looked extremely rocky for the Mudville
    nine that day;
The score stood two to four, with but an inning
    left to play.
So, when Cooney died at second, and Burrows
    did the same,
A pallor wreathed the features of the patrons of
    the game.

A straggling few got up to go, leaving there the
    rest,
With that hope which springs eternal within
    the human breast.
For they thought: "If only Casey could get a
    whack at that,"
They'd put even money now, with Casey at the
    bat.

But Flynn preceded Casey, and likewise so did
    Blake,
And the former was a pudd'n, and the latter
    was a fake,
So on that stricken multitude a deathlike
    silence sat;
For there seemed but little chance of Casey's
    getting to the bat.

But Flynn let drive a "single,' to the
    wonderment of all.
And the much-despised Blakey "tore the cover
    off the ball."
And when the dust had lifted, and they saw
    what had occurred,
There was Blakey safe at second, and Flynn a-
    huggin' third.

Then from the gladdened multitude went up a
    joyous yell—
It rumbled in the mountaintops, it rattled in the
    dell;
It struck up the hillside and rebounded on the
    flat;
For Casey, mighty Casey, was advancing to the
    bat.

There was ease in Casey's manner as he
    stepped into his place,

There was pride in Casey's bearing and a smile
    on Casey's face;
And when responding to the cheers he lightly
    doffed his hat,
No stranger in the crowd could doubt 'twas
    Casey at the bat.

Ten thousand eyes were on him as he rubbed
    his hands with dirt,
Five thousand tongues applauded when he
    wiped them on his shirt;
Then when the writhing pitcher ground the
    ball into his hip,
Defiance glanced in Casey's eye, a sneer curled
    Casey's lip.

And now the leather-covered sphere came
    hurtling through the air,
And Casey stood a-watching it in haughty
    grandeur there.
Close by the sturdy batsman the ball unheeded
    sped;
"That ain't my style," said Casey. "Strike one,"
    the umpire said.

From the benches, black with people, there
    went up a muffled roar,
Like the beating of the storm waves on the
    stern and distant shore.
"Kill him! kill the umpire!" shouted someone
    on the stand;
And it's likely they'd have killed him had not
    Casey raised his hand.

With a smile of Christian charity great Casey's
    visage shone;
He stilled the rising tumult, he made the game
    go on;
He signaled to the pitcher, and once more the
    spheroid flew;
But Casey still ignored it, and the umpire said,
    "Strike two."

"Fraud!" cried the maddened thousands, and
    the echo answered "Fraud!"
But one scornful look from Casey and the
    audience was awed;

They saw his face grow stern and cold, they
   saw his muscles strain,
And they knew that Casey wouldn't let the ball
   go by again.

The sneer is gone from Casey's lips, his teeth
   are clenched in hate,
He pounds with cruel vengeance his bat upon
   the plate;
And now the pitcher holds the ball, and now he
   lets it go,

And now the air is shattered by the force of
   Casey's blow.

Oh, somewhere in this favored land the sun is
   shining bright,
The band is playing somewhere, and
   somewhere hearts are light;
And somewhere men are laughing, and
   somewhere children shout,
But there is no joy in Mudville: Mighty Casey
   has struck out.

JAMES WHITCOMB RILEY

WHEN THE FROST IS ON THE PUNKIN

James Whitcomb Riley (1849–1916) grew up in Greenfield, Indiana, where he attended public schools and advanced as far as McGuffey's *Sixth Reader* (which was as far as one could go). He traveled about Indiana, painting advertisements on signs and acting in a traveling patent medicine show. All the while, he gathered local lore and observed the local dialect. He became a newspaperman, and worked for several Indiana journals. In 1877, he was fired for perpetrating a hoax, writing a poem that was allegedly by Edgar Allan Poe. At the Indianapolis *Journal*, he began writing Hoosier dialect poems that dealt with everyday concerns. Some of these poems were published in 1883 in a volume called *The Old Swimmin'-Hole and 'Leven More Poems*. He became a popular figure on the lecture circuit. His poems won a large following because of their cheerfulness, their rustic sentimentality, and their evocation of an innocent past. Riley's most popular poem was "When the Frost Is on the Punkin."

When the frost is on the punkin and the
   fodder's in the shock,
And you hear the kyouck and gobble of the
   struttin' turkey-cock
And the clackin' of the guineys, and the
   cluckin' of the hens,
And the rooster's hallylooyer as he tiptoes on
   the fence;
O, it's then's the times a feller is a-feelin' at his
   best,
With the risin' sun to greet him from a night of
   peaceful rest,
As he leaves the house, bareheaded, and goes
   out to feed the stock,
When the frost is on the punkin and the
   fodder's in the shock.

They's something kindo' harty-like about the
   atmusfere
When the heat of summer's over and the
   coolin' fall is here—
Of course we miss the flowers, and the
   blossums on the trees,
And the mumble of the hummin'-birds and
   buzzin' of the bees;
But the air's so appetizin'; and the landscape
   through the haze
Of a crisp and sunny morning of the airly
   autumn days
Is a pictur' that no painter has the colorin' to
   mock—
When the frost is on the punkin and the
   fodder's in the shock.

The husky, rusty russel of the tossels of the
  corn,
And the raspin' of the tangled leaves, as golden
  as the morn;
The stubble in the furries—kindo' lonesome-
  like, but still
A-preachin' sermons to us of the barns they
  growed to fill;
The strawstack in the medder, and the reaper
  in the shed;
The hosses in theyr stalls below—the clover
  overhead!—
O, it sets my hart a-clickin' like the tickin' of a
  clock,
When the frost is on the punkin and the
  fodder's in the shock!

Then your apples all is gethered, and the ones a
  feller keeps
Is poured around the cellar-floor in red and
  yeller heaps;
And your cider-makin' 's over, and your
  wimmern-folks is through
With their mince and apple-butter, and theyr
  souse and saussage, too!
I don't know how to tell it—but ef sich a thing
  could be
As the Angels wantin' boardin', and they'd call
  around on *me*—
I'd want to 'commodate 'em—all the whole-
  indurin' flock—
When the frost is on the punkin and the
  fodder's in the shock!

PAUL LAURENCE DUNBAR
WHEN DE CO'N PONE'S HOT

Paul Laurence Dunbar (1872–1906) was the first black American writer to commit himself to writing as a profession and also one of the first to achieve national renown. Both
his parents were former slaves; his father returned from refuge in Canada to fight in the
Civil War. Dunbar grew up in Dayton, Ohio, where he was the only black student in his
high school and editor of the school paper. While working as an elevator operator, he
paid for the publication in 1893 of his first volume of poetry, *Oak and Ivy,* and sold
copies to his passengers. A second volume, *Majors and Minors* (1895), received an ad-
miring review from William Dean Howells, the novelist, critic, and dean of late-nine-
teenth-century letters. Howells wrote the introduction to young Dunbar's third volume,
Lyrics of Lowly Life (1896), which included some of his earlier poems and brought him
national attention.

  After his new-found success, Dunbar lectured and gave poetry readings in the
United States and England. During the rest of his short life, he wrote four novels and
three more collections of poetry: *Lyrics of the Hearthside, Lyrics of Love and Laughter,*
and *Lyrics of Sunshine and Shadow.*

  Dunbar is best known for his dialect poetry; one of the best of his dialect poems is
"When de Co'n Pone's Hot." It shows the influence of James Whitcomb Riley by being
as much a celebration of black family life as "When The Frost Is on the Punkin" was a
celebration of Hoosier family life.

Dey is times in life when Nature
  Seems to slip a cog an' go,
Jes' a-rattlin' down creation,
  Lak an ocean's overflow;

When de worl' jes' stahts a-spinnin'
  Lak a picaninny's top,
An' yo' cup o' joy is brimmin'
  'Twell it seems about to slop,

An' you feel jes' lak a racah,
    Dat is trainin' fu' to trot—
When yo' mammy says de blessin'
    An' de co'n pone's hot.

When you set down at de table,
    Kin' o' weary lak an' sad,
An' you'se jes' a little tiahed
    An' purhaps a little mad;
How yo' gloom tu'ns into gladness,
    How yo' joy drives out de doubt
When de oven do' is opened,
    An' de smell comes po'in' out;
Why, de 'lectric light o' Heaven
    Seems to settle on de spot,
When yo' mammy says de blessin'
    An' de co'n pone's hot.

When de cabbage pot is steamin'
    An' de bacon good an' fat,
When de chittlins is a-sputter'n'
    So's to show you whah dey's at;

Tek away yo' sody biscuit
    Tek away yo' cake an' pie,
Fu' de glory time is comin',
    An' it's 'proachin' mighty nigh,
An' you want to jump an' hollah,
    Dough you know you'd bettah not,
When yo' mammy says de blessin'
    An' de co'n pone's hot.

I have hyeahd o' lots o' sermons,
    An' I've hyeahd o' lots o' prayers,
An' I've listened to some singin'
    Dat has tuck me up de stairs
Of de Glory-Lan' an' set me
    Jes' below de Mastah's th'one,
An' have lef' my hea't a-singin'
    In a happy aftah tone;
But dem wu'ds so sweetly murmured
    Seem to tech de softes' spot,
When my mammy says de blessin',
    An' de co'n pone's hot.

SAMUEL GOMPERS

WHAT DOES THE WORKING MAN WANT?

We want eight hours and nothing less. We have been accused of being selfish, and it has been said that we will want more; that last year we got an advance of ten cents and now we want more. We do want more.

Samuel Gompers (1850–1924) was born in London; he emigrated to New York in 1863, where he followed his father's trade as a cigar maker. As leader of the cigar makers' union, he took the union out of the Knights of Labor, an industrial union, and established the American Federation of Labor, a federation of craft unions, in 1886. Gompers was president of the AFL from 1886 to 1924, with the exception of only one year. He led the labor movement during a period in which the public was hostile to labor organizations and suspicious of radicalism. Under his leadership, the AFL avoided radical politics and concentrated on "bread-and-butter" issues like wages and working conditions. Employers bitterly resented labor unions and sought court injunctions to break strikes and boycotts. Gompers fought to shed the radical image that employers tried to pin on labor and to demonstrate that workers wanted what everyone else wanted: a better life, good wages, good working conditions, and time for self-cultivation.

This speech was delivered by Gompers on May 1, 1890, in Louisville, Kentucky, when Gompers was campaigning to establish the eight-hour workday.

. . . My friends, we have met here today to celebrate the idea that has prompted thousands of working-people of Louisville and New Albany to parade the streets of y[our city]; that prompts the toilers of Chicago to turn out by their fifty or hundred thousand of men; that prompts the vast army of wage-workers in New York to demonstrate their enthusiasm and appreciation of the importance of this idea; that prompts the toilers of England, Ireland, Germany, France, Italy, Spain, and Austria to defy the manifestos of the autocrats of the world and say that on May the first, 1890, the wage-workers of the world will lay down their tools in sympathy with the wage-workers of America, to establish a principle of limitations of hours of labor to eight hours for sleep [applause], eight hours for work, and eight hours for what we will. [Applause.]

It has been charged time and again that were we to have more hours of leisure we would merely devote it to debauchery, to the cultivation of vicious habits—in other words, that we would get drunk. I desire to say this in answer to that charge: As a rule, there are two classes in society who get drunk. One is the class who has no work to do in consequence of too much money; the other class, who also has no work to do, because it can't get any, and gets drunk on its face. [Laughter.] I maintain that that class in our social life that exhibits the greatest degree of sobriety is that class who are able, by a fair number of hours of day's work to earn fair wages—not overworked. The man who works twelve, fourteen, and sixteen hours a day requires some artificial stimulant to restore the life ground out of him in the drudgery of the day. [Applause.] . . .

We ought to be able to discuss this question on a higher ground, and I am pleased to say that the movement in which we are engaged will stimulate us to it. They tell us that the eight-hour movement can not be enforced, for the reason that it must check industrial and commercial progress. I say that the history of this country, in its industrial and commercial rela-

tions, shows the reverse. I say that is the plane on which this question ought to be discussed—that is the social question. As long as they make this question an economic one, I am willing to discuss it with them. I would retrace every step I have taken to advance this movement did it mean industrial and commercial stagnation. But it does not mean that. It means greater prosperity; it means a greater degree of progress for the whole people; it means more advancement and intelligence, and a nobler race of people. . . .

They say they can't afford it. Is that true? Let us see for one moment. If a reduction in the hours of labor causes industrial and commercial ruination, it would naturally follow increased hours of labor would increase the prosperity, commercial and industrial. If that were true, England and America ought to be at the tail end, and China at the head of civilization. [Applause.]

Is it not a fact that we find laborers in England and the United States, where the hours are eight, nine and ten hours a day—do we not find that the employers and laborers are more successful? Don't we find them selling articles cheaper? We do not need to trust the modern moralist to tell us those things. In all industries where the hours of labor are long, there you will find the least development of the power of invention. Where the hours of labor are long, men are cheap, and where men are cheap there is no necessity for invention. How can you expect a man to work ten or twelve or fourteen hours at his calling and then devote any time to the invention of a machine or discovery of a new principle or force? If he be so fortunate as to be able to read a paper he will fall asleep before he has read through the second or third line. [Laughter.]

Why, when you reduce the hours of labor, say an hour a day, just think what it means. Suppose men who work ten hours a day had the time lessened to nine, or men who work nine hours a day have it reduced to eight hours; what does it mean? It means millions of golden hours and opportunities for thought. Some men might say you will go to sleep. Well, some men might sleep sixteen hours a day; the ordinary man might try that, but he would soon find he could not do it long. He would have to do something. He would probably go to the theater one night, to a concert another night, but he could not do that every night. He would probably become interested in some study and the hours that have been taken from manual labor are devoted to mental labor, and the mental labor of one hour will produce for him more wealth than the physical labor of a dozen hours. [Applause.]

I maintain that this is a true proposition— that men under the short-hour system not only have opportunity to improve themselves, but to make a greater degree of prosperity for their employers. Why, my friends, how is it in China, how is it in Spain, how is it in India and Russia, how is it in Italy? Cast your eye throughout the universe and observe the industry that forces nature to yield up its fruits to man's necessities, and you will find that where the hours of labor are the shortest the progress of invention in machinery and the prosperity of the people are the greatest. It is the greatest impediment to progress to hire men cheaply. Wherever men are cheap, there you find the least degree of progress. It has only been under the great influence of our great republic, where our people have exhibited their great senses, that we can move forward, upward and onward, and are watched with interest in our movements of progress and reform. . . .

The man who works the long hours has no necessities except the barest to keep body and soul together, so he can work. He goes to sleep and dreams of work; he rises in the morning to go to work; he takes his frugal lunch to work; he comes home again to throw himself down on a miserable apology for a bed so that he can get that little rest that he may be able to go to work again. He is nothing but a veritable machine. He lives to work instead of working to live. [Loud applause.]

My friends, the only thing the working people need besides the necessities of life, is time. Time. Time with which our lives begin; time with which our lives close; time to cultivate the better nature within us; time to brighten our homes. Time, which brings us from the lowest condition up to the highest civilization; time, so that we can raise men to a higher plane.

My friends, you will find that it has been ascertained that there is more than a million of our brothers and sisters—able-bodied men and women—on the streets, and on the highways and byways of our country willing to work but who cannot find it. You know that it is the theory of our government that we can work or cease to work at will. It is only a theory. You know that it is only a theory and not a fact. It is true that we can cease to work when we want to, but I deny that we can work when we will, so long as there are a million idle men and women tramping the streets of our cities, searching for work. The theory that we can work or cease to work when we will is a delusion and a snare. It is a lie.

What we want to consider is, first, to make our employment more secure, and, secondly, to make wages more permanent, and, thirdly, to give these poor people a chance to work. The laborer has been regarded as a mere producing machine . . . but back of labor is the soul of man and honesty of purpose and aspiration. Now you can not, as the political economists and college professors, say that labor is a commodity to be bought and sold. I say we are American citizens with the heritage of all the great men who have stood before us; men who have sacrificed all in the cause except honor. Our enemies would like to see this movement thrust into hades, they would like to see it in a warmer climate [laughter], but I say to you that this labor movement has come to stay. [Loud applause.] Like Banquo's ghost, it will not down. [Applause.] I say the labor movement is a fixed fact. It has grown out of the necessities of the people, and, although some may desire to see it fail, still the labor movement will be found to have a strong lodgment in the hearts of the people, and we will go on until success has been achieved.

We want eight hours and nothing less. We have been accused of being selfish, and it has been said that we will want more; that last year we got an advance of ten cents and now we want more. We do want more. You will find that a man generally wants more. Go and ask a tramp what he wants, and if he doesn't want a drink he will want a good, square meal. You ask a workingman, who is getting two dollars a day, and he will say that he wants ten cents more. Ask a man who gets five dollars a day and he will want fifty cents more. The man who receives five thousand dollars a year wants six thousand dollars a year, and the man who owns eight or nine hundred thousand dollars will want a hundred thousand dollars more to make it a million, while the man who has his millions will want every thing he can lay his hands on and then raise his voice against the poor devil who wants ten cents more a day. We live in the latter part of the Nineteenth century. In the age of electricity and steam that has produced wealth a hundred fold, we insist that it has been brought about by the intelligence and energy of the workingmen, and while we find that it is now easier to produce it is harder to live. We do want more, and when it becomes more, we shall still want more. [Applause.] And we shall never cease to demand more until we have received the results of our labor. . . .

THE PLEDGE OF ALLEGIANCE

The pledge first appeared in the magazine *The Youth's Companion* on September 8, 1892, as part of a national commemoration of the four-hundredth anniversary of Christopher Columbus's voyage to the New World. It was widely adopted for use in patriotic exercises in schools. At that time, it read "I pledge allegiance to my Flag and the Republic for which it stands; one nation indivisible, with liberty and Justice for all." In 1924, the words "the flag of the United States of America" were substituted for "my Flag." In 1942, the United States government accorded official recognition to the pledge. President Dwight D. Eisenhower persuaded Congress to add the phrase "under God" to the pledge in 1954.

For years there was a dispute about the authorship of the pledge. James B. Upham and Francis Bellamy, who were both editors of *The Youth's Companion,* claimed credit. In 1957, a report by the U.S. Library of Congress supported Bellamy as the author.

According to a law passed by Congress in 1954, the person reciting the pledge is supposed to stand upright, remove any headgear, and put the right hand over the heart.

I pledge allegiance to the flag of the United States of America and to the Republic for which it stands, one nation under God, indivisible, with liberty and justice for all.

JOHN MUIR

THE MOUNTAINS OF CALIFORNIA

After ten years spent in the heart of it, rejoicing and wondering... it still seems to me above all others the Range of Light, the most divinely beautiful of all the mountain-chains I have ever seen.

Anyone who doubts the power of the written word need only consider the accomplishments of John Muir (1838–1914). Born in Scotland, he emigrated with his family to Wisconsin in 1849. He attended the University of Wisconsin and at first devoted himself to mechanical inventions, but switched careers when he nearly lost an eye in an accident. Muir became a passionate naturalist, especially devoted to forests, mountains, and glaciers. He walked from the Middle West to the Gulf of Mexico, taking notes as he traveled. In 1868, at the age of thirty, he had his first view of the Sierra Nevadas in California and found his greatest love.

He traveled throughout the western states, observing, cataloguing, and describing the natural life of the region. Many of his lyrical observations became essays and magazine articles. He urged the federal government to adopt a forest conservation policy and to protect the great natural resources from development. Due to his campaign, Sequoia and Yosemite national parks were established in 1890.

In 1892, Muir founded the Sierra Club, which turned his passion for nature into a national movement. Muir encouraged President Theodore Roosevelt's interest in conservation, and the president joined Muir for a camping trip into Yosemite in 1903. A great virgin stand of redwoods just north of San Francisco was donated to the U.S. National Park Service and named Muir Woods National Forest in 1908 in his honor.

The Mountains of California, published in 1894, was Muir's first book. It contains no advocacy, only accurate and vibrant descriptions of scenes that he loved. The book was an immediate success when it appeared; it expanded the ranks of conservationists across the nation. And it became John Muir's lasting testament to the mountains he loved and helped to save.

. . . Making your way through the mazes of the Coast Range to the summit of any of the inner peaks or passes opposite San Francisco, in the clear springtime, the grandest and most telling of all California landscapes is outspread before you. At your feet lies the great Central Valley glowing golden in the sunshine, extending north and south farther than the eye can reach, one smooth, flowery, lake-like bed of fertile soil. Along its eastern margin rises the mighty Sierra, miles in height, reposing like a smooth, cumulous cloud in the sunny sky, and so gloriously colored, and so luminous, it seems to be not clothed with light, but wholly composed of it, like the wall of some celestial city. Along the top, and extending a good way down, you see a pale, pearl-gray belt of snow; and below it a belt of blue and dark purple, marking the extension of the forests; and along the base of the range a broad belt of rose-purple and yellow, where lie the miner's goldfields and the foot-hill gardens. All these colored belts blending smoothly make a wall of light ineffably fine, and as beautiful as a rainbow, yet firm as adamant.

When I first enjoyed this superb view, one

glowing April day, from the summit of the Pacheco Pass, the Central Valley, but little trampled or plowed as yet, was one furred, rich sheet of golden compositae, and the luminous wall of the mountains shone in all its glory. Then it seemed to me the Sierra should be called not the Nevada, or Snowy Range, but the Range of Light. And after ten years spent in the heart of it, rejoicing and wondering, bathing in its glorious floods of light, seeing the sunbursts of morning among the icy peaks, the noonday radiance on the trees and rocks and snow, the flush of the alpenglow, and a thousand dashing waterfalls with their marvelous abundance of irised spray, it still seems to me above all others the Range of Light, the most divinely beautiful of all the mountain-chains I have ever seen.

The Sierra is about 500 miles long, 70 miles wide, and from 7000 to nearly 15,000 feet high. In general views no mark of man is visible on it, nor anything to suggest the richness of the life it cherishes, or the depth and grandeur of its sculpture. None of its magnificent forest-crowned ridges rises much above the general level to publish its wealth. No great valley or lake is seen, or river, or group of well-marked features of any kind, standing out in distinct pictures. Even the summit-peaks, so clear and high in the sky, seem comparatively smooth and featureless. Nevertheless, glaciers are still at work in the shadows of the peaks, and thousands of lakes and meadows shine and bloom beneath them, and the whole range is furrowed with cañons to a depth of from 2000 to 5000 feet, in which once flowed majestic glaciers, and in which now flow and sing a band of beautiful rivers.

Though of such stupendous depth, these famous cañons are not raw, gloomy, jagged-walled gorges, savage and inaccessible. With rough passages here and there they still make delightful pathways for the mountaineer, conducting from the fertile lowlands to the highest icy fountains, as a kind of mountain streets full of charming life and light, graded and sculptured by the ancient glaciers, and presenting, throughout all their courses, a rich variety of novel and attractive scenery, the most attractive that has yet been discovered in the mountain-ranges of the world.

In many places, especially in the middle region of the western flank of the range, the main cañons widen into spacious valleys or parks, diversified like artificial landscape-gardens, with charming groves and meadows, and thickets of blooming bushes, while the lofty, retiring walls, infinitely varied in form and sculpture, are fringed with ferns, flowering-plants of many species, oaks, and evergreens, which find anchorage on a thousand narrow steps and benches; while the whole is enlivened and made glorious with rejoicing streams that come dancing and foaming over the sunny brows of the cliffs to join the shining river that flows in tranquil beauty down the middle of each one of them.

The walls of these park valleys of the Yosemite kind are made up of rocks mountains in size, partly separated from each other by narrow gorges and side-cañons; and they are so sheer in front, and so compactly built together on a level floor, that, comprehensively seen, the parks they inclose look like immense halls or temples lighted from above. Every rock seems to glow with life. Some lean back in majestic repose; others, absolutely sheer, or nearly so, for thousands of feet, advance their brows in thoughtful attitudes beyond their companions, giving welcome to storms and calms alike, seemingly conscious yet heedless of everything going on about them, awful in stern majesty, types of permanence, yet associated with beauty of the frailest and most fleeting forms; their feet set in pine-groves and gay emerald meadows, their brows in the sky; bathed in light, bathed in floods of singing water, while snow-clouds, avalanches, and the winds shine and surge and wreathe about them as the years go by, as if into these mountain mansions Nature had taken pains to gather their choicest treasures to draw her lovers into close and confiding communion with her. . . .

KATHARINE LEE BATES

AMERICA THE BEAUTIFUL

Katharine Lee Bates (1850–1929) wrote "America the Beautiful" in 1893, and it was published in *The Congregationalist* in 1895. Bates revised the lyrics in 1904, and again in 1911 in her *America the Beautiful and Other Poems.* For most of her adult life, Bates was a professor of English at Wellesley College. She was also an editor, wrote children's books, and published several collections of poetry. However, her lasting fame comes from her authorship of the memorable verses to "America the Beautiful." The song is widely admired, and it has often been proposed as a substitute for "The Star-Spangled Banner" as the national anthem.

O beautiful for spacious skies,
    For amber waves of grain,
For purple mountain majesties
    Above the fruited plain!
America! America!
    God shed His grace on thee
And crown thy good with brotherhood
    From sea to shining sea!

O beautiful for pilgrim feet,
    Whose stern, impassioned stress
A thoroughfare for freedom beat
    Across the wilderness!
America! America!
    God mend thine every flaw,
Confirm thy soul in self-control,
    Thy liberty in law!

O beautiful for heroes proved
    In liberating strife,
Who more than self their country loved,
    And mercy more than life!
America! America!
    May God thy gold refine,
Till all success be nobleness
    And every gain divine!

O beautiful for patriot dream
    That sees beyond the years
Thine alabaster cities gleam
    Undimmed by human tears!
America! America!
    God shed His grace on thee,
And crown thy good with brotherhood
    From sea to shining sea!

BOOKER T. WASHINGTON

THE ATLANTA EXPOSITION ADDRESS

In all things that are purely social we can be separate as the fingers, yet one as the hand in all things essential to mutual progress.

Booker T. Washington (1856–1915) was born a slave. In 1872, he enrolled at Hampton Institute and paid his way by working in the school as a janitor. After teaching and further studies, he was chosen to lead Tuskegee Normal and Industrial Institute. Over the next thirty-four years, Washington built Tuskegee from an impoverished school into a major institution with 1,500 students.

Washington believed that the path to advancement for blacks was through industrial education, small-scale entrepreneurship, and hard work. The fact that he was invited to address a white audience at the Atlanta Exposition on September 18, 1895, was considered newsworthy. In his speech he counseled fellow blacks to cultivate "the common occupations of life," to develop friendly relations with their white neighbors, and to begin "at the bottom," not the top.

Black leaders like W.E.B. Du Bois rejected his counsel of patience and moderation and called his speech the "Atlanta Compromise"; these leaders also denounced Washington's emphasis on industrial education at the expense of academic education. At the time, black rights in the South were imperiled by the passage of Jim Crow laws. Black farmers were mainly tenant farmers, exploited by a system of sharecropping. Black workers in the cities were excluded from labor unions.

Whites, however, cheered Washington's speech, and he was fêted by white southerners and northerners. In 1901, he was invited to the White House by President Theodore Roosevelt. From 1895 until his death, he was considered the most powerful black American of the day. He wrote a dozen books, including his autobiography, *Up from Slavery.*

One-third of the population of the South is of the Negro race. No enterprise seeking the material, civil, or moral welfare of this section can disregard this element of our population and reach the highest success. I but convey to you, Mr. President and Directors, the sentiment of the masses of my race when I say that in no way have the value and manhood of the American Negro been more fittingly and generously recognized than by the managers of this magnificent Exposition at every stage of its progress. It is a recognition that will do more to cement the friendship of the two races than any occurrence since the dawn of our freedom.

Not only this, but the opportunity here afforded will awaken among us a new era of industrial progress. Ignorant and inexperienced, it is not strange that in the first years of our new life we began at the top instead of at the bottom; that a seat in Congress or the State Legislature was more sought than real estate or industrial skill; that the political convention or stump speaking had more attractions than starting a dairy farm or truck garden.

A ship lost at sea for many days suddenly sighted a friendly vessel. From the mast of the unfortunate vessel was seen a signal: "Water, water, we die of thirst." The answer from the friendly vessel at once came back, "Cast down your bucket where you are." A second time the signal, "Water, water, send us water," ran up from the distressed vessel and was answered, "Cast down your bucket where you are." And a third and fourth signal for water was answered "Cast down your bucket where you are." The captain of the distressed vessel, at last heeding the injunction, cast down his bucket and it came up full of fresh, sparkling water from the mouth of the Amazon River.

To those of my race who depend on bettering their condition in a foreign land, or who underestimate the importance of cultivating friendly relations with the Southern white man who is their next-door neighbor, I would say: Cast down your bucket where you are; cast it down in making friends, in every manly way, of the people of all races by whom we are surrounded. Cast it down in agriculture, mechanics, in commerce, in domestic service, and in the professions. And in this connection it is well to bear in mind that whatever other sins the South may be called upon to bear, when it comes to business pure and simple, it is in the South that the Negro is given a man's chance in the commercial world, and in nothing is this Exposition more eloquent than in emphasizing this chance. Our greatest danger is that, in the great leap from slavery to freedom, we may overlook the fact that the masses of us are to live by the productions of our hands and fail to keep in mind that we shall prosper in the proportion as we learn to dignify and glorify common labor, and put brains and skill into the common occupations of life; shall prosper in proportion as we learn to draw the line between the superficial and the substantial, the ornamental gewgaws of life and the useful. No race can prosper till it learns that there is as much dignity in tilling a field as in writing a poem. It is at the bottom of life we must begin, and not at the top. Nor should we permit our grievances to overshadow our opportunities.

To those of the white race who look to the incoming of those of foreign birth and strange tongue and habits for the prosperity of the South, were I permitted I would repeat what I say to my own race, "Cast down your bucket where you are." Cast it down among the 8,000,000 Negroes whose habits you know, whose fidelity and love you have tested in days when to have proved treacherous meant the ruin of your firesides. Cast down your bucket among these people who have, without strikes and labor wars, tilled your fields, cleared your forests, builded your railroads and cities, and brought forth treasures from the bowels of the earth and helped make possible this magnificent representation of the progress of the South. Casting down your bucket among my people, helping and encouraging them as you are doing on these grounds, and, with education of head, hand and heart, you will find that they will buy your surplus land, make blossom the waste places in your fields, and run your factories.

While doing this, you can be sure in the future, as in the past, that you and your families will be surrounded by the most patient, faithful, law-abiding, and unresentful people that the world has seen. As we have proved our loyalty to you in the past, in nursing your children, watching by the sick-bed of your mothers and fathers, and often following them with tear-dimmed eyes to their graves, so in the future, in

our humble way, we shall stand by you with a devotion that no foreigner can approach, ready to lay down our lives, if need be, in defense of yours; interlacing our industrial, commercial, civil, and religious life with yours in a way that shall make the interests of both races one. In all things that are purely social we can be as separate as the fingers, yet one as the hand in all things essential to mutual progress.

There is no defense or security for any of us except in the highest intelligence and development of all. If anywhere there are efforts tending to curtail the fullest growth of the Negro, let these efforts be turned into stimulating, encouraging and making him the most useful and intelligent citizen. Effort or means so invested will pay a thousand per cent interest. These efforts will be twice blessed—"blessing him that gives and him that takes."

There is no escape, through law of man or God, from the inevitable:

The laws of changeless justice bind
Oppressor with oppressed,
And close as sin and suffering joined
We march to fate abreast.

Nearly sixteen million hands will aid you in pulling the load upward, or they will pull against you the load downward. We shall constitute one-third and more of the ignorance and crime of the South, or one-third its intelligence and progress; we shall contribute one-third to the business and industrial prosperity of the South, or we shall prove a veritable body of death, stagnating, depressing, retarding every effort to advance the body politic.

Gentlemen of the Exposition: As we present to you our humble effort at an exhibition of our progress, you must not expect over much. Starting thirty years ago with ownership here and there in a few quilts and pumpkins and chickens (gathered from miscellaneous sources), remember: the path that has led us from these to the invention and production of agricultural implements, buggies, steam engines, newspapers, books, statuary, carving, paintings, the management of drugstores and banks, has not been trodden without contact with thorns and this-tles. While we take pride in what we exhibit as a result of our independent efforts, we do not for a moment forget that our part in this exhibition would fall far short of your expectations but for the constant help that has come to our educational life, not only from the Southern states, but especially from Northern philanthropists who have made their gifts a constant stream of blessing and encouragement.

The wisest among my race understand that the agitation of questions of social equality is the extremest folly, and that progress in the enjoyment of all the privileges that will come to us must be the result of severe and constant struggle rather than of artificial forcing. No race that has anything to contribute to the markets of the world is long in any degree ostracized. It is important and right that all privileges of the law be ours, but it is vastly more important that we be prepared for the exercise of those privileges. The opportunity to earn a dollar in a factory just now is worth infinitely more than the opportunity to spend a dollar in an opera house.

In conclusion, may I repeat that nothing in thirty years has given us more hope and encouragement and drawn us so near to you of the white race as this opportunity offered by the Exposition; and here bending, as it were, over the altar that represents the results of the struggles of your race and mine, both starting practically empty-handed three decades ago, I pledge that, in your effort to work out the great and intricate problem which God has laid at the doors of the South, you shall have at all times the patient, sympathetic help of my race. Only let this be constantly in mind that, while from representations in these buildings of the product of field, of forest, of mine, of factory, letters and art, much good will come—yet far above and beyond material benefits, will be that higher good, that let us pray God will come, in a blotting out of sectional differences and racial animosities and suspicions, in a determination to administer absolute justice, in a willing obedience among all classes to the mandates of law. This, coupled with material prosperity, will bring into our beloved South a new heaven and a new earth.

JOHN HOPE

REPLY TO BOOKER T. WASHINGTON

If we are not striving for equality, in heaven's name for what are we living?

John Hope (1868–1936) was born in Augusta, Georgia, and graduated from Worcester Academy in Massachusetts and then Brown University in 1894. When he wrote the following, he was a professor of classics and sciences at Roger Williams University in Nashville, Tennessee. Hope was one of the founders of the Niagara Movement, which preceded the National Association for the Advancement of Colored People. In 1906, he became the first black president of Atlanta Baptist College (Morehouse College), and in 1929, the president of Atlanta University.

Hope, a strong advocate of liberal education for blacks, opposed Booker T. Washington's advocacy of technical training. Hope heard Washington's famous Atlanta Exposition speech and disagreed strongly. On February 22, 1896, he delivered the following speech in rebuttal to Washington to a black debating society.

If we are not striving for equality, in heaven's name for what are we living? I regard it as cowardly and dishonest for any of our colored men to tell white people or colored people that we are not struggling for equality. If money, education, and honesty will not bring to me as much privilege, as much equality as they bring to any American citizen, then they are to me a curse, and not a blessing. God forbid that we should get the implements with which to fashion our freedom, and then be too lazy or pusillanimous to fashion it. Let us not fool ourselves nor be fooled by others. If we cannot do what other freemen do, then we are not free. Yes, my friends, I want equality. Nothing less. I want all that my God-given powers will enable me to get, then why not equality? Now, catch your breath, for I am going to use an adjective: I am going to say we demand social equality. In this Republic we shall be less than freemen, if we have a whit less than that which thrift, education, and honor afford other freemen. If equality, political, economic, and social, is the boon of other men in this great country of ours, then equality, political, economic, and social, is what we demand. Why build a wall to keep me out? I am no wild beast, nor am I an unclean thing.

Rise, Brothers! Come let us possess this land. Never say: "Let well enough alone." Cease to console yourselves with adages that numb the moral sense. Be discontented. Be dissatisfied. "Sweat and grunt" under present conditions. Be as restless as the tempestuous billows on the boundless sea. Let your discontent break mountain-high against the wall of prejudice, and swamp it to the very foundation. Then we shall not have to plead for justice nor on bended knee crave mercy; for we shall be men. Then and not until then will liberty in its highest sense be the boast of our Republic.

JOHN MARSHALL HARLAN
DISSENT FROM *PLESSY V. FERGUSON*

In view of the Constitution, in the eye of the law, there is in this country no superior, dominant, ruling class of citizens. There is no caste here. Our Constitution is color-blind, and neither knows nor tolerates classes among citizens.

After Reconstruction, whites regained control of southern legislatures and passed Jim Crow laws to enforce racial segregation and discrimination. The most important test of Jim Crow laws was the case of *Plessy v. Ferguson* in 1896, in which the Supreme Court upheld a Louisiana law segregating rail passengers by race. Eight of the nine justices reasoned that, so long as the facilities provided for the races were equal, there was nothing wrong with racial segregation. If colored persons chose to believe that "enforced separation of the two races stamps the colored race with a badge of inferiority," said the majority, "it is not by reason of anything found in the act, but solely because the colored race chooses to put that construction upon it." This decision endorsed "separate but equal" facilities. Since most southern blacks were disenfranchised and politically powerless, separate facilities were not, and could not be, equal.

The only Supreme Court justice to dissent from the *Plessy* decision was John Marshall Harlan (1833–1911). Harlan achieved a reputation as a forceful dissenter, particularly on matters involving the protection of black rights. His famous dissent in *Plessy v. Ferguson* was quoted in the early 1950s by lawyers for the National Association for the Advancement of Colored People in their successful legal attack on racial segregation.

... In respect of civil rights, common to all citizens, the Constitution of the United States does not, I think, permit any public authority to know the race of those entitled to be protected in the enjoyment of such rights. Every true man has pride of race, and under appropriate circumstances when the rights of others, his equals before the law, are not to be affected, it is his privilege to express such pride and to take such action based upon it as to him seems proper. But I deny that any legislative body or judicial tribunal may have regard to the race of citizens when the civil rights of those citizens are involved. Indeed, such legislation, as that here in question, is inconsistent not only with that equality of rights which pertains to citizenship, National and State, but with the personal liberty enjoyed by every one within the United States....

The white race deems itself to be the dominant race in this country. And so it is, in prestige, in achievements, in education, in wealth and in power. So, I doubt not, it will continue to be for all time, if it remains true to its great heritage and holds fast to the principles of constitutional liberty. But in view of the Constitution, in the eye of the law, there is in this country no superior, dominant, ruling class of citizens. There is no caste here. Our Constitution is color-blind, and neither knows nor tolerates classes among citizens. In respect of civil rights, all citizens are equal before the law. The humblest is the peer of the most powerful. The law regards man as man, and takes no account of his surroundings or of his color when his civil rights as guaranteed by the supreme law of the land are involved. It is, therefore, to be regretted that this high tribunal, the final expositor of the fundamental law of the land, has reached the conclusion that it is competent for a State to regulate the enjoyment by citizens of their civil rights solely upon the basis of race....

The arbitrary separation of citizens, on the basis of race, while they are on a public highway, is a badge of servitude wholly inconsistent with the civil freedom and the equality before the law established by the Constitution. It cannot be justified upon any legal grounds.

If evils will result from the commingling of the two races upon public highways established for the benefit of all, they will be infinitely less than those that will surely come from state legislation regulating the enjoyment of civil rights upon the basis of race. We boast of the freedom enjoyed by our people above all other peoples. But it is difficult to reconcile that boast with a state of the law which, practically, puts the brand of servitude and degradation upon a large class of our fellow-citizens, our equals before the law. The thin disguise of "equal" accommodations for passengers in railroad coaches will not mislead any one, nor atone for the wrong this day done....

THEODORE ROOSEVELT

IN PRAISE OF THE STRENUOUS LIFE

Far better it is to dare mighty things, to win glorious triumphs, even though checkered by failure, than to take rank with those poor spirits who neither enjoy much nor suffer much because they live in the gray twilight that knows neither victory nor defeat.

Theodore Roosevelt (1858–1919), born to a wealthy New York family, was a physical weakling as a child. With iron determination, he devoted himself to physical activity and became a vigorous outdoorsman. He graduated from Harvard College and briefly attended Columbia Law School, then chose a life of politics and historical writing. At

the age of twenty-three he was elected to the state legislature, and after several political defeats, spent two years ranching in the Dakota Territories. A stint as police commissioner in New York City was followed by service as assistant secretary of the navy in the McKinley administration. When the Spanish-American War began in 1898, he resigned to lead a troop of volunteers, known as the Rough Riders. His heroics in Cuba propelled him into the governorship of New York. There he alienated the Republican machine boss, who decided to get rid of him by making him the vice-presidential nominee on William McKinley's ticket in 1900. The relentless overachiever was supposed to fade into quiet oblivion, but when McKinley was assassinated in September 1901, Roosevelt became president.

Roosevelt delivered one of his most popular speeches on April 10, 1899, in Chicago, a few months after he was inaugurated as governor of New York. Only six weeks previously, William Jennings Bryan had spoken in Chicago, denouncing imperialism. Roosevelt responded to Bryan on Appomattox Day in a speech that merged his personal view of life as physical challenge with his conception of America's role in the world.

In speaking to you, men of the greatest city of the West, men of the state which gave to the country Lincoln and Grant, men who preeminently and distinctly embody all that is most American in the American character, I wish to preach not the doctrine of ignoble ease but the doctrine of the strenuous life; the life of toil and effort; of labor and strife; to preach that highest form of success which comes not to the man who desires mere easy peace but to the man who does not shrink from danger, from hardship, or from bitter toil, and who out of these wins the splendid ultimate triumph. . . .

As it is with the individual so it is with the nation. It is a base untruth to say that happy is the nation that has no history. Thrice happy is the nation that has a glorious history. Far better it is to dare mighty things, to win glorious triumphs, even though checkered by failure, than to take rank with those poor spirits who neither enjoy much nor suffer much because they live in the gray twilight that knows neither victory nor defeat. If in 1861 the men who loved the Union had believed that peace was the end of all things and war and strife a worst of all things, and had acted up to their belief, we would have saved hundreds of thousands of lives, we would have saved hundreds of millions of dollars. Moreover, besides saving all the blood and treasure we then lavished, we would

have prevented the heartbreak of many women, the dissolution of many homes; and we would have spared the country those months of gloom and shame when it seemed as if our armies marched only to defeat. We would have avoided all this suffering simply by shrinking from strife. And if we had thus avoided it we would have shown that we were weaklings and that we were unfit to stand among the great nations of the earth. Thank God for the iron in the blood of our fathers, the men who upheld the wisdom of Lincoln and bore sword or rifle in the armies of Grant! Let us, the children of the men who proved themselves equal to the mighty days— let us, the children of the men who carried the great Civil War to a triumphant conclusion, praise the God of our fathers that the ignoble counsels of peace were rejected, that the suffering and loss, the blackness of sorrow and despair, were unflinchingly faced and the years of strife endured; for in the end the slave was freed, the Union restored, and the mighty American Republic placed once more as a helmeted queen among nations.

We of this generation do not have to face a task such as that our fathers faced, but we have our tasks, and woe to us if we fail to perform them! We cannot, if we would, play the part of China, and be content to rot by inches in ignoble ease within our borders, taking no interest in what goes on beyond them; sunk in a scrambling commercialism; heedless of the higher life, the life of aspiration, of toil and risk; busying ourselves only with the wants of our bodies for the day; until suddenly we should find, beyond a shadow of question, what China has already found, that in this world the nation that has trained itself to a career of unwarlike and isolated ease is bound in the end to go down before other nations which have not lost the manly and adventurous qualities. If we are to be a really great people, we must strive in good faith to play a great part in the world. We cannot avoid meeting great issues. All that we can determine for ourselves is whether we shall meet them well or ill. Last year we could not help being brought face to face with the problem of war with Spain. All we could decide was whether we should shrink like cowards from the contest or enter into it as beseemed a brave and high-spirited people; and, once in, whether failure or success should crown our banners. So it is now. We cannot avoid the responsibilities that confront us in Hawaii, Cuba, Puerto Rico, and the Philippines. All we can decide is whether we shall meet them in a way that will redound to the national credit, or whether we shall make of our dealings with these new problems a dark and shameful page in our history. To refuse to deal with them at all merely amounts to dealing with them badly. We have a given problem to solve. If we undertake the solution there is, of course, always danger that we may not solve it aright, but to refuse to undertake the solution simply renders it certain that we cannot possibly solve it aright.

The timid man, the lazy man, the man who distrusts his country, the overcivilized man, who has lost the great fighting, masterful virtues, the ignorant man and the man of dull mind, whose soul is incapable of feeling the mighty lift that thrills "stern men with empires in their brains"—all these, of course, shrink from seeing the nation undertake its new duties; shrink from seeing us build a navy and army adequate to our needs; shrink from seeing us do our share of the world's work by bringing order out of chaos in the great, fair tropic islands from which the valor of our soldiers and sailors has driven the Spanish flag. These are the men who fear the strenuous life, who fear the only national life which is really worth leading....

I preach to you, then, my countrymen, that our country calls not for the life of ease, but for the life of strenuous endeavor. The twentieth century looms before us big with the fate of many nations. If we stand idly by, if we seek merely swollen, slothful ease, and ignoble peace, if we shrink from the hard contests where men must win at hazard of their lives and at the risk of all they hold dear, then the bolder and stronger peoples will pass us by and will win for themselves the domination of the world. Let us therefore boldly face the life of strife, resolute to do our duty well and manfully; resolute to uphold righteousness by deed and by word; resolute to be both honest and brave, to serve high ideals, yet to use practical methods. Above all, let us shrink from no strife, moral or physical, within or without the nation, provided we are certain that the strife is justified; for it is only through strife, through hard and dangerous endeavor, that we shall ultimately win the goal of true national greatness.

GEORGE FRISBIE HOAR

AGAINST IMPERIALISM

Let us at least have this to say . . . "The flag which we received without a rent we handed down without a stain."

In 1895, when Cuban nationalists launched a war of independence against Spain, American public opinion rallied to the side of the rebels. The sinking of the USS *Maine* in Havana harbor in February 1898 provoked outrage in the United States, fed by the "yellow press." By the end of April, the United States and Spain were at war. The U.S. Navy defeated the Spanish fleet in the Caribbean and in the Philippines. At the end of 1898, Spain renounced all claim to Cuba and turned over Guam, Puerto Rico, and the Philippines to the United States.

The Spanish-American War ignited a heated debate about America's imperial ambitions, particularly because it left the United States with overseas territories. No one was more articulate in opposing imperialism than George Frisbie Hoar (1826–1904), the Republican senator from Massachusetts. In arguing against the absorption of the Philippines, Hoar broke with his own party. The anti-imperialists lost the battle: Republican President McKinley decided that it was the duty of the United States to "uplift" the Filipinos. After the United States annexed the Philippines, 70,000 American troops were required to put down a native rebellion. The Philippines finallly achieved independence in 1946.

Hoar's speech was delivered in the Senate in May 1902.

Gentlemen talk about sentimentalities, about idealism. They like practical statesmanship better. But, Mr. President, this whole debate for the last four years has been a debate between two kinds of sentimentality. There has been practical statesmanship in plenty on both sides. Your side have carried their sentimentalities and ideals out in your practical statesmanship. The other side have tried and begged to be allowed to carry theirs out in practical statesmanship also. On one side have been sentimentalities. They were the ideals of the fathers of the revolutionary time, and from their day down till the day of Abraham Lincoln and Charles Sumner was over. The sentimentalities were that all men in political right were created equal; that governments derive their just powers from the consent of the governed, and are instituted to secure that equality; that every people—not every scattering neighborhood or settlement without or-

ganic life, not every portion of a people who may be temporarily discontented, but the political being that we call a people—has the right to institute a government for itself and to lay its foundation on such principles and organize its powers in such form as to it and not to any other people shall seem most likely to effect its safety and happiness. Now, a good deal of practical statesmanship has followed from these ideals and sentimentalities. They have built forty-five states on firm foundations. They have covered South America with republics. They have kept despotism out of the Western Hemisphere. They have made the United States the freest, strongest, richest of the nations of the world. They have made the word "republic" a name to conjure by the round world over. By their virtue the American flag—beautiful as a flower to those who love it; terrible as a meteor to those who hate it—floats everywhere over peaceful seas, and is welcomed everywhere in friendly ports as the emblem of peaceful supremacy and sovereignty in the commerce of the world. . . .

You also, my imperialistic friends, have had your ideals and your sentimentalities. One is that the flag shall never be hauled down where it has once floated. Another is that you will not talk or reason with a people with arms in their hands. Another is that sovereignty over an unwilling people may be bought with gold. And another is that sovereignty may be got by force of arms, as the booty of battle or the spoils of victory.

What has been the practical statesmanship which comes from your ideals and your sentimentalities? You have wasted six hundred millions of treasure. You have sacrificed nearly ten thousand American lives—the flower of our youth. You have devastated provinces. You have slain uncounted thousands of the people you

desire to benefit. You have established reconcentration camps. Your generals are coming home from their harvest, bringing their sheaves with them, in the shape of other thousands of sick and wounded and insane to drag out their miserable lives, wrecked in body and mind. You make the American flag in the eyes of a numerous people the emblem of sacrilege in Christian churches, and of the burning of human dwellings, and of the horror of the water torture . . . .

Your practical statesmanship has succeeded in converting a people who three years ago were ready to kiss the hem of the garment of the American and to welcome him as a liberator, who thronged after your men when they landed on those islands with benediction and gratitude, into sullen and irreconcilable enemies, possessed of a hatred which centuries cannot eradicate. . . .

I have sometimes fancied that we might

An 1898 cartoon from the Rocky Mountain News *portrays a self-satisfied Uncle Sam planting the flag on distant shores, embarking on imperialistic ventures.*

erect here in the capital of the country a column to American Liberty which alone might rival in height the beautiful and simple shaft which we have erected to the fame of the Father of the Country. I can fancy each generation bringing its inscription, which should recite its own contribution to the great structure of which the column should be but the symbol.

The generation of the Puritan and the Pilgrim and the Huguenot claims the place of honor at the base. "I brought the torch of Freedom across the sea. I cleared the forest. I subdued the savage and the wild beast. I laid in Christian liberty and law the foundations of empire."

The next generation says: "What my fathers founded I builded. I left the seashore to penetrate the wilderness. I planted schools and colleges and courts and churches."

Then comes the generation of the great colonial day: "I stood by the side of England on many a hard-fought field. I helped humble the power of France. I saw the lilies go down before the lion at Louisburg and Quebec. I carried the cross of St. George in triumph in Martinique and the Havana. I knew the stormy pathways of the ocean. I followed the whale from the Arctic to the Antarctic seas, among tumbling mountains of ice and under equinoctial heat, as the great English orator said, 'No sea not vexed by my fisheries; no climate not witness to my toils.' "

Then comes the generation of the revolutionary time: "I encountered the power of England. I declared and won the independence of my country. I placed that declaration on the eternal principles of justice and righteousness which all mankind have read, and on which all mankind will one day stand. I affirmed the dignity of human nature and the right of the people to govern themselves. I devised the securities against popular haste and delusion which made that right secure. I created the supreme court and the Senate. For the first time in history I made the right of the people to govern themselves safe, and established institutions for that end which will endure forever."

The next generation says: "I encountered England again. I vindicated the right of an American ship to sail the seas the wide world over without molestation. I made the American sailor as safe at the ends of the earth as my fathers had made the American farmer safe in his home. I proclaimed the Monroe Doctrine in the face of the Holy Alliance, under which sixteen republics have joined the family of nations. I filled the Western Hemisphere with republics from the Lakes to Cape Horn, each controlling its own destiny in safety and in honor."

Then comes the next generation: "I did the mighty deeds which in your younger years you saw and which your fathers told. I saved the Union. I put down the rebellion. I freed the slave. I made of every slave a freeman, and of every freeman a citizen, and of every citizen a voter."

Then comes another who did the great work in peace, in which so many of you had an honorable share: "I kept the faith. I paid the debt. I brought in conciliation and peace instead of war. I secured in the practice of nations the great doctrine of expatriation. I devised the homestead system. I covered the prairie and the plain with happy homes and with mighty states. I crossed the continent and joined together the seas with my great railroads. I declared the manufacturing independence of America, as my fathers affirmed its political independence. I built up our vast domestic commerce. I made my country the richest, freest, strongest, happiest people on the face of the earth."

And now what have we to say? What have we to say? Are we to have a place in that honorable company? Must we engrave on that column: "We repealed the Declaration of Independence. We changed the Monroe Doctrine from a doctrine of eternal righteousness and justice, resting on the consent of the governed, to a doctrine of brutal selfishness, looking only to our own advantage. We crushed the only republic in Asia. We made war on the only Christian people in the East. We converted a war of glory to a war of shame. We vulgarized the American flag. We introduced perfidy into the practice of war. We inflicted torture on unarmed men to extort confession. We put children to death. We established reconcentrado camps. We devastated provinces. We baffled the aspirations of a people for liberty."

No, Mr. President. Never! Never! Other and better counsels will yet prevail. The hours are long in the life of a great people. The irrevocable step is not yet taken.

Let us at least have this to say: "We, too, have kept the faith of the fathers. We took Cuba by the hand. We delivered her from her age-long bondage. We welcomed her to the family of nations. We set mankind an example never beheld before of moderation in victory. We led hesitating and halting Europe to the deliverance of their beleaguered ambassadors in China. We marched through a hostile country—a country cruel and barbarous—without anger or revenge. We returned benefit for injury, and pity for cruelty. We made the name of America beloved in the East as in the West. We kept faith with the Philippine people. We kept faith with our own history. We kept our national honor unsullied. The flag which we received without a rent we handed down without a stain." [Applause on the floor and in the galleries.]

JOSÉ DE DIEGO

NO

The no *must be and is the only saving word of the freedom and dignity of enslaved people.*

Until late in the nineteenth century, Puerto Rico was a Spanish colony. In response to pressures from Puerto Ricans, the Spanish granted the island broad powers of self-government in 1897. However, the following year American troops occupied Puerto Rico during the Spanish-American War, and control of the island was ceded to the United States at the war's end. Efforts to impose mainland culture on the island incurred the wrath of Puerto Rican patriots, who resented their return to colonial status. In 1917, the island gained limited powers of self-government and its inhabitants became American citizens. In 1948, the island won the right to elect its own governor. In 1952, it became a commonwealth associated with the United States. Whether the island will remain a commonwealth or become a state or gain independence is an unresolved issue to this day.

José de Diego (1866–1918) was a Puerto Rican statesman, poet, and political leader who experienced the transfer of power from Spain to the United States. He served in the cabinet during the brief period of Puerto Rican autonomy under Spain and also in the American colonial government. In his poems and speeches, he passionately defended Puerto Rican culture and political independence. The following essay, "No," has meaning for any people who live under a government that lacks the consent of the governed.

Brief, solid, affirmative as a hammer blow, this is the virile word, which must enflame lips and save the honor of our people, in these unfortunate days of anachronistic imperialism.

Two or three years ago Doctor Coll y Toste wrote some brilliant paragraphs to demonstrate that Puerto Ricans do not know and ought to know the protest of an energetic affirmation.

The knowledgeable doctor was wrong: our greatest moral affliction is an atavistic predisposition to the irreflexive concession and to weakness of will, which bend lovingly, like a rose bush to the sighs of the wind.

In truth, the affirmation has impelled and resolved great undertakings in science, in art, in philosophy, in religious sentiment: all the miracles of faith and love; the death of Christ and the life of Columbus; saintly wonders of affirmations, which were raised to the glorious summits of the rising spirit, to divine light.

In political evolution, in the struggle for freedom, the affirmative adverb is almost always useless and always disastrous, so soft in all languages, so sweet in the Romance tongues, superior in this sense to the mother Latin tongue. *Certe, quidem* do not have the brevity and the harmony of the Spanish, Italian, and Portuguese *sí* and the French *si,* when the latter substitutes for *oui* in the most expressive sentences; *si* in singing, a musical note (B), an arpeggio of the flute, a bird's trill, noble and good for melody, for rhythm, for dreaming, for love: more for the protest and impetus, for the paroxysm, for wrath, for anathema, for dry fulminating hate, like the scratching of a ray of light, the *no* is far better, the rude, bitter O vast, like a roar, round and ardent like a chaos producer of life through the conflagration of all the forces of the abyss.

From the almost prehistoric uprisings of savage tribes against chieftains of Asiatic empires, the negative to submission, the protest against the tyrant, the *no* of the oppressed has been the word, the genesis of the emancipation of peoples: and even when the impotency of the means and the efficacy of the goals, as in our homeland, separate the revolutionary fire from the vision of the ideal, the *no* must be and is the only saving word of the freedom and dignity of enslaved people.

We do not know how to say "no," and we are attracted, unconsciously, like a hypnotic suggestion, by the predominant *sí* of the word on thought, of the form on essence—artists and weak and kindly, as we have been made by the beauty and generosity of our land. Never, in general terms, does a Puerto Rican say, nor does he know how to say "no": "We'll see," "I'll study the matter," "I'll decide later"; when a Puerto Rican uses these expressions, it must be understood that he does not want to; at most, he joins the *sí* with the *no* and with the affirmative and negative adverbs makes a conditional conjunction, ambiguous, nebulous, in which the will fluctuates in the air, like a little bird aimless and shelterless on the flatness of a desert....

We have to learn to say "no," raise our lips, unburden our chest, put in tension all our vocal muscles and all our will power to fire this *o* of *no,* which will resound perhaps in America and the world, and will resound in the heavens with more efficacy than the rolling of cannons.

THE PROGRESSIVE AGE

Strikers for the International Ladies Garment Workers Union on the picket line in 1910.

ELIZABETH CADY STANTON

THE SOLITUDE OF SELF

The talk of sheltering woman from the fierce storms of life is the sheerest mockery, for they beat on her from every point of the compass, just as they do on man, and with more fatal results, for he has been trained to protect himself, to resist, and to conquer.

Elizabeth Cady Stanton lived a remarkable life, full of accomplishment and recognition as the nation's leading feminist. She delivered "The Solitude of Self" in 1892 when she was seventy-six years old. It is generally considered to be the finest statement of her feminist ideology. It contains no hint of complacency or self-congratulation. Instead, she is unrelenting in her demand for "self-sovereignty" for women in all spheres of their lives. Self-reliance is necessary because, ultimately, each of us is alone; each of us must be prepared to act on our own behalf, to think for ourselves, to take full responsibility for our lives.

The point I wish plainly to bring before you on this occasion is the individuality of each human soul; our Protestant idea, the right of individual conscience and judgment; our republican idea, individual citizenship. In discussing the rights of woman, we are to consider, first, what belongs to her as an individual, in a world of her own, the arbiter of her own destiny, an imaginary Robinson Crusoe, with her woman, Friday, on a solitary island. Her rights under such circumstances are to use all her faculties for her own safety and happiness.

Secondly, if we consider her as a citizen, as a member of a great nation, she must have the same rights as all other members, according to the fundamental principles of our Government.

Thirdly, viewed as a woman, an equal factor in civilization, her rights and duties are still the same—individual happiness and development.

Fourthly, it is only the incidental relations of life, such as mother, wife, sister, daughter, which may involve some special duties and training. . . .

The strongest reason for giving woman all the opportunities for higher education, for the full development of her faculties, her forces of mind and body; for giving her the most enlarged freedom of thought and action; a complete emancipation from all forms of bondage, of custom, dependence, superstition; from all the crippling influences of fear—is the solitude and personal responsibility of her own individual life. The strongest reason why we ask for woman a voice in the government under which she lives; in the religion she is asked to believe; equality in social life, where she is the chief factor; a place in the trades and professions, where she may earn her bread, is because of her birthright to self-sovereignty; because, as an individual, she must rely on herself. No matter how much women prefer to lean, to be protected and supported, nor how much men desire to have them do so, they must make the voyage of life alone, and for safety in an emergency, they must know something of the laws of navigation. To guide our own craft, we must be captain, pilot, engineer; with chart and compass to stand at the wheel; to watch the winds and waves, and know when to take in the sail, and to read the signs in the firmament over all. It matters not whether the solitary voyager is man or woman; nature, having endowed them equally, leaves them to their own skill and judgment in the hour of danger, and, if not equal to the occasion, alike they perish.

To appreciate the importance of fitting every

human soul for independent action, think for a moment of the immeasurable solitude of self. We come into the world alone, unlike all who have gone before us, we leave it alone, under circumstances peculiar to ourselves. No mortal ever has been, no mortal ever will be like the soul just launched on the sea of life. There can never again be just such a combination of prenatal influences; never again just such environments as make up the infancy, youth and manhood of this one. Nature never repeats herself, and the possibilities of one human soul will never be found in another. No one has ever found two blades of ribbon grass alike, and no one will ever find two human beings alike. Seeing, then, that what must be the infinite diversity in human character, we can in a measure appreciate the loss to a nation when any class of the people is uneducated and unrepresented in the government.

We ask for the complete development of every individual, first, for his own benefit and happiness. In fitting out an army, we give each soldier his own knapsack, arms, powder, his blanket, cup, knife, fork and spoon. We provide alike for all their individual necessities; then each man bears his own burden.

Again, we ask complete individual development for the general good; for the consensus of the competent on the whole round of human interests, on all questions of national life; and here each man must bear his share of the general burden. It is sad to see how soon friendless children are left to bear their own burdens, before they can analyze their feelings; before they can even tell their joys and sorrows, they are thrown on their own resources. The great lesson that nature seems to teach us at all ages is self-dependence, self-protection, self-support. . . .

We ask no sympathy from others in the anxiety and agony of a broken friendship or shattered love. When death sunders our nearest ties, alone we sit in the shadow of our affliction. Alike amid the greatest triumphs and darkest tragedies of life, we walk alone. On the divine heights of human attainment, eulogized and worshipped

as a hero or saint, we stand alone. In ignorance, poverty and vice, as a pauper or criminal, alone we starve or steal; alone we suffer the sneers and rebuffs of our fellows; alone we are hunted and hounded through dark courts and alleys, in by-ways and high-ways; alone we stand in the judgment seat; alone in the prison cell we lament our crimes and misfortunes; alone we expiate them on the gallows. In hours like these we realize the awful solitude of individual life, its pains, its penalties, its responsibilities, hours in which the youngest and most helpless are thrown on their own resources for guidance and consolation. Seeing, then, that life must ever be a march and a battle that each soldier must be equipped for his own protection, it is the height of cruelty to rob the individual of a single natural right.

To throw obstacles in the way of a complete education is like putting out the eyes; to deny the rights of poverty is like cutting off the hands. To refuse political equality is to rob the ostracized of all self-respect; of credit in the market place; of recompense in the world of work, of a voice in choosing those who make and administer the law, a choice in the jury before whom they are tried, and in the judge who decides their punishment. [Think of] . . . woman's position! Robbed of her natural rights, handicapped by law and custom at every turn, yet compelled to fight her own battles, and in the emergencies of life to fall back on herself for protection. . . .

The young wife and mother, at the head of some establishment, with a kind husband to shield her from the adverse winds of life, with wealth, fortune and position, has a certain harbor of safety, secure against the ordinary ills of life. But to manage a household, have a desirable influence in society, keep her friends and the affections of her husband, train her children and servants well, she must have rare common sense, wisdom, diplomacy, and a knowledge of human nature. To do all this, she needs the cardinal virtues and the strong points of character that the most successful statesman possesses. An uneducated woman trained to dependence, with no resources in herself, must make a failure of any position in life. But society says women do not need a knowledge of the world, the liberal training that experience in public life must give, all the advantages of collegiate education; but when for the lack of all this, the woman's happiness is wrecked, alone she bears her humiliation; and the solitude of the weak and ignorant is indeed pitiable. In the wild chase for the prizes of life, they are ground to powder.

In age, when the pleasures of youth are passed, children grown up, married and gone, the hurry and bustle of life in a measure over, when the hands are weary of active service, when the old arm chair and the fireside are the chosen resorts, then men and women alike must fall back on their own resources. If they cannot find companionship in books, if they have no interest in the vital questions of the hour, no interest in watching the consummation of reforms with which they might have been identified, they soon pass into their dotage. The more fully the faculties of the mind are developed and kept in use, the longer the period of vigor and active interests in all around us continues. If, from a life-long participation in public affairs, a woman feels responsible for the laws regulating our system of education, the discipline of our jails and prisons, the sanitary condition of our private homes, public building and thoroughfares, an interest in commerce, finance, our foreign relations, in any or all these questions, her solitude will at least be respectable, and she will not be driven to gossip or scandal for entertainment.

The chief reason for opening to every soul the doors to the whole round of human duties and pleasures is the individual development thus attained, the resources thus provided under all circumstances to mitigate the solitude that at times must come to everyone. . . .

Inasmuch, then, as woman shares equally the joys and sorrows of time and eternity, is it not the height of presumption in man to propose to represent her at the ballot box and the throne of grace, to do her voting in the state, her praying in the church, and to assume the position of high priest at the family altar?

Nothing strengthens the judgment and quickens the conscience like individual responsibility. Nothing adds such dignity to character as the recognition of one's self-sovereignty; the right to an equal place, everywhere conceded—a place earned by personal merit, not an artificial attainment by inheritance, wealth, family and position. Conceding, then, that the responsibilities of life rest equally on man and woman, that their destiny is the same, they need the same preparation for time and eternity. The talk of sheltering woman from the fierce storms of life is the sheerest mockery, for they beat on her from every point of the compass, just as they do on man, and with more fatal results, for he has been trained to protect himself, to resist, and to conquer. Such are the facts in human experience, the responsibilities of individual sovereignty. Rich and poor, intelligent and ignorant, wise and foolish, virtuous and vicious, man and woman; it is ever the same, each soul must depend wholly on itself.

Whatever the theories may be of woman's dependence on man, in the supreme moments of her life, he cannot bear her burdens. Alone she goes to the gates of death to give life to every man that is born into the world; no one can share her fears, no one can mitigate her pangs; and if her sorrow is greater than she can bear, alone she passes beyond the gates into the vast unknown. . . .

So it ever must be in the conflicting scenes of life, in the long, weary march, each one walks alone. We may have many friends, love, kindness, sympathy and charity, to smooth our pathway in everyday life, but in the tragedies and triumphs of human experience, each mortal stands alone. . . .

Women are already the equals of men in the whole realm of thought, in art, science, literature and government. . . . The poetry and novels of the century are theirs, and they have touched the keynote of reform, in religion, politics and social life. They fill the editor's and professor's chair, plead at the bar of justice, walk the wards of the hospital, speak from the pulpit and the platform. Such is the type of womanhood that an enlightened public sentiment welcomes to-day, and such the triumph of the facts of life over the false theories of the past.

Is it, then, consistent to hold the developed woman of this day within the same narrow political limits as the dame with the spinning wheel and knitting needles occupied in the past? No, no! Machinery has taken the labors of woman as well as man on its tireless shoulders; the loom and the spinning wheel are but dreams of the past; the pen, the brush, the easel, the chisel, have taken their places, while the hopes and ambitions of women are essentially changed.

We see reason sufficient in the outer conditions of human beings for individual liberty and development, but when we consider the self-dependence of every human soul, we see the need of courage, judgment and the exercise of every faculty of mind and body, strengthened and developed by use, in woman as well as man.

Whatever may be said of man's protecting power in ordinary conditions, amid all the terrible disasters by land and sea, in the supreme moments of danger, alone woman must ever meet the horrors of the situation. The Angel of Death even makes no royal pathway for her. Man's love and sympathy enter only into the sunshine of our lives. In that solemn solitude of self, that links us with the immeasurable and the eternal, each soul lives alone forever. . . .

And yet, there is a solitude which each and every one of us has always carried with him, more inaccessible than the ice-cold mountains, more profound than the midnight sea; the solitude of self. Our inner being which we call ourself, no eye nor touch of man or angel has ever pierced. It is more hidden than the caves of the gnome; the sacred adytum of the oracle; the hidden chamber of Eleusinian mystery, for to it only omniscience is permitted to enter.

Such is individual life. Who, I ask you, can take, dare take on himself the rights, the duties, the responsibilities of another human soul?

CHARLOTTE PERKINS GILMAN
WOMEN AND ECONOMICS

Wealth, power, social distinction, fame,—not only these, but home and happiness, reputation, ease and pleasure, her bread and butter,—all, must come to her through a small gold ring.

Charlotte Perkins Gilman (1860–1935) was the leading theoretician of feminism during the progressive era. Gilman had a miserable childhood. Her father deserted her mother and left the family nearly destitute. In 1884, she married, and gave birth to a daughter. Oppressed by household routine, she suffered a nervous collapse. She left her husband in 1888, taking the child. After her divorce, her husband married her best friend, and Gilman sent her daughter to live with them, freeing herself to work and lecture. She wrote short stories and poetry, and supported herself by lecturing on women, labor, and social organization.

In 1900, Gilman married again but maintained her busy career as lecturer and writer. From 1909 to 1916, she single-handedly wrote, edited, and published a feminist monthly magazine, the *Forerunner*. She also wrote a novel, *Herland,* and a fictionalized account of her nervous breakdown, *The Yellow Wallpaper.*

Her major work, *Women and Economics* (1898), excerpted here, is an argument for women's economic independence.

What we do modifies us more than what is done to us. The freedom of expression has been more restricted in women than the freedom of impression, if that be possible. Something of the world she lived in she has seen from her barred windows. Some air has come through the purdah's folds, some knowledge has filtered to her eager ears from the talk of men. Desdemona learned somewhat of Othello. Had she known more, she might have lived longer. But in the ever-growing human impulse to create, the power and will to make, to do, to express one's new spirit in new forms,—here she has been utterly debarred. She might work as she had worked from the beginning,—at the primitive labors of the household; but in the inevitable expansion of even those industries to professional levels we have striven to hold her back. To work with her own hands, for nothing, in direct body-service to her own family,—this has been permitted,—yes, compelled. But to be and to do anything further from this she has been forbidden. Her labor has not been limited in kind, but in degree. Whatever she has been allowed to do must be done in private and alone, the first-hand industries of savage times....

It is painfully interesting to trace the gradual cumulative effect of these conditions upon women: first, the action of large natural laws, acting on her as they would act on any other animal; then the evolution of social customs and laws (with her position as the active cause), following the direction of mere physical forces, and adding heavily to them; then, with increasing civilization, the unbroken accumulation of precedent, burnt into each generation by the growing force of education, made lovely by art, holy by religion, desirable by habit; and, steadily acting from beneath, the unswerving pressure of economic necessity upon which the whole structure rested. These are strong modifying conditions, indeed.

The process would have been even more effective and far less painful but for one important circumstance. Heredity has no Salic law. Each girl child inherits from her father a certain increasing percentage of human development, human power, human tendency; and each boy as well inherits from his mother the increasing percentage of sex-development, sex-power, sex-tendency. The action of heredity has been to equalize what every tendency of environment and education made to differ. This has saved us from such a female as the gypsy moth. It has held up the woman, and held down the man. It has set iron bounds to our absurd effort to make a race with one sex a million years behind the other. But it has added terribly to the pain and difficulty of human life,—a difficulty and a pain that should have taught us long since that we were living on wrong lines. Each woman born, re-humanized by the current of race activity carried on by her father and re-womanized by her traditional position, has had to live over again in her own person the same process of restriction, repression, denial; the smothering "no" which crushed down all her human desires to create, to discover, to learn, to express, to advance....

To the young man confronting life the world lies wide. Such powers as he has he may use, must use. If he chooses wrong at first, he may choose again, and yet again. Not effective or successful in one channel, he may do better in another. The growing, varied needs of all mankind call on him for the varied service in which he finds his growth. What he wants to be, he may strive to get. What he wants to get, he may strive to get. Wealth, power, social distinction, fame, —what he wants he can try for.

To the young woman confronting life there is the same world beyond, there are the same human energies and human desires and ambition within. But all that she may wish to have, all that she may wish to do, must come through a single channel and a single choice. Wealth, power, social distinction, fame,—not only these, but home and happiness, reputation, ease and pleasure, her bread and butter,—all, must come to her through a small gold ring. This is a heavy pressure. It has accumulated behind her through heredity, and continued about her through environment. It has been subtly trained into her through education, till she herself has come to think it a right condition, and pours its influence upon her daughter with increasing impetus. Is it any wonder that women are oversexed? But for the constant inheritance from the more human male, we should have been queen bees, indeed, long before this. But the daughter of the soldier and the sailor, of the artist, the inventor, the great merchant, has inherited in body and brain her share of his development in each generation, and so stayed somewhat human for all her femininity. . . .

EDWIN MARKHAM

THE MAN WITH THE HOE

Edwin Markham (1852–1940) grew up on a ranch in California and became a schoolteacher and administrator. In 1899, he achieved national fame with the publication of "The Man with the Hoe" in the *San Francisco Examiner*. Inspired by Jean-François Millet's painting of a French peasant, Markham's man-with-a-hoe became a symbol of the world's mute, oppressed, and exploited workers. Markham continued to write poetry for many years, but nothing else he wrote gained him as much attention as this one poem.

Bowed by the weight of centuries he leans
Upon his hoe and gazes on the ground,
The emptiness of ages in his face,
And on his back the burden of the world.
Who made him dead to rapture and despair,
A thing that grieves not and that never hopes,
Stolid and stunned, a brother to the ox?
Who loosened and let down this brutal jaw?
Whose was the hand that slanted back this
        brow?
Whose breath blew out the light within this
        brain?

Is this the Thing the Lord God made and gave
To have dominion over sea and land;
To trace the stars and search the heavens for
        power;
To feel the passion of Eternity?
Is this the dream He dreamed who shaped the
        suns
And pillared the blue firmament with light?
Down all the stretch of Hell to it's last gulf
There is no shape more terrible than this—
More tongued with censure of the world's
        blind greed—

More filled with signs and portents for the
        soul—
More fraught with menace to the universe.

What gulfs between him and the seraphim!
Slave of the wheel of labor, what to him
Are Plato and the swing of Pleiades?
What the long reaches of the peaks of song,
The rift of dawn, the reddening of the rose?
Through this dread shape the suffering ages
        look;
Time's tragedy is in that aching stoop;
Through this dread shape humanity betrayed,
Plundered, profaned, and disinherited,
Cries protest to the Judges of the World,
A protest that is also prophecy.

O masters, lords and rulers in all lands,
Is this the handiwork you give to God,
This monstrous thing distorted and soul-
        quenched?
How will you ever straighten up this shape;
Touch it again with immortality;
Give back the upward looking and the light;
Rebuild in it the music and the dream;

Make right the immemorial infamies,
Perfidious wrongs, immedicable woes?

O masters, lords and rulers in all lands,
How will the Future reckon with this Man?
How answer his brute question in that hour
When whirlwinds of rebellion shake the world?

How will it be with kingdoms and with kings—
With those who shaped him to the thing he
    is—
When this dumb Terror shall reply to God,
    After the silence of the centuries?

JAMES WELDON JOHNSON AND J. ROSAMOND JOHNSON
LIFT EV'RY VOICE AND SING

James Weldon Johnson (1871–1938) and his brother J. Rosamond Johnson (1873–1954) wrote "Lift Ev'ry Voice and Sing" in 1900 for a celebration of Lincoln's birthday. First sung by black schoolchildren in Jacksonville, Florida, it came to be known as "the Negro National Anthem." Rosamond Johnson became a successful composer, and James Weldon Johnson became a prominent author, poet, and civil rights leader.

Lift ev'ry voice and sing,
Till earth and heaven ring,
Ring with the harmonies of Liberty;
Let our rejoicing rise
High as the list'ning skies,
Let it resound loud as the rolling sea.
Sing a song full of the faith that the dark past
    has taught us
Sing a song full of the hope that the present has
    brought us
Facing the rising sun of our new day begun,
Let us march on till victory is won.

Stony the road we trod,
Bitter the chast'ning rod,
Felt in the days when hope unborn had died;
Yet with a steady beat,
Have not our weary feet
Come to the place for which our fathers
    sighed?
We have come over a way that with tears has
    been watered

We have come, treading our path thro' the
    blood of the slaughtered,
Out from the gloomy past, till now we stand at
    last
Where the white gleam of our bright star is
    cast.

God of our weary years,
God of our silent tears,
Thou who hast brought us thus far on the way;
Thou who hast by Thy might,
Led us into the light,
Keep us forever in the path, we pray.

Lest our feet stray from the places, our God,
    where we met Thee,
Lest our hearts, drunk with the wine of the
    world, we forget Thee;
Shadowed beneath Thy hand, may we forever
    stand,
True to our God, true to our native land.

M. CAREY THOMAS

SHOULD HIGHER EDUCATION FOR WOMEN DIFFER?

So long as men and women are to compete together, and associate together, in their professional life, women's preparation for the same profession cannot safely differ from men's.

M(artha) Carey Thomas (1857–1935) seems to have been born a feminist, for even as a child, she was determined to get a college education and to be independent. Born to a prominent Quaker family in Baltimore, Thomas was the oldest of nine children. She attended Cornell, then Johns Hopkins Graduate School (where she was excluded from seminars), and finally the University of Zurich, where she earned a doctorate in literature. Soon after her return to the United States, she was appointed dean of the new Bryn Mawr College in Pennsylvania. Eleven years later, in 1894, she became its president and set herself the goal of establishing the finest women's college in the country, with standards and curriculum as rigorous as the best men's colleges.

In 1899, Thomas gained national attention when she upbraided Charles W. Eliot, the president of Harvard University, for his claim that the great tradition of learning inherited from the past "was of no service in women's education" and that new models must be found. Thomas retorted that Eliot might as well have told women educators to invent "new symphonies and operas, a new Beethoven and Wagner, new statues and pictures, a new Phidias and a new Titian. . . . It would be easier to do all this than to create for women . . . a new intellectual heavens and earth."

In an article published in 1901, Thomas explained the rationale for a common curriculum for men and women in higher education.

Once granted that women are to compete with men for self-support as physicians or lawyers, . . . what is the best attainable training for the physician or the lawyer, man or woman? There is no reason to believe that typhoid or scarlet fever or phthisis can be successfully treated by a woman physician in one way and by a man physician in another way. There is indeed every reason to believe that unless treated in the best way the patient may die, the sex of the doctor affecting the result less even than the sex of the patient. The question needs only to be put for us to feel irrevocably sure that there is no special woman's way of dealing with disease. And so in law, in architecture, in electricity, in bridge-building, in all mechanic arts and technical sciences, our effort must be for

the most scientific instruction, the broadest basis of training that will enable men and women students to attain the highest possible proficiency in their chosen profession. Given two bridge-builders, a man and a woman, given a certain bridge to be built, and given as always the unchangeable laws of mechanics in accordance with which this special bridge and all other bridges must be built, it is simply inconceivable that the preliminary instruction given to the two bridge-builders should differ in quantity, quality, or method of presentation because while the bridge is building one will wear knickerbockers and the other a rainy-day skirt. You may say you do not think that God intended a woman to be a bridge-builder. You have, of course, a right to this prejudice; but as you live

The renowned astronomer Maria Mitchell, discoverer of a new comet, was a member of the faculty at the Vassar Female College from 1865 until 1888. She is shown here with her students. Women's opportunities for higher education were severely limited until the founding of women's colleges and coeducational state universities.

in America, and not in the interior of Asia or Africa, you will probably not be able to impose it on women who wish to build bridges. You may say that women's minds are such that they cannot build good bridges. If you are right in this opinion you need concern yourselves no further—bridges built by women, will on the whole, tend to fall down, and the competition of men who can build good bridges will force women out of the profession. Both of these opinions of yours are side issues, and, however they may be decided hereafter, do not in the remotest degree affect the main question of a common curriculum for men and women in technical and professional schools. But you may say that men and women should study bridge-building and medicine and law in separate

schools, and not together. You may be foolish enough, and wasteful enough, to think that all the expensive equipment of our technical and professional schools should be duplicated for women, when experience and practice have failed to bring forward a single valid objection to professional coeducation, and when the present trend of public opinion is overwhelmingly against you; and for the sake of argument let us grant that beside every such school for men is to be founded a similar school for women. But this duplication of professional schools for women leaves us just where we were in regard to the curriculum of professional study to be taught in such women's schools. So long as men and women are to compete together, and associate together, in their professional life, women's preparation for the same profession cannot safely differ from men's. If men's preparation is better, women, who are less well prepared, will be left behind in the race; if women's is better, men will suffer in competition with women. . . .

The above argument applies with equal force to the training given by the university graduate school of arts and sciences. Statistics indicate that an overwhelmingly large majority of men and women graduate students are fitting themselves for the profession of higher teaching, that over one-third of all graduate students in the United States are women, and that the annual increase of women graduate students is greater than that of men. In the lower grades of teaching men have almost ceased to compete with women; in the higher grade, that is, in college teaching, women are just beginning to compete with men, and this competition is beset with the bitterest professional jealousy that women have ever had to meet, except perhaps in medicine. There are in the United States only eleven independent colleges for women of at all the same grade as the three hundred and thirty-six coeducational colleges where women and men are taught together, yet only in these separate colleges for women have women an opportunity of competing with men for professors' chairs. It is very rare indeed for coeducational colleges to employ any women instructors, and even then only so many women are as a rule employed as are needed to look after the discipline or home life of the women students. Where women are teaching in coeducational colleges side by side with men their success is regarded by men teachers with profound dislike, and on account of this sex jealousy college presidents and boards of trustees (all of whom are, as a rule, men) cannot, even if they would, materially add to the number of women teachers or advance them. The working of the elective system, however, permits us to see that men students show no such jealousy, but recognize the able teaching of women by overcrowding their classes. Women have succeeded so brilliantly, on the whole so much better than men, as primary and secondary

teachers, that they will undoubtedly repeat this success in their college teaching so soon as artificial restrictions are removed. No one could seriously maintain that, handicapped as women now are by prejudice in the highest branches of a profession peculiarly their own, they should be further hampered by the professional training different from men's. . . .

But this line of reasoning will be incomplete unless we ask ourselves whether there are not some subjects peculiar to women in which we must maintain special women's technical schools. There are certainly three professional schools where women students already largely outnumber men: normal schools, including normal departments of universities, schools of nursing, and schools for library study. If cooking and domestic service ever become lucrative professions, and more especially if men of wealth ever come to choose their wives for culinary and sanitary lore instead as at present for social and intellectual charm, such schools will tend to spring up and, like normal schools, will undoubtedly be attended almost exclusively by women. They will beyond question be taught exactly in the same way as if they were to be attended exclusively by men. The method of teaching cooking is one and the same and does not depend on the sex of the cooks. . . .

The burden of proof is with those who believe that the college education of men and women should differ. For thirty years it has been as nearly as possible the same, with brilliantly satisfactory results, so far as concerns women. College women have married as generally as their non-college-bred sisters, and have as a rule married better than their sisters, because they have chosen a larger proportion of professional men; they have not died in childbirth, as was predicted; they have borne their proper proportion of children, and have brought up more than the usual proportion of those born; they have made efficient housekeepers and wives as well as mothers; their success as teachers has been so astonishingly great that already they are driving non-college-bred women teachers out of the field. There is, in short, not a word to be said against the success and efficiency and healthfulness of these women educated by men's curriculum. . . .

Undoubtedly the life of most women after leaving college will differ from that of men. About one-half will marry in a rather deliberate fashion, choosing carefully, and on the whole living very happily a life of comparative leisure, not of self-support; about one-third will become professional teachers, probably for life; and the greater part of the remainder will lead useful and helpful lives as unmarried women of leisure. And just because after leaving college only one-third, and that in the peculiarly limited profession of teaching, are to get the wider training of affairs that educates men engaged in business and in the professions all their lives thru, women while in college ought to have the broadest possible education. This college education should be the same as men's, not only because there is, I believe, but one best education, but because men and women are to live and work together as comrades and dear friends and married friends and lovers, and because their effectiveness and happiness and the welfare of the generation to come after them will be vastly increased if their college education has given them the same intellectual training and the same scholarly and moral ideals.

JACOB A. RIIS
THE BATTLE WITH THE SLUM

For it is one thing or the other: either wipe out the slum, or it wipes out us.

Jacob A. Riis (1849–1914) was born in Denmark and emigrated to the United States at the age of twenty-one. A few years later, he became a newspaper reporter in New York City, covering corruption, scandals, and life on the impoverished Lower East Side. His 1890 book, *How the Other Half Lives,* contributed to the passage of state legislation to reform tenement housing.

The Battle with the Slum was published in 1902 as a sequel to *How the Other Half Lives.* Riis was one of the first social commentators to recognize the vicious cycle of poverty and its pervasive influence on home, family, and community, as well as on opportunities for education and employment. He rallied his readers to battle the political bosses and to fight for social improvement. His belief in the power of the word to expose political corruption and social evils was characteristic of the progressive muckrakers.

The following excerpt is taken from Riis's *The Battle with the Slum.*

The slum is as old as civilization. Civilization implies a race to get ahead. In a race there are usually some who for one cause or another cannot keep up, or are thrust out from among their fellows. They fall behind, and when they have been left far in the rear they lose hope and ambition, and give up. Thenceforward, if left to their own resources, they are the victims, not the masters, of their environment; and it is a bad master. They drag one another always farther down. The bad environment becomes the heredity of the next generation. Then, given the crowd, you have the slum ready-made. The battle with the slum began the day civilization recognized in it her enemy. It was a losing fight until conscience joined forces with fear and self-interest against it. When common sense and the golden rule obtain among men as a rule of practice, it will be over. The two have not always been classed together, but here they are plainly seen to belong together. Justice to the individual is accepted in theory as the only safe groundwork of the commonwealth. When it is practised in dealing with the slum, there will shortly be no slum. We need not wait for the millennium, to get rid of it. We can do it now. All that is required is that it shall not be left to itself. That is justice to it and to us, since its grievous ailment is that it cannot help itself. When a man is drowning, the thing to do is to pull him out of the water; afterward there will be time for talking it over. We got at it the other way in dealing with our social problems. The wise men had their day, and they decided to let bad enough alone; that it was unsafe to interfere with "causes that operate sociologically," as one survivor of these unfittest put it to me. It was a piece of scientific humbug that cost the age which listened to it dear. "Causes that operate sociologically" are the opportunity of the political and every other kind of scamp who trades upon the depravity and helplessness of the slum, and the refuge of the pessimist who is useless in the fight against them. We have not done yet paying the bills he ran up for us. Some time since we turned to, to pull the drowning man out, and it was time. A little while longer, and we should hardly have escaped being dragged down with him.

The slum complaint had been chronic in all ages, but the great changes which the nineteenth century saw, the new industry, political freedom, brought on an acute attack which put that very freedom in jeopardy. Too many of us had supposed that, built as our commonwealth was on universal suffrage, it would be proof against the complaints that harassed older states; but in fact it turned out that there was extra hazard in that. Having solemnly resolved that all men are created equal and have certain inalienable rights, among them life, liberty, and the pursuit of happiness, we shut our eyes and waited for the formula to work. It was as if a man with a cold should take the doctor's prescription to bed with him, expecting it to cure him. The formula was all right, but merely repeating it worked no cure. When, after a hundred years, we opened our eyes, it was upon sixty cents a day as the living wage of the working-woman in our cities; upon "knee pants" at forty cents a dozen for the making; upon the Potter's Field taking tithe of our city life, ten per cent each year for the trench, truly the Lost Tenth of the slum. Our country had grown great and rich; through our ports was poured food for the millions of Europe. But in the back streets multitudes huddled in ignorance and want. The foreign oppressor had been vanquished, the fetters stricken from the black man at home; but his white brother, in his bitter plight, sent up a cry of distress that had in it a distinct note of menace. Political freedom we had won; but the problem of helpless poverty, grown vast with the added offscourings of the Old World, mocked us, unsolved. Liberty at sixty cents a day set presently its stamp upon the government of our cities, and it became the scandal and the peril of our political system. . . .

Slow work, yes! but be it ever so slow, the battle has got to be fought, and fought out. For it is one thing or the other: either wipe out the slum, or it wipes out us. Let there be no mistake about this. It cannot be shirked. Shirking means surrender, and surrender means the end of government by the people.

If any one believes this to be needless alarm, let him think a moment. Government by the people must ever rest upon the people's ability to govern themselves, upon their intelligence and public spirit. The slum stands for ignorance, want, unfitness, for mob-rule in the day of wrath. This at one end. At the other, hard-heartedness, indifference, self-seeking, greed. It is human nature. We are brothers whether we own it or not, and when the brotherhood is denied in Mulberry Street we shall look vainly for the virtue of good citizenship on Fifth Avenue. When the slum flourishes unchallenged in the cities, their wharves may, indeed, be busy, their treasure-houses filled—wealth and want go so together, —but patriotism among their people is dead.

As long ago as the very beginning of our

republic, its founders saw that the cities were danger-spots in their plan. In them was the peril of democratic government. At that time, scarce one in twenty-five of the people in the United States lived in a city. Now it is one in three. And to the selfishness of the trader has been added the threat of the slum. Ask yourself then how long before it would make an end of us, if let alone.

Put it this way: you cannot let men live like pigs when you need their votes as freemen; it is not safe. You cannot rob a child of its childhood, of its home, its play, its freedom from toil and care, and expect to appeal to the grown-up voter's manhood. The children are our to-morrow, and as we mould them to-day so will they deal with us then. Therefore that is not safe. Unsafest of all is any thing or deed that strikes at the home, for from the people's home proceeds citizen virtue, and nowhere else does it live. The slum is the enemy of the home. Because of it the chief city of our land came long ago to be called "The Homeless City." When this people comes to be truly called a nation without homes there will no longer be any nation.

Hence, I say, in the battle with the slum we win or we perish. There is no middle way. We shall win, for we are not letting things be the way our fathers did. But it will be a running fight, and it is not going to be won in two years, or in ten, or in twenty. For all that, we must keep on fighting, content if in our time we avert the punishment that waits upon the third and

A street scene in the early 1900s on the Lower East Side of New York City—a slum populated largely by immigrants from Eastern and Southern Europe.

the fourth generation of those who forget the brotherhood. As a man does in dealing with his brother so it is the way of God that his children shall reap, that through toil and tears we may make out the lesson which sums up all the commandments and alone can make the earth fit for the kingdom that is to come.

CARRIE CHAPMAN CATT
PREJUDICE AGAINST WOMEN

The whole aim of the woman movement has been to destroy the idea that obedience is necessary to women; to train women to such self-respect that they would not grant obedience and to train men to such comprehension of equity they would not exact it.

Carrie Chapman Catt (1859–1947) was born in Ripon, Wisconsin, and worked as a schoolteacher, high school principal, and school superintendent in Mason City, Iowa. Catt organized the Iowa Woman Suffrage Association, founded the International Woman Suffrage Association, and reorganized the National American Woman Suffrage

. . . The question of woman suffrage is a very simple one. The plea is dignified, calm and logical. Yet, great as is the victory over conservatism which is represented in the accomplishment of man suffrage, infinitely greater will be the attainment of woman suffrage. Man suffrage exists through the surrender of many a stronghold of ancient thought, deemed impregnable, yet these obstacles were the veriest Don Quixote windmills compared with the opposition which has stood arrayed against woman suffrage.

Woman suffrage must meet precisely the same objections which have been urged against man suffrage, but in addition, it must combat sex-prejudice, the oldest, the most unreasoning, the most stubborn of all human idiosyncracies. What *is* prejudice? An opinion, which is not based upon reason; a judgment, without having heard the argument; a feeling, without being able to trace from whence it came. And sex-prejudice is a pre-judgment against the rights, liberties and opportunities of women. A belief, without proof, in the incapacity of women to do that which they have never done. Sex-prejudice has been the chief hindrance in the rapid advance of the woman's rights movement to its present status, and it is still a stupendous obstacle to be overcome.

In the United States, at least, we need no longer argue woman's intellectual, moral and physical qualification for the ballot with the intelligent. The Reason of the best of our citizens has long been convinced. The justice of the argument has been admitted, but sex-prejudice is far from conquered.

When a great church official exclaims petulantly, that if women are no more modest in their demands men may be obliged to take to drowning female infants again; when a renowned United States Senator declares no

human being can find an answer to the arguments for woman suffrage, but with all the force of his position and influence he will oppose it; when a popular woman novelist speaks of the advocates of the movement as the "shrieking sisterhood;" when a prominent politician says "to argue against woman suffrage is to repudiate the Declaration of Independence," yet he hopes it may never come, the question flies entirely outside the domain of reason, and retreats within the realm of sex-prejudice, where neither logic nor common sense can dislodge it. . . .

Four chief causes led to the subjection of women, each the logical deduction from the theory that men were the units of the race—obedience, ignorance, the denial of personal liberty, and the denial of right to property and wages. These forces united in cultivating a spirit of egotism and tyranny in men and weak dependence in women. . . . In fastening these disabilities upon women, the world acted logically when reasoning from the premise that man is the race and woman his dependent. The perpetual tutelage and subjection robbed women of all freedom of thought and action, and all incentive for growth, and they logically became the inane weaklings the world would have them, and their condition strengthened the universal belief in their incapacity. This world taught woman nothing skillful and then said her work was valueless. It permitted her no opinions and said she did not know how to think. It forbade her to speak in public, and said the sex had no orators. It denied her the schools, and said the sex had no genius. It robbed her of every vestige of responsibility, and then called her weak. It taught her that every pleasure must come as a favor from men, and when to gain it she decked herself in paint and fine feathers, as she had been taught to do, it called her vain.

This was the woman enshrined in literature.

She was immortalized in song and story. Chivalry paid her fantastic compliments. As Diderot said: "when woman is the theme, the pen must be dipped in the rainbow, and the pages must be dried with a butterfly's wing." Surrounded by a halo of this kind of mysticism woman was encouraged to believe herself adored. This woman who was pretty, coquettish, affectionate, obedient, self effacive [*sic*], now gentle and meek, now furious and emotional, always ignorant, weak and silly, became the ideal woman of the world.

When at last the New Woman came, bearing the torch of truth, and with calm dignity asked a share in the world's education, opportunities and duties, it is no wonder these untrained weaklings should have shrunk away in horror. . . . Nor was it any wonder that man should arise to defend the woman of the past, whom he had learned to love and cherish. Her very weakness and dependence were dear to him and he loved to think of her as the tender clinging vine, while he was the strong and sturdy oak. He had worshiped her ideal through the age of chivalry as though she were a goddess, but he had governed her as though she were an idiot. Without the slightest comprehension of the inconsistency of his position, he believed this relation to be in accordance with God's command. . . .

The whole aim of the woman movement has been to destroy the idea that obedience is necessary to women; to train women to such self-respect that they would not grant obedience and to train men to such comprehension of equity they would not exact it. . . . As John Stuart Mill said in speaking of the conditions which preceded the enfranchisement of men: "The noble has been gradually going down on the social ladder and the commoner has been gradually going up. Every half century has brought them nearer to each other;" so we may say, for the past hundred years, man as the dominant power in the world has been going down the ladder and woman has been climbing up. Every decade has brought them nearer together. The opposition to the enfranchisement of women is the last defense of the old theory that obedience is necessary for women, because man alone is the creator of the race.

The whole effort of the woman movement has been to destroy obedience of woman in the home. That end has been very generally attained, and the average civilized woman enjoys the right of individual liberty in the home of her father, her husband, and her son. The individual woman no longer obeys the individual man. She enjoys self-government in the home and in society. The question now is, shall all women as a body obey all men as a body? Shall the woman who enjoys the right of self-government in every other department of life be permitted the right of self-government in the State? It is no more right for all men to govern all women than it was for one man to govern one woman. It is no more right for men to govern women than it was for one man to govern other men. . . .

W. E. B. DU BOIS
THE TALENTED TENTH

The Talented Tenth of the Negro race must be made leaders of thought and missionaries of culture among their people.

W. E. B. Du Bois (1868–1963) was the most influential black intellectual in the first half of the twentieth century. Born in Great Barrington, Massachusetts, Du Bois was educated at Fisk University and at Harvard, where he earned a Ph.D degree. In 1903, in his most famous book, *The Souls of Black Folk*, Du Bois accurately prophesied, "The problem of the Twentieth Century is the problem of the color line." Concluding that social science was an inadequate counter to Jim Crow laws, disenfranchisement, lynching, and other racist practices, he turned to political action to influence public opinion. A founder of the National Association for the Advancement of Colored People in 1909, Du Bois was editor of its magazine, *The Crisis,* from 1910 to 1934.

Through much of his life, Du Bois struggled to resolve conflicting tendencies in his identity as an African American. In *The Souls of Black Folk,* he wrote, "One ever feels his twoness—an American, a Negro; two souls, two thoughts, two unreconciled strivings; two warring ideals in one dark body, whose dogged strength alone keeps it from being torn asunder."

In *The Negro Problem,* published in 1903, Du Bois challenged Booker T. Washington's advocacy of industrial education for blacks. At issue was the question of the kind of education best fitted to lift the black population from poverty to equality. Du Bois proposed that "the talented tenth" be educated in colleges and universities to provide leadership and direction for the entire black race.

The Negro race, like all races, is going to be saved by its exceptional men. The problem of education, then, among Negroes must first of all deal with the Talented Tenth; it is the problem of developing the Best of this race that they may guide the Mass away from the contamination and death of the Worst, in their own and other races. Now the training of men is a difficult and intricate task. Its technique is a matter for educational experts, but its object is for the vision of seers. If we make money the object of man-training, we shall develop money-makers but not necessarily men; if we make technical skill the object of education, we may possess artisans but not, in nature, men. Men we shall have only as we make manhood the object of the work of the schools—intelligence, broad sympathy, knowledge of the world that was and is, and of the relation of men to it—this is the curriculum of that Higher Education which must underlie true life.... From the very first it has been the educated and intelligent of the Negro people that have led and elevated the mass, and the sole obstacles that nullified and retarded their efforts were slavery and race prejudice; for what is slavery but the legalized survival of the unfit and the nullification of the work of natural internal leadership? ...

It is the fashion of today to ... say that with freedom Negro leadership should have begun at the plow and not in the Senate—a foolish and mischievous lie; two hundred and fifty years that black serf toiled at the plow and yet that toiling was in vain till the Senate passed the war amendments; and two hundred and fifty years more the half-free serf of today may toil at his plow, but unless he have political rights and righteously guarded civic status, he will still remain the poverty-stricken and ignorant plaything of rascals, that he now is. This all sane men know even if they dare not say it. . . .

How then shall the leaders of a struggling people be trained and the hands of the risen few strengthened? There can be but one answer: The best and most capable of their youth must be schooled in the colleges and universities of the land. We will not quarrel as to just what the university of the Negro should teach or how it should teach it—I willingly admit that each soul and each race-soul needs its own peculiar curriculum. But this is true: A university is a human invention for the transmission of knowledge and culture from generation to generation, through the training of quick minds and pure hearts, and for this work no other human invention will suffice, not even trade and industrial schools.

All men cannot go to college but some men must; every isolated group or nation must have its yeast, must have for the talented few centers of training where men are not so mystified and befuddled by the hard and necessary toil of earning a living, as to have no aims higher than their bellies, and no God greater than Gold. This is true training, and thus in the beginning were the favored sons of the freedmen trained.... Where ought they to have begun to build? At the bottom, of course, quibbles the mole with his eyes in the earth. Aye! truly at the bottom, at the very bottom; at the bottom of knowledge, down in the very depths of knowledge there where the roots of justice strike into the lowest soil of Truth. And so they did begin; they founded colleges, and up from the colleges shot normal schools, and out from the normal schools went teachers, and around the normal teachers clustered other teachers to teach the public schools; the college trained in Greek and Latin and mathematics, 2,000 men; and these men trained full 50,000 others in morals and manners, and they in turn taught thrift and the alphabet to nine millions of men, who today hold $300,000,000 of property. It was a miracle —the most wonderful peace-battle of the nineteenth century, and yet today men smile at it, and in fine superiority tell us that it was all a strange mistake; that a proper way to found a system of education is first to gather the children and buy them spelling books and hoes; afterward men may look about for teachers, if haply they may find them; or again they would teach men Work, but as for Life—why, what has Work to do with Life, they ask vacantly....

The college-bred Negro . . . is, as he ought to be, the group leader, the man who sets the ideals of the community where he lives, directs its thoughts, and heads its social movements. It need hardly be argued that the Negro people need social leadership more than most groups; that they have no traditions to fall back upon, no long-established customs, no strong family ties, no well-defined social classes. All these things must be slowly and painfully evolved. The preacher was, even before the war, the group leader of the Negroes, and the church their greatest social institution. Naturally this preacher was ignorant and often immoral, and the problem of replacing the older type by bet-

ter educated men has been a difficult one. Both by direct work and by direct influence on other preachers, and on congregations, the college-bred preacher has an opportunity for reformatory work and moral inspiration, the value of which cannot be overestimated.

It has, however, been in the furnishing of teachers that the Negro college has found its peculiar function. Few persons realize how vast a work, how mighty a revolution has been thus accomplished. To furnish five millions and more of ignorant people with teachers of their own race and blood, in one generation, was not only a very difficult undertaking, but a very important one, in that it placed before the eyes of almost every Negro child an attainable ideal. It brought the masses of the blacks in contact with modern civilization, made black men the leaders of their communities and trainers of the new generation. In this work college-bred Negroes were first teachers, and then teachers of teachers. And here it is that the broad culture of college work has been of peculiar value. Knowledge of life and its wider meaning has been the point of Negroes' deepest ignorance, and the sending out of teachers whose training has not been simply for breadwinning, but also for human culture, has been of inestimable value in the training of these men. . . .

The main question, so far as the Southern Negro is concerned, is: What, under the present circumstance, must a system of education do in order to raise the Negro as quickly as possible in the scale of civilization? The answer to this question seems to me clear: It must strengthen the Negro's character, increase his knowledge, and teach him to earn a living. Now it goes without saying, that it is hard to do all these things simultaneously or suddenly, and that at the same time it will not do to give all the attention to one and neglect the others; we could give black boys trades, but that alone will not civilize a race of ex-slaves; we might simply increase their knowledge of the world, but this would not necessarily make them wish to use this knowledge honestly; we might seek to strengthen character and purpose, but to what end if this people have nothing to eat or to wear? . . . Schoolhouses do not teach themselves—piles of brick and mortar and machinery do not send out *men.* It is the trained, living human soul, cultivated and strengthened by long study and thought, that breathes the real breath of life into boys and girls and makes them human, whether they be black or white, Greek, Russian, or American. . . .

I would not deny, or for a moment seem to deny, the paramount necessity of teaching the Negro to work, and to work steadily and skill-fully; or seem to depreciate in the slightest de-gree the important part industrial schools must play in the accomplishment of these ends, but I *do* say, and insist upon it, that it is industrialism drunk with its vision of success to imagine that its work can be accomplished without providing for the training of broadly cultured men and women to teach its own teachers, and to teach the teachers of the public schools. . . .

I am an earnest advocate of manual training and trade teaching for black boys, and for white boys, too. I believe that next to the founding of Negro colleges the most valuable addition to Negro education since the war has been indus-trial training for black boys. Nevertheless, I in-sist that the object of all true education is not to make men carpenters, it is to make carpenters men; there are two means of making the carpen-ter a man, each equally important; the first is to give the group and community in which he works liberally trained teachers and leaders to teach him and his family what life means; the second is to give him sufficient intelligence and technical skill to make him an efficient work-man; the first object demands the Negro college and college-bred men—not a quantity of such colleges, but a few of excellent quality; not too many college-bred men, but enough to leaven the lump, to inspire the masses, to raise the Tal-ented Tenth to leadership; the second object demands a good system of common schools, well-taught, conveniently located, and properly equipped. . . .

Men of America, the problem is plain before you. Here is a race transplanted through the criminal foolishness of your fathers. Whether you like it or not the millions are here, and here they will remain. If you do not lift them up, they will pull you down. Education and work are the levers to uplift a people. Work alone will not do it unless inspired by the right ideals and guided by intelligence. Education must not simply teach work—it must teach Life. The Talented Tenth of the Negro race must be made leaders of thought and missionaries of culture among their people. No others can do this work and Negro colleges must train men for it. The Negro race, like all other races, is going to be saved by its exceptional men.

W. E. B. DU BOIS

ADVICE TO A BLACK SCHOOLGIRL

Ignorance is a cure for nothing.

A white high school teacher in Berwyn, Pennsylvania, wrote to Du Bois about a black student who was "very bright" but refused to study because she felt that she would "never have a chance to use her knowledge." Du Bois wrote to the student, Vernealia Fareira, on January 7, 1905, as follows.

I wonder if you will let a stranger say a word to you about yourself? I have heard that you are a young woman of some ability but that you are neglecting your school work because you have become hopeless of trying to do anything in the world. I am very sorry for this. How any human being whose wonderful fortune it is to live in the 20th century should under ordinarily fair advantages despair of life is almost unbelievable. And if in addition to this that person is, as I am, of Negro lineage with all the hopes and yearnings of hundreds of millions of human souls dependent in some degree on her striving, then her bitterness amounts to crime.

There are in the U.S. today tens of thousands of colored girls who would be happy beyond measure to have the chance of educating themselves that you are neglecting. If you train yourself as you easily can, there are wonderful chances of usefulness before you: you can join the ranks of 15,000 Negro women teachers, of hundreds of nurses and physicians, of the growing number of clerks and stenographers, and above all of the host of homemakers. Ignorance is a cure for nothing. Get the very best training possible & the doors of opportunity will fly open before you as they are flying before thousands of your fellows. On the other hand every time a colored person neglects an opportunity, it makes it more difficult for others of the race to get such an opportunity. Do you want to cut off the chances of the boys and girls of tomorrow?

THE NIAGARA MOVEMENT DECLARATION OF PRINCIPLES

Any discrimination based simply on race or color is barbarous, we care not how hallowed it be by custom, expediency or prejudice.

W. E. B. Du Bois was the moving force in the creation of the Niagara Movement, an organization of prominent African American leaders that first convened in the summer of 1905 at Niagara Falls. The purpose of the organization was to establish an assertive alternative to the accommodationist politics of Booker T. Washington. The group, however, was unable to develop enough funding to establish a permanent staff or headquarters and appeared to be heading for the same fate as previous efforts to organize a black protest organization.

But in 1908, race riots in Springfield, Illinois, the hometown of Abraham Lincoln, prompted a group of whites to plan an organization that would revive the abolitionist spirit on behalf of black rights. Mary White Ovington, a social worker; William English Walling, a journalist; and Oswald Garrison Villard, publisher of the *New York Post,* convened a national conference to renew "the struggle for political and civil liberty." The white leaders joined forces with the black leaders of the Niagara Movement to create the National Association for the Advancement of Colored People. The principles of the Niagara Movement became the principles of the new NAACP.

Progress: The members of the conference, known as the Niagara Movement, assembled in annual meeting at Buffalo, July 11th, 12th and 13th, 1905, congratulate the Negro-Americans on certain undoubted evidences of progress in the last decade, particularly the increase of intelligence, the buying of property, the checking of crime, the uplift in home life, the advance in literature and art, and the demonstration of constructive and executive ability in the conduct of great religious, economic and educational institutions.

Suffrage: At the same time, we believe that this class of American citizens should protest emphatically and continually against the curtailment of their political rights. We believe in manhood suffrage; we believe that no man is so good, intelligent or wealthy as to be entrusted wholly with the welfare of his neighbor.

Civil Liberty: We believe also in protest against the curtailment of our civil rights. All American citizens have the right to equal treatment in places of public entertainment according to their behavior and deserts.

Economic Opportunity: We especially complain against the denial of equal opportunities to us in economic life; in the rural districts of the South this amounts to peonage and virtual slavery; all over the South it tends to crush labor and small business enterprises; and everywhere American prejudice, helped often by iniquitous laws, is making it more difficult for Negro-Americans to earn a decent living.

Education: Common school education should be free to all American children and compulsory. High school training should be adequately provided for all, and college training should be the monopoly of no class or race in any section of our common country. We believe that, in defense of our own institutions, the United States should aid common school education, particularly in the South, and we especially recommend concerted agitation to this end. We urge an increase in public high school facilities in the South, where the Negro-Americans are almost wholly without such provisions. We favor well-equipped trade and technical schools for the training of artisans, and the need of adequate and liberal endowment for a few institutions of higher education must be patent to sincere well-wishers of the race.

Courts: We demand upright judges in courts, juries selected without discrimination on account of color and the same measure of punishment and the same efforts at reformation for black as for white offenders. We need orphanages and farm schools for dependent children,

juvenile reformatories for delinquents, and the abolition of the dehumanizing convict-lease system.

Public Opinion: We note with alarm the evident retrogression in this land of sound public opinion on the subject of manhood rights, republican government and human brotherhood, and we pray God that this nation will not degenerate into a mob of boasters and oppressors, but rather will return to the faith of the fathers, that all men were created free and equal, with certain unalienable rights.

Health: We plead for health—for an opportunity to live in decent houses and localities, for a chance to rear our children in physical and moral cleanliness.

Employers and Labor Unions: We hold up for public execration the conduct of two opposite classes of men: The practice among employers of importing ignorant Negro-American laborers in emergencies, and then affording them neither protection nor permanent employment; and the practice of labor unions in proscribing and boycotting and oppressing thousands of their fellow-toilers, simply because they are black. These methods have accentuated and will accentuate the war of labor and capital, and they are disgraceful to both sides.

Protest: We refuse to allow the impression to remain that the Negro-American assents to inferiority, is submissive under oppression and apologetic before insults. Through helplessness we may submit, but the voice of protest of ten million Americans must never cease to assail the ears of their fellows, so long as America is unjust.

Color-Line: Any discrimination based simply on race or color is barbarous, we care not how hallowed it be by custom, expediency or prejudice. Differences made on account of ignorance, immorality, or disease are legitimate methods of fighting evil, and against them we have no word of protest; but discriminations based simply and solely on physical peculiarities, place of birth, color of skin, are relics of that unreasoning human savagery of which the world is and ought to be thoroughly ashamed.

"Jim Crow" Cars: We protest against the

"Jim Crow" car, since its effect is and must be to make us pay first-class fare for third-class accommodations, render us open to insults and discomfort and to crucify wantonly our manhood, womanhood and self-respect.

Soldiers: We regret that this nation has never seen fit adequately to reward the black soldiers who, in its five wars, have defended their country with their blood, and yet have been systematically denied the promotions which their abilities deserve. And we regard as unjust, the exclusion of black boys from the military and naval training schools.

War Amendments: We urge upon Congress the enactment of appropriate legislation for securing the proper enforcement of those articles of freedom, the thirteenth, fourteenth and fifteenth amendments of the Constitution of the United States.

Oppression: We repudiate the monstrous doctrine that the oppressor should be the sole authority as to the rights of the oppressed. The Negro race in America stolen, ravished and degraded, struggling up through difficulties and oppression, needs sympathy and receives criticism; needs help and is given hindrance, needs protection and is given mob-violence, needs justice and is given charity, needs leadership and is given cowardice and apology, needs bread and is given a stone. This nation will never stand justified before God until these things are changed.

The Church: Especially are we surprised and astonished at the recent attitude of the church of Christ—of an increase of a desire to bow to racial prejudice, to narrow the bounds of human brotherhood, and to segregate black men to some outer sanctuary. This is wrong, unchristian and disgraceful to the twentieth century civilization.

Agitation: Of the above grievances we do not hesitate to complain, and to complain loudly and insistently. To ignore, overlook, or apologize for these wrongs is to prove ourselves unworthy of freedom. Persistent manly agitation is the way to liberty, and toward this goal the Niagara Movement has started and asks the cooperation of all men of all races.

Help: At the same time we want to acknowledge with deep thankfulness the help of our fellowmen from the Abolitionist down to those who today still stand for equal opportunity and who have given and still give of their wealth and of their poverty for our advancement.

Duties: And while we are demanding and ought to demand, and will continue to demand the rights enumerated above, God forbid that we should ever forget to urge corresponding duties upon our people:

The duty to vote.

The duty to respect the rights of others.

The duty to work.

The duty to obey the laws.

The duty to be clean and orderly.

The duty to send our children to school.

The duty to respect ourselves, even as we respect others.

This statement, complaint and prayer we submit to the American people, and Almighty God.

ALBERT VON TILZER AND JACK NORWORTH

TAKE ME OUT TO THE BALL GAME

"Take Me Out to the Ball Game" is the national anthem of the national pastime; it is the song played during "the seventh inning stretch." It was written in 1908 by two stalwarts of Tin Pan Alley, Albert Von Tilzer and Jack Norworth. Von Tilzer, who wrote the music, had never been to a baseball game. Von Tilzer collaborated with various lyricists to write some of the most popular songs of his time, such as "Teasing" (1904),

"Put Your Arms Around Me, Honey" (1910), and "I'll Be with You in Apple Blossom Time" (1920). Von Tilzer was a member of a musical family (whose real name was Gumm); his brother Harry wrote "I Want a Girl Just Like the Girl That Married Dear Old Dad" (1911) and "When My Baby Smiles at Me" (1920). Norworth was a veteran vaude-villian, a song-and-dance man, who wrote "Shine On, Harvest Moon" for the Ziegfeld Follies of 1908.

Katie Casey was baseball mad,
Had the fever and had it bad;
Just to root for the home town crew, ev'ry sou,
    Katie blew
On a Saturday, her young beau
Called to see if she'd like to go,
To see a show but Miss Kate said, "No,
I'll tell you what you can do":

CHORUS:
Take me out to the ball game,
Take me out with the crowd
Buy me some peanuts and crackerjack,
I don't care if I never get back,

Let me root, root, root for the home team,
If they don't win it's a shame
For it's one, two, three strikes you're out,
At the old ball game.

Katie Casey saw all the games,
Knew the players by their first names;
Told the umpire he was wrong, all along, good
    and strong
When the score was just two to two,
Katie Casey knew just what to do,
Just to cheer up the boys she knew,
She made the gang sing this song:

The first World Series was played in 1903 in Boston at the Huntington Avenue Baseball Grounds, now the site of Northeastern University. The Boston Americans beat the Pittsburgh Nationals. The games were interrupted several times by enthusiastic fans who broke through police lines around the field.

JOE HILL
THE PREACHER AND THE SLAVE

Joseph Hillstrom (c. 1879–1915) came to the United States from Sweden in 1902, drifted for a time, then joined the radical Industrial Workers of the World in 1910. The "Wobblies" opposed the American Federation of Labor, which accepted the capitalist system and refused to organize unskilled workers. Even the radical socialist leader Eugene Victor Debs withdrew from the IWW when its revolutionary zeal became too extreme for him. Although Hill worked as a labor organizer, he was better known for the parodies that he wrote, especially "The Preacher and the Slave." Hill was arrested in January 1914 on murder charges; convicted on the basis of circumstantial evidence, he spent nearly two years in jail while unsuccessfully appealing his conviction. The day before he faced a firing squad in November 1915, he wired Big Bill Haywood, the head of the IWW, "Don't waste any time in mourning. Organize!" After his death, he became a legendary figure, celebrated in Alfred Hayes's "I Dreamed I Saw Joe Hill Last Night."

"The Preacher and the Slave" is sung to the tune "Sweet Bye and Bye" and is included in the AFL-CIO official song book.

Long-haired preachers come out every night,
Try to tell you what's wrong and what's right;
But when asked how 'bout something to eat
They will answer with voices so sweet:

CHORUS:
You will eat, bye and bye,
In that glorious land above the sky;
Work and play, live on hay,
You'll get pie in the sky when you die.

And the starvation army they play,
And they sing and they clap and they pray.
Till they get all your coin on the drum,
Then they tell you when you are on the bum:

If you fight hard for children and wife—
Try to get something good in this life—
You're a sinner and bad man, they tell,
When you die you will sure go to hell.

Workingmen of all countries unite,
Side by side we for freedom will fight:
When the world and its wealth we have gained
To the grafters we'll sing this refrain:

LAST CHORUS:
You will eat, bye and bye.
When you've learned how to cook and to fry;
Chop some wood, 'twill do you good,
And you'll eat in the sweet bye and bye.

JOYCE KILMER
TREES

"Trees" is the best-known poem by Joyce Kilmer (1886–1918), a poet, journalist, and critic who died in World War I at the second Battle of the Marne. Born in New Brunswick, New Jersey, and educated at Rutgers and Columbia universities, Kilmer published his first volume of poetry, *Summer of Verse,* in 1911. "Trees" was first published in *Poetry* magazine in 1913. It was the title poem in a collection of Kilmer's poetry called

Trees and Other Poems (1914). His other books include *The Circus and Other Essays, Main Street and Other Poems, Literature in the Making,* and *Dreams and Images,* an anthology of modern Catholic poetry. Kilmer was posthumously awarded the Croix de Guerre.

I think that I shall never see
A poem lovely as a tree.

A tree whose hungry mouth is prest
Against the earth's sweet flowing breast;

A tree that looks at God all day,
And lifts her leafy arms to pray;

A tree that may in Summer wear
A nest of robins in her hair;

Upon whose bosom snow has lain;
Who intimately lives with rain.

Poems are made by fools like me,
But only God can make a tree.

WOODROW WILSON
THE NEW FREEDOM

Nations are renewed from the bottom, not from the top.

(Thomas) Woodrow Wilson (1856–1924) was born in Virginia, the son of a stern Presbyterian minister. In his youth, he lived in Georgia and South Carolina amid the devastation caused by the Civil War. He was educated at Davidson College in North Carolina, Princeton University, and Johns Hopkins University, where he earned a Ph.D. degree in history and government. His successful career as a professor led to the presidency of Princeton University in 1902. His speeches and writings on current issues brought him national recognition, and he was elected governor of New Jersey in 1910. His appeal to progressive forces in the Democratic Party brought him the Democratic nomination for president in 1912; because the Republican Party split between the followers of William Howard Taft and Theodore Roosevelt, Wilson won the election.

Wilson's campaign speeches were collected in a volume, excerpted here, called *The New Freedom,* which was the slogan of his progressive platform.

When I look back on the processes of history, when I survey the genesis of America, I see this written over every page: that the nations are renewed from the bottom, not from the top; that the genius which springs up from the ranks of unknown men is the genius which renews the youth and energy of the people. Everything I know about history, every bit of experience and observation that has contributed to my thought, has confirmed me in the conviction that the real wisdom of human life is compounded out of the experiences of ordinary men. The utility, the vitality, the fruitage of life does not come from the top to the bottom; it comes, like the natural growth of a great tree, from the soil, up through the trunk into the branches to the foliage and the fruit. The great struggling unknown masses of the men who are at the base of everything are the dynamic force that is lifting the levels of society. A nation is as great, and only as great, as her rank and file.

So the first and chief need of this nation of

ours to-day is to include in the partnership of government all those great bodies of unnamed men who are going to produce our future leaders and renew the future energies of America. And as I confess that, as I confess my belief in the common man, I know what I am saying. The man who is swimming against the stream knows the strength of it. The man who is in the mêlée knows what blows are being struck and what blood is being drawn. The man who is on the make is the judge of what is happening in America, not the man who has made good; not the man who has emerged from the flood; not the man who is standing on the bank looking on, but the man who is struggling for his life and for the lives of those who are dearer to him than himself. That is the man whose judgment will tell you what is going on in America; that is the man by whose judgment I, for one, wish to be guided.

We have had the wrong jury; we have had the wrong group,—no, I will not say the wrong group, but too small a group,—in control of the policies of the United States. The average man has not been consulted, and his heart had begun to sink for fear he never would be consulted, and his heart had begun to sink for fear he never would be consulted again. Therefore, we have got to organize a government whose sympathies will be open to the whole body of the people of the United States, a government which will consult as large a proportion of the people of the United States as possible before it acts. Because the great problem of government is to know what the average man is experiencing and is thinking about. Most of us are average men; very few of us rise, except by fortunate accident, above the general level of the community about us; and therefore the man who thinks common thoughts, the man who has had common experiences is almost always the man who interprets America aright. Isn't that the reason that we are proud of such stories as the story of Abraham Lincoln,—a man who rose out of the ranks and interpreted America better than any man had interpreted it who had risen out of the privi-leged classes or the educated classes of America?

The hope of the United States in the present and in the future is the same that it has always been: it is the hope and confidence that out of unknown homes will come men who will constitute themselves the masters of industry and of politics. The average hopefulness, the average welfare, the average enterprise, the average initiative, of the United States are the only things that make it rich. We are not rich because a few gentlemen direct our industry; we are rich because of our own intelligence and our own industry. America does not consist of men who get their names into the newspapers; America does not consist politically of the men who set themselves up to be political leaders; she does not consist of the men who do most of her talking,—they are important only so far as they speak for that great voiceless multitude of men who constitute the great body and the saving force of the nation. Nobody who cannot speak the common thought, who does not move by the common impulse, is the man to speak for America, or for any of her future purposes. Only he is fit to speak who knows the thoughts of the great body of citizens, the men who go about their business every day, the men who toil from morning till night, the men who go home tired in the evenings, the men who are carrying on the things we are so proud of.

You know how it thrills our blood sometimes to think how all the nations of the earth wait to see what America is going to do with her power, her physical power, her enormous resources, her enormous wealth. The nations hold their breath to see what this young country will do with her young unspoiled strength; we cannot help but be proud that we are strong. But what has made us strong? The toil of millions of men, the toil of men who do not boast, who are inconspicuous, but who live their lives humbly from day to day; it is the great body of toilers that constitutes the might of America. It is one of the glories of our land that nobody is able to predict from what family, from what region, from what race, even, the leaders of the country are going to come. The great leaders of this country have not come very often from the established, "successful" families.

I remember speaking at a school not long ago where I understood that almost all the young men were the sons of very rich people, and I told them I looked upon them with a great deal of pity, because, I said: "Most of you fellows are doomed to obscurity. You will not do anything. You will never try to do anything, and with all the great tasks of the country waiting to be done, probably you are the very men who will decline to do them. Some man who has been 'up against it,' some man who has come out of the crowd, somebody who has had the whip of necessity laid on his back, will emerge out of the crowd, will show that he understands the crowd, understands the interests of the nation, united and not separated, and will stand up and lead us."

If I may speak of my own experience, I have found audiences made up of the "common people" quicker to take a point, quicker to understand an argument, quicker to discern a tendency and to comprehend a principle, than many a college class that I have lectured to,—not because the college class lacked the intelligence, but because college boys are not in contact with the realities of life, while "common" citizens are in contact with the actual life of day by day; you do not have to explain to them what touches them to the quick.

There is one illustration of the value of the constant renewal of society from the bottom that has always interested me profoundly. The only reason why government did not suffer dry rot in the Middle Ages under the aristocratic system which then prevailed was that so many of the men who were efficient instruments of government were drawn from the church,—from that great religious body which was then the only church, that body which we now distinguish from other religious bodies as the Roman Catholic Church. The Roman Catholic Church was then, as it is now, a great democracy. There was no peasant so humble that he

might not become a priest, and no priest so obscure that he might not become Pope of Christendom; and every chancellery in Europe, every court in Europe, was ruled by these learned, trained and accomplished men,—the priesthood of that great and dominant body. What kept government alive in the Middle Ages was this constant rise of the sap from the bottom, from the rank and file of the great body of the people through the open channels of the priesthood. That, it seems to me, is one of the most interesting and convincing illustrations that could possibly be adduced of the thing that I am talking about.

The only way that government is kept pure is by keeping these channels open, so that nobody may deem himself so humble as not to constitute a part of the body politic, so that there will constantly be coming new blood into the veins of the body politic; so that no man is so obscure that he may not break the crust of any class he may belong to, may not spring up to higher levels and be counted among the leaders of the state. Anything that depresses, anything that makes the organization greater than the man, anything that blocks, discourages, dismays the humble man, is against all the principles of progress. When I see alliances formed, as they are now being formed, by successful men of business with successful organizers of politics, I know that something has been done that checks the vitality and progress of society. Such an alliance, made at the top, is an alliance made to depress the levels, to hold them where they are, if not to sink them; and, therefore, it is the constant business of good politics to break up such partnerships, to re-establish and reopen the connections between the great body of the people and the offices of government.

To-day, when our government has so far passed into the hands of special interests; to-day, when the doctrine is implicitly avowed that only select classes have the equipment necessary for carrying on government; to-day when the doctrine is implicitly avowed that only select classes have the equipment necessary for carrying on government; to-day, when so many

Industrialization and mass-production techniques changed the nature of the workplace for many Americans. In this classic photograph by Lewis Hine, a worker examines the hub of a transformer motor.

conscientious citizens, smitten with the scene of social wrong and suffering, have fallen victims to the fallacy that benevolent government can be meted out to the people by kind-hearted trustees of prosperity and guardians of the welfare of dutiful employees—to-day, supremely, does it behoove this nation to remember that a people shall be saved by the power that sleeps in its own deep bosom, or by none; shall be renewed in hope, in conscience, in strength, by waters welling up from its own sweet, perennial springs. Not from above; not by patronage of its aristocrats. The flower does not bear the root, but the root the flower. Everything that blooms in beauty in the air of heaven draws its fairness, its vigor, from its roots. Nothing living can blossom into fruitage unless through nourishing stalks deep-planted in the common soil. The rose is merely the evidence of the vitality of the root; and the real source of its beauty, the very blush that it wears upon its tender cheek, comes from those silent sources of life that lie hidden in the chemistry of the soil. Up from that soil, up from the silent bosom of the earth, rise the currents of life and energy. Up from the common soil, up from the quiet heart of the people, rise joyously to-day streams of hope and determination bound to renew the face of the earth in glory.

I tell you, the so-called radicalism of our times is simply the effort of nature to release the generous energies of our people. This great American people is at bottom just, virtuous, and hopeful; the roots of its being are in the soil of what is lovely, pure, and of good report, and the need of the hour is just that radicalism that will clear a way for the realization of the aspirations of a sturdy race.

WILLIAM MONROE TROTTER
PROTEST TO PRESIDENT WILSON

Have you a "new freedom" for white Americans and a new slavery for your Afro-American fellow citizens? God forbid!

Woodrow Wilson promised a "new freedom" when he campaigned for the presidency in 1912. As a candidate, he wrote to a black leader to pledge that, if elected, "The colored people . . . may count on me for absolute fair dealing." Soon after his election, however, the Wilson administration introduced racial segregation in the Treasury Department and the Post Office Department.

The fledgling National Association for the Advancement of Colored People sent a protest to Wilson, but to no avail. A year later, on November 12, 1914, the president met with a delegation of African Americans led by William Monroe Trotter (1872–1934), the editor of a black newspaper in Boston. Trotter delivered the following address. Wilson was so offended that he told the committee he would not meet with them again unless they got a new leader.

Born in Ohio, Trotter grew up in a middle-class family in a comfortable suburb of Boston. He went to Harvard, where he was the first black student elected to Phi Beta Kappa in his junior year. After a brief interlude in business, he launched the *Boston Guardian* and was a relentless crusader for racial equality. His speech to Wilson was reprinted in the nation's black press.

One year ago we presented a national petition, signed by Afro-Americans in thirty-eight states, protesting against the segregation of employes of the National government whose ancestry could be traced in whole or in part to Africa, as instituted under your administration in the treasury and postoffice departments. We then appealed to you to undo this race segregation in accord with your duty as president and with your pre-election pledges. We stated that there could be no freedom, no respect from others, and no equality of citizenship under segregation for races, especially when applied to but one of many racial elements in the government employ. For such placement of employes means a charge by the government of physical indecency or infection, or of being a lower order of beings, or a subjection to the prejudices of other citizens, which constitutes inferiority of status. We protested such segregation as to working conditions, eating tables, dressing rooms, rest rooms, lockers and especially public toilets in government buildings. We stated that such segregation was a public humiliation and degradation, entirely unmerited and far-reaching in its injurious effects, a gratuitous blow against ever-loyal citizens and against those many of whom aided and supported your elevation to the presidency of our common country.

At that time you stated you would investigate conditions for yourself. Now, after the lapse of a year, we have come back having found that all the forms of segregation of government employes of African extraction are still practiced in the treasury and postoffice department buildings, and to a certain extent have spread into other government buildings.

Under the treasury department, in the bureau of engraving and printing there is segregation not only in dressing rooms, but in working positions, Afro-American employes being herded at separate tables, in eating, and in toilets. In the navy department there is herding at desks and separation in lavatories. In the post-office department there is separation in work for Afro-American women in the alcove on the eighth floor, of Afro-American men in rooms on the seventh floor, with forbidding even of entrance into an adjoining room occupied by white clerks on the seventh floor, and of Afro-American men in separate rooms just instituted on the sixth floor, with separate lavatories for Afro-American men on the eighth floor; in the main treasury building in separate lavatories in the basement; in the interior department separate lavatories, which were specifically pointed out to you at our first hearing; in the state and other departments separate lavatories; in marine hospital service building in separate lavatories, though there is but one Afro-American clerk to use it; in the war department in separate lavatories; in the postoffice department building separate lavatories; in the sewing and bindery divisions of the government printing office on the fifth floor there is herding at working positions of Afro-American women and separation in lavatories, and new segregation instituted by the division chief since our first audience with you. This lavatory segregation is the most degrading, most insulting of all. Afro-American employes who use the regular public lavatories on

the floors where they work are cautioned and are then warned by superior officers against insubordination.

We have come by vote of this league to set before you this definite continuance of race segregation and to renew the protest and to ask you to abolish segregation of Afro-American employes in the executive department.

Because we cannot believe you capable of any disregard of your pledges we have been sent by the alarmed American citizens of color. They realize that if they can be segregated and thus humiliated by the national government at the national capital the beginning is made for the spread of that persecution and prosecution which makes property and life itself insecure in the South, the foundation of the whole fabric of their citizenship is unsettled.

They have made plain enough to you their opposition to segregation last year by a national anti-segregation petition, this year by a protest registered at the polls, voting against every Democratic candidate save those outspoken against segregation. The only Democrat elected governor in the eastern states, was Governor Walsh of Massachusetts, who appealed to you by letter to stop segregation. Thus have the Afro-Americans shown how they detest segregation.

In fact, so intense is their resentment that the movement to divide this solid race vote and make peace with the national Democracy, so suspiciously revived when you ran for the presidency, and which some of our families for two generations have been risking all to promote, bids fair to be undone.

Only two years ago you were heralded as perhaps the second Lincoln, and now the Afro-American leaders who supported you are hounded as false leaders and traitors to their race. What a change segregation has wrought!

You said that your "Colored fellow citizens could depend upon you for everything which would assist in advancing the interests of their race in the United States." Consider this pledge in the face of the continued color segregation! Fellow citizenship means congregation. Segregation destroys fellowship and citizenship. Consider that any passerby on the streets of the national capital, whether he be black or white, can enter and use the public lavatories in government buildings while citizens of color who do the work of the government are excluded.

As equal citizens and by virtue of your public promises we are entitled at your hands to freedom from discrimination, restriction, imputation and insult in government employ. Have you a "new freedom" for white Americans and a new slavery for your Afro-American fellow citizens? God forbid!

We have been delegated to ask you to issue an executive order against any and all segregation of government employes because of race and color, and to ask whether you will do so. We await your reply, that we may give it to the waiting citizens of the United States of African extraction.

EDGAR LEE MASTERS
ANNE RUTLEDGE

Edgar Lee Masters (1869–1950) grew up on a farm in Illinois and became a lawyer. Although he wrote many poems, plays, novels, and biographies, he is best remembered for his *Spoon River Anthology* (1915). That collection consists of a series of free-verse monologues, each representing the epitaph of a citizen of the fictional town of Spoon River, each revealing the frustrations and disappointments of his or her life in a small town. Perhaps the best known was the epitaph for "Anne Rutledge," the sweetheart of Abraham Lincoln's youth, who died in 1835 at the age of about nineteen.

Out of me unworthy and unknown
The vibrations of deathless music;
"With malice toward none, with charity
    for all."
Out of me the forgiveness of millions
    toward millions,
And the beneficent face of a nation
Shining with justice and truth.

I am Anne Rutledge who sleep beneath
    these weeds,
Beloved in life of Abraham Lincoln,
Wedded to him, not through union,
But through separation.
Bloom forever, O Republic,
From the dust of my bosom!

ROBERT FROST
THE ROAD NOT TAKEN

Robert Frost (1874–1963) went to high school in Lawrence, Massachusetts, and briefly attended college at Dartmouth and Harvard. Until he achieved success as a poet, Frost alternated between farming and teaching Greek and Latin in high school. His first collection of poems was published in 1913. From 1916 on, he held posts in distinguished academic institutions, usually as a poet in residence. Frost's poetry is admired in part because he is accessible to readers without academic training; while many other poets became experimental, he continued to use ordinary language and to describe everyday events, closely observed. Many of his poems reflect his closeness to nature, through which he expressed symbolic meaning, rather than bucolic nostalgia. "The Road Not Taken," one of Frost's best-known poems, was written in 1915.

Two roads diverged in a yellow wood,
And sorry I could not travel both
And be one traveler, long I stood
And looked down one as far as I could
To where it bent in the undergrowth;

Then took the other, as just as fair,
And having perhaps the better claim,
Because it was grassy and wanted wear;
Though as for that the passing there
Had worn them really about the same,

And both that morning equally lay
In leaves no step had trodden black.
Oh, I kept the first for another day!
Yet knowing how way leads on to way,
I doubted if I should ever come back.

I shall be telling this with a sigh
Somewhere ages and ages hence;
Two roads diverged in a wood, and I—
I took the one less traveled by,
And that has made all the difference.

ALICE DUER MILLER
EVOLUTION

Alice Duer Miller (1874–1942) was born in New York City, and she graduated from Barnard College in 1899. She wrote light poetry on behalf of the suffrage movement, bringing wit to a cause that was often accused of being humorless. The following poem comes from her collection *Are Women People? A Book of Rhymes for Suffrage Times*, published in 1915.

Said Mr. Jones in 1910:
"Women, subject yourselves to men."
Nineteen-Eleven heard him quote:
"They rule the world without the vote."
By Nineteen-Twelve, he would submit
"When all the women wanted it."
By Nineteen-Thirteen, looking glum,

He said that it was bound to come.
This year I heard him say with pride:
"No reasons on the other side!"
By Nineteen-Fifteen, he'll insist
He's always been a suffragist.
And what is really stranger, too,
He'll think that what he says is true.

CARL SANDBURG
CHICAGO

Born in Galesburg, Illinois, to Swedish immigrant parents, Carl Sandburg (1878–1967) worked as a laborer, fought in the Spanish-American War, then put himself through Lombard College in Galesburg. He was a journalist, an advertising writer, an organizer for the Social Democratic Party in Wisconsin, and an aide to the socialist mayor of Milwaukee.

His poems were first printed in *Poetry* magazine in 1914. Two years later he published *Chicago Poems,* and "Chicago" was one of this first collection. After another collection, *Cornhuskers,* appeared in 1918, Sandburg was recognized by fellow poets and the poetry-loving public as an important new poet. His simple, direct language, his use of colloquialisms, and his free verse established him as an original voice. Sandburg published two collections of ballads and folksongs. He won the Pulitzer Prize for poetry in 1919 and in 1950, and he was awarded the Pulitzer Prize in 1939 for his massive, six-volume biography of Lincoln.

Hog Butcher for the World,
Tool maker, Stacker of Wheat,
Player with Railroads and the Nation's Freight
    Handler;
Stormy, husky, brawling,
City of the Big Shoulders:

They tell me you are wicked and I believe
    them, for I have seen your painted
    women under the gas lamps luring the
    farm boys.
And they tell me you are crooked and I answer:
    Yes, it is true I have seen the gunman
    kill and go free to kill again.
And they tell me you are brutal and my reply
    is: On the faces of women and children I
    have seen the marks of wanton hunger.
And having answered so I turn once more to
    those who sneer at this my city, and I
    give them back the sneer and say to
    them:
Come and show me another city with lifted
    head singing so proud to be alive and
    coarse and strong and cunning.
Flinging magnetic curses amid the toil of piling

job on job, here is a tall bold slugger set
    vivid against the little soft cities;
Fierce as a dog with tongue lapping for action,
    cunning as a savage pitted against the
    wilderness,
        Bareheaded,
        Shoveling,
        Wrecking,
        Planning,
        Building, breaking, rebuilding,
Under the smoke, dust all over his mouth,
    laughing with white teeth,
Under the terrible burden of destiny laughing
    as a young man laughs,
Laughing even as an ignorant fighter laughs
    who has never lost a battle,
Bragging and laughing that under his wrist is
    the pulse, and under his ribs the heart of
    the people,
        Laughing!
Laughing the stormy, husky, brawling laughter
    of Youth, half-naked, sweating, proud to
    be Hog Butcher, Tool Maker, Stacker of
    Wheat, Player with Railroads and Freight
    Handler to the Nation.

RALPH CHAPLIN

SOLIDARITY FOREVER

"Solidarity Forever" is known as the anthem of the labor movement. It was written by Ralph Chaplin (1888–1961), a poet, writer, artist, and organizer for the Industrial Workers of the World ("Wobblies"). The Wobblies believed in change through violent class struggle; they were active from 1905 until about 1920, and were known equally for their revolutionary activism and for their songs. The Wobblies favored organizing all workers into one big industrial union, while the moderate leadership of the American Federation of Labor preferred to organize workers by their crafts. The leaders of the IWW were prosecuted and persecuted, particularly for their opposition to America's entry into World War I. "Solidarity Forever" was the best-known Wobbly song. Chaplin wrote it in 1915 while he was in West Virginia, helping to organize a coal miners' strike. It is sung to the tune of "John Brown's Body."

When the Union's inspiration through the
    workers' blood shall run
There can be no power greater anywhere
    beneath the sun.
Yet what force on earth is weaker than the
    feeble strength of one?
But the Union makes us strong.

CHORUS:
Solidarity forever!
Solidarity forever!
Solidarity forever!
For the Union makes us strong.

They have taken untold millions, that they
    never toiled to earn,
But without our brain and muscle not a single
    wheel could turn;
We can break their haughty power, gain our
    freedom when we learn—
That the Union makes us strong.

In our hands is placed a power greater than
    their hoarded gold;
Greater than the might of armies magnified a
    thousand fold,
We can bring to birth a new world from the
    ashes of the old.
For the Union makes us strong.

WORLD WAR I AND AFTER

Americans All, *a Liberty Loan poster by Howard Chandler Christy, 1919, encouraged Americans to buy war bonds.*

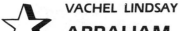

VACHEL LINDSAY

ABRAHAM LINCOLN WALKS AT MIDNIGHT and THE LEADEN-EYED

Vachel Lindsay (1879–1931) was born in Springfield, Illinois, and attended Hiram College in Ohio and art schools in Chicago and New York. He thought about becoming a missionary, but turned instead to poetry, which he infused with the missionary spirit. In 1912, he walked from Illinois to New Mexico, reading his poems in exchange for food and shelter. His first public recognition as a poet came in 1913, when he published his poem "General William Booth Enters Heaven," about the founder of the Salvation Army. He attempted to revive poetry as an oral art form, accessible to common people. At his poetry readings, he invited the audience to join in the refrain. Listeners clamored to hear him recite poems like "Bryan, Bryan, Bryan," "The Congo," and "The Santa Fe Trail."

One of his most popular poems, "Abraham Lincoln Walks at Midnight," was written in 1914, as the Great War began in Europe. "The Leaden-Eyed" was published in Lindsay's *The Congo and Other Poems* (1915).

Abraham Lincoln Walks at Midnight

(In Springfield, Illinois)

It is portentous, and a thing of state
That here at midnight, in our little town
A mourning figure walks, and will not rest,
Near the old court-house pacing up and down,

Or by his homestead, or in shadowed yards
He lingers where his children used to play,
Or through the market, on the well-worn
 stones
He stalks until the dawn-stars burn away.

A bronzed, lank man! His suit of ancient black,
A famous high top-hat and plain worn shawl
Make him the quaint great figure that men love,
The prairie-lawyer, master of us all.

He cannot sleep upon his hillside now.
He is among us:—as in times before!
And we who toss and lie awake for long
Breathe deep, and start, to see him pass the
 door.

His head is bowed. He thinks on men and
 kings.

Yea, when the sick world cries, how can he
 sleep?
Too many peasants fight, they know not why,
Too many homesteads in black terror weep.

The sins of all the war-lords burn his heart.
He sees the dreadnaughts scouring every main.
He carries on his shawl-wrapped shoulders
 now
The bitterness, the folly and the pain.

He cannot rest until a spirit-dawn
Shall come;—the shining hope of Europe free:
The league of sober folk, the Workers' Earth,
Bringing long peace to Cornland, Alp and Sea.

It breaks his heart that kings must murder still,
That all his hours of travail here for men
Seem yet in vain. And who will bring white
 peace
That he may sleep upon his hill again?

The Leaden-Eyed

Let not young souls be smothered out before
They do quaint deeds and fully flaunt their
 pride.

It is the world's one crime its babes grow dull,
Its poor are oxlike, limp and leaden-eyed.
Not that they starve, but starve so dreamlessly;

Not that they sow, but that they seldom reap;
Not that they serve, but have no gods to serve;
Not that they die, but that they die like sheep.

ALFRED BRYAN AND AL PIANTADOSI
I DIDN'T RAISE MY BOY TO BE A SOLDIER

Alfred Bryan wrote the lyrics, and Al Piantadosi wrote the music for the hit song of 1915, "I Didn't Raise My Boy to Be a Soldier," which captured the public's desire to stay out of the war raging in Europe. Bryan was a successful lyricist, whose songs include "Peg 'o My Heart," "Come Josephine in My Flying Machine," and "Daddy, You've Been a Mother to Me." Piantadosi, a New Yorker, played the piano in saloons and accompanied vaudeville performers. He wrote a number of commercially successful songs, including three with ethnic themes ("I'm a Yiddish Cowboy," "I'm Awfully Glad I'm Irish," and "That Italian Rag"). Two of his ballads sold over a million copies of sheet music ("That's How I Need You" and "The Curse of an Aching Heart").

Ten million soldiers to the war have gone,
Who may never return again.
Ten million mothers' hearts must break
For the ones who died in vain.
Head bowed down in sorrow
In her lonely years,
I heard a mother murmur thro' her tears:

CHORUS:
I didn't raise my boy to be a soldier,
I brought him up to be my pride and joy,
Who dares to put a musket on his shoulder,
To shoot some other mother's darling boy?

Let nations arbitrate their future troubles,
It's time to lay the sword and gun away,
There'd be no war today,
If mothers all would say,
I didn't raise my boy to be a soldier.

What victory can cheer a mother's heart,
When she looks at her blighted home?
What victory can bring her back
All she cared to call her own?
Let each mother answer
In the year to be,
Remember that my boy belongs to me!

ALAN SEEGER
I HAVE A RENDEZVOUS WITH DEATH

Alan Seeger (1888–1916) was born in New York. He graduated from Harvard in 1910, went to Paris in 1913, and enlisted in the French Foreign Legion when the war began. He was killed in the Battle of the Somme. "I Have a Rendezvous with Death" was the most famous of his war poems. It was originally published in the *North American Review,* October 1916.

I have a rendezvous with Death
At some disputed barricade,
When Spring comes back with rustling shade
And apple blossoms fill the air—
I have a rendezvous with Death
When Spring brings back blue days and fair.

It may be he shall take my hand,
And lead me into his dark land,
And close my eyes and quench my breath—
It may be I shall pass him still.
I have a rendezvous with Death
On some scarred slope of battered hill,

When Spring comes round again this year
And the first meadow flowers appear.
God knows 'twere better to be deep
Pillowed in silk and scented down,
Where Love throbs out in blissful sleep,
Pulse nigh to pulse, and breath to breath,
Where hushed awakenings are dear . . .
But I've a rendezvous with Death
At midnight in some flaming town,
When Spring trips north again this year;
And I to my pledged word am true,
I shall not fail that rendezvous.

WOODROW WILSON
WAR MESSAGE TO CONGRESS

The world must be made safe for democracy.

In the summer of 1914, war broke out in Europe between the Central Powers (Germany and Austria-Hungary) and the Entente Powers (Britain, France, and Russia). Americans had never become involved in a European war, and President Woodrow Wilson declared that Americans should be "neutral in fact as well as in name . . . impartial in thought as well as in action." The Great Rule of Washington and Jefferson, reinforced by the Monroe Doctrine, was that America should remain aloof from international politics. Neutrality proved difficult, however. Public opinion was outraged in May 1915, when a German submarine sank the British liner *Lusitania,* with a loss of nearly 1,200 lives, including 128 Americans.

Wilson ran for reelection successfully in 1916 on the slogan "He kept us out of war." Wilson thought that he could bring the warring sides together, and he sent aides to Europe to try to find terms on which the war might end. In January 1917, he addressed Congress and spoke of his efforts to find a formula for "peace without victory," a settlement without winners or losers, a settlement that would be guaranteed by an international "League for Peace." Wilson warned prophetically that a vindictive peace would sow the seeds of yet another European conflict.

Germany pledged not to attack unarmed ships without warning, but in early 1917 resumed unrestricted submarine warfare and sank several American merchant vessels. Wilson found the German policy intolerable. So, on April 2, 1917, Wilson asked Congress for a declaration of war. Wilson's war message, excerpted here, committed more than one million American troops to one of the bloodiest conflicts in world history.

At the end of the war, Wilson advocated the creation of a League of Nations. When he returned home from the peace conference in Europe, he had the burden of drumming up popular support for the peace treaty and for the League of Nations, since the

Republicans had gained control of the Senate. His rigorous schedule of cross-country travel destroyed his health; he collapsed in September 1919 and was incapacitated for the balance of his term of office.

. . . On the third of February last I officially laid before you the extraordinary announcement of the Imperial German Government that on and after the first day of February it was its purpose to put aside all restraints of law or of humanity and use its submarines to sink every vessel that sought to approach either the ports of Great Britain and Ireland or the western coasts of Europe or any of the ports controlled by the enemies of Germany within the Mediterranean. That had seemed to be the object of the German submarine warfare earlier in the war, but since April of last year the Imperial Government had somewhat restrained the commanders of its undersea craft in conformity with its promise then given to us that passenger boats should not be sunk and that due warning would be given to all other vessels which its submarines might seek to destroy, when no resistance was offered or escape attempted, and care taken that their crews were given at least a fair chance to save their lives in their open boats. The precautions taken were meager and haphazard enough, as was proved in distressing instance after instance in the progress of the cruel and unmanly business, but a certain degree of restraint was observed. The new policy has swept every restriction aside. Vessels of every kind, whatever their flag, their character, their cargo, their destination, their errand, have been ruthlessly sent to the bottom without warning and without thought of help or mercy for those on board, the vessels of friendly neutrals along with those of belligerents. Even hospital ships and ships carrying relief to the sorely bereaved and stricken people of Belgium, though the latter were provided with safe conduct through the proscribed areas by the German Government itself and were distinguished by unmistakable marks of identity, have been sunk with the same reckless lack of compassion or of principle.

I was for a little while unable to believe that such things would in fact be done by any government that had hitherto subscribed to the humane practices of civilized nations. International law had its origin in the attempt to set up some law which would be respected and observed upon the seas, where no nation had right of dominion and where lay the free highways of the world. . . . This minimum of right the German Government has swept aside under the plea of retaliation and necessity and because it had no weapons which it could use at sea except these which it is impossible to employ as it is employing them without throwing to the winds all scruples of humanity or of respect for the understandings that were supposed to underlie the intercourse of the world. I am not now thinking of the loss of property involved, immense and serious as that is, but only of the wanton and wholesale destruction of the lives of non-combatants, men, women, and children, engaged in pursuits which have always, even in the darkest periods of modern history, been deemed innocent and legitimate. Property can be paid for; the lives of peaceful and innocent people cannot be. The present German submarine warfare against commerce is a warfare against mankind.

It is a war against all nations. American ships have been sunk, American lives taken, in ways which it has stirred us very deeply to learn of, but the ships and people of other neutral and friendly nations have been sunk and overwhelmed in the waters in the same way. There has been no discrimination. The challenge is to all mankind. Each nation must decide for itself how it will meet it. The choice we make for ourselves must be made with a moderation of counsel and a temperateness of judgment befitting our character and our motives as a nation. We must put excited feeling away. Our motive will not be revenge or the victorious assertion of the physical might of the nation, but only the vindication of right, of human right, of which we are only a single champion. . . .

With a profound sense of the solemn and even tragical character of the step I am taking and of the grave responsibilities which it involves, but in unhesitating obedience to what I deem my constitutional duty, I advise that the Congress declare the recent course of the Imperial German Government to be in fact nothing less than war against the government and people of the United States; that it formally accept the status of belligerent which has thus been thrust upon it; and that it take immediate steps not only to put the country in a more thorough state of defense but also to exert all its power and employ all its resources to bring the Government of the German Empire to terms and end the war. . . .

While we do these things, these deeply momentous things, let us be very clear, and make very clear to all the world what our motives and our objects are. . . . Our object . . . is to vindicate the principles of peace and justice in the life of the world as against selfish and autocratic power and to set up amongst the really free and self-governed peoples of the world such a concert of purpose and of action as will henceforth insure the observance of those principles. Neutrality is no longer feasible or desirable where the peace of the world is involved and the freedom of its peoples, and the menace to that peace and freedom lies in the existence of autocratic governments backed by organized force which is controlled wholly by their will, not by the will of their people. We have seen the last of neutrality in such circumstances. We are at the beginning of an age in which it will be insisted that the same standards of conduct and of responsibility for wrong done shall be observed among nations and their governments that are observed among the individual citizens of civilzed states.

We have no quarrel with the German people. We have no feeling towards them but one of sympathy and friendship. It was not upon their impulse that their government acted in entering this war. It was not with their previous knowledge or approval. It was a war determined upon as wars used to be determined upon in the old, unhappy days when peoples were nowhere consulted by their rulers and wars were provoked and waged in the interest of dynasties or of little groups of ambitious men who were accustomed to use their fellow men as pawns and tools. . . .

We are accepting this challenge of hostile purpose because we know that in such a Government, following such methods, we can never have a friend; and that in the presence of its organized power, always lying in wait to accomplish we know not what purpose, there can be no assured security for the democratic Governments of the world. We are now about to accept gauge of battle with this natural foe to liberty and shall, if necessary, spend the whole force of the nation to check and nullify its pretensions and its power. We are glad, now that we see the facts with no veil of false pretense about them, to fight thus for the ultimate peace of the world and for the liberation of its peoples, the German peoples included: for the rights of nations great and small and the privilege of men everywhere to choose their way of life and of obedience. The world must be made safe for democracy. Its peace must be planted upon the tested foundations of political liberty. We have no selfish ends to serve. We desire no conquest, no dominion. We seek no indemnities for ourselves, no material compensation for the sacrifices we shall freely make. We are but one of the champions of the rights of mankind. We shall be satisfied when those rights have been made as secure as the faith and the freedom of nations can make them. . . .

There are, it may be, many months of fiery trial and sacrifice ahead of us. It is a fearful thing to lead this great peaceful people into war, into the most terrible and disastrous of all wars, civilization itself seeming to be in the balance. But the right is more precious than peace, and we shall fight for the things which we have always carried nearest our hearts,—for democracy, for the right of those who submit to authority to have a voice in their own Governments, for the rights and liberties of small nations, for a universal dominion of right by such a concert of free peoples as shall bring peace and safety to all nations and make the world itself at last free. To such a task we can dedicate our lives and our fortunes, everything that we are and everything that we have, with the pride of those who know that the day has come when America is privileged to spend her blood and her might for the principles that gave her birth and happiness and the peace which she has treasured. God helping her, she can do no other.

GEORGE NORRIS

AGAINST ENTRY INTO THE WAR

We are taking a step today that is fraught with untold danger. We are going into war upon the command of gold.

Many Americans opposed the nation's entry into the European war. Some thought that the decision was made to benefit the rich; some opposed war on principle either as pacifists or as socialists (or both); some opponents were of Irish or German descent and did not want their nation helping Britain or fighting Germany.

George William Norris (1861–1944), a progressive Republican, denounced the decision to enter the war as a tragic mistake, promoted by rapacious Wall Street financiers. Born in Ohio, Norris practiced law in Nebraska, where he was elected to Congress in 1902. In 1912, he won election to the Senate, where he established himself as a reformer and maverick for the next three decades. Norris opposed entry into the world war and opposed the Treaty of Versailles. He initiated the Twentieth Amendment to the Constitution, eliminating the lame duck session of Congress by advancing the president's inauguration from March to January. He led the fight for presidential primaries and direct election of U.S. senators. An advocate of public ownership of hydroelectric power, he introduced the bill creating the Tennessee Valley Authority.

The following speech was delivered by Norris on April 4, 1917, two days after Wilson asked Congress for a declaration of war. Anti-war sentiment was unpopular in the country, but Norris was regularly reelected by his constituents in Nebraska.

There are a great many American citizens who feel that we owe it as a duty to humanity to take part in this war. Many instances of cruelty and inhumanity can be found on both sides. Men are often biased in their judgment on account of their sympathy and their interests. To my mind, what we ought to have maintained from the beginning was the strictest neutrality. If we had done this I do not believe we would have been on the verge of war at the present time. We had a right as a nation, if we desired, to cease at any time to be neutral. We had a technical right to respect the English war zone and to disregard the German war zone, but we could not do that and be neutral. I have no quarrel to find with the man who does not desire our country to remain neutral. While many such people are moved by selfish motives and hopes of gain, I have no doubt but that in a great many instances, through what I believe to be a misunderstanding of the real condition, there are many honest, patriotic citizens who think we ought to engage in this war and who are behind the President in his demand that we should declare war against Germany. I think such people err in judgment and to a great extent have been misled as to the real history and the true facts by the almost unanimous demand of the great combination of wealth that has a direct financial interest in our participation in the war. We have loaned many hundreds of millions of dollars to the allies in this controversy. While such action was legal and countenanced by international law, there is no doubt in my mind but the enormous amount of money loaned to the allies in this country has been instrumental in bringing about a public sentiment in favor of our country taking a course that would make every bond worth a hundred cents on the dollar and making the payment of every debt certain and sure. Through this instrumentality and also through the instrumentality of others who have not only made millions out of the war in the manufacture of munitions, etc., and who would expect to make millions more if our country can be drawn into the catastrophe, a large number of the great newspapers and news agencies of the country have been controlled and enlisted in the greatest propaganda that the world has ever known, to manufacture sentiment in favor of war. It is now demanded that the American citizens shall be used as insurance policies to guarantee the safe delivery of munitions of war to belligerent nations. The enormous profits of munition manufacturers, stockbrokers, and bond dealers must be still further increased by our entrance into the war. This has brought us to the present moment, when Congress, urged by the President and backed by the artificial sentiment, is about to declare war and engulf our country in the greatest holocaust that the world has ever known. . . .

During World War I, millions of Americans bought Liberty Bonds to finance the war and planted "victory gardens" to increase food production. Boys and girls in St. Louis, Missouri, conserved food by joining canning clubs.

To whom does the war bring prosperity? Not to the soldier who for the munificent compensation of $16 per month shoulders his musket and goes into the trench, there to shed his blood and to die if necessary; not to the broken-hearted widow who waits for the return of the mangled body of her husband; not to the mother who weeps at the death of her brave boy; not to the little children who shiver with cold; not to the babe who suffers from hunger; nor to the millions of mothers and daughters who carry broken hearts to their graves. War brings no prosperity to the great mass of common and patriotic citizens. It increases the cost of living of those who toil and those who already must strain every effort to keep soul and body together. War brings prosperity to the stock gambler on Wall street—to those who are already in possession of more wealth than can be realized or enjoyed. [A Wall Street broker] says if we can not get war, "it is nevertheless good opinion that the preparedness program will compensate in good measure for the loss of the stimulus of actual war." That is, if we can not get war, let us go as far in that direction as possible. If we can not get war, let us cry for additional ships, additional guns, additional munitions, and everything else that will have a tendency to bring us as near as possible to the verge of war. And if war comes do such men as these shoulder the musket and go into the trenches?

Their object in having war and in preparing for war is to make money. Human suffering and the sacrifice of human life are necessary, but Wall Street considers only the dollars and the cents. The men who do the fighting, the people who make the sacrifices, are the ones who will not be counted in the measure of this great prosperity he depicts. The stock brokers would not, of course, go to war, because the very object they have in bringing on the war is profit, and therefore they must remain in their Wall Street offices in order to share in that great prosperity which they say war will bring. The volunteer officer, even the drafting officer, will not find them. They will be concealed in their palatial offices on Wall Street, sitting behind mahogany desks, covered up with clipped coupons—coupons soiled with the sweat of honest toil, coupons stained with mothers' tears, coupons dyed in the lifeblood of their fellow men.

We are taking a step today that is fraught with untold danger. We are going into war upon the command of gold. We are going to run the risk of sacrificing millions of our countrymen's lives in order that other countrymen may coin their lifeblood into money. And even if we do not cross the Atlantic and go into the trenches, we are going to pile up a debt that the toiling masses that shall come many generations after us will have to pay. Unborn millions will bend their backs in toil in order to pay for the terrible step we are now about to take. We are about to do the bidding of wealth's terrible mandate. By our act we will make millions of our countrymen suffer, and the consequences of it may well be that millions of our brethren must shed their lifeblood, millions of broken-hearted women must weep, millions of children must suffer with cold, and millions of babes must die from hunger, and all because we want to preserve the commercial right of American citizens to deliver munitions of war to belligerent nations.

GEORGE M. COHAN
OVER THERE

George M. Cohan (1878–1942) was born on the third of July, but he changed his birthdate by twenty-four hours so he could say that he really was, like the title of one of his hit songs, a "Yankee Doodle Dandy." As a child, he was on the vaudeville circuit with his parents and his sister. The quintessential song-and-dance man, Cohan became known as "Mr. Broadway"; many of his songs became classics, including "You're a Grand Old Flag," "Give My Regards to Broadway," and "Mary is a Grand Old Name."

Cohan's "Over There" was the theme song of World War I for Americans. It was first performed at the New York Hippodrome in late 1917, where it was received with "frenzied enthusiasm." The music is an adaptation of a bugle call, summoning the troops to the battle front. Cohan received a Congressional Medal of Honor for composing it.

Johnnie get your gun, get your gun, get your
    gun,
Take it on the run, on the run, on the run;
Hear them calling you and me;
Ev'ry son of liberty.
Hurry right away, no delay, go today,
Make your daddy glad, to have had such a lad,
Tell your sweetheart not to pine,
To be proud her boy's in line.

CHORUS:
Over there, over there,
Send the word, send the word over there,
That the Yanks are coming,
the Yanks are coming,
The drums rum-tumming ev'ry where—

So prepare, say a pray'r,
Send the word, send the word to beware,
We'll be over, we're coming over,
And we won't come back till it's over over
    there.

Johnnie get your gun, get your gun, get your
    gun,
Johnnie show the Hun, you're a son-of-a-gun,
Hoist the flag and let her fly,
Like true heroes, do or die.
Pack your little kit, show your grit, do your bit,
Soldiers to the ranks from the towns and the
    tanks,
Make your mother proud of you,
And to liberty be true.

IRVING BERLIN

OH, HOW I HATE TO GET UP IN THE MORNING

Irving Berlin (1888–1989) was born in Russia and was brought to the United States in 1893. He left school at the age of eight when his father died, and young Israel Baline had to earn money to help his family. At first he sold newspapers, and later sang for tips in bars on New York's Lower East Side. When he was nineteen, he published his first song, and his name was mistakenly printed as "I. Berlin," which he decided to keep. His first hit was "Alexander's Ragtime Band" (1911). Before he was thirty, Berlin was one of the most successful songwriters in American musical history. Although he never learned to read or write music, Berlin wrote over 1,500 songs, including the immensely popular "Blue Skies" (1927), "God Bless America" (1938), and "White Christmas" (1942).

During World War I, Irving Berlin was drafted and served as a sergeant in the infantry at Camp Upton on Long Island in New York. While in uniform, he staged a morale-boosting, all-soldier show called *Yip, Yip, Yaphank*, which included "Oh, How I Hate to Get Up in the Morning" (1917). The song was reintroduced in his 1942 musical, *This is the Army*.

The other day I chanced to meet a soldier
    friend of mine,
He'd been in camp for sev'ral weeks and he
    was looking fine;
His muscles had developed and his cheeks
    were rosy red,
I asked him how he liked the life and this is
    what he said:

CHORUS:
Oh! How I hate to get up in the morning,
Oh! how I'd love to remain in bed;
For the hardest blow of all, is to hear the
    bugler call;
"You've got to get up, you've got to get up,
    you've got to get up this morning!"

Someday I'm going to murder the bugler,

Someday they're going to find him dead;
I'll amputate his reveille, and step upon it
    heavily,
And spend the rest of my life in bed.

A bugler in the army is the luckiest of men,
He wakes the boys at five and then goes back
    to bed again;
He doesn't have to blow again until the
    afternoon,
If ev'rything goes well with me I'll be a bugler
    soon.

Oh! boy the minute the battle is over,
Oh! boy the minute the foe is dead;
I'll put my uniform away, and move to
    Philadelphia,
And spend the rest of my life in bed.

THE MARINES' HYMN

The origin of "The Marines' Hymn" is uncertain, but its tremendous popularity as a martial song is not. The music of the song has been traced to a song called "Couplets des deux hommes d'armes" in Jacques Offenbach's opera *Geneviève de Brabant* (1868). The opera was performed in New York City on October 22, 1868. The lyrics have been attributed to several different people, but none holds a copyright. The earliest known printing of the lyrics was in *The National Police Gazette*, June 16, 1917. The Marines' newspaper *The Quantico Leatherneck* printed the first stanza in July 1918. The Marine Corps itself printed the entire song, music and lyrics, on August 1, 1918.

From the halls of Montezuma
To the shores of Tripoli;
We fight our country's battles
On the land as on the sea;
First to fight for right and freedom
And to keep our honor clean;
We are proud to claim the title
Of United States Marine.

Our flag's unfurl'd to every breeze
From dawn to setting sun;
We have fought in ev'ry clime and place
Where we could take a gun;

In the snow of far off Northern land
And in sunny tropic scenes;
You will find us always on the job
The United States Marines.

Here's health to you and to our Corps
Which we are proud to serve;
In many a strife we've fought for life
And never lost our nerve;
If the Army and the Navy
Ever look on Heaven's scenes;
They will find the streets are guarded
By United States Marines.

EDMUND L. GRUBER
THE FIELD ARTILLERY SONG

"The Field Artillery Song" is better known as "The Caisson Song." It was written by Lieutenant (later Brigadier General) Edmund L. Gruber in 1907, while he was serving in the Philippines. The great bandmaster and composer John Philip Sousa produced an instrumental version of the song in 1918 and helped to popularize it. A spirited marching song, "The Field Artillery Song" was enormously popular among the troops and people on the home front during both World War I and World War II.

Over hill, over dale,
As we hit the dusty trail,
And the caissons go rolling along.
In and out, hear them shout
Counter march and right about,
And the caissons go rolling along.

Then it's hi! hi! hee! in the field artillery
Shout out your numbers loud and strong,
For where e'er you go,
You will always know
That the caissons go rolling along.

CARL SANDBURG
GRASS

Carl Sandburg's "Grass" was one of the most affecting and memorable poems about the Great War. It was published as part of *Cornhuskers,* which appeared in 1918.

Pile the bodies high at Austerlitz and Waterloo.
Shovel them under and let me work—
    I am the grass; I cover all.

And pile them high at Gettysburg
And pile them high at Ypres and Verdun.
Shovel them under and let me work.

Two years, ten years, and passengers ask the
    conductor:
        What place is this?
        Where are we now?

        I am the grass.
        Let me work.

EUGENE VICTOR DEBS
STATEMENT TO THE COURT

And while there is a soul in prison, I am not free.

Eugene Victor Debs (1855-1926) was a labor organizer, a founder of the Socialist Party, and five times the Socialist candidate for president. Born in Terre Haute, Indiana, Debs went to work for the railroad as a boy of fourteen, eventually becoming a locomotive fireman. By the time he was twenty, he was involved in organizing the Brotherhood of Locomotive Firemen. In 1893, he was elected president of the new American Railway Union, and the next year Debs led a major strike against the Pullman Palace Car Company, which ended with federal troops in Chicago and Debs in jail for six months for contempt of court. While in jail, Debs read widely in socialist literature, and in 1898, helped to found what was later called the Socialist Party of America and became its presidential candidate in 1900.

Debs and other Socialists opposed American entry into the World War in 1917. For his scathing criticism of the Wilson administration, Debs was arrested in June 1918 for violating the Espionage Act of 1917 and was charged with sedition. After Debs gave the following speech, the judge sentenced him to ten years in prison; his sentence was commuted by President Harding in 1921. As a presidential candidate in 1920, Debs received his highest total (915,000 votes), even though he was in federal prison.

Your honor, years ago I recognized my kinship with all living beings, and I made up my mind that I was not one bit better than the meanest on earth. I said then, and I say now, that while there is a lower class, I am in it, while there is a criminal element, I am of it, and while there is a soul in prison, I am not free.

I listened to all that was said in this court in support and justification of this prosecution, but my mind remains unchanged. I look upon the Espionage Law as a despotic enactment in flagrant conflict with democratic principles and with the spirit of free institutions. . . .

Your Honor, I have stated in this court that I am opposed to the social system in which we live; that I believe in a fundamental change—but if possible by peaceable and orderly means. . . .

Standing here this morning, I recall my boyhood. At fourteen I went to work in a railroad shop; at sixteen I was firing a freight engine on a railroad. I remember all the hardships and privations of that earlier day, and from that time until now my heart has been with the working class. I could have been in Congress long ago. I have preferred to go to prison. . . .

I am thinking this morning of the men in the mills and factories; of the men in the mines and on the railroads. I am thinking of the women who for a paltry wage are compelled to work out their barren lives; of the little children who in this system are robbed of their childhood and

in their tender years are seized in the remorseless grasp of Mammon and forced into the industrial dungeons, there to feed the monster machines while they themselves are being starved and stunted, body and soul. I see them dwarfed and diseased and their little lives broken and blasted because in this high noon of our twentieth-century Christian civilization money is still so much more important than the flesh and blood of childhood. In very truth gold is god today and rules with pitiless sway in the affairs of men.

In this country, the most favored beneath the bending skies—we have vast areas of the richest and most fertile soil, material resources in inexhaustible abundance, the most marvelous productive machinery on earth, and millions of eager workers ready to apply their labor to that machinery to produce an abundance for every man, woman, and child—and if there are still vast numbers of our people who are the victims of poverty and whose lives are an unceasing struggle all the way from youth to old age, until at last death comes to their rescue and stills their aching hearts and lulls these hapless victims to dreamless sleep, it is not the fault of the Almighty: it cannot be charged to nature, but it is due entirely to the outgrown social system in which we live, that ought to be abolished not only in the interest of the toiling masses but in the higher interest of all humanity. . . .

I believe, Your Honor, in common with all

Socialists, that this nation ought to own and control its own industries. I believe, as all Socialists do, that all things that are jointly needed and used ought to be jointly owned—that industry, the basis of our social life, instead of being the private property of the few and operated for their enrichment, ought to be the common property of all, democratically administered in the interest of all. . . .

I am opposing a social order in which it is possible for one man who does absolutely nothing that is useful to amass a fortune of hundreds of millions of dollars, while millions of men and women who work all the days of their lives secure barely enough for a wretched existence.

This order of things cannot always endure. I have registered my protest against it. I recognize the feebleness of my effort, but fortunately I am not alone. There are multiplied thousands of others who, like myself, have come to realize that before we may truly enjoy the blessings of civilized life, we must reorganize society upon a mutual and co-operative basis; and to this end we have organized a great economic and political movement that spreads over the face of all the earth.

There are today upwards of sixty millions of Socialists, loyal, devoted adherents to this cause, regardless of nationality, race, creed, color, or sex. They are all making common cause. They are spreading with tireless energy the propaganda of the new social order. They are waiting, watching, and working hopefully through all the hours of the day and the night. They are still in a minority. But they have learned how to be patient and to bide their time. They feel—they know, indeed—that the time is coming, in spite of all opposition, all persecution, when this emancipating gospel will spread among all the peoples, and when this minority will become the triumphant majority and, sweeping into power, inaugurate the greatest social and economic change in history.

In that day we shall have the universal commonwealth—the harmonious co-operation of every nation with every other nation on earth. . . .

MARGARET SANGER

THE RIGHT TO ONE'S BODY

No woman can call herself free who does not own and control her body.

Margaret Sanger (1883–1966) achieved an international reputation as a tireless crusader for birth control. Born in Corning, New York, she was the sixth of eleven children. She worked as a nurse in the impoverished Lower East Side of New York City, where she saw high mortality rates among both mothers and infants. Sanger campaigned against laws that made it criminal to provide information about birth control.

Sanger published a magazine in 1914 called *The Woman Rebel* (later retitled *Birth Control Review*) and produced a pamphlet, *Family Limitation.* Since it was illegal to print or distribute such information, she was indicted for mailing illegal materials, but her case was dismissed. She opened the nation's first birth-control clinic in Brooklyn in 1916; Sanger was arrested for maintaining a "public nuisance" and spent thirty days in the workhouse.

Sanger traveled all over the world to publicize the importance of birth control. As time went by, many states liberalized access to information about birth control. In 1973, the Supreme Court in *Roe v. Wade* struck down laws restricting abortion. However, the Supreme Court in 1989 ruled that the states were permitted to narrow access to abortion.

The following excerpt is from Sanger's *Woman and the New Race* (1920).

The problem of birth control has arisen directly from the effort of the feminine spirit to free itself from bondage. Woman herself has wrought that bondage through her reproductive powers and while enslaving herself has enslaved the world. The physical suffering to be relieved is chiefly woman's. Hers, too, is the love life that dies first under the blight of too prolific breeding. Within her is wrapped up the future of the race—it is hers to make or mar. All of these considerations point unmistakably to one fact—it is woman's duty as well as her privilege to lay hold of the means of freedom. Whatever men may do, she cannot escape the responsibility. For ages she has been deprived of the opportunity to meet this obligation. She is now emerging from her helplessness. Even as no one can share the suffering of the overburdened mother, so no one can do this work for her. Others may help, but she and she alone can free herself.

The basic freedom of the world is woman's freedom. A free race cannot be born of slave mothers. A woman enchained cannot choose but give a measure of that bondage to her sons and daughters. No woman can call herself free who does not own and control her body. No woman can call herself free until she can choose consciously whether she will or will not be a mother.

It does not greatly alter the case that some women call themselves free because they earn their own livings, while others profess freedom because they defy the conventions of sex relationship. She who earns her own living gains a sort of freedom that is not to be undervalued, but in quality and in quantity it is of little account beside the untrammeled choice of mating or not mating, or being a mother or not being a mother. She gains food and clothing and shelter, at least, without submitting to the charity of her companion, but the earning of her own living

does not give her the development of her inner sex urge, far deeper and more powerful in its outworkings than any of these externals. In order to have that development, she must still meet and solve the problem of motherhood.

With the so-called "free" woman, who chooses a mate in defiance of convention, freedom is largely a question of character and audacity. If she does attain to an unrestricted choice of a mate, she is still in a position to be enslaved through her reproductive powers. Indeed, the pressure of law and custom upon the woman not legally married is likely to make her more of a slave than the woman fortunate enough to marry the man of her choice.

Look at it from any standpoint you will, suggest any solution you will, conventional or unconventional, sanctioned by law or in defiance of law, woman is in the same position, fundamentally, until she is able to determine for herself whether she will be a mother and to fix the number of her offspring. This unavoidable situation is alone enough to make birth control, first of all, a woman's problem. On the very face of the matter, voluntary motherhood is chiefly the concern of the woman.

It is persistently urged, however, that since sex expression is the act of two, the responsibility of controlling the results should not be placed upon woman alone. Is it fair, it is asked, to give her, instead of the man, the task of protecting herself when she is, perhaps, less rugged in physique than her mate, and has, at all events, the normal, periodic inconveniences of her sex?

We must examine this phase of her problem in two lights—that of the ideal, and of the conditions working toward the ideal. In an ideal society, no doubt, birth control would become the concern of the man as well as the woman. The hard, inescapable fact which we encounter to-day is that man has not only refused any such responsibility, but has individually and collectively sought to prevent woman from obtaining knowledge by which she could assume this responsibility for herself. She is still in the position of a dependent to-day because her mate has refused to consider her as an individual apart from his needs. She is still bound because she has in the past left the solution of the problem to him. Having left it to him, she finds that instead of rights, she has only such privileges as she has gained by petitioning, coaxing and cozening. Having left it to him, she is exploited, driven and enslaved to his desires.

While it is true that he suffers many evils as the consequence of this situation, she suffers vastly more. While it is true that he should be awakened to the cause of these evils, we know that they come home to her with crushing force every day. It is she who has the long burden of carrying, bearing and rearing the unwanted children. . . . It is her heart that the sight of the deformed, the subnormal, the undernourished, the overworked child smites first and oftenest and hardest. It is *her* love life that dies first in the fear of undesired pregnancy. It is her opportunity for self expression that perishes first and most hopelessly because of it.

Conditions, rather than theories, facts, rather than dreams, govern the problem. They place it squarely upon the shoulders of woman. She has learned that whatever the moral responsibility of the man in this direction may be, he does not discharge it. She has learned that, lovable and considerate as the individual husband may be, she has nothing to expect from men in the mass, when they make laws and decree customs. She knows that regardless of what ought to be, the brutal, unavoidable fact is that she will never receive her freedom until she takes it for herself.

Having learned this much, she has yet something more to learn. Women are too much inclined to follow in the footsteps of men, to try to think as men think, to try to solve the general problems of life as men solve them. If after attaining their freedom, women accept conditions in the spheres of government, industry, art, morals and religion as they find them, they will be

Poster by Charles Stelze, 1918. A constitutional amendment prohibiting the sale, manufacture, or importation of liquor was adopted in 1919. The effort to keep the nation dry failed, however, leading to widespread evasion of the law and to smuggling, backyard stills, gang warfare, and speakeasies. Prohibition was repealed in 1933.

but taking a leaf out of man's book. The woman is not needed to do man's work. She is not needed to think man's thoughts. She need not fear that the masculine mind, almost universally dominant, will fail to take care of its own. Her mission is not to enhance the masculine spirit, but to express the feminine; hers is not to preserve a man-made world, but to create a human world by the infusion of the feminine element into all of its activities.

Woman must not accept; she must challenge. She must not be awed by that which has been built up around her; she must reverence that within her which struggles for expression. Her eyes must be less upon what is and more clearly upon what should be. She must listen only with a frankly questioning attitude to the dogmatized opinions of man-made society. When she chooses her new, free course of action, it must be in the light of her own opinion —of her own intuition. Only so can she give play to the feminine spirit. Only thus can she free her mate from the bondage which he wrought for himself when he wrought hers. Only thus can she restore to him that of which he robbed himself in restricting her. Only thus can she remake the world. . . .

EDNA ST. VINCENT MILLAY
FIRST FIG

As a child growing up in Maine, Edna St. Vincent Millay (1892–1950) contributed poems to *St. Nicholas,* a literary magazine for children. She and her two sisters were raised by their mother, who supported them by working as a practical nurse. Millay did not expect to go to college, in view of her family's limited finances. But in 1912, her poem "Renascence" won a national competition, and young Edna (or Vincent as she called herself) received financial assistance from a patron in New York, whose support enabled her to enroll in college. Already recognized as an accomplished poet as a freshman, Millay graduated from Vassar College in 1917. Millay lived and worked in Greenwich Village in New York City, where she became a central figure among literary rebels of the age. Her first volume of poetry, *Renascence and Other Poems,* was published in 1917. She won the Pulitzer Prize for poetry in 1923 for *The Harp-Weaver and Other Poems.* Although she wrote many beautiful lyric poems, the Millay poem that is most often quoted is "First Fig," from *A Few Figs from Thistles* (1920). For many people, Edna St. Vincent Millay personified the new liberated woman of the 1920s, and this poem captured the romantic and cynical spirit of the restless youth of the era.

My candle burns at both ends;
    It will not last the night;
But ah, my foes, and oh, my friends—
    It gives a lovely light!

POEMS OF ANGEL ISLAND

Chinese immigrants began to arrive on the West Coast in the mid-nineteenth century when gold was discovered, and many helped to build the Central Pacific Railroad. However, racial prejudice and competition for jobs led to anti-Chinese legislation by localities and the state of California. Although many of these discriminatory laws were struck down by the courts, anti-Chinese sentiment prompted passage of the Chinese Exclusion Act of 1882, which barred most Chinese immigration.

Despite restrictive legislation, thousands of Chinese immigrants came to the United States between 1910 and 1940. Their arrival point was Angel Island in San Francisco

Bay, which was known as the Ellis Island of the West. Angel Island was both an entry point and a detention center for Chinese and Japanese immigrants awaiting admission and for those who were awaiting deportation. Some of the detainees wrote poems on the wooden barracks walls, recording their feelings about their voyage, their longing for home, and their detention.

In this poem, the "Flowery Flag" is a Cantonese term for the United States, referring to its colorful flag.

I used to admire the land of the Flowery Flag
    as a country of abundance.
I immediately raised money and started my
    journey.
For over a month, I have experienced enough
    winds and waves.
Now on an extended sojourn in jail, I am
    subject to the ordeals of prison life.

I look up and see Oakland so close by.
I wish to go back to my motherland to carry
    the farmer's hoe.
Discontent fills my belly and it is difficult for
    me to sleep.
I just write these few lines to express what is
    on my mind.

YOUNGHILL KANG

A KOREAN DISCOVERS NEW YORK

It was always of New York I dreamed—not Paris nor London nor Berlin nor Munich nor Vienna nor age-buried Rome.

Younghill Kang (1903–1972) was born in Korea and emigrated to the United States in 1921. A teacher, translator, novelist, and memoirist, he attempted to explain the Asian world to an American audience through his writings. His first publication was *Translations of Oriental Poetry* (1929). He was the author of several books, including the autobiographical *The Grass Roof* (1931) and *East Goes West* (1937), from which this classic account of the immigrant experience is excerpted.

From an old walled Korean city some thousand years old—Seoul—famous for poets and scholars, to New York. I did not come directly. But almost. A large steamer from the Orient landed me in Vancouver, Canada, and I travelled over three thousand miles across the American continent, a journey more than half as far as from Yokohama to Vancouver. At Halifax, straightway I took another liner. And this time for New York. It was in New York I felt I was destined really "to come off from the boat." The beginning of my new existence must be founded here. In Korea *to come out from the boat* is an idiom meaning to be born, as the word "pai" for "womb" is the same as "pai" for "boat"; and there is the story of a Korean humorist who had no money, but who needed to get across a river. On landing him on the other side, the ferryman asked for his money. But the Korean humorist said to the ferryman who too had just stepped out, "You wouldn't charge your brother, would you? We both came from the same boat." And so he travelled free. My only plea for a planet-ride among the white-skinned majority of this New World is the same facetious argument. I brought little money, and no prestige, as I entered a practical country with small respect for the dark side of the moon. I got in just in time before the law against Oriental immigration was passed.

But New York, that magic city on rock yet ungrounded, nervous, flowing, million-hued as a dream, became, throughout the years I am recording, the vast mechanical incubator of me.

It was always of New York I dreamed—not Paris nor London nor Berlin nor Munich nor Vienna nor age-buried Rome. I was eighteen, green with youth, and there was some of the mystery of nature in my simple immediate response to what was for me just a name . . . like the dogged moth that directs its flight by some unfathomable law. But I said to myself, "I want neither dreams nor poetry, least of all tradition, never the full moon." Korea even in her shattered state had these. And beyond them stood waiting—death. I craved swiftness, unimpeded action, fluidity, and amorphous New. Out of action rises the dream, rises the poetry. Dream without motion is the only wasteland that can sustain nothing. So I came adoring the crescent, not the full harvest moon, with winter over the horizon and its waning to a husk.

"New York at last!" I heard from the passengers around me. And the information was not needed. In unearthly white and mauve, shadow of white, the city rose, like a dream dreamed overnight, new, remorselessly new, impossibly new . . . and yet there in all the arrogant pride of rejoiced materialism. These young, slim, stately things a thousand houses high (or so it seemed to me, coming from an architecture that had never defied the earth), a tower of Babel each one, not one tower of Babel but many, a city of Babel towers, casually, easily strewn end up against the skies—they stood at the brink, close-crowded, the brink of America, these Giant-esses, these Fates, which were not built for a king nor a ghost nor any man's religion, but were materialized by those hard, cold, magic words—opportunity, enterprise, prosperity, success—just business words out of world-wide commerce from a land rich in natural resource. Buildings that sprang white from the rock. No earth clung to their skirts. They leaped like Athene from the mind synthetically; they spurned the earth. And there was no monument to the machine-age like America.

I could not have come farther from home than this New York. Our dwellings, low, weathered, mossed, abhorring the lifeless line—the definite, the finite, the aloof—loving rondures and an upward stroke, the tilt of a roof like a boat always aware of the elements in which it is swinging—most fittingly my home was set a hemisphere apart, so far over the globe that to have gone on would have meant to go nearer not farther. How far my little grass-roofed, hill-wrapped village from this gigantic rebellion which was New York! And New York's rebellion called to me excitedly, this savagery which piled great concrete block on concrete block, topping at the last moment as in an afterthought, with crowns as delicate as pinnacled ice; this lavishness which, without a prayer, pillaged coal mines and waterfalls for light, festooning the great nature-severed city with diamonds of frozen electrical phenomena—it fascinated me, the Asian man, and in it I saw not Milton's Satan, but the one of Blake.

STEPHEN VINCENT BENÉT
AMERICAN NAMES

Stephen Vincent Benét (1898–1943) was born in Pennsylvania; he graduated from Yale College in 1919. His father was a military man who loved poetry and read poetry aloud to the Benét children, all of whom grew up to be writers. Stephen Vincent Benét published his first book when he was seventeen. He was a prolific poet who also wrote novels, short stories, and librettos. He and his wife, Rosemary, wrote *A Book of Americans* in 1933, which portrayed historical characters for children. He twice received the Pulitzer Prize for his poetry. Both of his Pulitzer Prize–winning poems—"John Brown's Body" and "Western Star"—were about the American past.

I have fallen in love with American names,
The sharp names that never get fat,
The snakeskin-titles of mining-claims,
The plumed war-bonnet of Medicine Hat,
Tucson and Deadwood and Lost Mule Flat.

Seine and Piave are silver spoons,
But the spoonbowl-metal is thin and worn,
There are English counties like hunting-tunes
Played on the keys of a posthoy's horn,
But I will remember where I was born.

I will remember Carquinez Straits,
Little French Lick and Lundy's Lane,
The Yankee ships and the Yankee dates
And the bullet-towns of Calamity Jane.
I will remember Skunktown Plain.

I will fall in love with a Salem tree
And a rawhide quirt from Santa Cruz,
I will get me a bottle of Boston sea

And a blue-gum nigger to sing me blues.
I am tired of loving a foreign muse.

Rue des Martyrs and Bleeding-Heart-Yard,
Senlis, Pisa, and Blindman's Oast,
It is a magic ghost you guard
But I am sick for a newer ghost,
Harrisburg, Spartanburg, Painted Post.

Henry and John were never so
And Henry and John were always right?
Granted, but when it was time to go
And the tea and the laurels had stood all night,
Did they never watch for Nantucket Light?

I shall not rest quiet in Montparnasse.
I shall not lie easy at Winchelsea.
You may bury my body in Sussex grass,
You may bury my tongue at Champmédy.
I shall not be there. I shall rise and pass.
Bury my heart at Wounded Knee.

CLAUDE MCKAY
AMERICA

Claude McKay (1889–1948) was one of the first—and the angriest—voices of the Harlem Renaissance in the 1920s. This was a period of enormous creativity among African American writers, musicians, performers, and artists, many of whom lived and worked in New York City's Harlem. McKay was born in Jamaica, where he was educated by an older brother and by an Englishman who taught him French and the world's great classics of literature. As a young man, he published two volumes of verse. After arriving in the United States in 1912, he studied at Tuskegee and at Kansas State Teachers College. He went to New York in 1914, where he became involved in the avant-garde movement in politics and the arts. In addition to writing poetry, McKay wrote novels and short stories. He spent a year in the Soviet Union in 1922–23, where he was lionized by the leaders of the Russian Revolution. He then spent several years in Spain, Morocco, and France. But McKay became disillusioned with Communism, and after his return to the United States in 1934, found that he was at odds with many of his former allies. His autobiography, *A Long Way from Home,* was published in 1937. In 1944, he converted to Roman Catholicism. He spent his last years ill and destitute.

Although she feeds me bread of bitterness,
And sinks into my throat her tiger's tooth,
Stealing my breath of life, I will confess
I love this cultured hell that tests my youth!
Her vigor flows like tides into my blood,
Giving me strength erect against her hate.
Her bigness sweeps my being like a flood.
Yet as a rebel fronts a king in state,
I stand within her walls with not a shred
Of terror, malice, not a word of jeer.
Darkly I gaze into the days ahead,
And see her might and granite wonders there,
Beneath the touch of Time's unerring hand,
Like priceless treasures sinking in the sand.

A children's fashion show in New York City's Harlem in the 1920s. This time was known as the Harlem Renaissance because of the unusual creativity of an entire generation of black artists, writers, musicians, and performers.

COUNTEE CULLEN
YET DO I MARVEL

Countee Cullen (1903–1946) was born in New York City, where he garnered many honors as a poet. As a boy in school, he won a citywide poetry contest, and at New York University he won a major poetry prize and was elected to Phi Beta Kappa. He achieved national recognition as a poet in 1925 with his first collection of poems, *Color,* and became one of the leading figures of the Harlem Renaissance of the 1920s. In addition to several volumes of poetry, he wrote a novel, *One Way to Heaven,* and several children's books. After 1934, he taught in a New York City junior high school.

I doubt not God is good, well-meaning, kind,
And did He stoop to quibble could tell why
The little buried mole continues blind,
Why flesh that mirrors Him must some day die,
Make plain the reason tortured Tantalus
Is baited by the fickle fruit, declare
If merely brute caprice dooms Sisyphus
To struggle up a never-ending stair.
Inscrutable His ways are, and immune
To catechism by a mind too strewn
With petty cares to slightly understand
What awful brain compels His awful hand.
Yet do I marvel at this curious thing:
To make a poet black, and bid him sing!

JAMES WELDON JOHNSON
O BLACK AND UNKNOWN BARDS

James Weldon Johnson (1871–1938), born in Jacksonville, Florida, was a man of remarkable gifts. He was trained in music and other subjects by his mother, who was a schoolteacher. He received his bachelor's degree in 1894 from Atlanta University; studied the law and was admitted to practice law in Florida in 1897 (the first African American to gain entry to the Florida bar since Reconstruction); and earned a master's degree from Atlanta University in 1904. During this same period, he was principal of the black high school in Jacksonville for several years. Johnson and his brother John Rosamond Johnson began writing songs together, and in 1901, the brothers left for New York, where they wrote some two hundred songs for Broadway.

For most people, this might have been a lifetime of professional activity, but Johnson overflowed with creative energy. In 1906, he was appointed U.S. consul to Puerto Cabello, Venezuela, and he served in the diplomatic corps in Latin America until 1914. He then taught at Fisk University, wrote a novel, and in 1916 joined the staff of the National Association for the Advancement of Colored People as executive secretary. In addition to writing poetry, Johnson prepared major anthologies of black poetry and spirituals. "O Black and Unknown Bards" was part of *Saint Peter Relates an Incident of the Resurrection Day* (1930).

O black and unknown bards of long ago,
How came your lips to touch the sacred fire?
How, in your darkness, did you come to know
The power and beauty of the minstrel's lyre?
Who first from midst his bonds lifted his eyes?
Who first from out the still watch, lone and
        long,
Feeling the ancient faith of prophets rise
Within his dark-kept soul, burst into song?

Heart of what slave poured out such melody
As "Steal away to Jesus"? On its strains
His spirit must have nightly floated free,
Though still about his hands he felt his chains.
Who heard great "Jordan roll"? Whose starward
        eye
Saw chariot "swing low"? And who was he
That breathed that comforting, melodic sigh,
"Nobody knows de trouble I see"?

What merely living clod, what captive thing,
Could up toward God through all its darkness
        grope,
And find within its deadened heart to sing
These songs of sorrow, love and faith, and
        hope?
How did it catch that subtle undertone,
That note in music heard not with the ears?
How sound the elusive reed so seldom blown,
Which stirs the soul or melts the heart to tears.

Not that great German master in his dream
Of harmonies that thundered amongst the stars
At the creation, ever heard a theme
Nobler than "Go down, Moses." Mark its bars
How like a mighty trumpet-call they stir
The blood. Such are the notes that men have
        sung
Going to valorous deeds; such tones there
        were
That helped make history when Time was
        young.

There is a wide, wide wonder in it all,
That from degraded rest and servile toil
The fiery spirit of the seer should call
These simple children of the sun and soil.
O black slave singers, gone, forgot, unfamed,
You—you alone, of all the long, long line
Of those who've sung untaught, unknown,
        unnamed,
Have stretched out upward, seeking the divine.

You sang not deeds of heroes or of kings;
No chant of bloody war, no exulting paean
Of arms-won triumphs; but your humble
        strings
You touched in chord with music empyrean.
You sang far better than you knew; the songs
That for your listeners' hungry hearts sufficed
Still live,—but more than this to you belongs:
You sang a race from wood and stone to Christ.

LANGSTON HUGHES

THE NEGRO SPEAKS OF RIVERS and I, TOO

(James) Langston Hughes (1902–1967) was a writer of many talents. Poet, essayist,
journalist, novelist, short-story writer, playwright, anthologist, translator (of Spanish
and French literature), lyricist, and newspaper columnist, Hughes achieved international renown. Best known as a poet, he won recognition at an early age. His poem
"The Negro Speaks of Rivers" appeared in *The Crisis* in 1921; his first volume of poems,
The Weary Blues, appeared in 1926. Hughes, one of the most gifted poets of the Harlem
Renaissance, sensitively explored the African heritage of black Americans. He ultimately
published nine volumes of his collected poems. His poem "I, Too" was first published in

New Negro in 1925; it is a response to Walt Whitman's "I Sing America," an affirmation that "the darker brother" also sings an American song and will gain a place at the American table.

The Negro Speaks of Rivers

I've known rivers:
I've known rivers ancient as the world and
        older than the
    flow of human blood in human veins.

My soul has grown deep like the rivers.

I bathed in the Euphrates when dawns were
        young.
I built my hut near the Congo and it lulled me
        to sleep.
I looked upon the Nile and raised the pyramids
        above it.
I heard the singing of the Mississippi when Abe
        Lincoln
    went down to New Orleans, and I've seen
        its muddy
    bosom turn all golden in the sunset.

I've known rivers:
Ancient, dusky rivers.

My soul has grown deep like the rivers.

I, Too

I, too, sing America.
I am the darker brother.
They send me to eat in the kitchen
When company comes,
But I laugh,
And eat well,
And grow strong.

Tomorrow,
I'll be at the table
When company comes.
Nobody'll dare
Say to me,
"Eat in the kitchen,"
Then.

Besides,
They'll see how beautiful I am
And be ashamed—

I, too, am America.

HERBERT HOOVER

THE AMERICAN SYSTEM OF SELF-GOVERNMENT

Liberalism is a force truly of the spirit, a force proceeding from the deep realization that economic freedom cannot be sacrificed if political freedom is to be preserved.

Herbert Hoover (1874–1964) was born in Iowa, raised in Oregon, and educated as an engineer at Stanford University. Hoover gained an international reputation for his work distributing $100 million worth of food and other assistance to devastated areas of Europe during and after World War I. When he received the Republican presidential nomination in 1928, Hoover was known as a progressive, pragmatic leader. His background in relief activities should have prepared him for the national calamity that began with the stock market crash in October 1929, but Hoover opposed massive public works projects and direct federal aid to the unemployed.

    Hoover's defeat at the polls by Franklin D. Roosevelt in 1932 led many to conclude that his philosophy of limited government was decisively repudiated. But even though the New Deal vastly expanded the role of the federal government in the economy, it did not destroy self-government and private initiative, as Hoover feared. The ideas Hoover expressed remained a basic theme in the American self-image and gained new international credibility in the late 1980s as socialist states began to abandon central planning and to experiment with political pluralism, market economies, and private enterprise.

This speech was delivered during Hoover's successful 1928 campaign.

... During 150 years we have builded up a form of self-government and a social system which is peculiarly our own. It differs essentially from all others in the world. It is the American system. It is just as definite and positive a political and social system as has ever been developed on earth. It is founded upon a particular conception of self-government in which decentralized local responsibility is the very base. Further than this, it is founded upon the conception that only through ordered liberty, freedom and equal opportunity to the individual will his initiative and enterprise spur on the march of progress. And in our insistence upon equality of opportunity has our system advanced beyond all the world.

During the war we necessarily turned to the Government to solve every difficult economic problem. The Government having absorbed every energy of our people for war, there was no other solution. For the preservation of the State, the Federal Government became a centralized despotism which undertook unprecedented responsibilities, assumed autocratic powers, and took over the business of citizens. To a large degree we regimented our whole people temporarily into a socialistic state. However justified in time of war if continued in peace time it would destroy not only our American system but with it our progress and freedom as well.

When the war closed, the most vital of all issues both in our own country and throughout the world was whether Governments should continue their wartime ownership and operation of many instrumentalities of production and distribution. We were challenged with a peace-time choice between the American system of rugged individualism and a European philosophy of diametrically opposed doctrines—doctrines of paternalism and state socialism. The acceptance of these ideas would have meant the destruction of self-government through centralization of government. It would have meant the undermining of the individual initiative and enterprise through which our people have grown to unparalleled greatness. . . .

When the Republican Party came into full power it went at once resolutely back to our fundamental conception of the State and the rights and responsibilities of the individual. Thereby it restored confidence and hope in the American people, it freed and stimulated enterprise, it restored the Government to its position as an umpire instead of a player in the economic game. For these reasons the American people have gone forward in progress while the rest of the world has halted, and some countries have even gone backwards. If anyone will study the causes of retarded recuperation in Europe, he will find much of it due to the stifling of private initiative on one hand, and overloading of the Government with business on the other.

There has been revived in this campaign, however, a series of proposals which, if adopted, would be a long step toward the abandonment of our American system and a surrender to the destructive operation of governmental conduct of commercial business. Because the country is faced with difficulty and doubt over certain national problems—that is, prohibition, farm relief and electrical power—our opponents propose that we must thrust government a long way into the businesses which give rise to these problems. In effect, they abandon the tenets of their own party and turn to State socialism as a solu-

Automobiles line the road along the coast near San Francisco in the 1920s. The automobile brought vast changes to American life: concrete roads, traffic lights, vacations, tourism, filling stations, suburbs, and greater mobility.

tion for the difficulties presented by all three. It is proposed that we shall change from prohibition to the State purchase and sale of liquor. If their agricultural relief program means anything, it means that the Government shall directly or indirectly buy and sell and fix prices of agricultural products. And we are to go into the hydro-electric-power business. In other words, we are confronted with a huge program of government in business.

There is, therefore, submitted to the American people a question of fundamental principle. That is: shall we depart from the principles of our American political and economic system, upon which we have advanced beyond all the

rest of the world, in order to adopt methods based on principles destructive of its very foundations? . . .

I should like to state to you the effect that this projection of government in business would have upon our system of self-government and our economic system. That effect would reach to the daily life of every man and woman. It would impair the very basis of liberty and freedom not only for those left outside the fold of expanded bureaucracy but for those embraced within it. . . .

It is a false liberalism that interprets itself into the Government operation of commercial business. Every step of burcaucratizing of the business of our country poisons the very roots of liberalism—that is, political equality, free speech, free assembly, free press, and equality of opportunity. It is the road not to more liberty, but to less liberty. Liberalism should be found not striving to spread bureaucracy but striving to set bounds to it. True liberalism seeks all legitimate freedom, first in the confident belief that without such freedom the pursuit of all other blessings and benefits is vain. That belief is the foundation of all American progress, political as well as economic.

Liberalism is a force truly of the spirit, a force proceeding from the deep realization that economic freedom cannot be sacrificed if political freedom is to be preserved. Even if Governmental conduct of business could give us more efficiency instead of less efficiency, the fundamental objection to it would remain unaltered and unabated. It would destroy political equality. It would increase rather than decrease abuse and corruption. It would stifle initiative and invention. It would undermine the development of leadership. It would cramp and cripple the mental and spiritual energies of our people. It would extinguish equality and opportunity. It would dry up the spirit of liberty and progress. For these reasons primarily it must be resisted. For a hundred and fifty years liberalism has found its true spirit in the American system, not in the European systems.

I do not wish to be misunderstood in this statement. I am defining a general policy. It does not mean that our Government is to part with one iota of its national resources without complete protection to the public interest. . . .

Nor do I wish to be misinterpreted as believing that the United States is free-for-all and devil-take-the-hind-most. The very essence of equality of opportunity and of American individualism is that there shall be no domination by any group or combination in this Republic, whether it be business or political. On the contrary, it demands economic justice as well as political and social justice. It is no system of laissez faire.

I feel deeply on this subject because during the war I had some practical experience with governmental operation and control. I have witnessed not only at home but abroad the many failures of Government in business. I have seen its tyrannies, its injustices, its destructions of self-government, its undermining of the very instincts which carry our people forward to progress. I have witnessed the lack of advance, the lowered standards of living, the depressed spirits of people working under such a system. My objection is based not upon theory or upon a failure to recognize wrong or abuse, but I know the adoption of such methods would strike at the very roots of American life and would destroy the very basis of American progress. . . .

And what have been the results of our American system? Our country has become the land of opportunity to those born without inheritance, not merely because of the wealth of its resources and industry, but because of this freedom of initiative and enterprise. Russia has natural resources equal to ours. Her people are equally industrious, but she has not had the blessings of 150 years of our form of government and of our social system. . . .

The greatness of America has grown out of a political and social system and a method of control of economic forces distinctly its own—our American system—which has carried this great experiment in human welfare further than ever before in all history. We are nearer today to the ideal of the abolition of poverty and fear from the lives of men and women than ever before in any land. And I again repeat that the departure from our American system by injecting principles destructive to it which our opponents propose will jeopardize the very liberty and freedom of our people, will destroy equality of opportunity, not alone to ourselves but to our children.

THE DEPRESSION AND
WORLD WAR II

An unemployed man selling apples on a street corner during the Great Depression. When Roosevelt was elected, fifteen million were unemployed, and a third of the nation's banks had failed.

MILTON AGER AND JACK YELLEN
HAPPY DAYS ARE HERE AGAIN

"Happy Days Are Here Again" was introduced on the eve of the stock market crash in October 1929, which plunged the nation into the Great Depression. While "Happy Days" were far away, people needed cheering up. The song became famous as the theme song of Democrat Franklin D. Roosevelt's presidential campaigns and has regularly been a staple at national conventions of the Democratic Party. The song was composed by Milton Ager, with words by Jack Yellen. The duo also wrote "Ain't She Sweet?" in 1927, and Ager wrote the music for "I'm Nobody's Baby" in 1921.

So long, sad times;
Go 'long, bad times!
We are rid of you at last.
Howdy, gay times!
Cloudy gray times,
You are now a thing of the past.

'Cause happy days are here again!
The skies above are clear again.
Let us sing a song of cheer again
Happy days are here again!

Altogether shout it now!
There's no one who can doubt it now,
So let's tell the world about it now
Happy days are here again!

Your cares and troubles are gone;
There'll be no more from now on.
Happy days are here again,
The skies above are clear again;
Let us sing a song of cheer again
Happy days arc here again!

FRANKLIN DELANO ROOSEVELT
FIRST INAUGURAL ADDRESS

The only thing we have to fear is fear itself—nameless, unreasoning, unjustified terror which paralyzes needed efforts to convert retreat into advance.

Franklin Delano Roosevelt (1882–1945) was the only person to be elected president four times. He led the nation through two major traumas, the Great Depression and World War II. A descendant of a distinguished New York family, Roosevelt graduated from Harvard College, married his distant cousin Eleanor Roosevelt, and studied at Columbia University Law School. Although crippled by polio in 1921, he was elected governor of New York in 1928. In 1932, Roosevelt was elected to the presidency, defeating the incumbent, Republican Herbert Hoover. Roosevelt was president during one of the most tumultuous and crisis-ridden periods of American history. Assailed by extremists from both left and right, he retained great popularity until his death in office on April 12, 1945.

When Roosevelt was inaugurated as president on March 4, 1933, the nation was in the grip of a devastating economic depression. Millions of people were out of work, and confidence in the future was at a low ebb. He confronted two huge tasks: first, to

uplift the spirit of the nation, which he did with his own buoyant and vital personality; second, to bring relief to the needy and to revive the economy. Toward this second goal, Roosevelt used the powers of the federal government to intervene actively in the economy and to create an array of social and economic programs, which was called the New Deal. In doing so, the new president soon set aside the pledges in this speech that he would cut government spending and balance the federal budget.

I am certain that my fellow Americans expect that on my induction into the Presidency I will address them with a candor and a decision which the present situation of our Nation impels. This is preeminently the time to speak the truth, the whole truth, frankly and boldly. Nor need we shrink from honestly facing conditions in our country to-day. This great Nation will endure as it has endured, will revive and will prosper. So, first of all, let me assert my firm belief that the only thing we have to fear is fear itself—nameless, unreasoning, unjustified terror which paralyzes needed efforts to convert retreat into advance. In every dark hour of our national life a leadership of frankness and vigor has met with that understanding and support of the people themselves which is essential to victory. I am convinced that you will again give the support to leadership in these critical days.

In such a spirit on my part and on yours we face our common difficulties. They concern, thank God, only material things. Values have shrunken to fantastic levels; taxes have risen; our ability to pay has fallen; government of all kinds is faced by serious curtailment of income; the means of exchange are frozen in the currents of trade; the withered leaves of industrial enterprise lie on every side; farmers find no markets for their produce; the savings of many years in thousands of families are gone.

More important, a host of unemployed citizens face the grim problem of existence, and an equally great number toil with little return. Only a foolish optimist can deny the dark realities of the moment.

Yet our distress comes from no failure of substance. We are stricken by no plague of locusts. Compared with the perils which our forefathers conquered because they believed and

were not afraid, we have still much to be thankful for. Nature still offers her bounty and human efforts have multiplied it. Plenty is at our doorsteps, but a generous use of it languishes in the very sight of the supply. Primarily this is because the rulers of the exchange of mankind's goods have failed, through their own stubbornness and their own incompetence, have admitted their failure, and abdicated. Practices of the unscrupulous money changers stand indicted in the court of public opinion, rejected by the hearts and minds of men. . . .

Happiness lies not in the mere possession of money; it lies in the joy of achievement, in the thrill of creative effort. The joy and moral stimulation of work no longer must be forgotten in the mad chase of evanescent profits. These dark days will be worth all they cost us if they teach us that our true destiny is not to be ministered unto but to minister to ourselves and to our fellow men. . . .

Our greatest primary task is to put people to work. This is no unsolvable problem if we face it wisely and courageously. It can be accomplished in part by direct recruiting by the Government itself, treating the task as we would treat the emergency of a war, but at the same time, through this employment, accomplishing greatly needed projects to stimulate and reorganize the use of our natural resources.

Hand in hand with this we must frankly recognize the overbalance of population in our industrial centers and, by engaging on a national scale in a redistribution, endeavor to provide a better use of the land for those best fitted for the land. The task can be helped by definite efforts to raise the values of agricultural products and with this the power to purchase the output of our cities. It can be helped by preventing realistically the tragedy of the growing loss through foreclosure of our small homes and our farms. It can be helped by insistence that the Federal, State, and local governments act forthwith on the demand that their cost be drastically reduced. It can be helped by the unifying of relief activities which to-day are often scattered, uneconomical, and unequal. It can be helped by national planning for and supervision of all forms of transportation and of communications and other utilities which have a definitely public character. There are many ways in which it can be helped, but it can never be helped merely by talking about it. We must act and act quickly.

Finally, in our progress toward a resumption of work we require two safeguards against a return of the evils of the old order; there must be a strict supervision of all banking and credits and investments; there must be an end to speculation with other people's money, and there must be provision for an adequate but sound currency.

There are the lines of attack. I shall presently urge upon a new Congress in special session detailed measures for their fulfillment, and I shall seek the immediate assistance of the several States. Through this program of action we address ourselves to putting our own national house in order and making income balance outgo. . . .

In the winter of 1937, flooding throughout the Ohio Valley claimed four hundred lives and left thousands homeless. This photograph, by Margaret Bourke-White, shows refugees lined up for supplies at an emergency relief station.

In the field of world policy I would dedicate this Nation to the policy of the good neighbor —the neighbor who resolutely respects himself and, because he does so, respects the rights of others—the neighbor who respects his obligations and respects the sanctity of his agreements in and with a world of neighbors.

If I read the temper of our people correctly, we now realize as we have never realized before our interdependence on each other; that we can not merely take but we must give as well; that if we are to go forward, we must move as a trained and loyal army willing to sacrifice for the good of a common discipline, because without such discipline no progress is made, no leadership becomes effective. We are, I know, ready and willing to submit our lives and property to such discipline, because it makes possible a leadership which aims at a larger good. This I propose to offer, pledging that the larger purposes will bind upon us all as a sacred obligation with a unity of duty hitherto evoked only in time of armed strife.

With this pledge taken, I assume unhesitatingly the leadership of this great army of our people dedicated to a disciplined attack upon our common problems.

Action in this image and to this end is feasible under the form of government which we have inherited from our ancestors. Our Constitution is so simple and practical that it is possible always to meet extraordinary needs by changes in emphasis and arrangement without loss of essential form. That is why our constitutional system has proved itself the most superbly enduring political mechanism the modern world has produced. It has met every stress of vast expansion of territory, of foreign wars, of bitter internal strife, of world relations.

It is to be hoped that the normal balance of executive and legislative authority may be wholly adequate to meet the unprecedented task before us. But it may be that an unprecedented demand and need for undelayed action may call for temporary departure from that normal balance of public procedure.

I am prepared under my constitutional duty to recommend the measures that a stricken nation in the midst of a stricken world may require. These measures, or such other measures as the Congress may build out of its experience and wisdom, I shall seek, within my constitutional authority, to bring to speedy adoption.

But in the event that the Congress shall fail to take one of these two courses, and in the event that the national emergency is still critical, I shall not evade the clear course of duty that will then confront me. I shall ask the Congress for the one remaining instrument to meet the crisis—broad Executive power to wage a war against the emergency, as great as the power that would be given to me if we were in fact invaded by a foreign foe.

For the trust reposed in me I will return the courage and the devotion that befit the time. I can do no less. . . .

FRANKLIN DELANO ROOSEVELT
SECOND INAUGURAL ADDRESS

I see one-third of a nation ill-housed, ill-clad, ill-nourished.

In 1936, Roosevelt won an overwhelming victory at the polls over Alfred Landon, the governor of Kansas (a Republican progressive). At Roosevelt's second inaugural, on January 20, 1937, he struck a tone of confidence and pragmatism, portraying an administration that was busily seeking solutions and solving problems. But he acknowledged *the continuing human toll of the Depression, which blighted lives while the Roosevelt administration battled the courts to create new executive agencies to provide social security for the aged, work for the unemployed, and price supports for agricultural products.*

When four years ago we met to inaugurate a President, the Republic, single-minded in anxiety, stood in spirit here. We dedicated ourselves to the fulfillment of a vision—to speed the time when there would be for all the people that security and peace essential to the pursuit of happiness. We of the Republic pledged ourselves to drive from the temple of our ancient faith those who have profaned it; to end by action, tireless and unafraid, the stagnation and despair of that day. We did those first things first.

Our covenant with ourselves did not stop there. Instinctively we recognized a deeper need—the need to find through government the instrument of our united purpose to solve for the individual the ever-rising problems of a complex civilization. Repeated attempts at their solution without the aid of government had left us baffled and bewildered. For, without that aid, we had been unable to create those moral controls over the services of science which are necessary to make science a useful servant instead of a ruthless master of mankind. To do this we knew that we must find practical controls over blind economic forces and blindly selfish men.

We of the Republic sensed the truth that democratic government has innate capacity to protect its people against disasters once considered inevitable, to solve problems once considered unsolvable. We would not admit that we could not find a way to master economic epidemics just as, after centuries of fatalistic suffering, we had found a way to master epidemics of disease. We refused to leave the problems of our common welfare to be solved by the winds of chance and the hurricanes of disaster. . . .

Four years of new experience have not belied our historic instinct. They hold out the clear hope that government within communities, government within the separate States, and government of the United States can do the

things the times require, without yielding its democracy. Our tasks in the last four years did not force democracy to take a holiday. . . .

Have we reached the goal of our vision of that fourth day of March, 1933? Have we found our happy valley?

I see a great nation, upon a great continent, blessed with a great wealth of natural resources. Its hundred and thirty million people are at peace among themselves; they are making their country a good neighbor among the nations. I see a United States which can demonstrate that, under democratic methods of government, national wealth can be translated into a spreading volume of human comforts hitherto unknown, and the lowest standard of living can be raised far above the level of mere subsistence.

But here is the challenge to our democracy: In this nation I see tens of millions of its citizens—a substantial part of its whole population—who at this very moment are denied the greater part of what the very lowest standards of today call the necessities of life.

I see millions of families trying to live on incomes so meager that the pall of family disaster hangs over them day by day.

I see millions whose daily lives in city and on farm continue under conditions labeled indecent by a so-called polite society half a century ago.

I see millions denied education, recreation, and the opportunity to better their lot and the lot of their children.

I see millions lacking the means to buy the products of farm and factory and by their poverty denying work and productiveness to many other millions.

I see one-third of a nation ill-housed, ill-clad, ill-nourished.

It is not in despair that I paint you that picture. I paint it for you in hope—because the

Nation, seeing and understanding the injustice in it, proposes to paint it out. We are determined to make every American citizen the subject of his country's interest and concern; and we will never regard any faithful law-abiding group within our borders as superfluous. The test of our progress is not whether we add more to the abundance of those who have much; it is whether we provide enough for those who have too little.

If I know aught of the spirit and purpose of our Nation, we will not listen to Comfort, Opportunism, and Timidity. We will carry on....

Today we reconsecrate our country to long-cherished ideals in a suddenly changed civilization. In every land there are always at work forces that drive men apart and forces that draw men together. In our personal ambitions we are individualists. But in our seeking for economic and political progress as a nation, we all go up, or else we all go down, as one people....

E. Y. HARBURG AND JAY GORNEY
BROTHER, CAN YOU SPARE A DIME?

E. Y. (Yip) Harburg wrote the lyrics, and Jay Gorney wrote the music to this song, which was introduced in *Americana,* a musical revue; it opened on October 5, 1932, at the Shubert Theatre in New York, and ran for seventy-seven performances. The show was remembered mainly for this song, which became the anthem of the Depression. Harburg later wrote the lyrics to *Finian's Rainbow;* his many popular songs include "Over the Rainbow" and "Only a Paper Moon." Jay Gorney wrote songs for Broadway and Hollywood.

They used to tell me I was building a dream,
And so I followed the mob
When there was earth to plough or guns to
      bear
I was always there right there on the job.

They used to tell me I was building a dream
With peace and glory ahead
Why should I be standing in line
Just waiting for bread?

Once I built a railroad, made it run,
Made it race against time.
Once I built a railroad,
Now it's done
Brother, can you spare a dime?

Once I built a tower, to the sun.
Brick and rivet and lime,
Once I built a tower,
Now it's done,
Brother, can you spare a dime?

Once in khaki suits
Gee, we looked swell
Full of that Yankee Doodle-de-dum.
Half a million boots went sloggin' thru Hell,
I was the kid with the drum.
Say, don't you remember, they called me Al
It was Al all the time
Say, don't you remember I'm your Pal!
Buddy, can you spare a dime?

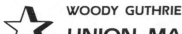

WOODY GUTHRIE

UNION MAID and SO LONG, IT'S BEEN GOOD TO KNOW YUH (DUSTY OLD DUST)

Woody Guthrie (1912–1967), born Woodrow Wilson Guthrie, became a legend in his own time as a singer and composer. He wrote more than one thousand songs, mostly about the struggles of common people and the dispossessed, many of which became American standards. Born in Okemah, Oklahoma, Guthrie left home as a teenager to hitchhike, ride freight trains, live in hobo camps, and follow migrant workers. He witnessed the effect of the Great Dust Bowl on people's lives and followed "Okies" to California. Guthrie's career was cut short by Huntington's chorea, a hereditary degenerative disease, which caused him to die a slow, lingering death.

"Union Maid," written in 1940, was one of Guthrie's most popular union songs. Guthrie wrote "So Long, It's Been Good to Know Yuh" in 1936, as he observed the devastation the Dust Bowl wrought on the people of Oklahoma.

Union Maid

There once was a union maid
Who never was afraid
Of goons and ginks and company finks
And the deputy sheriffs who made the raids;
She went to the union hall
When a meeting it was called,
And when the company boys came 'round
She always stood her ground.

CHORUS:
Oh, you can't scare me.
I'm sticking to the union,
I'm sticking to the union,
I'm sticking to the union.
Oh, you can't scare me.
I'm sticking to the union,
I'm sticking to the union
Till the day I die.

This union maid was wise
To the tricks of company spies.
She never got fooled by a company stool,
She'd always organize the guys.
She always got her way
When she struck for higher pay,
She'd show her union card to the company
    guard
And this is what she'd say:

You gals who want to be free,
Just take a little tip from me:
Get you a man who's a union man
And join the Ladies' Auxiliary;
Married life ain't hard
When you've got a union card,
A union man has a happy life
When he's got a union wife.

So Long, It's Been Good to Know Yuh (Dusty Old Dust)

I've sung this song, but I'll sing it again,
Of the place that I lived on the wild, windy
    plains.
In the month called April, the county called
    Gray,
And here's what all of the people there say:

CHORUS:
So long, it's been good to know you;
So long, it's been good to know you;
So long, it's been good to know you,
This dusty old dust is a-getting my home,
And I've got to be driftin' along.

A dust storm hit, and it hit like thunder;
It dusted us over, and it covered us under;
Blocked out the traffic and blocked out the sun.

Straight for home all the people did run.

The sweethearts sat in the dark and they
    sparked,
They hugged and they kissed in that dusty old
    dark.
They sighed and cried, hugged and kissed,
Instead of marriage, they talked like this:
    Honey,

Now, the telephone rang, and it jumped off the
    wall;

That was the preacher a-making his call.
He said, "Kind friend, this may be the end;
You've got your last chance of salvation of sin."

The churches was jammed, and the churches
    was packed,
And that dusty old dust storm blowed so black;
The preacher could not read a word of his text,
And he folded his specs and he took up
    collection, said:

FLORENCE REECE

WHICH SIDE ARE YOU ON?

According to Alan Lomax, who collected folk songs for the Archive of American Folk Song at the Library of Congress, this song was written by the twelve-year-old daughter of a miner who was on strike in Harlan County, Kentucky. He wrote that she sang it to him in front of the family hearth of a log cabin in 1937. The music is a variation of an old English tune, "Jack Munro." It became very popular with labor groups, who admired its unabashed militancy.

Come all of you good workers.
Good news to you I'll tell,
Of how the good old union
Has come in here to dwell.

CHORUS:
Which side are you on,
Tell me, which side are you on?

My daddy was a miner,
He's now in the air an' sun,
Stick with him, brother miners,
Until this battle's won.

They say in Harlan county,
There are no neutrals there,
You'll either be a union man,
Or a thug for J. H. Blair.

O gentlemen, can you stand it,
O tell me if you can,
Will you be a lousy scab,
Or will you be a man?

Don't scab for the bosses,
Don't listen to their lies.
Us poor folks haven't got a chance,
Unless we organize.

ALFRED HAYES

I DREAMED I SAW JOE HILL LAST NIGHT

Alfred Hayes (1911–) was born in England and grew up in New York City, where he worked for newspapers, magazines, and radio. He has written novels, plays, poetry, and movie scripts, but nothing else he has written has as much fame and notoriety as

"I Dreamed I Saw Joe Hill Last Night." Joe Hill (Joseph Hillstrom) emigrated from Sweden to the United States in 1902, and several years later became a member of the radical Industrial Workers of the World ("Wobblies"). In 1914, Hill was convicted of murdering a Salt Lake City grocer. Despite massive protests about the fairness of his trial, Hill was executed by a five-man firing squad at the Utah State Penitentiary. "I Dreamed I Saw Joe Hill Last Night" was written during the Great Depression (1938) and became a favorite of the union movement.

I dreamed I saw Joe Hill last night
Alive as you and me.
Says I, "But Joe, you're ten years dead."
"I never died," says he.
"I never died," says he.

"In Salt Lake, Joe," says I to him,
Him standing by my bed,
"They framed you on a murder charge."
Says Joe, "But I ain't dead."
Says Joe, "But I ain't dead."

"The copper bosses killed you, Joe,
They shot you, Joe," says I.
"Takes more than guns to kill a man,"
Says Joe, "I didn't die,"
Says Joe, "I didn't die."

And standing there as big as life
And smiling with his eyes,
Joe says, "What they forgot to kill

Went on to organize,
Went on to organize."

"Joe Hill ain't dead," he says to me,
"Joe Hill ain't never died.
Where working men are out on strike
Joe Hill is at their side,
Joe Hill is at their side."

"From San Diego up to Maine,
In every mine and mill,
Where workers strike and organize,"
Says he, "You'll find Joe Hill,"
Says he, "You'll find Joe Hill."

I dreamed I saw Joe Hill last night,
Alive as you or me.
Says I, "But Joe, you're ten years dead,"
"I never died," says he,
"I never died," says he.

IRVING BERLIN

GOD BLESS AMERICA and THIS IS THE ARMY, MR. JONES

One of Irving Berlin's biggest hits was "God Bless America." He had originally written it in 1917 for his Army musical, *Yip, Yip, Yaphank*, but did not use it. It remained tucked away for twenty-one years, until the popular singer Kate Smith asked him for a patriotic song for a national radio broadcast in 1938. It was an overnight sensation; many people suggested that it should be the national anthem, and both political parties played it at their national conventions in 1940. Over the years, it has been considered America's unofficial national anthem, since "The Star-Spangled Banner" has difficult lyrics and a difficult tune. Berlin assigned the royalties for the song to the God Bless America Fund, which supports the Boy Scouts and Girl Scouts.

He wrote "This Is the Army, Mr. Jones" in 1942 during the Second World War and introduced it in his musical *This Is the Army.* Its royalties, too, are donated to the Boy Scouts and Girl Scouts.

God Bless America

While the storm clouds gather
Far across the sea,
Let us swear allegiance
To a land that's free,
Let us all be grateful
For a land so fair,
As we raise our voices
In a solemn prayer.

God bless America
Land that I love.
Stand beside her and guide her,
Thru the night with a light from above.
From the mountains to the prairies
To the oceans white with foam,
God bless America
My home sweet home
God bless America
My home sweet home.

This Is the Army, Mr. Jones

A bunch of frightened rookies were list'ning
    filled with awe,
They listened while a sergeant was laying down
    the law.
They stood there at attention,
Their faces turning red,
The sergeant looked them over and this is what
    he said.

This is the Army, Mister Jones,
No private rooms or telephones.
You had your breakfast in bed before
But you won't have it there anymore.

This is the Army, Mister Green,
We like the barracks nice and clean.
You had a housemaid to clean your floor
But she won't help you out anymore.

Do what the buglers command,
They're in the army and not in a band.

This is the Army, Mister Brown,
You and your baby went to town.
She had you worried
But this is war and she won't worry you
    anymore.

WOODY GUTHRIE

THIS LAND IS YOUR LAND

Woody Guthrie wrote the lyrics to what eventually became "This Land is Your Land" in a dingy hotel room near New York City's Times Square on February 23, 1940. According to his biographer, Joe Klein, Guthrie was "angry, frustrated, and feeling sorry for himself," and "took it out on Irving Berlin." The song was titled "God Blessed America" and each verse ended with the line, "God Blessed America for me." The song was intended as a parodic response to Berlin's wildly popular "God Bless America." The music was taken from the song "Little Darlin', Pal of Mine" by the Carter Family (a popular country music group in the 1920s and 1930s), which was based on an old Baptist hymn, "Oh My Lovin' Brother."

After Guthrie wrote the song, he forgot about it for a few years, then recorded it in the spring of 1944. He titled it "This Land is Your Land." The song was a favorite of the civil rights movement in the 1960s, and (like several other songs) it has even been suggested as a substitute for "The Star-Spangled Banner."

This land is your land, this land is my land
From California to the New York island,
From the redwood forest to the Gulf Stream
　　waters;
This land was made for you and me.

As I was walking that ribbon of highway
I saw above me that endless skyway;
I saw below me that golden valley;
This land was made for you and me.

I've roamed and rambled and I followed my
　　footsteps
To the sparkling sands of her diamond deserts;
And all around me a voice was sounding;
This land was made for you and me.

One bright Sunday morning in the shadows of
　　the steeple
By the Relief Office I seen my people;

As they stood there hungry, I stood there
　　whistling;
This land was made for you and me.

When the sun came shining, and I was strolling,
And the wheat fields waving and the dust
　　clouds rolling.
As the fog was lifting a voice was chanting:
This land was made for you and me.

Nobody living can ever stop me,
As I go walking that freedom highway;
Nobody living can ever make me turn back,
This land was made for you and me.

As I went walking, I saw a sign there,
And on the sign it said, "No Trespassing,"
But on the other side it didn't say nothing,
That side was made for you and me.

E. B. WHITE
FREEDOM

A writer goes about his task today with the extra satisfaction which comes from know-ing that he will be the first to have his head lopped off.

E. B. White (1899–1985), born in Mount Vernon, New York, graduated from Cornell University. For many years he was a staff writer for *The New Yorker* magazine. He was an accomplished essayist, humorist, poet, and satirist. He is well known to generations of American children for his classic children's books, *Stuart Little* (1945) and *Charlotte's Web* (1952). He is familiar to generations of students and writers as co-author (and reviser) of *The Elements of Style,* an invaluable handbook on composition and usage originally written by William Strunk, Jr., who had been White's English professor at Cornell. The essay "Freedom" was first published in *Harper's* magazine in July 1940, before the United States had entered the war against Nazism and during the period of the Nazi–Soviet pact, when both the right and the left chose to ignore the totalitarian threat to democracy. The essay was included in White's collection titled *One Man's Meat* (1942).

I have often noticed on my trips up to the city that people have recut their clothes to follow the fashion. On my last trip, however, it seemed to me that people had remodeled their ideas too —taken in their convictions a little at the waist, shortened the sleeves of their resolve, and fitted themselves out in a new intellectual ensemble copied from a smart design out of the very latest page of history. It seemed to me they had strung along with Paris a little too long.

I confess to a disturbed stomach. I feel sick when I find anyone adjusting his mind to the new tyranny which is succeeding abroad. Because of its fundamental strictures, fascism does not seem to me to admit of any compromise or any rationalization, and I resent the patronizing air of persons who find in my plain belief in freedom a sign of immaturity. If it is boyish to believe that a human being should live free, then I'll gladly arrest my development and let the rest of the world grow up.

I shall report some of the strange remarks I heard in New York. One man told me that he thought perhaps the Nazi ideal was a sounder ideal than our constitutional system "because have you ever noticed what fine alert young faces the young German soldiers have in the newsreel?" He added: "Our American youngsters spend all their time at the movies—they're a mess." That was his summation of the case, his interpretation of the new Europe. Such a remark leaves me pale and shaken. If it represents the peak of our intelligence, then the steady march of despotism will not receive any considerable setback at our shores.

Another man informed me that our democratic notion of popular government was decadent and not worth bothering about—"because England is really rotten and the industrial towns there are a disgrace." That was the only reason he gave for the hopelessness of democracy; and he seemed mightily pleased with himself, as though he were more familiar than most with the anatomy of decadence, and had detected subtler aspects of the situation than were discernible to the rest of us.

Another man assured me that anyone who took *any* kind of government seriously was a gullible fool. You could be sure, he said, that there is nothing but corruption "because of the way Clemenceau acted at Versailles." He said it didn't make any difference really about this war. It was just another war. Having relieved himself of this majestic bit of reasoning, he subsided.

Another individual, discovering signs of zeal creeping into my blood, berated me for having lost my detachment, my pure skeptical point of view. He announced that he wasn't going to be swept away by all this nonsense, but would prefer to remain in the role of innocent bystander, which he said was the duty of any intelligent person. (I noticed, that he phoned later to qualify his remark, as though he had lost some of his innocence in the cab on the way home.)

Those are just a few samples of the sort of talk that seemed to be going round—talk which was full of defeatism and disillusion and sometimes of a too studied innocence. Men are not merely annihilating themselves at a great rate these days, but they are telling one another enormous lies, grandiose fibs. Such remarks as I heard are fearfully disturbing in their cumulative effect. They are more destructive than dive bombers and mine fields, for they challenge not merely one's immediate position but one's main defenses. They seemed to me to issue either from persons who could never have really come to grips with freedom so as to understand her, or from renegades. Where I expected to find indignation, I found paralysis, or a sort of dim acquiescence, as in a child who is duly swallowing a distasteful pill. I was advised of the growing anti-Jewish sentiment by a man who seemed to be watching the phenomenon of intolerance not through tears of shame but with a clear intellectual gaze, as through a well-ground lens.

The least a man can do at such a time is to declare himself and tell where he stands. I believe in freedom with the same burning delight, the same faith, the same intense abandon which attended its birth on this continent more than a century and a half ago. I am writing my declara-

A newsstand in New York City in 1935 displays a slice of American popular culture: movie magazines, romance magazines, detective magazines, Baby Ruths, Chiclets, and Moxie.

tion rapidly, much as though I were shaving to catch a train. Events abroad give a man a feeling of being pressed for time. Actually I do not believe I am pressed for time, and I apologize to the reader for a false impression that may be created. I just want to tell, before I get slowed down, that I am in love with freedom and that it is an affair of long standing and that it is a fine state to be in, and that I am deeply suspicious of people who are beginning to adjust to fascism and dictators merely because they are succeeding in war. From such adaptable natures a smell rises. I pinch my nose.

For as long as I can remember I have had a sense of living somewhat freely in a natural world. I don't mean I enjoyed freedom of action, but my existence seemed to have the quality of free-ness. I traveled with secret papers pertaining to a divine conspiracy. Intuitively I've always been aware of the vitally important pact which a man has with himself, to be all things to himself, and to be identified with all things, to stand self-reliant, taking advantage of his haphazard connection with a planet, riding his luck, and following his bent with the tenacity of a hound. My first and greatest love affair was with this thing we call freedom, this lady of infinite allure, this dangerous and beautiful and sublime being who restores and supplies us all.

It began with the haunting intimation

(which I presume every child receives) of his mystical inner life; of God in man; of nature publishing herself through the "I." This elusive sensation is moving and memorable. It comes early in life: a boy, we'll say, sitting on the front steps on a summer night, thinking of nothing in particular, suddenly hearing as with a new perception and as though for the first time the pulsing sound of crickets, overwhelmed with the novel sense of identification with the natural company of insects and grass and night, conscious of a faint answering cry to the universal perplexing question: "What is 'I'?" Or a little girl, returning from the grave of a pet bird leaning with her elbows on the window sill, inhaling the unfamiliar draught of death, suddenly seeing herself as part of the complete story. Or to an older youth, encountering for the first time a great teacher who by some chance word or mood awakens something and the youth beginning to breathe as an individual and conscious of strength in his vitals. I think the sensation must develop in many men as a feeling of identity with God—an eruption of the spirit caused by allergies and the sense of divine existence as distinct from mere animal existence. This is the beginning of the affair with freedom.

But a man's free condition is of two parts: the instinctive free-ness he experiences as an animal dweller on a planet, and the practical liberties he enjoys as a privileged member of human society. The latter is, of the two, more generally understood, more widely admired, more violently challenged and discussed. It is the practical and apparent side of freedom. The United States, almost alone today, offers the liberties and the privileges and the tools of freedom. In this land the citizens are still invited to write plays and books, to paint their pictures, to meet for discussion, to dissent as well as to agree, to mount soapboxes in the public square, to enjoy education in all subjects without censorship, to hold court and judge one another, to compose music, to talk politics with their neighbors without wondering whether the secret police are listening, to exchange ideas as well as goods, to kid the government when it needs kidding, and to read real news of real events instead of phony news manufactured by a paid agent of the state. This is a fact and should give every person pause.

To be free, in a planetary sense, is to feel that you belong to earth. To be free, in a social sense, is to feel at home in a democratic framework. In Adolph Hitler, although he is a freely flowering individual, we do not detect either type of sensibility. From reading his book I gather that his feeling for earth is not a sense of communion but a driving urge to prevail. His feeling for men is not that they co-exist, but that they are capable of being arranged and standardized by a superior intellect—that their existence suggests not a fulfillment of their personalities but a submersion of their personalities in the common racial destiny. His very great absorption in the destiny of the German people somehow loses some of its effect when you discover, from his writings, in what vast contempt he holds *all* people. "I learned," he wrote, ". . . to gain an insight into the unbelievably primitive opinions and arguments of the people." To him the ordinary man is a primitive, capable only of being used and led. He speaks continually of people as sheep, halfwits, and impudent fools—the same people from whom he asks the utmost in loyalty, and to whom he promises the ultimate in prizes.

Here in America, where our society is based on belief in the individual, not contempt for him, the free principle of life has a chance of surviving. I believe that it must and will survive. To understand freedom is an accomplishment which all men may acquire who set their minds in that direction; and to love freedom is a tendency which many Americans are born with. To live in the same room with freedom, or in the same hemisphere, is still a profoundly shaking experience for me.

One of the earliest truths (and to him most valuable) that the author of *Mein Kampf* discovered was that it is not the written word, but the spoken word, which in heated moments moves great masses of people to noble or ignoble action. The written word, unlike the spoken word, is something which every person examines privately and judges calmly by his own intellectual standards, not by what the man standing next to him thinks. "I know," wrote Hitler, "that one is able to win people far more by the spoken than by the written word. . . ." Later he adds contemptuously: "For let it be said to all knights of the pen and to all the political dandies, especially of today: the greatest changes in this world have never been brought about by a goose quill! No, the pen has always been reserved to motivate these changes theoretically."

Luckily I am not out to change the world—that's being done for me, and at a great clip. But I know that the free spirit of man is persistent in nature; it recurs, and has never successfully been wiped out, by fire or flood. I set down the above remarks merely (in the words of Mr. Hitler) to motivate that spirit, theoretically. Being myself a knight of the goose quill, I am under no misapprehension about "winning people"; but I am inordinately proud these days of the quill, for it has shown itself, historically, to be the hypodermic which inoculates men and keeps the germ of freedom always in circulation, so that there are individuals in every time in every land who are the carriers, the Typhoid Marys, capable of infecting others by mere contact and example. These persons are feared by every tyrant—who shows his fear by burning the books and destroying the individuals. A writer goes about his task today with the extra satisfaction which comes from knowing that he will be the first to have his head lopped off—even before the political dandies. In my own case this is a double satisfaction, for if freedom were denied me by force of earthly circumstance, I am the same as dead and would infinitely prefer to go into fascism without my head than with it, having no use for it any more and not wishing to be saddled with so heavy an encumberance.

JOHN GILLESPIE MAGEE, JR.

HIGH FLIGHT

John Gillespie Magee, Jr. (1922–1941) was born in Shanghai, where his father was a Protestant Episcopal missionary. His father was an American from Pittsburgh, and his mother was English. Although Magee was an American, he attended schools in England, where he excelled in poetry. At Rugby, he won the poetry prize that thirty-four years earlier had been won by Rupert Brooke, his personal hero. When war came in 1939, Magee joined the Royal Canadian Air Force. While in the service, he continued to write poetry. One of the poems that he mailed to his parents, then living in Washington, D.C., was "High Flight." He saw combat in England and was killed in an aerial accident on December 13, 1941.

Although a biography was written about Magee in 1942, he and his poem drifted into obscurity. Then, forty-five years after his death, his words were spoken by the President of the United States. On January 28, 1986, the space shuttle Challenger lifted off from its launching pad and exploded less than two minutes later, while the nation watched in horror. That evening, President Ronald Reagan postponed his scheduled State of the Union message and spoke words of consolation to a grieving nation. He ended his speech by saying of the crew, "We will never forget them nor the last time we saw them this morning as they prepared for their journey and waved goodbye and 'slipped the surly bonds of Earth—and touched the face of God.' "

Oh! I have slipped the surly bonds of Earth
   And danced the skies on laughter-silvered
      wings;
Sunward I've climbed, and joined the tumbling
    mirth
   Of sun-split clouds,—and done a hundred
     things
You have not dreamed of—wheeled and soared
    and swung
   High in the sunlit silence. Hov'ring there,

I've chased the shouting wind along, and flung
   My eager craft through footless halls of
     air. . . .

Up, up the long, delirious, burning blue
   I've topped the wind-swept heights with
     easy grace,
Where never lark, or even eagle flew—
   And, while with silent, lifting mind I've trod
   The high untrespassed sanctity of space,
Put out my hand and touched the face of God.

CHARLES A. ZIMMERMAN

ANCHORS AWEIGH

"Anchors Aweigh" was originally written in 1906 as a football marching song in honor of the senior class at the United States Naval Academy. The music was composed by Lieutenant Charles A. Zimmerman, bandmaster of the Academy, and the words were by a senior, Alfred H. Miles. It was Bandmaster Zimmerman's practice to write a march each year in honor of the graduating class. Lieutenant Zimmerman was very popular with the cadets, and each year the graduating class honored him with a medal in gratitude for the march that he had given them. The official history of Annapolis states that Zimmerman had so many medals that he would have drowned instantly if he ever fell overboard in full dress uniform.

   Midshipman Miles told Bandmaster Zimmerman that his classmates wanted a zesty piece of music that would serve well as a football marching song. The two sat together at the chapel organ, and the piece was written in November 1906, in time for the epic Army–Navy game. That year, for the first time in many years, Navy beat Army, and that convinced many Navy men that the song was a winner.

   For many years, the song was sung only at the Naval Academy, but in 1926, it was published in a collection of navy songs and became nationally known as the navy theme song. Periodically the lyrics were revised, first to make them more of a naval song than a football song, and later versions added pointed comments about the nation's foes. The song now exists in several versions. In the version printed here, the last stanza was one of those originally written by Midshipman Miles. The navy was always pleased that the army never had a song that was as popular as "Anchors Aweigh."

Anchors Aweigh, my boys, Anchors Aweigh,
Farewell to college joys,
We sail at break of day-day-day-day!
Through our last night on shore,
Drink to the foam,
Until we meet once more

Here's wishing you a happy voyage home.

Sail Navy down the bay
Anchors Aweigh
We'll never change our course
We're from the U.S.A. ay-ay-ay
We've got a job to do

Over the sea
Anchors Aweigh, today
As we go sailing on to victory.

Stand Navy down the field
Sail set to the sky
We'll never change our course

So Army you steer shy-y-y-y
Roll up the score Navy
Anchors Aweigh
Sail Navy down the field
And sink the Army, sink the Army grey.

FRANKLIN DELANO ROOSEVELT

THE FOUR FREEDOMS

We look forward to a world founded upon four essential human freedoms. The first is freedom of speech and expression—everywhere in the world. The second is freedom of every person to worship God in his own way—everywhere in the world. The third is freedom from want... everywhere in the world. The fourth is freedom from fear... anywhere in the world.

In his State of the Union speech on January 6, 1941, Roosevelt described America's response to the spreading world conflict. Only months earlier, France had fallen to Hitler's forces; even as Roosevelt spoke, Great Britain steadfastly continued to resist Nazi air attacks. Through these tense months, the military collapse of Great Britain was a real and frightening possibility. In this speech, Roosevelt prepared public opinion for active assistance to America's allies. By March 1941, Congress had enacted Lend-Lease, a program that enabled the United States to supply tanks, trucks, airplanes, and food to its endangered allies. Although the program was enacted mainly to help Great Britain, most Lend-Lease assistance went to the British Commonwealth countries and the Soviet Union.

. . . I suppose that every realist knows that the democratic way of life is at this moment being directly assailed in every part of the world —assailed either by arms or by secret spreading of poisonous propaganda by those who seek to destroy unity and promote discord in nations that are still at peace.

During sixteen months this assault has blotted out the whole pattern of democratic life in an appalling number of independent nations, great and small. And the assailants are still on the march, threatening other nations, great and small. . . .

Our national policy is this:

First, by an impressive expression of the public will and without regard to partisanship, we are committed to all-inclusive national defense.

Second, by an impressive expression of the public will and without regard to partisanship, we are committed to full support of all those resolute people everywhere who are resisting aggression and are thereby keeping war away from our hemisphere. By this support we express our determination that the democratic cause shall prevail, and we strengthen the defense and the security of our own nation.

Third, by an impressive expression of the public will and without regard to partisanship, we are committed to the proposition that principles of morality and considerations for our own security will never permit us to acquiesce in a peace dictated by aggressors and sponsored by appeasers. We know that enduring peace cannot be bought at the cost of other people's freedom. . . .

Therefore, the immediate need is a swift and driving increase in our armament production. . . .

Let us say to the democracies: "We Americans are vitally concerned in your defense of freedom. We are putting forth our energies, our resources and our organizing powers to give you the strength to regain and maintain a free world. We shall send you in ever-increasing numbers, ships, planes, tanks, guns. That is our purpose and our pledge." . . .

As men do not live by bread alone, they do not fight by armaments alone. Those who man our defenses and those behind them who build our defenses must have the stamina and the courage which come from an unshakable belief in the manner of life which they are defending. The mighty action that we are calling for cannot be based on a disregard of all the things worth fighting for.

The nation takes great satisfaction and much strength from the things which have been done to make its people conscious of their individual stake in the preservation of democratic life in America. Those things have toughened the fibre of our people, have renewed their faith and strengthened their devotion to the institutions we make ready to protect.

Certainly this is no time for any of us to stop thinking about the social and economic problems which are the root cause of the social revolution which is today a supreme factor in the world. For there is nothing mysterious about the foundations of a healthy and strong democracy.

The basic things expected by our people of

The final inspection of mass-produced propellers for military aircraft. During World War II, women replaced men in war industries.

their political and economic systems are simple. They are:

Equality of opportunity for youth and for others.

Jobs for those who can work.

Security for those who need it.

The ending of special privilege for the few.

The preservation of civil liberties for all.

The enjoyment of the fruits of scientific progress in a wider and constantly rising standard of living.

These are the simple, the basic things that must never be lost sight of in the turmoil and unbelievable complexity of our modern world. The inner and abiding strength of our economic and political systems is dependent upon the degree to which they fulfill these expectations. . . .

In the future days which we seek to make secure, we look forward to a world founded upon four essential human freedoms.

The first is freedom of speech and expression—everywhere in the world.

The second is freedom of every person to worship God in his own way—everywhere in the world.

The third is freedom from want—which, translated into world terms, means economic understandings which will secure to every nation a healthy peacetime life for its inhabitants —everywhere in the world.

The fourth is freedom from fear, which, translated into world terms, means a world-wide reduction of armaments to such a point and in such a thorough manner that no nation will be in a position to commit an act of physical aggression against any neighbor—anywhere in the world.

That is no vision of a distant millennium. It is a definite basis for a kind of world attainable in our own time and generation. That kind of world is the very antithesis of the so-called "new order" of tyranny which the dictators seek to create with the crash of a bomb.

To that new order we oppose the greater conception—the moral order. A good society is able to face schemes of world domination and foreign revolutions alike without fear.

Since the beginning of our American history we have been engaged in change, in a perpetual, peaceful revolution, a revolution which goes on steadily, quietly, adjusting itself to changing conditions without the concentration camp or the quick-lime in the ditch. The world order which we seek is the co-operation of free countries, working together in a friendly, civilized society.

This nation has placed its destiny in the hands, heads and hearts of its millions of free men and women, and its faith in freedom under the guidance of God. Freedom means the supremacy of human rights everywhere. Our support goes to those who struggle to gain those rights and keep them. Our strength is in our unity of purpose.

To that high concept there can be no end save victory.

FRANKLIN DELANO ROOSEVELT

WAR MESSAGE TO CONGRESS

Yesterday, December 7, 1941—a date which will live in infamy—the United States of America was suddenly and deliberately attacked by naval and air forces of the empire of Japan.

On December 7, 1941, the Japanese military launched a surprise aerial attack on an American naval base at Pearl Harbor on Oahu Island in Hawaii. Because the attack began early on a Sunday morning, there was a tremendous loss of life—more than

2,300 Americans were killed—and destruction of ships in the harbor and airplanes on the ground. The American public was outraged. In response to Roosevelt's "day of infamy" speech, Congress voted overwhelmingly to declare war on Japan. Since Japan was part of the Axis powers, with Germany and Italy, war with Japan guaranteed that America would be a major participant in the world war.

Yesterday, December 7, 1941—a date which will live in infamy—the United States of America was suddenly and deliberately attacked by naval and air forces of the empire of Japan.

The United States was at peace with that nation and, at the solicitation of Japan, was still in conversation with its government and its emperor looking toward the maintenance of peace in the Pacific.

Indeed, one hour after Japanese air squadrons had commenced bombing in the American Island of Oahu the Japanese Ambassador to the United States and his colleague delivered to our Secretary of State a formal reply to a recent American message. And, while this reply stated that it seemed useless to continue the existing diplomatic negotiations, it contained no threat or hint of war or of armed attack.

It will be recorded that the distance of Hawaii from Japan makes it obvious that the attack was deliberately planned many days or even weeks ago. During the intervening time the Japanese Government has deliberately sought to deceive the United States by false statements and expressions of hope for continued peace.

The attack yesterday on the Hawaiian Islands has caused severe damage to American naval and military forces. I regret to tell you that very many American lives have been lost. In addition American ships have been reported torpedoed on the high seas between San Francisco and Honolulu.

Yesterday the Japanese Government also launched an attack against Malaya.

Last night Japanese forces attacked Hong Kong.

Last night Japanese forces attacked Guam.

Last night Japanese forces attacked the Philippine Islands.

Last night the Japanese attacked Wake Island.

And this morning the Japanese attacked Midway Island.

Japan has therefore undertaken a surprise offensive extending throughout the Pacific area. The facts of yesterday and today speak for themselves. The people of the United States have already formed their opinions and well understand the implications to the very life and safety of our nation.

As Commander in Chief of the Army and Navy I have directed that all measures be taken for our defense.

Always will our whole nation remember the character of the onslaught against us.

No matter how long it may take us to overcome this premeditated invasion, the American people in their righteous might, will win through to absolute victory.

I believe that I interpret the will of the Congress and of the people when I assert that we will not only defend ourselves to the uttermost but will make it very certain that this form of treachery shall never again endanger us.

Hostilities exist. There is no blinking at the fact that our people, our territory and our interests are in grave danger.

With confidence in our armed forces, with the unbounding determination of our people, we will gain the inevitable triumph. So help us God.

I ask that the Congress declare that since the unprovoked and dastardly attack by Japan on Sunday, Dec. 7, 1941, a state of war has existed between the United States and the Japanese Empire.

POEMS OF THE ISSEI

In the aftermath of the Japanese government's surprise attack on the American naval base at Pearl Harbor, the federal government ordered a mass evacuation of all Japanese-Americans on the West Coast. The decision was motivated by racial prejudice, rather than national security, since no Japanese-American had committed any act of sabotage and no comparable policy was established for German-Americans or Italian-Americans. President Roosevelt issued an executive order establishing the War Relocation Authority on March 18, 1942. This agency supervised the mass evacuation of 110,000 Japanese-Americans from their homes on the West Coast to relocation centers inland. There, men, women, and children lived in sparsely furnished military barracks, surrounded by barbed wire, until the war ended. Two-thirds of those who were forced

During the war, Japanese-Americans were removed from their homes on the west coast, classified as security risks, and relocated to internment camps inland. Forty-five years later, the federal government paid millions of dollars in compensation to the evacuees for their property losses.

to abandon their homes and businesses were American citizens. In 1944, the Supreme Court upheld the evacuation and internment order. Thousands of internees volunteered to serve in the military and did so with distinction.

Eventually the federal government acknowledged the injustice of this wartime policy and paid compensation to the evacuees, but no amount of money could right the wrong that had been done.

The first generation of Japanese immigrants to the United States is known as Issei; many of their poems, written in the camps, were collected and printed in the *Amerasia Journal.* They are written in a terse form called senryu, a three-line poem that compresses intense emotion into a brief statement.

Thirty years
in America
become a dream.
—SASABUNE

As one
of the Japanese
I gather my belongings.
—KEIHO

Enduring
and still enduring
the color of my skin.
—KIKYO

ROBERT CRAWFORD
THE ARMY AIR CORPS

Robert Crawford (1899–1961) was born in the Yukon Territory and educated at Princeton University and the Juilliard School of Music. He was director of the Princeton Glee Club and conductor of a number of choral groups. In 1939, the Army Air Corps offered a prize for the best song to serve as its theme. Crawford's entry won. During the Second World War, he served as a major in the Air Corps.

Off we go, into the wild blue yonder,
Climbing high, into the sun;
Here they come, zooming to meet our thunder,
At 'em, boys
Give 'er the gun!
Down we dive,
Spouting our flame from under,
Off with one helluva roar!
We live in fame
Or go down in flame
NOTHING'LL STOP THE ARMY AIR CORPS!

Minds of men fashioned a crate of thunder,
Sent it high into the blue;
Hands of men blasted the world asunder;

How they lived God only knew!
Souls of men dreaming of skies to conquer
Gave us wings, ever to soar!
With scouts before and bombers galore,
NOTHING'LL STOP THE ARMY AIR CORPS!

Off we go into the wild sky yonder,
Keep the wings level and true;
If you'd live to be a gray-haired wonder
Keep the nose out of the blue!
Flying men, guarding the nation's border,
We'll be there, followed by more!
In echelon we carry on.
NOTHING'LL STOP THE ARMY AIR CORPS!

FRANK LOESSER
PRAISE THE LORD AND PASS THE AMMUNITION

Frank Loesser (1910–1969) was one of the nation's most successful songwriters. Among his credits were the Broadway productions *Guys and Dolls* and *The Most Happy Fella*, as well as such popular songs as "Baby, It's Cold Outside" and "On a Slow Boat to China." He wrote the words and music for "Praise the Lord and Pass the Ammunition," which was one of the few martial songs to become a hit during the Second World War. The American public favored escapist and romantic songs like "White Christmas," "Paper Doll," and "Oh, What a Beautiful Morning."

Down went the gunner, a bullet was his fate,
Down went the gunner, and then the gunner's
     mate.
Up jumped the sky pilot, gave the boys a look.
And manned the gun himself as he laid aside
     The Book,

                         Shouting

CHORUS:
"Praise the Lord, and pass the ammunition!
Praise the Lord, and pass the ammunition!
Praise the Lord, and pass the ammunition
     And we'll all stay free!
Praise the Lord, and swing into position.
Can't afford to sit around a-wishin'.

Praise the Lord, we're all between perdition
     And the deep blue sea!"

     Yes, the sky pilot said it,
     You've got to give him credit
     For a son-of-a-gun of a gunner was he,

                         Shouting

"Praise the Lord, we're on a mighty mission!
All aboard! We're not a-goin' fishin'.
Praise the Lord, and pass the ammunition
     And we'll all stay free!"

LEARNED HAND
THE SPIRIT OF LIBERTY

The spirit of liberty is the spirit which is not too sure that it is right.

Although he was never appointed to the Supreme Court, Learned Hand (1872–1961) is considered one of the greatest judges in American history. Born in Albany, New York, he graduated from Harvard and Harvard Law School.

Learned Hand was first appointed to the federal bench in 1909, then elevated to the United States Court of Appeals in 1924. As chief judge of that court from 1939 to 1951, he became one of the most influential jurists in the nation, by virtue of his intellect, his wisdom, and his profound faith in democratic principles.

On May 21, 1944, Judge Hand was invited to address a huge gathering in Central Park in New York City, to honor "I Am an American Day." His speech, delivered during the critical days of the war, was widely reprinted and anthologized.

We have gathered here to affirm a faith, a faith in a common purpose, a common conviction, a common devotion. Some of us have chosen America as the land of our adoption; the rest have come from those who did the same. For this reason we have some right to consider ourselves a picked group, a group of those who had the courage to break from the past and brave the dangers and the loneliness of a strange land. What was the object that nerved us, or those who went before us, to this choice? We sought liberty; freedom from oppression, freedom from want, freedom to be ourselves. This we then sought; this we now believe that we are by way of winning. What do we mean when we say that first of all we seek liberty? I often wonder whether we do not rest our hopes too much upon constitutions, upon laws and upon courts. These are false hopes; believe me, these are false hopes. Liberty lies in the hearts of men and women; when it dies there, no constitution, no law, no court can save it; no constitution, no law, no court can even do much to help it. While it lies there it needs no constitution, no law, no court to save it. And what is this liberty which must lie in the hearts of men and women? It is not the ruthless, the unbridled will; it is not freedom to do as one likes. That is the denial of liberty, and leads straight to its overthrow. A society in which men recognize no check upon their freedom soon becomes a society where freedom is the possession of only a savage few; as we have learned to our sorrow.

What this is the spirit of liberty? I cannot define it; I can only tell you my own faith. The spirit of liberty is the spirit which is not too sure that it is right; the spirit of liberty is the spirit which seeks to understand the minds of other men and women; the spirit of liberty is the spirit which weighs their interests alongside its own without bias; the spirit of liberty remembers that not even a sparrow falls to earth unheeded; the spirit of liberty is the spirit of Him who, near two thousand years ago, taught mankind that lesson it has never learned, but has never quite forgotten; that there may be a kingdom where the least shall be heard and considered side by side with the greatest. And now in that spirit, that spirit of an America which has never been, and which may never be; nay, which never will be except as the conscience and courage of Americans create it; yet in the spirit of that America which lies hidden in some form in the aspirations of us all; in the spirit of that America for which our young men are at this moment fighting and dying; in that spirit of liberty and of America I ask you to rise and with me pledge our faith in the glorious destiny of our beloved country.

 KARL SHAPIRO

ELEGY FOR A DEAD SOLDIER

Karl Shapiro (1913–   ), born in Baltimore, published his first volume of poetry in 1935. Two more collections of poetry were published in 1942. In 1945, Shapiro won the Pulitzer Prize for *V-Letter and Other Poems,* which was written while he was a soldier in the South Pacific. After the war, Shapiro published numerous volumes of poetry, literary criticism, essays, and fiction and served as editor of *Poetry.* He has received numerous honors and awards for his poetry. He has taught at several universities, including the University of Nebraska and the University of California at Davis.

"Elegy for a Dead Soldier" was included in *V-Letter and Other Poems.*

I

A white sheet on the tail-gate of a truck
Becomes an altar; two small candlesticks
Sputter at each side of the crucifix
Laid round with flowers brighter than the
     blood,
Red as the red of our apocalypse,
Hibiscus that a marching man will pluck
To stick into his rifle or his hat,
And great blue morning-glories pale as lips
That shall no longer taste or kiss or swear.
The wind begins a low magnificat,
The chaplain chats, the palmtrees swirl their
     hair,
The columns come together through the mud.

II

We too are ashes as we watch and hear
The psalm, the sorrow, and the simple praise
Of one whose promised thoughts of other days
Were such as ours, but now wholly destroyed,
The service record of his youth wiped out,
His dream dispersed by shot, must disappear.
What can we feel but wonder at a loss
That seems to point at nothing but the doubt
Which flirts our sense of luck into the ditch?
Reader of Paul who prays beside this fosse,
Shall we believe our eyes or legends rich
With glory and rebirth beyond the void?

III

For this comrade is dead, dead in the war,
A young man out of millions yet to live,
One cut away from all that war can give,
Freedom of self and peace to wander free.
Who mourns in all this sober multitude
Who did not feel the bite of it before
The bullet found its aim? This worthy flesh,
This boy laid in a coffin and reviewed—
Who has not wrapped himself in this same flag,
Heard the light fall of dirt, his wound still fresh,
Felt his eyes closed, and heard the distant brag
Of the last volley of humanity?

IV

By chance I saw him die, stretched on the
     ground,

A tattooed arm lifted to take the blood
Of someone else sealed in a tin. I stood
During the last delirium that stays
The intelligence a tiny moment more,
And then the strangulation, the last sound.
The end was sudden, like a foolish play,
A stupid fool slamming a foolish door,
The absurd catastrophe, half-prearranged,
And all the decisive things still left to say.
So we disbanded, angrier and unchanged,
Sick with the utter silence of dispraise.

V

We ask for no statistics of the killed,
For nothing political impinges on
This single casualty, or all those gone,
Missing or healing, sinking or dispersed,
Hundreds of thousands counted, millions lost.
More than an accident and less than willed
Is every fall, and this one like the rest.
However others calculate the cost,
To us the final aggregate is *one*,
One with a name, one transferred to the blest;
And though another stoops and takes the gun,
We cannot add the second to the first.

. . . .

XI

The time to mourn is short that best becomes
The military dead. We lift and fold the flag,
Lay bare the coffin with its written tag,
And march away. Behind, four others wait
To lift the box, the heaviest of loads.
The anesthetic afternoon benumbs,
Sickens our senses, forces back our talk.
We know that others on tomorrow's roads
Will fall, ourselves perhaps, the man beside,
Over the world the threatened, all who walk:
And could we mark the grave of him who died
We would write this beneath his name and
     date:

EPITAPH

Underneath this wooden cross there lies
A Christian killed in battle. You who read,
Remember that this stranger died in pain;
And passing here, if you can lift your eyes
Upon a peace kept by a human creed,
Know that one soldier has not died in vain.

AFTER WORLD WAR II

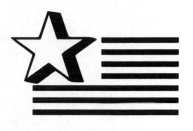

Moving day in a new suburb of Los Angeles in 1953. This scene was repeated in suburbs across the nation in the years following World War II, thanks to new highways, low-cost housing mortgages, and the desire of millions of people for homes of their own.

BERNARD BARUCH

THE BARUCH PLAN FOR CONTROL OF ATOMIC ENERGY

We are here to make a choice between the quick and the dead.

At the end of World War II, the United States had a monopoly on knowledge of the atomic bomb. An American plan to place atomic energy under international control was presented to the United Nations Atomic Energy Commission on June 14, 1946, by Bernard Baruch, the American representative. Baruch (1870–1965) was a wealthy financier who had served as an adviser to President Wilson and President Roosevelt. The term "elder statesman" seems to have been invented to describe him.

The Soviet Union blocked the Baruch Plan, because it required international inspection. Ruled by the dictator Joseph Stalin, the Soviet Union called instead for immediate destruction of existing atomic weapons and a ban on future production, but without inspection. The Soviet position prevented international cooperation until the signing of the Nuclear Test Ban Treaty by the U.S., the U.S.S.R., and Great Britain in 1963.

So, the Baruch Plan failed. One can only imagine how the world might have differed, whether there would have been an international arms race, and how the world's resources might have been spent, had the plan succeeded.

We are here to make a choice between the quick and the dead. That is our business.

Behind the black portent of the new atomic age lies a hope which, seized upon with faith, can work our salvation. If we fail, then we have damned every man to be the slave of fear. Let us not deceive ourselves: We must elect world peace or world destruction.

Science has torn from nature a secret so vast in its potentialities that our minds cower from the terror it creates. Yet terror is not enough to inhibit the use of the atomic bomb. The terror created by weapons has never stopped man from employing them, for each new weapon a defense has been produced, in time. But now we face a condition in which adequate defense does not exist.

Science, which gave us this dread power, shows that it *can* be made a giant help to humanity, but science does *not* show us how to prevent its baleful use. So we have been appointed to obviate that peril by finding a meet-ing of the minds and the hearts of our peoples. Only in the will of mankind lies the answer.

It is to express this will and make it effective that we have been assembled. We must provide the mechanism to assure that atomic energy is used for peaceful purposes and preclude its use in war. To that end, we must provide immediate, swift, and sure punishment of those who violate the agreements that are reached by the nations. Penalization is essential if peace is to be more than a feverish interlude between wars. And, too, the United Nations can prescribe individual responsibility and punishment on the principles applied at Nuremberg by the Union of Soviet Socialist Republics, the United Kingdom, France, and the United States—a formula certain to benefit the world's future.

In this crisis, we represent not only our governments but, in a larger way, we represent the peoples of the world. We must remember that the peoples do not belong to the governments but that the governments belong to the peoples.

We must answer their demands; we must answer the world's longing for peace and security.

In that desire, the United States shares ardently and hopefully. The search of science for the absolute weapon has reached fruition in this country. But she stands ready to proscribe and destroy this instrument—to lift its use from death to life—if the world will join in a pact to that end. . . .

Now, if ever, is the time to act for the common good. Public opinion supports the world movement toward security. If I read the sign aright, the peoples want a program not composed merely of pious thoughts but of enforceable sanctions—an international law with teeth in it.

We of this nation, desirous of helping to bring peace to the world and realizing the heavy obligations upon us arising from our possession of the means of producing the bomb and from the fact that it is a part of our armament, are prepared to make our full contribituion toward effective control of atomic energy. . . .

But before a country is ready to relinquish any winning weapons, it must have more than words to reassure it. It must have a guarantee of safety, not only against the offenders in the atomic area but against the illegal users of other weapons—bacteriological, biological, gas—perhaps—and why not?—against war itself.

In the elimination of war lies our solution, for only then will nations cease to compete with one another in the production and use of dread "secret" weapons which are evaluated solely by their capacity to kill. This devilish program takes us back, not merely to the Dark Ages but from cosmos to chaos. If we succeed in finding a suitable way to control atomic weapons, it is reasonable to hope that we may also preclude the use of other weapons adaptable to mass destruction. When a man learns to say "A" he can, if he chooses, learn the rest of the alphabet, too.

Let this be anchored in our minds: Peace is never long preserved by weight of metal or by an armament race. Peace can be made tranquil and secure only by understanding and agreement fortified by sanctions. We must embrace international cooperation or international disintegration. . . .

DAVID LILIENTHAL

CONFIRMATION HEARINGS

This I deeply believe.

In 1948, the Democratic Party was in a quandary. President Franklin D. Roosevelt had died in 1945, and his successor, Harry Truman, was unable to hold together the party's fractious coalition of forces. Its left wing detached itself to form the Progressive Party, with Henry Wallace as its candidate; its right wing—which included the key electoral votes of the deep South—warned that it would bolt the convention if the Democrats adopted a civil rights plank in their party platform.

To the Democratic convention in Philadelphia came Hubert Horatio Humphrey (1911–1978), the exuberant young mayor of Minneapolis who was running for the U.S. Senate. At one time a pharmacist, then a teacher, Humphrey was elected mayor in 1945. On July 14, 1948, Humphrey delivered the following impassioned plea for a bold stance on civil rights. When the convention sided with him, the southern Democrats

This I DO carry in my head, Senator.

I will do my best to make it clear. My convictions are not so much concerned with what I am against as what I am for; and that excludes a lot of things automatically.

Traditionally, democracy has been an affirmative doctrine rather than merely a negative one.

I believe—and I conceive the Constitution of the United States to rest, as does religion, upon the fundamental proposition of the integrity of the individual; and that all government and all private institutions must be designed to promote and protect and defend the integrity and the dignity of the individual; that that is the essential meaning of the Constitution and the Bill of Rights, as it is essentially the meaning of religion.

Any form of government, therefore, and any other institutions which make men means rather than ends, which exalt the state or any other institutions above the importance of men, which place arbitrary power over men as a fundamental tenet of government are contrary to that conception, and, therefore, I am deeply opposed to them.

The communistic philosophy as well as the communistic form of government falls within this category, for their fundamental tenet is quite to the contrary. The fundamental tenet of communism is that the state is an end in itself, and that therefore the powers which the state exercises over the individual are without any ethical standard to limit them.

That I deeply disbelieve.

It is very easy simply to say that one is not a Communist. And, of course, if despite my record it is necessary for me to state this very affirmatively, then it is a great disappointment to me.

It is very easy to talk about being against communism. It is equally important to believe those things which provide a satisfying and effective alternative. Democracy is that satisfying, affirmative alternative.

Its hope in the world is that it is an affirmative belief, rather than being simply a belief against something else and nothing more.

One of the tenets of democracy that grows out of this central core of a belief that the individual comes first, that all men are the children of God and that their personalities are therefore sacred, is a deep belief in civil liberties and their protection, and a repugnance to anyone who would steal from a human being that which is most precious to him—his good name—either by imputing things to him by innuendo or by insinuation. And it is especially an unhappy circumstance that occasionally that is done in the name of democracy. This, I think, can tear our country apart and destroy it if we carry it further.

I deeply believe in the capacity of democracy to surmount any trials that may lie ahead, provided only that we practice it in our daily lives.

And among the things we must practice is this: that while we seek fervently to ferret out the subversive and anti-democratic forces in the country, we do not at the same time, by hysteria, by resort to innuendo, and smears, and other unfortunate tactics, besmirch the very cause that we believe in, and cause a separation among our people—cause one group and one individual to hate another, based on mere attacks, mere unsubstantiated attacks upon their loyalty.

I want also to add that part of my conviction is based on my training as an Anglo-American common lawyer. It is the very basis and the great heritage of the English people to this country, which we have maintained, that we insist on the strictest rules of credibility of witnesses and on the avoidance of hearsay, and that gossip shall be excluded, in the courts of justice. And that, too, is an essential of our democracy.

Whether by administrative agencies acting arbitrarily against business organizations, or whether by investigating activities of legislative branches, whenever those principles fail, those principles of the protection of an individual and his good name against besmirchment by gossip, hearsay, and the statements of witnesses who are not subject to cross-examination—then, too, we have failed in carrying forward our ideals in respect to democracy.

This I deeply believe.

HUBERT HUMPHREY

A PLEA FOR CIVIL RIGHTS

The time has arrived for the Democratic party to get out of the shadow of states' rights and walk forthrightly into the bright sunshine of human rights.

In 1948, the Democratic Party was in a quandary. President Franklin D. Roosevelt had died in 1945, and his successor, Harry Truman, was unable to hold together the party's fractious coalition of forces. Its left wing detached itself to form the Progressive Party, with Henry Wallace as its candidate; its right wing—which included the key electoral votes of the white South—warned that it would bolt the convention if the Democrats adopted a civil rights plank in their party platform.

To the Democratic convention in Philadelphia came Hubert Horatio Humphrey (1911–1978), the exuberant young mayor of Minneapolis who was running for the U.S. Senate. At one time a pharmacist, then a teacher, Humphrey was elected mayor in 1945. On July 14, 1948, Humphrey delivered the following impassioned plea for a bold stance on civil rights. When the convention sided with him, the southern Democrats bolted the convention and the party. Despite the defections from the party, Truman eked out a victory over Dewey, and Humphrey was elected to the Senate, where he served for the next sixteen years with distinction.

I realize that I am dealing with a charged issue—with an issue which has been confused by emotionalism on all sides. I realize that there are those here—friends and colleagues of mine, many of them—who feel as deeply as I do about this issue and who are yet in complete disagreement with me.

My respect and admiration for these men and their views was great when I came here.

It is now far greater because of the sincerity, the courtesy and the forthrightness with which they have argued in our discussions.

Because of this very respect—because of my profound belief that we have a challenging task to do here—because good conscience demands it—I feel I must rise at this time to support this report—a report that spells out our democracy, a report that the people will understand and enthusiastically acclaim.

Let me say at the outset that this proposal is made with no single region, no single class, no single racial or religious group in mind.

All regions and all states have shared in the precious heritage of American freedom. All states and all regions have at least some infringements of that freedom—all people, all groups have been the victims of discrimination.

The masterly statement of our keynote

A turning point in the desegregation of Southern public schools occurred in Little Rock, Arkansas, in 1957, when President Dwight D. Eisenhower sent federal troops to enforce a court order admitting nine black pupils to Central High School in Little Rock, Arkansas.

speaker, the distinguished United States senator from Kentucky, Alben Barkley, made that point with great force. Speaking of the founder of our party, Thomas Jefferson, he said:

"He did not proclaim that all white, or black, or red, or yellow men are equal; that all Christian or Jewish men are equal; that all Protestant and Catholic men are equal; that all rich or poor men are equal; that all good or bad men are equal.

"What he declared was that all men are equal; and the equality which he proclaimed was equality in the right to enjoy the blessings of free government in which they may participate and to which they have given their consent."

We are here as Democrats. But more important, as Americans—and I firmly believe that as men concerned with our country's future, we must specify in our platform the guarantees which I have mentioned.

Yes, this is far more than a party matter. Every citizen has a stake in the emergence of the United States as the leader of the free world. That world is being challenged by the world of slavery. For us to play our part effectively, we must be in a morally sound position.

We cannot use a double standard for measuring our own and other people's policies. Our demands for democratic practices in other lands will be no more effective than the guarantees of those practiced in our own country.

We are God-fearing men and women. We place our faith in the brotherhood of man under the fatherhood of God.

I do not believe that there can be any compromise of the guarantees of civil rights which I have mentioned.

In spite of my desire for unanimous agreement on the platform there are some matters which I think must be stated without qualification. There can be no hedging—no watering down.

There are those who say to you—we are rushing this issue of civil rights. I say we are 172 years late.

There are those who say—this issue of civil rights is an infringement on states' rights. The time has arrived for the Democratic party to get out of the shadow of states' rights and walk forthrightly into the bright sunshine of human rights.

People—human beings—this is the issue of the 20th century. People—all kinds and all sorts of people—look to America for leadership—for help—for guidance.

My friends—my fellow Democrats—I ask you for a calm consideration of our historic opportunity. Let us forget the evil passions, the blindness of the past. In these times of world economic, political and spiritual—above all, spiritual crisis, we cannot—we must not, turn from the path so plainly before us.

That path has already led us through many valleys of the shadow of death. Now is the time to recall those who were left on that path of American freedom.

For all of us here, for the millions who have sent us, for the whole two billion members of the human family—our land is now, more than ever, the last best hope on earth. I know that we can—I know that we shall—begin here the fuller and richer realization of that hope—that promise of a land where all men are free and equal, and each man uses his freedom and equality wisely and well.

HARRY S. TRUMAN

INAUGURAL ADDRESS

Only by helping the least fortunate of its members to help themselves can the human family achieve the decent, satisfying life that is the right of all people.

The election of Harry S. Truman (1884–1972) in 1948 was one of the biggest upsets in American political history. Truman overcame both a resurgent Republican party, led by New York's Governor Thomas Dewey, and a deep split in his own party. A scrappy populist, Truman confounded the pollsters and the pundits by defeating Dewey, Henry Wallace of the Progressive Party, and Strom Thurmond of the Dixiecrat party.

Son of a Missouri farm family, Truman finished high school but could not afford to go to college. He tried and failed in a variety of business ventures, served with distinction in World War I, then succeeded in local politics with the support of the local Democratic machine. Truman was elected to the United States Senate in 1934 and was chosen as Franklin D. Roosevelt's vice-president in 1944. When Roosevelt died on April 12, 1945, Truman became president.

In his inaugural address, Truman proposed a massive international program of economic and technical assistance to nations in Latin America, Asia, the Middle East, and Africa. With the launching of the Point Four Program, the United States embarked on a new role in world affairs.

. . . Each period of our national history has had its special challenges. Those that confront us now are as momentous as any in the past. Today marks the beginning not only of a new administration, but of a period that will be eventful, perhaps decisive, for us and for the world.

It may be our lot to experience, and in large measure to bring about, a major turning point in the long history of the human race. The first half of this century, has been marked by unprecedented and brutal attacks on the rights of man, and by the two most frightful wars in history. The supreme need of our time is for men to learn to live together in peace and harmony.

The peoples of the earth face the future with grave uncertainty, composed almost equally of great hopes and great fears. In this time of doubt, they look to the United States as never before for good will, strength, and wise leadership.

It is fitting, therefore, that we take this occasion to proclaim to the world the essential principles of the faith by which we live, and to declare our aims to all peoples.

The American people stand firm in the faith which has inspired this Nation from the beginning. We believe that all men have a right to equal justice under law and equal opportunity to share in the common good. We believe that all men have the right to freedom of thought and expression. We believe that all men are created equal because they are created in the image of God.

From this faith we will not be moved.

The American people desire, and are determined to work for, a world in which all nations and all peoples are free to govern themselves as they see fit and to achieve a decent and satisfying life. About all else, our people desire, and are determined to work for, peace on earth—a just and lasting peace—based on genuine agreement freely arrived at by equals.

In the pursuit of these aims, the United States and other like-minded nations find themselves directly opposed by a regime with contrary aims and a totally different concept of life.

That regime adheres to a false philosophy which purports to offer freedom, security, and greater opportunity to mankind. Misled by this philosophy, many peoples have sacrificed their liberties only to learn to their sorrow that deceit and mockery, poverty and tyranny, are their reward.

That false philosophy is communism.

Communism is based on the belief that man is so weak and inadcquate that he is unable to govern himself, and therefore requires the rule of strong masters.

Democracy is based on the conviction that man has the moral and intellectual capacity, as well as the inalienable right, to govern himself with reason and justice.

Communism subjects the individual to arrest without lawful cause, punishment without trial, and forced labor as the chattel of the state. It decrees what information he shall receive, what art he shall produce, what leaders he shall follow, and what thoughts he shall think.

Democracy maintains that government is established for the benefit of the individual, and is charged with the responsibility of protecting the rights of the individual and his freedom in the exercise of his abilities.

Communism maintains that social wrongs can be corrected only by violence.

Democracy has proved that social justice can be achieved through peaceful change.

Communism holds that the world is so deeply divided into opposing classes that war is inevitable.

Democracy holds that free nations can settle differences justly and maintain lasting peace.

These differences between communism and democracy do not concern the United States alone. People everywhere are coming to realize that what is involved is material well-being, human dignity, and the right to believe in and worship God.

I state these differences, not to draw issues of belief as such, but because the actions resulting from the Communist philosophy are a threat to the efforts of free nations to bring about world recovery and lasting peace.

Since the end of hostilities, the United States has invested its substance and its energy in a great constructive effort to restore peace, stability, and freedom in the world.

We have sought no territory and we have imposed our will on none. We have asked for no privileges we would not extend to others.

We have constantly and vigorously supported the United Nations and related agencies as a means of applying democratic principles to international relations. We have consistently advocated and relied upon peaceful settlement of disputes among nations.

We have made every effort to secure agreement on effective international control of our most powerful weapon, and we have worked steadily for the limitation and control of all armaments.

We have encouraged, by precept and example, the expansion of world trade on a sound and fair basis.

Almost a year ago, in company with 16 free nations of Europe, we launched the greatest cooperative economic program in history. The purpose of that unprecedented effort is to invigorate and strengthen democracy in Europe, so that the free people of that continent can resume their rightful place in the forefront of civilization and can contribute once more to the security and welfare of the world.

Our efforts have brought new hope to all mankind. We have beaten back despair and defeatism. We have saved a number of countries from losing their liberty. Hundreds of millions of people all over the world now agree with us, that we need not have war—that we can have peace. . . .

In the coming years, our program for peace and freedom will emphasize four major courses of action.

First. We will continue to give unfaltering support to the United Nations and related agencies, and we will continue to search for ways to strengthen their authority and increase their ef-

fectiveness. We believe that the United Nations will be strengthened by the new nations which are being formed in lands now advancing toward self-government under democratic principles.

Second. We will continue our programs for world economic recovery.

This means, first of all, that we must keep our full weight behind the European recovery program. We are confident of the success of this major venture in world recovery. We believe that our partners in this effort will achieve the status of self-supporting nations once again.

In addition, we must carry out our plans for reducing the barriers to world trade and increasing its volume. Economic recovery and peace itself depend on increased world trade.

Third. We will strengthen freedom-loving nations against the dangers of aggression. We are now working out with a number of countries a joint agreement designed to strengthen the security of the North Atlantic area. Such an agreement would take the form of a collective defense arrangement within the terms of the United Nations Charter. . . .

Fourth. We must embark on a bold new program for making the benefits of our scientific advances and industrial progress available for the improvement and growth of underdeveloped areas.

More than half the people of the world are living in conditions approaching misery. Their food is inadequate. They are victims of disease. Their economic life is primitive and stagnant. Their poverty is a handicap and a threat both to them and to more prosperous areas.

For the first time in history humanity possesses the knowledge and the skill to relieve the suffering of these people.

The United States is preeminent among nations in the development of industrial and scientific techniques. The material resources which we can afford to use for the assistance of other peoples are limited. But our imponderable resources in technical knowledge are constantly growing and are inexhaustible.

I believe that we should make available to

peace-loving peoples the benefits of our store of technical knowledge in order to help them realize their aspirations for a better life. And, in cooperation with other nations, we should foster capital investment in areas needing development.

Our aim should be to help the free peoples of the world, through their own efforts, to produce more food, more clothing, more materials for housing, and more mechanical power to lighten their burdens.

We invite other countries to pool their technological resources in this undertaking. Their contributions will be warmly welcomed. This should be a cooperative enterprise in which all nations work together through the United Nations and its specialized agencies wherever practicable. It must be a world-wide effort for the achievement of peace, plenty, and freedom. . . .

All countries, including our own, will greatly benefit from a constructive program for the bet-ter use of the world's human and natural resources. Experience shows that our commerce with other countries expands as they progress industrially and economically.

Greater production is the key to prosperity and peace. And the key to greater production is a wider and more vigorous application of modern scientific and technical knowledge.

Only by helping the least fortunate of its members to help themselves can the human family achieve the decent, satisfying life that is the right of all people.

Democracy alone can supply the vitalizing force to stir the peoples of the world into triumphant action, not only against their human oppressors, but also against their ancient enemies —hunger, misery, and despair.

On the basis of these four major courses of action we hope to help create the conditions that will lead eventually to personal freedom and happiness for all mankind. . . .

MARGARET CHASE SMITH

DECLARATION OF CONSCIENCE

I do not want to see the Republican party ride to political victory on the Four Horsemen of Calumny—fear, ignorance, bigotry, and smear.

In 1950, Senator Joseph R. McCarthy of Wisconsin initiated a crusade to rid the Government of suspected Communists. He cast himself as a patriot, defending America against its enemies within and abroad; his critics accused him of recklessly destroying people's careers and reputations on the basis of rumor and innuendo. McCarthy, a Republican, repeatedly alleged that the Truman administration was "soft on Communism" and that its appointees in the State Department were traitors who had "lost" or "given away" countries where Communists came to power. For nearly five years—from February 1950, when he first claimed that the State Department was riddled with subversives, until December 1954, when Senator McCarthy was condemned by his colleagues in the Senate—the country was embroiled in bitter controversy over "McCarthyism."

Many in government and out were cowed by the senator's accusations. But not everyone was. Seven Republican senators—Charles Tobey of New Hampshire, George D. Aiken of Vermont, Wayne L. Morse of Oregon, Edward J. Thye of Minnesota, Irving M. Ives of New York, Robert C. Hendrickson of New Jersey, and Margaret Chase Smith

Mr. President, I would like to speak briefly and simply about a serious national condition. It is a national feeling of fear and frustration that could result in national suicide and the end of everything that we Americans hold dear. It is a condition that comes from the lack of effective leadership either in the legislative branch or the executive branch of our Government. That leadership is so lacking that serious and responsible proposals are being made that national advisory commissions be appointed to provide such critically needed leadership.

I speak as briefly as possible because too much harm has already been done with irresponsible words of bitterness and selfish political opportunism. I speak as simply as possible because the issue is too great to be obscured by eloquence. I speak simply and briefly in the hope that my words will be taken to heart.

Mr. President, I speak as a Republican. I speak as a woman. I speak as a United States Senator. I speak as an American.

The United States Senate has long enjoyed world-wide respect as the greatest deliberative body in the world. But recently that deliberative character has too often been debased to the level of a forum of hate and character assassination sheltered by the shield of congressional immunity.

It is ironical that we Senators can in debate in the Senate, directly or indirectly, by any form of words, impute to any American who is not a Senator any conduct or motive unworthy or unbecoming an American—and without that non-Senator American having any legal redress against us—yet if we say the same thing in the Senate about our colleagues we can be stopped on the grounds of being out of order.

It is strange that we can verbally attack anyone else without restraint and with full protection, and yet we hold ourselves above the same type of criticism here on the Senate floor. Surely the United States Senate is big enough to take self-criticism and self-appraisal. Surely we should be able to take the same kind of character attacks that we "dish out" to outsiders.

I think that it is high time for the United States Senate and its Members to do some real soul searching and to weigh our consciences as to the manner in which we are performing our duty to the people of America and the manner in which we are using or abusing our individual powers and privileges.

I think it is high time that we remembered that we have sworn to uphold and defend the Constitution. I think it is high time that we remembered that the Constitution, as amended, speaks not only of the freedom of speech but also of trial by jury instead of trial by accusation.

Whether it be a criminal prosecution in court or a character prosecution in the Senate, there is little practical distinction when the life of a person has been ruined.

Those of us who shout the loudest about Americanism in making character assassinations are all too frequently those who, by our own words and acts, ignore some of the basic principles of Americanism—

The right to criticize.

The right to hold unpopular beliefs.

The right to protest.

The right of independent thought.

The exercise of these rights should not cost one single American citizen his reputation or his right to a livelihood nor should he be in danger of losing his reputation or livelihood merely because he happens to know someone who holds unpopular beliefs. Who of us does not? Otherwise none of us could call our souls our own. Otherwise thought control would have set in.

The American people are sick and tired of being afraid to speak their minds lest they be politically smeared as Communists or Fascists by their opponents. Freedom of speech is not what it used to be in America. It has been so abused by some that it is not exercised by others.

The American people are sick and tired of seeing innocent people smeared and guilty people whitewashed. But there have been enough proved cases, such as the Amerasia case, the Hiss case, the Coplon case, the Gold case, to cause Nation-wide distrust and strong suspicion that there may be something to the unproved, sensational accusations.

As a Republican, I say to my colleagues on this side of the aisle that the Republican Party faces a challenge today that is not unlike the challenge which it faced back in Lincoln's day. The Republican Party so successfully met that challenge that it emerged from the Civil War as the champion of a united nation—in addition to being a party which unrelentingly fought loose spending and loose programs.

Today our country is being psychologically divided by the confusion and the suspicions that are bred in the United States Senate to spread like cancerous tentacles of "know nothing, suspect everything" attitudes. Today we have a Democratic administration which has developed a mania for loose spending and loose programs. History is repeating itself—and the Republican Party again has the opportunity to emerge as the champion of unity and prudence.

The record of the present Democratic administration has provided us with sufficient campaign issues without the necessity of resorting to political smears. America is rapidly losing its position as leader of the world simply because the Democratic administration has pitifully failed to provide effective leadership.

The Democratic administration has completely confused the American people by its daily contradictory grave warnings and optimistic assurances, which show the people that our Democratic administration has no idea of where it is going.

The Democratic administration has greatly lost the confidence of the American people by its complacency to the threat of communism here at home and the leak of vital secrets to Russia through key officials of the Democratic administration. There are enough proved cases to make this point without diluting our criticism with unproved charges.

Surely these are sufficient reasons to make it clear to the American people that it is time for a change and that a Republican victory is necessary to the security of the country. Surely it is clear that this Nation will continue to suffer so long as it is governed by the present ineffective Democratic adminstration.

Yet to displace it with a Republican regime embracing a philosophy that lacks political integrity or intellectual honesty would prove equally disastrous to the Nation. The Nation sorely needs a Republican victory. But I do not want to see the Republican Party ride to

A Chicago kindergarten teacher supervises an air-raid drill, known as "duck and cover." Students crouched, covered their heads, and stayed away from windows. Such drills were frequent in public schools at the height of Cold War tensions.

political victory on the Four Horsemen of Calumny—fear, ignorance, bigotry, and smear.

I doubt if the Republican Party could do so, simply because I do not believe the American people will uphold any political party that puts political exploitation above national interest. Surely we Republicans are not so desperate for victory.

I do not want to see the Republican Party win that way. While it might be a fleeting victory for the Republican Party, it would be a more lasting defeat for the American people. Surely it would ultimately be suicide for the Republican Party and the two-party system that has pro-

tected our American liberties from the dictator-ship of a one-party system.

As members of the minority party, we do not have the primary authority to formulate the pol-icy of our Government. But we do have the re-sponsibility of rendering constructive criticism, of clarifying issues, of allaying fears by acting as reponsible citizens.

As a woman, I wonder how the mothers, wives, sisters, and daughters feel about the way in which members of their families have been politically mangled in Senate debate—and I use the word "debate" advisedly.

As a United States Senator, I am not proud of

A teenager and friends in his first car, 1958. The 1950s marked the emergence of a youth culture, with enough disposable income to influence styles in music, movies, and dress.

the way in which the Senate has been made a publicity platform for irresponsible sensationalism. I am not proud of the reckless abandon in which unproved charges have been hurled from this side of the aisle. I am not proud of the obviously staged, undignified countercharges which have been attempted in retaliation from the other side of the aisle.

I do not like the way the Senate has been made a rendezvous for vilification, for selfish political gain at the sacrifice of individual reputations and national unity. I am not proud of the way we smear outsiders from the floor of the Senate and hide behind the cloak of congressional immunity and still place ourselves beyond criticism on the floor of the Senate.

As an American, I am shocked at the way Republicans and Democrats alike are playing directly into the Communist design of "confuse, divide, and conquer." As an American, I do not want a Democratic administration white wash or cover up any more than I want a Republican smear or witch hunt.

As an American, I condemn a Republican Fascist just as much as I condemn a Democrat Communist. I condemn a Democrat Fascist just as much as I condemn a Republican Communist. They are equally dangerous to you and me and to our country. As an American, I want to see our Nation recapture the strength and unity it once had when we fought the enemy instead of ourselves. . . .

LOUIS SIMPSON

THE SILENT GENERATION

Louis Simpson (1923–   ) was born in Jamaica, served in World War II, then graduated from Columbia University. He has published several volumes of poetry, fiction, critical works, and an autobiography. He received the Pulitzer Prize for poetry in 1963 for *At the End of the Open Road*.

After World War II, political quietism settled over much of American life. As in the period after the First World War, Americans were eager to return to "normalcy" and to improve their standard of living. Young people coming of age in the 1950s entered a world in which the great issues seemed to have been settled and in which ideological and political conflict was passé. The youth of the Eisenhower era were dubbed "the silent generation." They were apathetic, not alienated, the children of an age of conformity and comfort.

"The Silent Generation" appeared in Simpson's collection of poems *A Dream of Governors* (1959).

When Hitler was the Devil
He did as he had sworn
With such enthusiasm
That even, donnerwetter,
The Germans say, "Far better
Had he been never born!"

It was my generation
That put the Devil down
With great enthusiasm.

But now our occupation
Is gone. Our education
Is wasted on the town.

We lack enthusiasm.
Life seems a mystery;
It's like the play a lady
Told me about: "It's not . . .
It doesn't have a plot,"
She said, "It's history."

LANGSTON HUGHES

REFUGEE IN AMERICA and HARLEM

Since Langston Hughes began publishing poetry in 1921, when he was only nineteen years old, his productive career spanned more than four decades. "Refugee in America" was published in *The Saturday Evening Post* in 1943. "Harlem" was published in 1951, as part of a collection called *Montage of a Dream Deferred*.

Refugee in America

There are words like *Freedom*
Sweet and wonderful to say.
On my heart-strings freedom sings
All day everyday.

There are words like *Liberty*
That almost make me cry.
If you had known what I knew
You would know why.

Harlem

What happens to a dream deferred?

Does it dry up
like a raisin in the sun?
Or fester like a sore—
And then run?
Does it stink like rotten meat?
Or crust and sugar over—
like a syrupy sweet?

Maybe it just sags
like a heavy load.

Or does it explode?

BROWN V. BOARD OF EDUCATION

We conclude that in the field of public education the doctrine of "separate but equal" has no place.

On May 17, 1954, the Supreme Court unanimously ruled that racial segregation in the public schools was unconstitutional. The Supreme Court had previously outlawed racial segregation in higher education. At the time of the decision, the public schools in seventeen states were segregated by law; four other states permitted racial segregation by school districts. The court's ruling overturned segregation laws not only in Topeka, Kansas, where Linda Brown had been denied entry to her all-white neighborhood school, but in South Carolina, Delaware, Virginia, and the District of Columbia. Some districts in the border states between North and South moved promptly to end segregation. Most of the South, however, refused to comply.

From the time of *Brown* until the mid-1960s, the federal courts engaged in constant conflict with recalcitrant southern districts as one locality after another fought (and lost) the battle to maintain segregated schools.

The reach of the *Brown* decision went far beyond public schools. It provided the legal foundation for court challenges to racial segregation in every aspect of American

life. By ending states' power to segregate people by race and by bringing black Americans into the political process, it altered the daily life of the American people more than any other Supreme Court decision.

These cases come to us from the states of Kansas, South Carolina, Virginia, and Delaware. They are premised on different facts and different local conditions, but a common legal question justifies their consideration together in this consolidated opinion.

In each of the cases, minors of the Negro race, through their legal representatives, seek the aid of the courts in obtaining admission to the public schools of their community on a non-segregated basis. In each instance, they have been denied admission to schools attended by white children under laws requiring or permitting segregation according to race. This segregation was alleged to deprive the plaintiffs of the equal protection of the laws under the Fourteenth Amendment. In each of the cases other than the Delaware case, a three-judge federal district court denied relief to the plaintiffs on the so-called "separate but equal" doctrine announced by this Court in Plessy v. Ferguson.... Under that doctrine, equality of treatment is accorded when the races are provided substantially equal facilities, even though these facilities be separate....

The plaintiffs contend that segregated public schools are not "equal" and cannot be made "equal," and that hence they are deprived of the equal protection of the laws. Because of the obvious importance of the question presented, the Court took jurisdiction....

There are findings below that the Negro and white schools involved have been equalized, or are being equalized, with respect to buildings, curricula, qualifications and salaries of teachers, and other "tangible" factors. Our decision, therefore, cannot turn on merely a comparison of these tangible factors in the Negro and white schools involved in each of the cases. We must look instead to the effect of segregation itself on public education.

In approaching this problem, we cannot turn the clock back to 1868 when the Amendment was adopted, or even to 1896 when Plessy v. Ferguson was written. We must consider public education in the light of its full development and its present place in American life throughout the nation. Only in this way can it be determined if segregation in public schools deprives these plaintiffs of the equal protection of the laws.

Today, education is perhaps the most important function of state and local governments. Compulsory school attendance laws and the great expenditures for education both demonstrate our recognition of the importance of education to our democratic society. It is required in the performance of our most basic public responsibilities, even service in the armed forces. It is the very foundation of good citizenship. Today it is a principal instrument in awakening the child to cultural values, in preparing him for later professional training, and in helping him to adjust normally to his environment. In these days, it is doubtful that any child may reasonably be expected to succeed in life if he is denied the opportunity of an education. Such an opportunity, where the state has undertaken to provide it, is a right which must be made available to all on equal terms.

We come then to the question presented: Does segregation of children in public schools solely on the basis of race, even though the physical facilities and other "tangible" factors may be equal, deprive the children of the minority group of equal educational opportunities? We believe that it does.

In Sweatt v. Painter, ... in finding that a segregated law school for Negroes could not provide them equal educational opportunities, this Court relied in large part on "those qualities which are incapable of objective measurement but which make for greatness in a law school." In McLaurin v. Oklahoma State Regents, ... the

Court, in requiring that a Negro admitted to a white graduate school be treated like all other students, again resorted to intangible considerations: "... his ability to study, to engage in discussions and exchange views with other students, and, in general, to learn his profession." Such considerations apply with added force to children in grade and high schools. To separate them from others of similar age and qualifications solely because of their race generates a feeling of inferiority as to their status in the community that may affect their hearts and minds in a way unlikely ever to be undone. The effect of this separation on their educational opportunities was well stated by a finding in the Kansas case by a court which nevertheless felt compelled to rule against the Negro plaintiffs:

"Segregation of white and colored children in public schools has a detrimental effect upon the colored children. The impact is greater when it has the sanction of the law; for the policy of separating the races is usually interpreted as denoting the inferiority of the Negro group. A sense of inferiority affects the motivation of a child to learn. Segregation with the sanction of law, therefore, has a tendency to retard the educational and mental development of Negro children and to deprive them of some of the benefits they would receive in a racially integrated school system."

Whatever may have been the extent of psychological knowledge at the time of Plessy v. Ferguson, this finding is amply supported by modern authority. Any language in Plessy v. Ferguson contrary to this finding is rejected.

We conclude that in the field of public education the doctrine of "separate but equal" has no place. Separate educational facilities are inherently unequal. Therefore, we hold that the plaintiffs and others similarly situated for whom the actions have been brought are, by reason of the segregation complained of, deprived of the equal protection of the laws guaranteed by the Fourteenth Amendment....

DWIGHT D. EISENHOWER

FAREWELL ADDRESS

We must guard against the acquisition of unwarranted influence, whether sought or unsought, by the military-industrial complex.

Dwight D. Eisenhower (1890–1969) achieved the pinnacles of power during his lifetime, first in serving as supreme commander of the Allied military forces during World War II, and then as a popular two-term president of the United States. Born in Denison, Texas, the third of seven sons, Eisenhower grew up in Abilene, Kansas, in a family that was poor but hard-working and religious. He graduated from the United States Military Academy in 1915.

After World War II, he returned a popular hero and briefly assumed the presidency of Columbia University. In 1952, he was elected president. During his presidency, Democrats complained about Eisenhower's avoidance of racial controversies, his basic conservatism in domestic and foreign affairs, and even his syntax. But "Ike," as he was known, remained immensely popular.

On January 17, 1961, just before he retired from the presidency, Eisenhower gave his farewell address. Eisenhower described a shift in American politics caused by the rise of a "military-industrial complex" and a "scientific-technological elite." It was his

Three days from now, after half a century in the service of our country, I shall lay down the responsibilities of office as, in traditional and solemn ceremony, the authority of the Presidency is vested in my successor....

We now stand ten years past the midpoint of a century that has witnessed four major wars among great nations. Three of them involved our own country. Despite these holocausts America is today the strongest, the most influential and most productive nation in the world. Understandably proud of this pre-eminence we yet realize that America's leadership and prestige depend, not merely upon our unmatched material progress, riches and military strength, but on how we use our power in the interests of world peace and human betterment.

Throughout America's adventure in free government, our basic purposes have been to keep the peace; to foster progress in human achievement, and to enhance liberty, dignity and integrity among people and among nations. To strive for less would be unworthy of a free and religious people. Any failure traceable to arrogance, or our lack of comprehension or readiness to sacrifice would inflict upon us grievous hurt both at home and abroad.

Progress toward these noble goals is persistently threatened by the conflict now engulfing the world. It commands our whole attention, absorbs our very beings. We face a hostile ideology—global in scope, atheistic in character, ruthless in purpose, and insidious in method. Unhappily the danger it poses promises to be of indefinite duration. To meet it successfully, there is called for, not so much the emotional and transitory sacrifices of crisis, but rather those which enable us to carry forward steadily, surely, and without complaint the burdens of a prolonged and complex struggle—with liberty the stake. Only thus shall we remain, despite every provocation, on our charted course toward permanent peace and human betterment....

A vital element in keeping the peace is our military establishment. Our arms must be mighty, ready for instant action, so that no potential aggressor may be tempted to risk his own destruction.

Our military organization today bears little relation to that known by any of my predecessors in peacetime, or indeed by the fighting men of World War II or Korea.

Until the latest of our world conflicts, the United States had no armaments industry. American makers of plowshares could, with time and as required, make swords as well. But now we can no longer risk emergency improvisation of national defense; we have been compelled to create a permanent armaments industry of vast proportions. Added to this, three and a half million men and women are directly engaged in the defense establishment. We annually spend on military security more than the net income of all United States corporations.

This conjunction of an immense military establishment and a large arms industry is new in the American experience. The total influence—economic, political, even spiritual—is felt in every city, every statehouse, every office of the federal government. We recognize the imperative need for this development. Yet we must not fail to comprehend its grave implications. Our toil, resources, and livelihood are all involved; so is the very structure of our society.

In the councils of government, we must guard against the acquisition of unwarranted influence, whether sought or unsought, by the military-industrial complex. The potential for the disastrous rise of misplaced power exists and will persist.

We must never let the weight of this combination endanger our liberties or democratic processes. We should take nothing for granted.

An audience watches the premiere of Bwana Devil, *wearing Polaroid spectacles to enjoy the three-dimensional (3-D) sequences.*

Only an alert and knowledgeable citizenry can compel the proper meshing of the huge industrial and military machinery of defense with our peaceful methods and goals, so that security and liberty may prosper together.

Akin to, and largely responsible for the sweeping changes in our industrial-military posture, has been the technological revolution during recent decades.

In this revolution, research has become cen-

tral; it also becomes more formalized, complex, and costly. A steadily increasing share is conducted for, by, or at the direction of, the federal government. . . .

The prospect of domination of the nation's scholars by federal employment, project allocations, and the power of money is ever present —and is gravely to be regarded.

Yet, in holding scientific research and discovery in respect, as we should, we must also be alert to the equal and opposite danger that public policy could itself become the captive of a scientific-technological elite.

It is the task of statesmanship to mold, to balance, and to integrate these and other forces, new and old, within the principles of our democratic system—ever aiming toward the supreme goals of our free society.

Another factor in maintaining balance involves the element of time. As we peer into society's future, we—you and I, and our government—must avoid the impulse to live only for today, plundering, for our own ease and convenience, the precious resources of tomorrow. We cannot mortgage the material assets of our grandchildren without risking the loss also of their political and spiritual heritage. We want democracy to survive for all generations to come, not to become the insolvent phantom of tomorrow.

Down the long lane of the history yet to be written America knows that this world of ours, ever growing smaller, must avoid becoming a community of dreadful fear and hate, and be, instead, a proud confederation of mutual trust and respect.

Such a confederation must be one of equals. The weakest must come to the conference table with the same confidence as do we, protected as we are by our moral, economic, and military strength. That table, though scarred by many past frustrations, cannot be abandoned for the certain agony of the battlefield.

Disarmament, with mutual honor and confidence, is a continuing imperative. Together we must learn how to compose differences, not with arms, but with intellect and decent purpose. Because this need is so sharp and apparent I confess that I lay down my official responsibilities in this field with a definite sense of disappointment. As one who has witnessed the horror and the lingering sadness of war—as one who knows that another war could utterly destroy this civilization which has been so slowly and painfully built over thousands of years—I wish I could say tonight that a lasting peace is in sight.

Happily, I can say that war has been avoided. Steady progress toward our ultimate goal has been made. But, so much remains to be done. As a private citizen, I shall never cease to do what little I can to help the world advance along that road. . . .

 GWENDOLYN BROOKS
THE MOTHER

Gwendolyn Brooks (1917–   ) was born in Topeka, Kansas, and raised in the slums of Chicago. Her first poem was published when she was only thirteen, in a magazine called *American Childhood.* Her many collections of poetry Include *A Street in Bronzeville* (1945), *Annie Allen* (1949), *The Bean Eaters* (1960), *Collected Poems* (1963), *In the Mecca* (1968), *Riot* (1969), *Family Pictures* (1970), and *Aloneness* (1971). She received the Pulitzer Prize for *Annie Allen.* Most of her poetry deals with the lives and problems of black people.

Abortions will not let you forget.
You remember the children you got that you
	did not get,
The damp small pulps with a little or with no
	hair,
The singers and workers that never handled
	the air.
You will never neglect or beat
Them, or silence or buy with a sweet.
You will never wind up the sucking-thumb
Or scuttle off ghosts that come.
You will never leave them, controlling your
	luscious sigh,
Return for a snack of them, with gobbling
	mother-eye.

I have heard in the voices of the wind the
	voices of my dim killed children.
I have contracted. I have eased
My dim dears at the breasts they could never
	suck.
I have said, Sweets, if I sinned, if I seized
Your luck
And your lives from your unfinished reach,

If I stole your births and your names,
Your straight baby tears and your games,
Your stilted or lovely loves, your tumults, your
	marriages, aches, and your deaths,
If I poisoned the beginnings of your breaths,
Believe that even in my deliberateness I was
	not deliberate.
Though why should I whine,
Whine that the crime was other than mine?—
Since anyhow you are dead.
Or rather, or instead,
You were never made.
But that too, I am afraid,
Is faulty: oh, what shall I say, how is the truth
	to be said?
You were born, you had body, you died.
It is just that you never giggled or planned or
	cried.

Believe me, I loved you all.
Believe me, I knew you, though faintly, and I
	loved, I loved you
All.

☆ IT COULD BE A WONDERFUL WORLD

One of the perennial favorites at hootenannies and union songfests during the heyday of folk music was "It Could Be a Wonderful World." It was written in 1947 by Hy Zaret and Lou Singer. Zaret, the lyricist, won many awards for songs that promoted brotherhood and public service; in addition to writing many hit songs, he wrote the theme song for the Hit Parade ("So Long for A While"), the official marching song for the U.S. Army Chaplains Corps ("Soldiers of God"), and the official song of Brotherhood Week ("Let's Get Together"). The music was written by Lou Singer, who had many successful musical compositions to his credit.

If each little kid could have fresh milk each
    day;
If each working man had enough time for play;
If each homeless soul had a good place to stay
It could be a wonderful world.

CHORUS:
    If we could consider each other
    A neighbor, a friend, or a brother
    It could be a wonderful, wonderful world
    It could be a wonderful world.

If there were no poor and the rich were
    content;
If strangers were welcome wherever they
    went;
If each of us knew what true brotherhood
    meant
It would be a wonderful world!

TROUBLED TIMES

A demonstrator against the war in Vietnam puts flowers in the rifles of military policemen guarding the Pentagon. The 1960s was a time of protests, marches, and demonstrations against racial segregation and against the war; the era was notable, too, for the appearance of the counterculture, with its distinctive mode of dress and behavior.

JOHN F. KENNEDY

INAUGURAL ADDRESS

Ask not what your country can do for you—ask what you can do for your country.

John F. Kennedy (1917–1963) was born in Brookline, Massachusetts, and educated at Harvard University. He saw combat in the Pacific while serving in the navy during World War II. Kennedy was elected to Congress after the war. After three terms in the House of Representatives, Kennedy was elected to the Senate in 1952. In 1960, he was elected president, narrowly defeating Vice-President Richard Nixon.

As a candidate, Kennedy projected an image of youth and dynamism. In his campaign, he promised "to get the country moving again," and in his acceptance speech at the Democratic convention, he said, "We stand on the edge of a New Frontier." His inaugural address encompassed the major themes of his campaign and his brief presidency, which was ended by an assassin's bullet on November 22, 1963.

We observe today not a victory of party but a celebration of freedom—symbolizing an end as well as a beginning—signifying renewal as well as change. For I have sworn before you and Almighty God the same solemn oath our forebears prescribed nearly a century and three-quarters ago.

The world is very different now. For man holds in his mortal hands the power to abolish all forms of human poverty and all forms of human life. And yet the same revolutionary beliefs for which our forebears fought are still at issue around the globe—the belief that the rights of man come not from the generosity of the state but from the hand of God.

We dare not forget today that we are the heirs of that first revolution. Let the word go forth from this time and place, to friend and foe alike, that the torch has been passed to a new generation of Americans—born in this century, tempered by war, disciplined by a hard and bitter peace, proud of our ancient heritage—and unwilling to witness or permit the slow undoing of those human rights to which this nation has always been committed, and to which we are committed today at home and around the world.

Let every nation know, whether it wishes us well or ill, that we shall pay any price, bear any burden, meet any hardship, support any friend, oppose any foe to assure the survival and the success of liberty.

This much we pledge—and more.

To those old allies whose cultural and spiritual origins we share, we pledge the loyalty of faithful friends. United, there is little we cannot do in a host of co-operative ventures. Divided, there is little we can do—for we dare not meet a powerful challenge at odds and split asunder.

To those new states whom we welcome to the ranks of the free, we pledge our word that one form of colonial control shall not have passed away merely to be replaced by a far more iron tyranny. We shall not always expect to find them supporting our view. But we shall always hope to find them strongly supporting their own freedom—and to remember that, in the past, those who foolishly sought power by riding the back of the tiger ended up inside.

To those people in the huts and villages of half the globe struggling to break the bonds of mass misery, we pledge our best efforts to help them help themselves, for whatever period is required—not because the Communists may be doing it, not because we seek their votes, but because it is right. If a free society cannot help the many who are poor, it cannot save the few who are rich.

To our sister republics south of the border, we offer a special pledge—to convert our good words into good deeds—in a new alliance for progress—to assist free men and free governments in casting off the chains of poverty. But this peaceful revolution of hope cannot become the prey of hostile powers. Let all our neighbors know that we shall join with them to oppose aggression or subversion anywhere in the Americas. And let every other power know that this hemisphere intends to remain the master of its own house.

To that world assembly of sovereign states, the United Nations, our last best hope in an age where the instruments of war have far outpaced the instruments of peace, we renew our pledge of support—to prevent it from becoming merely a forum for invective—to strengthen its shield of the new and the weak—and to enlarge the area in which its writ may run.

Finally, to those nations who would make themselves our adversary, we offer not a pledge but a request: that both sides begin anew the quest for peace, before the dark powers of destruction unleashed by science engulf all humanity in planned or accidental self-destruction.

We dare not tempt them with weakness. For only when our arms are sufficient beyond doubt can we be certain beyond doubt that they will never be employed.

But neither can two great and powerful groups of nations take comfort from our present course—both sides overburdened by the cost of modern weapons, both rightly alarmed by the steady spread of the deadly atom, yet both racing to alter that uncertain balance of terror that stays the hand of mankind's final war.

So let us begin anew—remembering on both sides that civility is not a sign of weakness, and sincerity is always subject to proof. Let us never negotiate out of fear. But let us never fear to negotiate.

Let both sides explore what problems unite us instead of belaboring those problems which divide us.

Let both sides, for the first time, formulate serious and precise proposals for the inspection and control of arms—and bring the absolute power to destroy other nations under the absolute control of all nations.

Let both sides seek to invoke the wonders of science instead of its terrors. Together let us explore the stars, conquer the deserts, eradicate disease, tap the ocean depths, and encourage the arts and commerce.

Let both sides unite to heed in all corners of the earth the command of Isaiah—to "undo the heavy burdens . . . [and] let the oppressed go free."

And if a beachhead of co-operation may push back the jungle of suspicion, let both sides join in creating a new endeavor, not a new balance of power, but a new world of law, where the strong are just and the weak secure and the peace preserved.

All this will not be finished in the first one hundred days. Nor will it be finished in the first one thousand days, nor in the life of this administration, nor even perhaps in our lifetime on this planet. But let us begin.

In your hands, my fellow citizens, more than mine, will rest the final success or failure of our course. Since this country was founded, each generation of Americans has been summoned to give testimony to its national loyalty. The graves of young Americans who answered the call to service surround the globe.

Now the trumpet summons us again—not as a call to bear arms, though arms we need,—not as a call to battle, though embattled we are—but a call to bear the burden of a long twilight struggle, year in and year out, "rejoicing in hope, patient in tribulation"—a struggle against the common enemies of man: tyranny, poverty, disease, and war itself.

Can we forge against these enemies a grand and global alliance, North and South, East and West, that can assure a more fruitful life for all mankind? Will you join in that historic effort?

In the long history of the world, only a few generations have been granted the role of defending freedom in its hour of maximum danger.

I do not shrink from this responsibility—I welcome it. I do not believe that any of us would exchange places with any other people or any other generation. The energy, the faith, the devotion which we bring to this endeavor will light our country and all who serve it—and the glow from that fire can truly light the world.

And so, my fellow Americans: ask not what your country can do for you—ask what you can do for your country.

My fellow citizens of the world: ask not what America will do for you, but what together we can do for the freedom of man.

Finally, whether you are citizens of America or citizens of the world, ask of us here the same high standards of strength and sacrifice which we ask of you. With a good conscience our only sure reward, with history the final judge of our deeds, let us go forth to lead the land we love, asking His blessing and His help, but knowing that here on earth God's work must truly be our own.

PETE SEEGER

WHERE HAVE ALL THE FLOWERS GONE?

Pete Seeger (1919–   ) was born in New York City to a musical family. His father was a distinguished musicologist, and his mother was a violinist. Seeger attended Harvard briefly in the 1930s but left to travel the country and to immerse himself in the world of folk music. He learned to play the five-string banjo and developed a large repertoire of spirituals, ballads, work songs, and other kinds of folk music. In 1940, he and Woody Guthrie formed the Almanac Singers, which specialized in protest songs.

In the late 1940s, Seeger and three others—Lee Hays, Ronnie Gilbert, and Fred Hellerman—formed the Weavers, which became the most successful folk group in the country and sparked a national revival of folk music. The group broke up in 1952 when the entertainment industry blacklisted performers who had been involved in left-wing politics, but the group was reunited a few years later. It finally disbanded in 1963, performing together again only for reunion concerts.

Ever the political activist, Seeger used song to inspire the civil rights movement, the anti-war movement, and—during the 1970s and 1980s—the environmental movement.

Where have all the flowers gone?
Long time passing.
Where have all the flowers gone?
Long time ago.
Where have all the flowers gone?
The girls have picked them ev'ryone.
Oh, when will you ever learn?
Oh, when will you ever learn?

Where have all the young girls gone?
Long time passing.
Where have all the young girls gone?
Long time ago.
Where have all the young girls gone?

They've taken husbands everyone.
Oh, when will you ever learn?
Oh, when will you ever learn?

Where have all the young men gone?
Long time passing.
Where have all the young men gone?
Long time ago.
Where have all the young men gone?
They're all in uniform.
Oh, when will you ever learn?
Oh, when will you ever learn?

Where have all the soldiers gone?
Long time passing.

Where have all the soldiers gone?
Long time ago.
Where have all the soldiers gone?
They've gone to graveyards every one.
Oh, when will they ever learn?
Oh, when will they ever learn?

Where have all the graveyards gone?
Long time passing.
Where have all the graveyards gone?
Long time ago.
Where have all the graveyards gone?

They're covered with flowers every one.
Oh, when will they ever learn?
Oh, when will they ever learn?

Where have all the flowers gone?
Long time passing.
Where have all the flowers gone?
Long time ago.
Where have all the flowers gone?
Young girls picked them, every one,
Oh, when will they ever learn?
Oh, when will they ever learn?

NEWTON MINOW

ADDRESS TO THE BROADCASTING INDUSTRY

I invite you to sit down in front of your television set... and keep your eyes glued to that set until the station signs off. I can assure you that you will observe a vast wasteland.

Newton Minow (1926–   ) was appointed by President John Kennedy as chairman of the Federal Communications Commission, the agency responsible for regulating the use of the public airwaves. On May 9, 1961, he spoke to 2,000 members of the National Association of Broadcasters and told them that the daily fare on television was "a vast wasteland." Minow's indictment of commercial television launched a national debate about the quality of programming. After Minow's speech, the television critic for *The New York Times* wrote: "Tonight some broadcasters were trying to find dark explanations for Mr. Minow's attitude. In this matter the viewer possibly can be a little helpful; Mr. Minow has been watching television."

. . . Your industry possesses the most powerful voice in America. It has an inescapable duty to make that voice ring with intelligence and with leadership. In a few years this exciting industry has grown from a novelty to an instrument of overwhelming impact on the American people. It should be making ready for the kind of leadership that newspapers and magazines assumed years ago, to make our people aware of their world.

Ours has been called the jet age, the atomic age, the space age. It is also, I submit, the television age. And just as history will decide whether the leaders of today's world employed the atom to destroy the world or rebuild it for mankind's benefit, so will history decide whether today's broadcasters employed their powerful voice to enrich the people or debase them. . . .

Like everybody, I wear more than one hat. I am the chairman of the FCC. I am also a television viewer and the husband and father of other television viewers. I have seen a great many television programs that seemed to me eminently worthwhile, and I am not talking about the much-bemoaned good old days of "Playhouse 90" and "Studio One."

I am talking about this past season. Some

were wonderfully entertaining, such as "The Fabulous Fifties," the "Fred Astaire Show" and the "Bing Crosby Special"; some were dramatic and moving, such as Conrad's "Victory" and "Twilight Zone"; some were marvelously informative, such as "The Nation's Future," "CBS Reports," and "The Valiant Years." I could list many more—programs that I am sure everyone here felt enriched his own life and that of his family. When television is good, nothing—not the theater, not the magazines or newspapers—nothing is better.

But when television is bad, nothing is worse. I invite you to sit down in front of your television set when your station goes on the air and stay there without a book, magazine, newspaper, profit-and-loss sheet, or rating book to distract you—and keep your eyes glued to that set until the station signs off. I can assure you that you will observe a vast wasteland.

You will see a procession of game shows, violence, audience participation shows, formula comedies about totally unbelievable families, blood and thunder, mayhem, violence, sadism, murder, Western badmen, Western good men, private eyes, gangsters, more violence and cartoons. And, endlessly, commercials—many screaming, cajoling, and offending. And, most of all, boredom. True, you will see a few things you will enjoy. But they will be very, very few. And if you think I exaggerate, try it.

Is there one person in this room who claims that broadcasting can't do better? . . .

Why is so much of television so bad? I have heard many answers: demands of your advertisers; competition for ever higher ratings; the need always to attract a mass audience; the high cost of television programs; the insatiable appetite for programming material—these are some of them. Unquestionably these are tough problems not susceptible to easy answers.

But I am not convinced that you have tried hard enough to solve them. I do not accept the idea that the present overall programming is aimed accurately at the public taste. The ratings tell us only that some people have their television sets turned on, and, of that number, so many are tuned to one channel and so many to another. They don't tell us what the public might watch if they were offered half a dozen additional choices. A rating, at best, is an indication of how many people saw what you gave them. Unfortunately it does not reveal the depth of the penetration or the intensity of reaction, and it never reveals what the acceptance would have been if what you gave them had been better—if all the forces of art and creativity and daring and imagination had been unleashed. I believe in the people's good sense and good taste, and I am not convinced that the people's taste is as low as some of you assume. . . .

Certainly I hope you will agree that ratings should have little influence where children are concerned. The best estimates indicate that during the hours of 5 to 6 P.M., 60 percent of your audience is composed of children under twelve. And most young children today, believe it or not, spend as much time watching television as they do in the schoolroom. I repeat—let that sink in—most young children today spend as much time watching television as they do in the schoolroom. It used to be said that there were three great influences on a child: home, school, and church. Today there is a fourth great influence, and you ladies and gentlemen control it.

If parents, teachers, and ministers conducted their responsibilities by following the ratings, children would have a steady diet of ice cream, school holidays, and no Sunday school. What about your responsibilities? Is there no room on television to teach, to inform, to uplift, to stretch, to enlarge the capacities of our children? Is there no room for programs deepening their understanding of children in other lands? Is there no room for a children's news show explaining something about the world to them at their level of understanding? Is there no room for reading the great literature of the past, teaching them the great traditions of freedom? There are some fine children's shows, but they are drowned out in the massive doses of cartoons, violence, and more violence. Must these be your trademarks? Search your consciences and see if you cannot offer more to your young beneficiaries whose future you guide so many hours each and every day.

What about adult programming and ratings? You know, newspaper publishers take popularity ratings too. The answers are pretty clear; it is almost always the comics, followed by the advice-to-the-lovelorn columns. But, ladies and gentlemen, the news is still on the front page of all newspapers, the editorials are not replaced by more comics, the newspapers have not become one long collection of advice to the lovelorn. Yet newspapers do not need a license from the government to be in business—they do not use public property. But in television—where your responsibilities as public trustees are so plain—the moment that the ratings indicate that Westerns are popular, there are new imitations of Westerns on the air faster than the old coaxial cable could take us from Hollywood to New York. . . .

Let me make clear that what I am talking about is balance. I believe that the public interest is made up of many interests. There are many people in this great country, and you must serve all of us. You will get no argument from me if you say that, given a choice between a Western and a symphony, more people will watch the Western. I like Westerns and private eyes too—but a steady diet for the whole country is obviously not in the public interest. We all know that people would more often prefer to be entertained than stimulated or informed. But your obligations are not satisfied if you look only to popularity as a test of what to broadcast. You are not only in show business; you are free to communicate ideas as well as relaxation. You must provide a wider range of choices, more diversity, more alternatives. It is not enough to cater to the nation's whims—you must also serve the nation's needs. . . .

Let me address myself now to my role, not as a viewer but as chairman of the FCC. . . . I want to make clear some of the fundamental principles which guide me.

First, the people own the air. They own it as much in prime evening time as they do at 6 o'clock Sunday morning. For every hour that the people give you, you owe them something. I intend to see that your debt is paid with service.

Second, I think it would be foolish and wasteful for us to continue any worn-out wrangle over the problems of payola, rigged quiz shows, and other mistakes of the past. . . .

Third, I believe in the free enterprise system. I want to see broadcasting improved and I want you to do the job. . . .

Fourth, I will do all I can to help educational television. There are still not enough educational stations, and major centers of the country still lack usable educational channels. . . .

Fifth, I am unalterably opposed to governmental censorship. There will be no suppression of programming which does not meet with bureaucratic tastes. Censorship strikes at the taproot of our free society.

Sixth, I did not come to Washington to idly observe the squandering of the public's airwaves. The squandering of our airwaves is no less important than the lavish waste of any precious natural resource. . . .

What you gentlemen broadcast through the people's air affects the people's taste, their knowledge, their opinions, their understanding of themselves and of their world. And their future. The power of instantaneous sight and sound is without precedent in mankind's history. This is an awesome power. It has limitless capabilities for good—and for evil. And it carries with it awesome responsibilities—responsibilities which you and I cannot escape. . . .

TOM HAYDEN

THE PORT HURON STATEMENT

We are people of this generation, bred in at least modest comfort, housed now in universities, looking uncomfortably to the world we inherit.

In 1962, college students who had been active in the civil rights movement and the peace movement created Students for a Democratic Society. SDS represented what was called the New Left. At its organizing meeting in Port Huron, Michigan, SDS adopted a manifesto drafted by Tom Hayden (1939–   ), a graduate student at the University of Michigan. The Port Huron statement was a wide-ranging critique of American society —of racial injustice, the dangers of nuclear war, the failure to develop peaceful atomic energy, the Cold War, the maldistribution of wealth, the political apathy of students, and the exhaustion of liberal ideology. The introduction to the Port Huron statement is printed below. It was an influential document among student radicals in the 1960s and early 1970s.

Tom Hayden was elected to the California legislature in 1982.

We are people of this generation, bred in at least modest comfort, housed now in universities, looking uncomfortably to the world we inherit.

When we were kids the United States was the wealthiest and strongest country in the world; the only one with the atom bomb, the least scarred by modern war, an initiator of the United Nations that we thought would distribute Western influence throughout the world. Freedom and equality for each individual, government of, by, and for the people—these American values we found good, principles by which we could live as men. Many of us began maturing in complacency.

As we grew, however, our comfort was penetrated by events too troubling to dismiss. First, the permeating and victimizing fact of human degradation, symbolized by the Southern struggle against racial bigotry, compelled most of us from silence to activism. Second, the enclosing fact of the Cold War, symbolized by the presence of the Bomb, brought awareness that we ourselves, and our friends, and millions of abstract "others" we knew more directly because of our common peril, might die at any time. We might deliberately ignore, or avoid, or fail to feel

all other human problems, but not these two, for these were too immediate and crushing in their impact, too challenging in the demand that we as individuals take the responsibility for encounter and resolution.

While these and other problems either directly oppressed us or rankled our consciences and became our own subjective concern, we began to see complicated and disturbing paradoxes in our surrounding America. The declaration "all men are created equal..." rang hollow before the facts of Negro life in the South and the big cities of the North. The proclaimed peaceful intentions of the United States contradicted its economic and military investments in the Cold War status quo.

We witnessed, and continue to witness, other paradoxes. With nuclear energy whole cities can easily be powered, yet the dominant nation-states seem more likely to unleash destruction greater than that incurred in all wars of human history. Although our own technology is destroying old and creating new forms of social organization, men still tolerate meaningless work and idleness. While two-thirds of mankind suffers undernourishment, our own upper classes revel amidst superfluous abundance. Although world population is expected to double in forty years, the nations still tolerate anarchy as a major principle of international conduct and uncontrolled exploitation governs the sapping of the earth's physical resources. Although mankind desperately needs revolutionary leadership, America rests in national stalemate, its goals ambiguous and tradition-bound instead of informed and clear, its democratic system apathetic and manipulated rather than "of, by, and for the people."

Not only did tarnish appear on our image of American virtue, not only did disillusion occur when the hypocrisy of American ideals was discovered, but we began to sense that what we had originally seen as the American Golden Age was actually the decline of an era. The worldwide outbreak of revolution against colonialism and imperialism, the entrenchment of totalitarian states, the menace of war, overpopulation, international disorder, supertechnology—these trends were testing the tenacity of our own commitment to democracy and freedom and our abilities to visualize their application to a world in upheaval.

Our work is guided by the sense that we may be the last generation in the experiment with living. But we are a minority—the vast majority of our people regard the temporary equilibriums of our society and world as eternally functional parts. In this is perhaps the outstanding paradox: we ourselves are imbued with urgency, yet the message of our society is that there is no viable alternative to the present. Beneath the reassuring tones of the politicians, beneath the common opinion that America will "muddle through," beneath the stagnation of those who have closed their minds to the future, is the pervading feeling that there simply are no alternatives, that our times have witnessed the exhaustion not only of Utopias, but of any new departures as well. Feeling the press of complexity upon the emptiness of life, people are fearful of the thought that at any moment things might be thrust out of control. They fear change itself, since change might smash whatever invisible framework seems to hold back chaos for them now. For most Americans, all crusades are suspect, threatening. The fact that each individual sees apathy in his fellows perpetuates the common reluctance to organize for change. The dominant institutions are complex enough to blunt the minds of their potential critics, and entrenched enough to swiftly dissipate or entirely repel the energies of protest and reform, thus limiting human expectancies. Then, too, we are a materially improved society, and by our own improvements we seem to have weakened the case for further change.

Some would have us believe that Americans feel contentment amidst prosperity—but might it not better be called a glaze above deeply felt anxieties about their role in the new world? And if these anxieties produce a developed indifference to human affairs, do they not as well produce a yearning to believe there *is* an alternative to the present, that something *can* be done to change circumstances in the school, the workplaces, the bureaucracies, the government? It is to this latter yearning, at once the spark and engine of change, that we direct our present appeal. The search for truly democratic alternatives to the present, and a commitment to social experimentation with them, is a worthy and fulfilling human enterprise, one which moves us and, we hope, others today. On such a basis do we offer this document of our convictions and analysis: as an effort in understanding and changing the conditions of humanity in the late twentieth century, an effort rooted in the ancient, still unfulfilled conception of man attaining determining influence over his circumstances of life.

ED MCCURDY

LAST NIGHT I HAD THE STRANGEST DREAM

Ed McCurdy (1919–) was born in Willow Hall, Pennsylvania. A singer and composer, he has performed on radio and television, in cafés and in theaters. His song "Last Night I Had the Strangest Dream" was written in 1950 but achieved great popularity during the 1960s among opponents of the war in Vietnam. Since it was written without reference to any particular conflict, it has remained popular over the years for its simply stated pacifism.

Last night I had the strangest dream,
I'd never dreamed before,
I dreamed the world had all agreed
To put an end to war.

I dreamed I saw a mighty room
And the room was full of men,
And the paper they were signing said
They'd never fight again.

And when the paper was all signed,
And a million copies made,
They all joined hands and bowed their heads
And grateful prayers were prayed.

And the people in the streets below
Were dancing 'round and 'round.
While swords and guns and uniforms
Were scattered on the ground.

RACHEL CARSON

SILENT SPRING

The "control of nature" is a phrase conceived in arrogance, born of the Neanderthal age of biology and philosophy, when it was supposed that nature exists for the convenience of man.

In the early 1960s, Rachel Carson's book *Silent Spring* created international concern about the dangers of environmental pollution. More than any other individual at that time, Carson alerted the world to the human and natural toll that was exacted by indiscriminate use of chemicals. Carson (1907–1964) was a biologist who had a long career with the U.S. Bureau of Fisheries. She was also a successful writer. In 1951, she won the National Book Award for *The Sea Around Us*. Her most enduring legacy, however, was created by the publication in 1962 of *Silent Spring*, which was instrumental in launching the environmental movement in the United States.

The history of life on earth has been a history of interaction between living things and their surroundings. To a large extent, the physical form and the habits of the earth's vegetation and its animal life have been molded by the environment. Considering the whole span of earthly time, the opposite effect, in which life actually modifies its surroundings, has been relatively slight. Only within the moment of time represented by the present century has one species —man—acquired significant power to alter the nature of his world.

During the past quarter century this power has not only increased to one of disturbing magnitude but it has changed in character. The most alarming of all man's assaults upon the environment is the contamination of air, earth, rivers, and sea with dangerous and even lethal materials. This pollution is for the most part irrecoverable; the chain of evil it initiates not only in the world that must support life but in living tissues is for the most part irreversible. In this now universal contamination of the environment, chemicals are the sinister and little-recognized partners of radiation in changing the very nature of the world—the very nature of its life. Strontium 90, released through nuclear explosions into the air, comes to the earth in rain or drifts down as fallout, lodges in soil, enters into the grass or corn or wheat grown there, and in time takes up its abode in the bones of a human being, there to remain until his death. Similarly, chemicals sprayed on croplands or forests or gardens lie long in the soil, entering into living organisms, passing from one to another in a chain of poisoning and death. Or they pass mysteriously by underground streams until they emerge and, through the alchemy of air and sunlight, combine into new forms that kill vegetation, sicken cattle, and work unknown harm on those who drink from once pure wells. As Albert Schweitzer has said, "Man can hardly even recognize the devils of his own creation."

It took hundreds of millions of years to produce the life that now inhabits the earth—eons of time in which that developing and evolving and diversifying life reached a state of adjustment and balance with its surroundings. The environment, rigorously shaping and directing the life it supported, contained elements that were hostile as well as supporting. Certain rocks gave out dangerous radiation; even within the light of the sun, from which all life draws its energy, there were short-wave radiations with power to injure. Given time—time not in years but in millennia—life adjusts, and a balance has been reached. For time is the essential ingredient; but in the modern world there is no time.

The rapidity of change and the speed with which new situations are created follow the impetuous and heedless pace of man rather than the deliberate pace of nature. Radiation is no longer merely the background radiation of rocks, the bombardment of cosmic rays, the ultraviolet of the sun that have existed before there was any life on earth; radiation is now the unnatural creation of man's tampering with the atom. The chemicals to which life is asked to make its adjustment are no longer merely the calcium and silica and copper and all the rest of the minerals washed out of the rocks and carried in rivers to the sea; they are the synthetic creations of man's inventive mind, brewed in his laboratories, and having no counterparts in nature.

To adjust to these chemicals would require time on the scale that is nature's; it would require not merely the years of a man's life but the life of generations. And even this, were it by some miracle possible, would be futile, for the new chemicals come from our laboratories in an endless stream; almost five hundred annually find their way into actual use in the United States alone. The figure is staggering and its implications are not easily grasped—500 new chemicals to which the bodies of men and animals are required somehow to adapt each year, chemicals totally outside the limits of biologic experience.

Among them are many that are used in man's war against nature. Since the mid-1940's over 200 basic chemicals have been created for use in killing insects, weeds, rodents, and other organisms described in the modern vernacular as "pests"; and they are sold under several thousand different brand names.

These sprays, dusts, and aerosols are now applied almost universally to farms, gardens, forests, and homes—nonselective chemicals that have the power to kill every insect, the "good" and the "bad," to still the song of birds and the leaping of fish in the streams, to coat the leaves with a deadly film, and to linger on in the soil—all this though the intended target may be only a few weeds or insects. Can anyone believe it is possible to lay down such a barrage of poisons on the surface of the earth without making it unfit for all life? They should not be called "insecticides," but "biocides."

The whole process of spraying seems caught up in an endless spiral. Since DDT was released for civilian use, a process of escalation has been going on in which ever more toxic materials must be found. This has happened because insects, in a triumphant vindication of Darwin's principle of the survival of the fittest, have evolved super races immune to the particular insecticide used, hence a deadlier one has always to be developed—and then a deadlier one than that. . . .

The "control of nature" is a phrase conceived in arrogance, born of the Neanderthal age of biology and philosophy, when it was supposed that nature exists for the convenience of man. The concepts and practices of applied entomology for the most part date from that Stone Age of science. It is our alarming misfortune that so primitive a science has armed itself with the most modern and terrible weapons, and that in turning them against the insects it has also turned them against the earth.

MARTIN LUTHER KING, JR.,
LETTER FROM BIRMINGHAM CITY JAIL

Injustice anywhere is a threat to justice everywhere.

Martin Luther King, Jr., (1929–1968) was born in Atlanta, Georgia, the son and grandson of Baptist ministers. He entered Morehouse College at the age of fifteen in a program for gifted students then earned a divinity degree at Crozer Theological Seminary in Chester, Pennsylvania, and a doctorate in philosophy from Boston University.

King was pastor of the Dexter Avenue Baptist Church in Montgomery, Alabama, when a boycott of public buses began. His leadership of the boycott for a year made him a national figure. He then organized the Southern Christian Leadership Conference and became the leader of the rapidly spreading civil rights movement.

In 1963, King brought a campaign of nonviolence and passive resistance to Birmingham, where racial segregation and discrimination were pervasive. During protest demonstrations, hundreds of people were arrested. King chose to go to jail rather than to obey a court order to end the demonstrations. While in solitary confinement, he responded to a letter written to him by eight leading clergymen. They had asked him to call off the demonstrations and to rely instead on negotiations and the courts. King spent Easter weekend drafting his response.

For his leadership of the civil rights movement, King was awarded the Nobel Peace Prize in 1964. He was assassinated in 1968 while directing a strike in Memphis, Tennessee.

While confined here in the Birmingham City Jail, I came across your recent statement calling our present activities "unwise and untimely." . . .

I think I should give the reason for my being in Birmingham, since you have been influenced by the argument of "outsiders coming in." . . . I am here, along with several members of my staff, because we were invited here. I am here because I have basic organizational ties here. Beyond this, I am in Birmingham because injustice is here. Just as the 8th century prophets left their little villages and carried their "thus saith the Lord" far beyond the boundaries of their home town, and just as the Apostle Paul left his little village of Tarsus and carried the gospel of Jesus Christ to practically every hamlet and city of the Graeco-Roman world, I too am compelled to carry the gospel of freedom beyond my particular home town....Injustice anywhere is a threat to justice everywhere....

You deplore the demonstrations that are presently taking place in Birmingham. But I am sorry that your statement did not express a similar concern for the conditions that brought the demonstrations into being. I am sure that each of you would want to go beyond the superficial social analyst who looks merely at effects, and does not grapple with underlying causes. I would not hesitate to say that it is unfortunate that so-called demonstrations are taking place in Birmingham at this time, but I would say in more emphatic terms that it is even more unfortunate that the white power structure of this city left the Negro community with no other alternative.

In any nonviolent campaign there are four basic steps: 1) collection of the facts to determine whether injustices are alive; 2) negotiation; 3) self-purification; and 4) direct action. We have gone through all of these steps in Birmingham. There can be no gainsaying of the fact that racial injustice engulfs this community. Birmingham is probably the most thoroughly segregated city in the United States. Its ugly record of police brutality is known in every section of this country. Its unjust treatment of Negroes in the courts is a notorious reality. There have been more unsolved bombings of Negro homes and churches in Birmingham than any city in this nation. These are the hard, brutal, and unbelievable facts....

We know through painful experience that freedom is never voluntarily given by the oppressor; it must be demanded by the oppressed. Frankly I have never yet engaged in a direct action movement that was "well timed," according to the timetable of those who have not suffered unduly from the disease of segregation. For years now I have heard the word "Wait!" It rings in the ear of every Negro with a piercing familiarity. This "wait" has almost always meant "never." It has been a tranquilizing Thalidomide, relieving the emotional stress for a moment, only to give birth to an ill-formed infant of frustration. We must come to see with the distinguished jurist of yesterday that "justice too long delayed is justice denied." We have waited for more than 340 years for our constitutional and God-given rights. The nations of Asia and Africa are moving with jet-like speed toward the goal of political independence, and we still creep at horse and buggy pace toward the gaining of a cup of coffee at a lunch counter....

You express a greal deal of anxiety over our willingness to break laws. This is certainly a legitimate concern. Since we so diligently urge people to obey the Supreme Court's decision of 1954 outlawing segregation in the public schools, it is rather strange and paradoxical to find us consciously breaking laws. One may well ask, "How can you advocate breaking some laws and obeying others?" The answer is found in the fact that there are two types of laws: There are *just* laws and there are *unjust* laws. I would be the first to advocate obeying just laws. One has not only a legal but a moral responsibility to obey just laws. Conversely, one has a moral responsibility to disobey unjust laws. I would agree with Saint Augustine that "An unjust law is no law at all."

Now what is the difference between the two? How does one determine when a law is just or unjust? A just law is a man-made code that squares with the moral law or the law of God. An unjust law is a mode that is out of harmony with the moral law. To put it in the terms of Saint Thomas Aquinas, an unjust law is a human law that is not rooted in eternal and natural law. Any law that uplifts human personality is just. Any law that degrades human personality is unjust.

All segregation statutes are unjust because segregation distorts the soul and damages the personality. It gives the segregator a false sense

On February 1, 1960, four black college students staged the first "sit-in" at a segregated lunch counter in Greensboro, North Carolina. Similar demonstrations across the South—in restaurants, hotels, movie theaters, beaches, churches, and amusement parks—helped to destroy legal racial segregation.

of superiority and the segregated a false sense of inferiority. To use the words of Martin Buber, the great Jewish philosopher, segregation substitutes an "I-it" relationship for the "I-thou" relationship, and ends up relegating persons to the status of things. So segregation is not only politically, economically, and sociologically unsound, but it is morally wrong and sinful. Paul Tillich has said that sin is separation. Isn't segregation an existential expression of man's tragic separation, an expression of his awful estrangement, his terrible sinfulness? So I can urge men to obey the 1954 decision of the Supreme Court because it is morally right, and I can urge them to disobey segregation ordinances because they are morally wrong. . . .

Let me give another explanation. An unjust law is a code inflicted upon a minority which that minority had no part in enacting or creating because it did not have the unhampered right to vote. Who can say the Legislature of Alabama which set up the segregation laws was democratically elected? Throughout the state of Alabama all types of conniving methods are used to prevent Negroes from becoming registered voters and there are some counties without a single Negro registered to vote despite the fact that the Negro constitutes a majority of the population. Can any law set up in such a state be considered democratically structured? . . .

We can never forget that everything Hitler did in Germany was "legal" and everything the Hungarian freedom fighters did in Hungary was "illegal." It was "illegal" to aid and comfort a Jew in Hitler's Germany. But I am sure that, if I had lived in Germany during that time, I would have aided and comforted my Jewish brothers even though it was illegal. If I lived in a Communist country today where certain principles dear to the Christian faith are suppressed, I believe I would openly advocate disobeying these anti-religious laws. . . .

We will have to repent in this generation not merely for the vitriolic words and actions of the bad people, but for the appalling silence of good people. We must come to see that human progress never rolls in on wheels of inevitability. It comes through the tireless efforts and persistent work of men willing to be co-workers with God, and without this hard work time itself becomes an ally of the forces of social stagnation. . . .

You spoke of our activity in Birmingham as extreme. At first I was rather disappointed that fellow clergymen would see my nonviolent efforts as those of the extremist. I started thinking about the fact that I stand in the middle of two opposing forces in the Negro community. One is a force of complacency made up of Negroes who, as a result of long years of oppression, have been so completely drained of self-respect and a sense of "somebodiness" that they have adjusted to segregation, and of a few Negroes in the middle class who, because of a degree of academic and economic security, and because at points they profit by segregation, have unconsciously become insensitive to the problems of the masses. The other force is one of bitterness and hatred and comes perilously close to advocating violence. It is expressed in the various black nationalist groups that are springing up over the nation, the largest and best known being Elijah Muhammad's Muslim movement. This movement is nourished by the contemporary frustration over the continued existence of racial discrimination. It is made up of people who have lost faith in America, who have absolutely repudiated Christianity, and who have concluded that the white man is an incurable "devil."

I have tried to stand between these two forces saying that we need not follow the "do-nothingism" of the complacent or the hatred and despair of the black nationalist. There is the more excellent way of love and nonviolent protest. I'm grateful to God that, through the Negro church, the dimension of nonviolence entered our struggle. If this philsosphy had not emerged I am convinced that by now many streets of the South would be flowing with floods of blood. And I am further convinced that if our white brothers dismiss us as "rabble rousers" and "outside agitators"—those of us who are working through the channels of nonviolent direct action—and refuse to support our nonviolent efforts, millions of Negroes, out of frustration and despair, will seek solace and security in black nationalist ideologies, a development that will lead inevitably to a frightening racial nightmare.

Oppressed people cannot remain oppressed forever. The urge for freedom will eventually come. This is what has happened to the American Negro. Something within has reminded him of his birthright of freedom; something without has reminded that he can gain it. . . .

But as I continued to think about the matter I gradually gained a bit of satisfaction from being considered an extremist. Was not Jesus an extremist in love? "Love your enemies, bless them that curse you, pray for them that despitefully use you." Was not Amos an extremist for justice —"Let justice roll down like waters and righteousness like a mighty stream." Was not Paul an extremist for the gospel of Jesus Christ—"I bear in my body the marks of the Lord Jesus." Was not Martin Luther an extremist—"Here I stand; I can do none other so help me God." Was not John Bunyan an extremist—"I will stay in jail to the end of my days before I make a butchery of my conscience." Was not Abraham Lincoln an extremist—"This nation cannot survive half slave and half free." Was not Thomas Jefferson an extremist—"We hold these truths to be self evident that all men are created equal."

So the question is not whether we will be extremist but what kind of extremist will we be. Will we be extremists for hate or will we be extremists for love? Will we be extremists for the preservation of injustice—or will we be extremists for the cause of justice? . . .

I have traveled the length and breadth of Alabama, Mississippi, and all the other Southern states. On sweltering summer days and crisp autumn mornings I have looked at her beautiful churches with their spires pointing heavenward. I have beheld the impressive outlay of her massive religious education buildings. Over and over again I have found myself asking: "Who worships here? Who is their God? Where were their voices when the lips of Governor Barnett dripped with words of interposition and nullification? Where were they when Governor Wallace gave the clarion call for defiance and hatred? . . . The contemporary Church is so often a weak, ineffectual voice with an uncertain sound. It is so often the arch-supporter of the *status quo*. Far from being disturbed by the presence of the Church, the power structure of the average community is consoled by the Church's silent and often vocal sanction of things as they are.

But the judgment of God is upon the Church as never before. If the Church of today does not recapture the sacrificial spirit of the early Church, it will lose its authentic ring, forfeit the loyalty of millions and be dismissed as an irrelevant social club with no meaning for the 20th century. . . . I am thankful to God that some noble souls from the ranks of organized religion have broken loose from the paralyzing chains of conformity and joined us as active partners in the struggle for freedom . . . they have gone with the faith that right defeated is stronger than evil triumphant. These men have been the leaven in the lump of the race. Their witness has been the spiritual salt that has preserved the true meaning of the Gospel in these troubled times. They have carved a tunnel of hope through the dark mountain of disappointment. . . . But even if the Church does not come to the aid of justice, I have no despair about the future. I have no fear about the outcome of our struggle in Birmingham, even if our motives are presently misunderstood. We will reach the goal of freedom in Birmingham and all over the nation, because the goal of America is freedom. Abused and scorned though we may be, our destiny is tied up with the destiny of America. . . . One day the South will recognize its real heroes. They will be the James Merediths, courageously and with a majestic sense of purpose, facing jeering and hostile mobs and the agonizing loneliness that characterizes the life of the pioneer. They will be old, oppressed, battered Negro women, symbolized in a 72-year-old woman of Montgomery, Alabama, who rose up with a sense of dignity and with her people decided not to ride the segregated buses, and responded to one who inquired about her tiredness with ungrammatical profundity: "My feets is tired, but my soul is rested." They will be young high school and college students, young ministers of the Gospel and a host of the elders, courageously and nonviolently sitting in at lunch counters and willingly going to jail for conscience's sake. One day the South will know that when these disinherited children of God sat down at lunch counters they were in reality standing up for the best in the American dream and the most sacred values in our Judeo-Christian heritage, and thus carrying our whole nation back to great wells of democracy which were dug deep by the founding fathers in the formulation of the Constitution and the Declaration of Independence. . . .

I hope this letter finds you strong in the faith. I also hope that circumstances will soon make it possible for me to meet each of you, not as an integrationist or a civil rights leader, but as a fellow clergyman and a Christian brother. Let us all hope that the dark clouds of racial prejudice will soon pass away, that the deep fog of misunderstanding will be lifted from our fear-drenched communities, and that in some not too distant tomorrow the radiant stars of love and brotherhood will shine over our great nation with all of their scintillating beauty.

JOHN F. KENNEDY

SPEECH AT THE BERLIN WALL

Ich bin ein Berliner.

On the night of August 12–13, 1961, the government of East Germany erected the Berlin Wall to divide East and West Berlin. At first it was a simple barbed-wire barrier, intended to prevent the flow of East Germans to West Germany. But the barbed wire was soon replaced by a massive concrete wall, patrolled by armed guards. The wall stood as an ugly reminder of the postwar division of Europe between East and West. Many would-be escapees died trying to cross the border to the West.

When President Kennedy visited Europe in 1963, the high point of his trip occurred on June 26 when he stood before the Berlin Wall and declared: "Ich bin ein Berliner" —"I am a Berliner."

Twenty-eight years later, on November 9, 1989, the East German government opened the Berlin Wall in a paradoxical effort to stop the exodus of people fleeing their repressive society across the Hungarian border. During that remarkable year, the East European Communist regimes collapsed. Throughout Europe and the rest of the world, the opening of the Berlin Wall was hailed as symbolic of the end of the Cold War.

Two thousand years ago the proudest boast was "Civitas Romanus sum." Today, in the world of freedom, the proudest boast is "Ich bin ein Berliner."

There are many people in the world who really don't understand, or say they don't, what is the great issue between the free world and the Communist world. Let them come to Berlin. There are some who say that Communism is the wave of the future. Let them come to Berlin. And there are some who say in Europe and elsewhere we can work with the Communists. Let them come to Berlin. And there are even a few who say that it is true that Communism is an evil system, but it permits us to make economic progress. "Lasst sie nach Berlin kommen."

Freedom has many difficulties and democracy is not perfect, but we have never had to put a wall up to keep our people in, to prevent them from leaving us. I want to say, on behalf of my countrymen, who live many miles away on the other side of the Atlantic, who are far distant from you, that they take the greatest pride that they have been able to share with you, even

from a distance, the story of the last eighteen years. I know of no town, no city, that has been besieged for eighteen years that still lives with the vitality and the force, and the hope and the determination of the city of West Berlin. While the wall is the most obvious and vivid demonstration of the failures of the Communist system, for all the world to see, we take no satisfaction in it, for it is an offense not only against history but an offense against humanity, separating families, dividing husbands and wives and brothers and sisters, and dividing a people who wish to be joined together.

What is true of this city is true of Germany —real, lasting peace in Europe can never be assured as long as one German out of four is denied the elementary right of free men, and that is to make a free choice. In eighteen years of peace and good faith, this generation of Germans has earned the right to be free, including the right to unite their families and their nation in lasting peace with good will to all people. You live in a defended island of freedom, but your life is part of the main. So let me ask you, as I close, to lift your eyes beyond the dangers of today to the hopes of tomorrow, beyond the freedom merely of this city of Berlin, or your country of Germany, to the advance of freedom everywhere, beyond the wall to the day of peace with justice, beyond yourselves and ourselves to all mankind. Freedom is indivisible, and when one man is enslaved, all are not free. When all are free, then we can look forward to that day when this city will be joined as one—and this country, and this great continent of Europe—in a peaceful and hopeful glow. When that day finally comes, as it will, the people of West Berlin can take sober satisfaction in the fact that they were in the front lines for almost two decades.

All free men, wherever they may live, are citizens of Berlin, and, therefore, as a free man, I take pride in the words "Ich bin ein Berliner."

MARTIN LUTHER KING, JR.
THE MARCH ON WASHINGTON ADDRESS

I have a dream.

On August 28, 1963, more than 200,000 Americans gathered in the nation's capital, demonstrating in peaceful assembly on the mall between the Lincoln Memorial and the Washington Monument on behalf of equal justice for all. In a day of stirring speeches, Martin Luther King, Jr.'s "I have a dream" speech was electrifying. His soaring eloquence and his conscious fusing of religious rhetoric and familiar patriotic symbols conveyed a prophetic and uplifting sense of a world that might yet be. The "I Have a Dream" speech quickly entered the American language and national consciousness as a pithy evocation of the goals of the civil rights movement.

Five score years ago, a great American, in whose symbolic shadow we stand, signed the Emancipation Proclamation. This momentous decree came as a great beacon light of hope to millions of Negro slaves who had been seared in the flames of withering injustice. It came as a joyous daybreak to end the long night of captivity.

But one hundred years later, we must face the tragic fact that the Negro is still not free. One hundred years later, the life of the Negro is still sadly crippled by the manacles of segregation and the chains of discrimination. One hundred years later, the Negro lives on a lonely island of poverty in the midst of a vast ocean of material prosperity. One hundred years later, the Negro is still languished in the corners of American society and finds himself an exile in his own land. So we have come here today to dramatize an appalling condition.

In a sense we have come to our nation's Capital to cash a check. When the architects of our republic wrote the magnificent words of the Constitution and the Declaration of Independence, they were signing a promissory note to which every American was to fall heir. This note was a promise that all men would be guaranteed the unalienable rights of life, liberty, and the pursuit of happiness.

It is obvious today that America has defaulted on this promissory note insofar as her citizens of color are concerned. Instead of honoring this sacred obligation, America has given the Negro people a bad check; a check which has come back marked "insufficient funds." But we refuse to believe that the bank of justice is bankrupt. We refuse to believe that there are insufficient funds in the great vaults of opportunity of this nation. So we have come to cash this check—a check that will give us upon demand the riches of freedom and the security of justice.

We have also come to this hallowed spot to remind America of the fierce urgency of *now*. This is not time to engage in the luxury of cooling off or to take the tranquilizing drug of gradualism. *Now* is the time to make real the promises of democracy. *Now* is the time to rise from the dark and desolate valley of segregation to the sunlit path of racial justice. *Now* is the time to open the doors of opportunity to all of God's children. *Now* is the time to lift our nation from the quicksands of racial injustice to the solid rock of brotherhood.

It would be fatal for the nation to overlook the urgency of the moment and to underestimate the determination of the Negro. This sweltering summer of the Negro's legitimate discontent will not pass until there is an invigorating autumn of freedom and equality. Nineteen sixty-three is not an end, but a beginning. Those who hope that the Negro needed to blow off steam and will now be content will have a rude awakening if the nation returns to business as usual. There will be neither rest nor tranquillity in America until the Negro is granted his citizenship rights. The whirlwinds of revolt will continue to shake the foundations of our nation until the bright day of justice emerges.

But there is something that I must say to my people who stand on the warm threshold which leads into the palace of justice. In the process of gaining our rightful place we must not be guilty of wrongful deeds. Let us not seek to satisfy our thirst for freedom by drinking from the cup of bitterness and hatred. We must forever conduct our struggle on the high plane of dignity and discipline. We must not allow our creative protest to degenerate into physical violence. Again and again we must rise to the majestic heights of meeting physical force with soul force.

The marvelous new militancy which has en-

gulfed the Negro community must not lead us to a distrust of all white people, for many of our white brothers, as evidenced by their presence here today, have come to realize that their freedom is inextricably bound to our freedom. We cannot walk alone.

And as we walk, we must make the pledge that we shall march ahead. We cannot turn back. There are those who are asking the devotees of civil rights, "When will you be satisfied?"

We can never be satisfied as long as the Negro is the victim of the unspeakable horrors of police brutality.

We can never be satisfied as long as our bodies, heavy with fatigue of travel, cannot gain lodging in the motels of the highways and the cities.

We cannot be satisfied as long as the Negro's basic mobility is from a smaller ghetto to a larger one.

We can never be satisfied as long as a Negro in Mississippi cannot vote and a Negro in New York believes he has nothing for which to vote.

No, no, we are not satisfied, and we will not be satisfied until justice rolls down like waters and righteousness like a mighty stream.

I am not unmindful that some of you have come here out of great trials and tribulations. Some of you have come fresh from narrow jail cells. Some of you have come from areas where your quest for freedom left you battered by the storms of persecution and staggered by the winds of police brutality. You have been the veterans of creative suffering. Continue to work with the faith that unearned suffering is redemptive.

Go back to Mississippi, go back to Alabama, go back to South Carolina, go back to Georgia, go back to Louisiana, go back to the slums and ghettos of our Northern cities, knowing that somehow this situation can and will be changed. Let us not wallow in the valley of despair.

I say to you today, my friends, that in spite of the difficulties and frustrations of the moment I still have a dream. It is a dream deeply rooted in the American dream.

I have a dream that one day this nation will rise up and live out the true meaning of its creed: "We hold these truths to be self-evident; that all men are created equal."

I have a dream that one day on the red hills of Georgia the sons of former slaves and the sons of former slaveowners will be able to sit down together at the table of brotherhood.

I have a dream that one day even the state of Mississippi, a desert state sweltering with the heat of injustice and oppression, will be transformed into an oasis of freedom and justice.

I have a dream that my four little children will one day live in a nation where they will not be judged by the color of their skin but by the content of their character.

I have a dream today.

I have a dream that one day the state of Alabama, whose governor's lips are presently dripping with the words of interposition and nullification, will be transformed into a situation where little black boys and black girls will be able to join hands with little white boys and girls and walk together as sisters and brothers.

I have a dream today.

I have a dream that one day every valley shall be exalted, every hill and mountain shall be made low, the rough places will be made plain, and the crooked places will be made straight, and the glory of the Lord shall be revealed, and all flesh shall see it together.

This is our hope. This is the faith with which I return to the South. With this faith we will be able to hew out of the mountain of despair a stone of hope. With this faith we will be able to transform the jangling discords of our nation into a beautiful symphony of brotherhood.

With this faith we will be able to work together, to pray together, to struggle together, to go to jail together, to stand up for freedom together, knowing that we will be free one day.

This will be the day when all of God's children will be able to sing with new meaning, "My country 'tis of thee, sweet land of liberty, of thee I sing. Land where my father died, land of the

American astronauts landed on the moon on July 20, 1969. The first man on the moon, Astronaut Neil Armstrong, said, "That's one small step for a man, one giant leap for mankind."

Pilgrims' pride, from every mountainside, let freedom ring."

And if America is to be a great nation, this must become true. So let freedom ring from the prodigious hilltops of New Hampshire. Let freedom ring from the mighty mountains of New York. Let freedom ring from the heightening Alleghenies of Pennsylvania!

Let freedom ring from the snowcapped Rockies of Colorado! Let freedom ring from the curvaceous peaks of California! But not only that; let freedom ring from Stone Mountain of Georgia! Let freedom ring from Lookout Mountain of Tennessee!

Let freedom ring from every hill and molehill of Mississippi. From every mountainside, let freedom ring.

When we let freedom ring, when we let it ring from every village and every hamlet, from every state and every city, we will be able to speed up that day when all of God's children, black men and white men, Jews and Gentiles, Protestants and Catholics, will be able to join hands and sing in the words of the old Negro spiritual, "Free at last! Free at last! Thank God Almighty, we are free at last!"

WE SHALL OVERCOME

"We Shall Overcome" was known as the anthem of the civil rights movement in the 1960s. Whenever civil rights workers gathered, or whenever mass demonstrations were convened, people inevitably held hands, swaying side to side, and sang "We Shall Overcome." It was the theme song of the March on Washington, August 28, 1963, the day that Martin Luther King, Jr., gave his famous "I Have a Dream" speech. The song originated as a black spiritual in the nineteenth century. Like so many folk-protest songs, the lyrics were varied to fit the occasion, and there are many other verses.

We shall overcome,
We shall overcome,
We shall overcome,
Someday.
Oh, deep in my heart,
I do believe, that
We shall overcome
Someday.

We'll walk hand in hand,
We'll walk hand in hand,
We'll walk hand in hand,
Someday.
Oh, deep in my heart,
I do believe, that
We shall overcome
Someday.

We are not afraid,
We are not afraid,
We are not afraid,
Oh, no, no, no,
'Cause, deep in my heart,
I do believe, that
We shall overcome,
Someday.

O FREEDOM

This was one of the leading folk-protest songs of the 1960s. It originated in the nineteenth century among blacks as a folk spiritual. Some sources think that it is a freedman's song, since the lyrics express personal freedom in the present rather than freedom in the next life. During the 1960s, the song was adapted for the situation, and it can be found in many different versions.

O Freedom!
O Freedom!
O Freedom over me!
And before I'd be a slave,
I'd be buried in my grave,
And go home to my Lord and be free!

No more mournin'
No more weepin'
No more misery over me.
And before I'd be a slave,
I'd be buried in my grave,
And go home to my Lord and be free.

LEE HAYS AND PETE SEEGER
IF I HAD A HAMMER

Lee Hays and Pete Seeger were members of the Almanac Singers in 1940 and then members of the Weavers, the latter being the most popular folk quartet in the nation in the mid-twentieth century. The multi-talented Seeger was a major force in the popular revival of folk music in America after World War II. Hays sang bass, played the piano, and wrote folk music. Together with Seeger, he wrote the words and music for "If I Had a Hammer," which was one of the best-known protest songs of the 1960s.

If I had a hammer, I'd hammer in the morning,
I'd hammer in the evening—all over this land.
I'd hammer out danger, I'd hammer out
    warning,
I'd hammer out love between my brothers and
    my sisters
All over this land.

If I had a bell, I'd ring it in the morning
I'd ring it in the evening—all over this land.
I'd ring out danger, I'd ring out warning,
I'd ring out love between my brothers and my
    sisters
All over this land.

If I had a song, I'd sing it in the morning,
I'd sing it in the evening—all over this land.
I'd sing out danger, I'd sing out warning,
I'd sing out love between my brothers and my
    sisters
All over this land.

Well, I've got a hammer, and I've got a bell,
And I've got a song, All over this land,
It's the hammer of justice, it's the bell of
    freedom,
It's the song about love between my brothers
    and my sisters
All over this land.

BOB DYLAN
BLOWIN' IN THE WIND

Bob Dylan was born in Duluth, Minnesota, in 1941; his name at birth was Robert Allan Zimmerman. After a year at the University of Minnesota, he changed his name and entered the folk music scene. He has been widely recognized as the most influential American singer and songwriter of the 1960s. He wrote protest songs, love songs, folk songs, and rock music. "Blowin' in the Wind" (1963) has been called the unofficial anthem of the civil rights movement, and it was also popular in the anti-war movement.

How many roads must a man walk down
Before you call him a man?
Yes, 'n' how many seas must a white dove sail
Before she sleeps in the sand?

Yes, 'n' how many times must the cannon balls
    fly
Before they're forever banned?
The answer, my friend, is blowin' in the wind,
The answer is blowin' in the wind.

How many times must a man look up
Before he can see the sky?
Yes, 'n' how many ears must one man have
Before he can hear people cry?
Yes 'n' how many deaths will it take till he
    knows
That too many people have died?
The answer, my friend, is blowin' in the wind.
The answer is blowin' in the wind.

How many years can a mountain exist
Before it's washed to the sea?
Yes, 'n' how many years can some people exist
Before they're allowed to be free?
Yes, 'n' how many times can a man turn his
    head,
Pretending he just doesn't see?
The answer, my friend, is blowin' in the wind,
The answer is blowin' in the wind.

DUDLEY RANDALL

BALLAD OF BIRMINGHAM

Dudley Randall (1914–   ), born in Washington, D.C., received the B.A. degree in English from Wayne State University and the M.A. degree in library science from the University of Michigan in 1951. As founder and editor of the Broadside Press in Detroit, the leading publisher of black poetry in the country, he has played a major role in encouraging other black poets. He has edited several collections of black poetry, including *The Black Poets,* and has published several collections of his own poetry, including *Cities Burning.* His poem "Ballad of Birmingham" was written in response to the bombing of a black church in Birmingham, Alabama, on September 15, 1963, which killed four small girls. Those who planted the bomb expected to impede the civil rights campaign against segregation in Birmingham, but the murders mobilized national opinion on behalf of the civil rights movement.

"Mother, dear, may I go downtown
instead of out to play,
and march the streets of Birmingham
in a freedom march today?"

"No, baby, no, you may not go,
for the dogs are fierce and wild,
and clubs and hoses, guns and jails
ain't good for a little child."

"But, mother, I won't go alone.
Other children will go with me,
and march the streets of Birmingham
to make our country free."

"No, baby, no, you may not go,
for I fear those guns will fire.
But you may go to church instead,
and sing in the children's choir."

She has combed and brushed her nightdark hair,
and bathed rose petal sweet,
and drawn white gloves on her small brown hands,
and white shoes on her feet.

The mother smiled to know her child
was in the sacred place,
but that smile was the last smile
to come upon her face.

For when she heard the explosion,
her eyes grew wet and wild.
She raced through the streets of Birmingham
calling for her child.

She clawed through bits of glass and brick,
then lifted out a shoe.
"O, here's the shoe my baby wore,
but, baby, where are you?"

BETTY FRIEDAN

THE FEMININE MYSTIQUE

It . . . is time to stop giving lip service to the idea that there are no battles left to be fought for women in America.

The publication of Betty Friedan's book *The Feminine Mystique* in 1963 helped to launch the modern women's movement. Friedan (1921–) was born in Illinois, and she graduated from Smith College in 1942. The book appeared at a time when growing numbers of women were entering the labor force, and when women were making inroads into male-dominated professions. While *The Feminine Mystique* was aimed at middle- and even upper-middle-class women who could afford to be full-time housewives, it had a catalytic effect on the way women's issues in general were viewed and on the formation of a political lobby for women's interests. Friedan was a founder of the National Organization of Women, a leader in the unsuccessful political battle for the Equal Rights Amendment, and author of *It Changed My Life* and *The Second Stage.*

The problem lay buried, unspoken, for many years in the minds of American women. It was a strange stirring, a sense of dissatisfaction, a yearning that women suffered in the middle of the twentieth century in the United States. Each suburban wife struggled with it alone. As she made the beds, shopped for groceries, matched slipcover material, ate peanut butter sandwiches with her children, chauffeured Cub Scouts and Brownies, lay beside her husband at night—she was afraid to ask even of herself the silent question—"Is this all?"

For over fifteen years there was no word of this yearning in the millions of words written about women, for women, in all the columns, books and articles by experts telling women their role was to seek fulfillment as wives and mothers. Over and over women heard in voices of tradition and of Freudian sophistication that they could desire no greater destiny than to glory in their own femininity. Experts told them how to catch a man and keep him, how to breastfeed children and handle their toilet training, how to cope with sibling rivalry and adolescent rebellion; how to buy a dishwasher, bake bread, cook gourmet snails, and build a swimming pool with their own hands; how to dress, look, and act more feminine and make marriage more exciting; how to keep their husbands from dying young and their sons from growing into delinquents. They were taught to pity the neurotic, unfeminine, unhappy women who wanted to be poets or physicists or presidents. They learned that truly feminine women do not want careers, higher education, political rights—the independence and the opportunities that the old-fashioned feminists fought for. Some women, in their forties and fifties, still remembered painfully giving up those dreams, but most of the younger women no longer even thought about them. A thousand expert voices applauded their femininity, their adjustment, their new maturity. All they had to do was devote their lives from earliest girlhood to finding a husband and bearing children. . . .

The feminine mystique says that the highest value and the only commitment for women is the fulfillment of their own femininity. It says that the great mistake of Western culture, through most of its history, has been the undervaluation of this femininity. It says this femininity is so mysterious and intuitive and close to the creation and origin of life that man-made science may never be able to understand it. But however special and different, it is in no way inferior to the nature of man; it may even in certain respects be superior. The mistake, says the mystique, the root of women's troubles in the past is that women envied men, women tried to be like men, instead of accepting their own nature, which can find fulfillment only in sexual passivity, male domination, and nurturing maternal love....

The logic of the feminine mystique redefined the very nature of woman's problem. When woman was seen as a human being of limitless human potential, equal to man, anything that kept her from realizing her full potential was a problem to be solved: barriers to higher education and political participation, discrimination or prejudice in law or morality. But now that woman is seen only in terms of her sexual role, the barriers to the realization of her full potential, the prejudices which deny her full participation in the world, are no longer problems. The only problems now are those that might disturb her adjustment as a housewife. So career is a problem, education is a problem, political interest, even the very admission of women's intelligence and individuality is a problem. And finally there is the problem that has no name, a vague undefined wish for "something more" than washing dishes, ironing, punishing and praising the children....

If an able American woman does not use her human energy and ability in some meaningful pursuit (which necessarily means competition, for there is competition in every serious pursuit of our society), she will fritter away her energy in neurotic symptoms, or unproductive exercise, or destructive "love."

It ... is time to stop giving lip service to the idea that there are no battles left to be fought for women in America, that women's rights have already been won. It is ridiculous to tell girls to keep quiet when they enter a new field, or an old one, so the men will not notice they are there. In almost every professional field, in business and in the arts and sciences, women are still treated as second-class citizens. It would be a great service to tell girls who plan to work in society to expect this subtle, uncomfortable discrimination—tell them not to be quiet, and hope it will go away, but fight it. A girl should not expect special privileges because of her sex, but neither should she "adjust" to prejudice and discrimination.

She must learn to compete then, not as a woman, but as a human being. Not until a great many women move out of the fringes into the mainstream will society itself provide the arrangements for their new life plan....

MALVINA REYNOLDS
LITTLE BOXES

Malvina Reynolds (1900–1978) was born in San Francisco; she attended the University of California at Berkeley, where she received the B.A., M.A., and Ph.D. degree. Because of her leftist political activism, she was blacklisted and had difficulty getting employment. While writing political songs, she worked as a tailor, a social worker, a teacher, and a steelworker. She wrote more than five hundred songs and enjoyed a successful career as a performer, both in the United States and abroad. Several of her songs were popular hits, including Joan Baez's recording of "What Have they Done to the Rain?" in 1962 and Pete Seeger's recording of "Little Boxes" in 1963. The latter song criticized conformity, consumerism, and political indifference, as symbolized by the "ticky tacky houses" in the spreading suburbs. It was especially well liked by college students and others who had grown up in the "ticky tacky houses" and who wanted to demonstrate that they had not "come out all the same."

Marchers parade on behalf of the Equal Rights Amendment to the Constitution in New York City. The amendment was not adopted, but the women's movement nonetheless had a dramatic effect on family life and on the status of women in the workplace.

Little boxes on the hillside, little boxes made
    of ticky tacky
Little boxes on the hillside, little boxes all the
    same
There's a green one and a pink one and a blue
    one and a yellow one
And they're all made out of ticky tacky and
    they all look just the same.

And the people in the houses
All went to the university,
Where they were put in boxes
And they came out all the same,
And there's doctors and there's lawyers,
And business executives,
And they're all made out of ticky tacky
And they all look just the same.

And they all play on the golf course
And drink their martinis dry,
And they all have pretty children
And the children go to school,
And the children go to summer camp
And then to the university,
Where they are put in boxes and they come
    out all the same.

And the boys go into business
and marry and raise a family
In boxes made of ticky tacky
And they all look just the same.

LYNDON B. JOHNSON

HOWARD UNIVERSITY ADDRESS

You do not take a person who for years has been hobbled by chains and liberate him, bring him up to the starting line of a race and then say, "you are free to compete with all the others."

When John F. Kennedy was assassinated, Lyndon Johnson (1908-1973) became president. The most pressing domestic issue was civil rights, and Johnson became an effective advocate of social legislation, which he called his "Great Society" program. In response to his leadership, Congress passed a major civil rights act, federal aid to education, an antipoverty program, and federal protection for voting rights.

Johnson devoted his commencement address at Howard University on June 4, 1965, to explaining why legal equality was not enough to satisfy the aspirations of black Americans for full participation in American society. Johnson wanted to be remembered for his contributions to the health, education, and welfare of the American people, but his administration became ensnared by the Vietnam War, which consumed his energies and a large portion of the national budget. After completing one full term in office, Johnson did not run again for the presidency.

In far too many ways American Negroes have been another nation; deprived of freedom, crippled by hatred, the doors of opportunity closed to hope.

In our time change has come to this nation. The American Negro, acting with impressive restraint, has peacefully protested and marched, entered the courtrooms and the seats of government, demanding a justice that has long been denied. The voice of the Negro was the call to action. But it is a tribute to America that, once aroused, the courts and the Congress, the President and most of the people, have been the allies of progress....

The voting rights bill will be the latest, and among the most important, in a long series of victories. But this victory—as Winston Churchill said of another triumph for freedom—"is not the end. It is not even the beginning of the end. But it is, perhaps, the end of the beginning."

That beginning is freedom; and the barriers to that freedom are tumbling down. Freedom is the right to share, share fully and equally, in American society—to vote, to hold a job, to enter a public place, to go to school. It is the right to be treated in every part of our national life as a person equal in dignity and promise to all others.

But freedom is not enough. You do not wipe away the scars of centuries by saying: Now you are free to go where you want, and do as you desire, and choose the leaders you please.

You do not take a person who for years has been hobbled by chains and liberate him, bring him up to the starting line of a race and then say, "you are free to compete with all the others," and still justly believe that you have been completely fair.

Thus it is not enough just to open the gates of opportunity. All our citizens must have the ability to walk through those gates.

This is the next and the more profound stage of the battle for civil rights. We seek not just freedom but opportunity. We seek not just legal equity but human ability, not just equality as a right and a theory but equality as a fact and equality as a result....

Of course Negro Americans as well as white

Americans have shared in our rising national abundance. But the harsh fact of the matter is that in the battle for true equality too many—far too many—are losing ground every day.

We are not completely sure why this is. We know the causes are complex and subtle. But we do know the two broad basic reasons. And we do know that we have to act.

First, Negroes are trapped—as many whites are trapped—in inherited, gateless poverty. They lack training and skills. They are shut in, in slums, without decent medical care. Private and public poverty combine to cripple their capacities.

We are trying to attack these evils through our poverty program, through our education program, through our medical care and our other health programs, and a dozen more of the Great Society programs that are aimed at the root causes of this poverty.

We will increase, and we will accelerate, and we will broaden this attack in years to come until this most enduring of foes finally yields to our unyielding will.

But there is a second cause—much more difficult to explain, more deeply grounded, more desperate in its force. It is the devastating heritage of long years of slavery; and a century of oppression, hatred, and injustice.

For Negro poverty is not white poverty. Many of its causes and many of its cures are the same. But there are differences—deep, corrosive, obstinate differences—radiating painful roots into the community, and into the family, and the nature of the individual.

These differences are not racial differences. They are solely and simply the consequence of ancient brutality, past injustice, and present prejudice. They are anguishing to observe. For the Negro they are a constant reminder of oppression. For the white they are a constant reminder of guilt. But they must be faced and they must be dealt with and they must be overcome, if we are ever to reach the time when the only difference between Negroes and whites is the color of their skin.

Nor can we find a complete answer in the experience of other American minorities. They made a valiant and a largely successful effort to emerge from poverty and prejudice.

The Negro, like these others, will have to rely mostly upon his own efforts. But he just cannot do it alone. For they did not have the heritage of centuries to overcome, and they did not have a cultural tradition which had been twisted and battered by endless years of hatred and hopelessness, nor were they excluded—these others—because of race or color—a feeling whose dark intensity is matched by no other prejudice in our society.

Nor can these differences be understood as isolated infirmities. They are a seamless web. They cause each other. They result from each other. They reinforce each other.

Much of the Negro community is buried under a blanket of history and circumstance. It is not a lasting solution to lift just one corner of that blanket. We must stand on all sides and we must raise the entire cover if we are to liberate our fellow citizens. . . .

Perhaps most important—its influence radiating to every part of life—is the breakdown of the Negro family structure. For this, most of all, white America must accept responsibility. It flows from centuries of oppression and persecution of the Negro man. It flows from the long years of degradation and discrimination, which have attacked his dignity and assaulted his ability to produce for his family. . . .

The family is the cornerstone of our society. More than any other force it shapes the attitude, the hopes, the ambitions, and the values of the child. And when the family collapses it is the children that are usually damaged. When it happens on a massive scale the community itself is crippled.

So, unless we work to strengthen the family, to create conditions under which most parents will stay together, all the rest—schools, and playgrounds, and public assistance, and private concern—will never be enough to cut completely the circle of despair and deprivation.

There is no single easy answer to all of these problems.

Jobs are part of the answer. They bring the income which permits a man to provide for his family.

Decent homes in decent surroundings and a chance to learn—an equal chance to learn—are part of the answer.

Welfare and social programs better designed to hold families together are part of the answer.

Care for the sick is part of the answer.

An understanding heart by all Americans is another big part of the answer.

And to all of these fronts—and a dozen more—I will dedicate the expanding efforts of the Johnson Administration.

RODOLFO GONZALES
I AM JOAQUÍN

During the 1960s, many ethnic groups rejected the goal of assimilation as symbolized by the melting pot. "I Am Joaquín," a poem by Rodolfo Gonzales (1928–   ), is a strong expression of the Mexican-American rejection of cultural assimilation. Published in 1967, the poem became a manifesto of the Chicano political movement. It is a long meditation on the history of the Chicano people, connecting them to their Aztec and Indian heritage, and using that history to bolster ethnic solidarity.

Born in Denver, Gonzales was a prize-fighter and a laborer as a youth, then owned a neighborhood bar. He became active in the Democratic Party in Denver, ran a bail-bond business, and became chairman of Denver's antipoverty program in the early 1960s. In 1966, he founded the Crusade for Justice, a Mexican-American civil rights organization.

Originally Gonzales printed the poem himself and distributed more than 100,000 copies. It attracted so much attention among Chicano audiences that in 1972 it was published as a book. It is excerpted below.

I am Joaquín,
Lost in a world of confusion,
Caught up in a whirl of a
          gringo society.
Confused by the rules,
Scorned by attitudes,
Suppressed by manipulations,
And destroyed by modern society.
My fathers
     have lost the economic battle
and won
     the struggle of cultural survival.
And now!
     I must choose
          Between

the paradox of
Victory of the spirit,
despite physical hunger
          Or
to exist in the grasp
of American social neurosis,
sterilization of the soul
     and a full stomach.
. . . .
I shed tears of anguish
as I see my children disappear
behind the shroud of mediocrity
never to look back to remember me.
I am Joaquín.
          I must fight

And win this struggle
for my sons, and they
must know from me
Who I am.
Part of the blood that runs deep in me
Could not be vanquished by the Moors
I defeated them after five hundred years,
and I endured.
        The part of blood that is mine
        has labored endlessly five-hundred
        years under the heel of lustful
                Europeans
                I am still here!
I have endured in the rugged mountains
    of our country
I have survived the toils and slavery
    of the fields.
            I have existed
in the barrios of the city,
in the suburbs of bigotry,
in the mines of social snobbery,
in the prisons of dejection,
in the muck of exploitation
and
in the fierce heat of racial hatred.

And now the trumpet sounds,
The music of the people stirs the
        Revolution,
Like a sleeping giant it slowly
rears its head
to the sound of
            Tramping feet
            Clamouring voices

        Mariachi strains
        Fiery tequila explosions
        The smell of chile verde and
        Soft brown eyes of expectation for a
                        better life.
And in all the fertile farm lands,
            the barren plains,
the mountain villages,
smoke smeared cities
                We start to MOVE.
    La Raza!
Mejicano!
    Español!
        Latino!
            Hispano!
                Chicano!
or whatever I call myself,
                I look the same
                I feel the same
                I cry
                        and
                Sing the same

I am the masses of my people and
I refuse to be absorbed.
            I am Joaquín
The odds are great
but my spirit is strong
                    My faith unbreakable
                    My blood is pure
I am Aztec Prince and Christian Christ
            I SHALL ENDURE!
            I WILL ENDURE!

ROBERT F. KENNEDY

AGAINST THE WAR IN VIETNAM

At the end of it all, there will only be more Americans killed . . . so that they may say, as Tacitus said of Rome: "They made a desert, and called it peace."

Robert F. Kennedy (1925–1968) was attorney general in the cabinet of his older brother, President John F. Kennedy. In 1964, Robert Kennedy was elected senator from New York and became a leading critic of the Vietnam War and a spokesman for liberal

Democrats. On March 16, 1968, he announced his candidacy for the Democratic nomination for president and two days later delivered this stinging attack on American policy in Vietnam. Two weeks later, President Lyndon Johnson announced that he would not run again.

When President Johnson escalated American involvement in the war in 1965, it became the most divisive issue in American life. By 1968 there were more than 500,000 American troops in Vietnam. The war spawned an angry antiwar movement and undermined public trust in government, the military, and other institutions. Long after the United States withdrew its last combatants in 1975, the shadow of the war continued to affect popular culture and national politics.

. . . This is a year of choice—a year when we choose not simply who will lead us, but where we wish to be led; the country we want for ourselves—and the kind we want for our children. If in this year of choice we fashion new politics out of old illusions, we insure for ourselves nothing but crisis for the future—and we bequeath to our children the bitter harvest of those crises. . . .

Today I would speak to you . . . of the war in Vietnam. I come here . . . to discuss with you why I regard our policy here as bankrupt. . . .

I do not want—as I believe most Americans do not want—to sell out American interests, to simply withdraw, to raise the white flag of surrender. That would be unacceptable to us as a country and as a people. But I am concerned—as I believe most Americans are concerned—that the course we are following at the present time is deeply wrong. I am concerned—as I believe most Americans are concerned—that we are acting as if no other nations existed, against the judgment and desires of neutrals and our historic allies alike. I am concerned—as I believe most Americans are concerned—that our present course will not bring victory; will not bring peace; will not stop the bloodshed; and will not advance the interests of the United States or the cause of peace in the world.

I am concerned that, at the end of it all, there will only be more Americans killed; more of our treasure spilled out; and because of the bitterness and hatred on every side of this war, more hundreds of thousands of Vietnamese slaughtered; so that they may say, as Tacitus said of Rome: "They made a desert, and called it peace."

And I do not think that is what the American spirit is really all about.

Let me begin this discussion with a note both personal and public. I was involved in many of the early decisions on Vietnam, decisions which helped set us on our present path. It may be that the effort was doomed from the start; that it was never really possible to bring all the people of South Vietnam under the rule of the successive governments we supported—governments, one after another, riddled with corruption, inefficiency, and greed; governments which did not and could not successfully capture and energize the national feeling of their people. If that is the case, as it well may be, then I am willing to bear my share of the responsibility, before history and before my fellow-citizens. But past error is no excuse for its own perpetuation. Tragedy is a tool for the living to gain wisdom, not a guide by which to live. Now as ever, we do ourselves best justice when we measure ourselves against ancient tests, as in the Antigone of Sophocles: "All men make mistakes, but a good man yields when he knows his course is wrong, and repairs the evil. The only sin is pride."

The reversals of the last several months have led our military to ask for 206,000 more troops. This weekend, it was announced that some of them—a "moderate" increase, it was said—would soon be sent. But isn't this exactly what we have always done in the past? If we examine the history of this conflict, we find the dismal story repeated time after time. Every time—at every crisis—we have denied that anything was wrong; sent more troops; and issued more confident communiques. Every time, we have been assured that this one last step would bring victory. And every time, the predictions and promises have failed and been forgotten, and the demand has been made again for just one more step up the ladder.

But all the escalations, all the last steps, have brought us no closer to success than we were before. Rather, as the scale of the fighting has increased, South Vietnamese society has become less and less capable of organizing or defending itself, and we have more and more assumed the whole burden of the war.

And once again, the President tells us, as we have been told for twenty years, that "we are going to win;" "victory" is coming.

But what are the true facts? What is our present situation? . . .

The point of our pacification operations was always described as "winning the hearts and minds" of the people. We recognized that giving the countryside military security against the Viet Cong would be futile—indeed that it would be impossible—unless the people of the countryside themselves came to identify their interests with ours, and to assist not the Viet Cong, but the Saigon government. For this we recognized that their minds would have to be *changed*—that their natural inclination would be to support the Viet Cong, or at best remain passive, rather than sacrifice for foreign white men, or the remote Saigon government.

It is this effort that has been most gravely set back in the last month. We cannot change the minds of the people in villages controlled by the enemy. . . . If, in the years those villages and hamlets were controlled by Saigon, the government had brought honesty, social reform, land —if that had happened, if the many promises of a new and better life for the people had been fulfilled—then, in the process of reconquest, we might appear as liberators: just as we did in Europe, despite the devastation of war, in 1944–45. But the promises of reform were not kept.

Corruption and abuse of administrative power have continued to this day. Land reform has never been more than an empty promise. Viewing the performance of the Saigon government over the last three years, there is no reason for the South Vietnamese peasant to fight for the extension of its authority or to view the further devastation that effort will bring as anything but a calamity. . . .

The second evident fact of the last two months is that the Saigon government is no more or better an ally than it was before; that it may even be less; and that the war inexorably is growing more, not less, an American effort. . . . The facts are that thousands of young South Vietnamese buy their deferments from military service while American Marines die at Khe Sanh.

The facts are that the government has arrested monks and labor leaders, former Presidential candidates and government officials— including prominent members of the Committee for the Preservation of the Nation, in which American officials placed such high hopes just a few weeks ago.

Meanwhile, the government's enormous corruption continues, debilitating South Vietnam and crippling our effort to help its people. . . .

Third, it is becoming more evident with every passing day that the victories we achieve will only come at the cost of destruction for the nation we once hoped to help. . . .

An American commander said of the town of Ben Tre, "it became necessary to destroy the town in order to save it." It is difficult to quarrel with the decision of American commanders to use air power and artillery to save the lives of their men; if American troops are to fight for Vietnamese cities, they deserve protection. What I cannot understand is why the responsibility for the recapture and attendant destruction of Hue, and Ben Tre and the others, should fall to American troops in the first place.

If Communist insurgents or invaders held New York or Washington or San Francisco, we would not leave it to foreigners to take them back, and destroy them and their people in the process. . . .

If the government's troops will not or cannot carry the fight for their cities, we cannot ourselves destroy them. That kind of salvation is not an act we can presume to perform for them. For we must ask our government—we must ask ourselves: where does such logic end? If it becomes "necessary" to destroy all of South Vietnam in order to "save" it, will we do that too? And if we care so little about South Vietnam that we are willing to see the land destroyed and its people dead, then why are we there in the first place?

Can we ordain to ourselves the awful majesty of God—to decide what cities and villages are to be destroyed, who will live and who will die, and who will join the refugees wandering in a desert of our own creation? . . .

Let us have no misunderstanding. The Viet Cong are a brutal enemy indeed. Time and time again, they have shown their willingness to sacrifice innocent civilians, to engage in torture and murder and despicable terror to achieve their ends. This is a war almost without rules or quarter. There can be no easy moral answer to this war, no one-sided condemnation of American actions. What we must ask ourselves is whether we have a right to bring so much destruction to another land, without clear and convincing evidence that this is what its people want. But that is precisely the evidence we do not have. What they want is peace, not dominated by any outside forces. And that is what we are really committed to help bring them, not in some indefinite future, but while some scraps of life remain still to be saved from the holocaust.

The fourth fact that is now more clear than ever is that the war in Vietnam, far from being the last critical test for the United States is in fact weakening our position in Asia and around the world, and eroding the structure of international cooperation which has directly supported our security for the past three decades. . . . We set out to prove our willingness to keep our commitments everywhere in the world. What we are ensuring instead is that it is most unlikely that the American people would ever again be willing to . . . engage in this kind of struggle. Meanwhile our oldest and strongest allies pull back to their own shores, leaving us alone to police all of Asia. . . .

We are entitled to ask—we are required to ask—how many more men, how many more lives, how much more destruction will be asked, to provide the military victory that is always just around the corner, to pour into this bottomless pit of our dreams?

But this question the Administration does not and cannot answer. It has no answer—none but the ever-expanding use of military force and the lives of our brave soldiers, in a conflict where military force has failed to solve anything in the past. . . .

It is long past time to ask: what is this war doing to us? Of course it is costing us money—fully one-fourth of our federal budget—but that is the smallest price we pay. The cost is in our young men, the tens of thousands of their lives cut off forever. The cost is in our world position—in neutrals and allies alike, every day more baffled by and estranged from a policy they cannot understand.

Higher yet is the price we pay in our innermost lives, and in the spirit of our country. For the first time in a century, we have open resistance to service in the cause of the nation. For the first time perhaps in our history, we have desertions from our army on political and moral grounds. The front pages of our newspapers show photographs of American soldiers torturing prisoners. Every night we watch horror on the evening news. Violence spreads inexorably across the nation, filling our streets and crippling our lives. And whatever the costs to us, let us think of the young men we have sent there: not just the killed, but those who have to kill; not just the maimed, but also those who must look upon the results of what they do. . . .

The costs of the war's present course far outweigh anything we can reasonably hope to gain by it, for ourselves or for the people of Vietnam. It must be ended, and it can be ended, in a peace of brave men who have fought each other with a terrible fury, each believing that he alone was in the right. We have prayed to different gods, and the prayers of neither have been answered fully. Now, while there is still time for some of them to be partly answered, now is the time to stop.

And the fact is that much can be done. We can—as I have urged for two years, but as we have never done—negotiate with the National Liberation Front. We can—as we have never done—assure the Front a genuine place in the political life of South Vietnam. We can—as we are refusing to do today—begin to deescalate the war, concentrate on protecting populated areas, and thus save American lives and slow down the destruction of the countryside. We can—as we have never done—insist that the Government of South Vietnam broaden its base, institute real reforms, and seek an honorable settlement with their fellow countrymen. . . .

Even this modest and reasonable program is impossible while our present leadership, under the illusion that military victory is just ahead, plunges deeper into the swamp that is our present course. . . .

ROBERT F. KENNEDY

ON THE DEATH OF MARTIN LUTHER KING, JR.

What we need . . . is not division . . . not hatred . . . not violence . . . but love and wisdom, and compassion.

On April 4, 1968, Dr. Martin Luther King, Jr., was assassinated in Memphis. That evening, Senator Robert Kennedy was scheduled to speak in a poor black neighborhood in Indianapolis on behalf of his campaign for the Democratic presidential nomination. The police warned Kennedy not to go that night, since they could not guarantee his safety. When Kennedy arrived, he realized that the crowd had not heard about King's assassination. His spontaneous remarks that evening reflected the personal loss that he had sustained when his own brother was killed by a sniper's bullet.

Three months later, on June 4, 1968, Kennedy celebrated a major triumph in the important California primary. He seemed to be headed for the Democratic nomination on the night that he addressed his followers in Los Angeles' Ambassador Hotel. As he left through a kitchen hallway, he was shot by an embittered Palestinian immigrant; he died two days later.

I have bad news for you, for all of our fellow citizens, and people who love peace all over the world, and that is that Martin Luther King was shot and killed tonight.

Martin Luther King dedicated his life to love and to justice for his fellow human beings, and he died because of that effort.

In this difficult day, in this difficult time for the United States, it is perhaps well to ask what kind of a nation we are and what direction we want to move in. For those of you who are black —considering the evidence there evidently is that there were white people who were responsible—you can be filled with bitterness, with hatred, and a desire for revenge. We can move in that direction as a country, in great polarization—black people amongst black, white people amongst white, filled with hatred toward one another.

Or we can make an effort, as Martin Luther King did, to understand and to comprehend, and to replace that violence, that stain of bloodshed that has spread across our land, with an effort to understand with compassion and love.

For those of you who are black and are tempted to be filled with hatred and distrust at the injustice of such an act, against all white people, I can only say that I feel in my own heart the same kind of feeling. I had a member of my family killed, but he was killed by a white man. But we have to make an effort in the United States, we have to make an effort to understand, to go beyond these rather difficult times.

My favorite poet was Aeschylus. He wrote: "In our sleep, pain which cannot forget falls drop by drop upon the heart until, in our own despair, against our will, comes wisdom through the awful grace of God."

What we need in the United States is not division; what we need in the United States is not hatred; what we need in the United States is not violence or lawlessness, but love and wisdom, and compassion toward one another, and a feeling of justice towards those who still suffer within our country, whether they be white or they be black.

So I shall ask you tonight to return home, to say a prayer for the family of Martin Luther King, that's true, but more importantly to say a prayer for our own country, which all of us love—a prayer for understanding and that compassion of which I spoke.

We can do well in this country. We will have difficult times. We've had difficult times in the past. We will have difficult times in the future. It is not the end of violence; it is not the end of lawlessness; it is not the end of disorder.

But the vast majority of white people and the vast majority of black people in this country want to live together, want to improve the quality of our life, and want justice for all human beings who abide in our land.

Let us dedicate ourselves to what the Greeks wrote so many years ago: to tame the savageness of man and to make gentle the life of this world.

Let us dedicate ourselves to that, and say a prayer for our country and for our people.

ABELARDO DELGADO
STUPID AMERICA

Abelardo Delgado (1931–   ) was born in Chihuahua, Mexico; he emigrated to the United States with his mother in 1943, and lived in El Paso, Texas, where he attended public schools and the University of Texas. He was one of the leading writers of the Chicano political movement of the late 1960s and early 1970s. Delgado, who signs his poetry "Abelardo," has published numerous books of poetry. "Stupid America" appeared in his first collection, *Chicano: 25 Pieces of a Chicano Mind,* published in 1969.

Stupid america, see that chicano
with a big knife
in his steady hand
he doesn't want to knife you
he wants to sit on a bench
and carve christfigures
but you won't let him.
stupid america, hear that chicano
shouting curses on the street
he is a poet
without paper and pencil
and since he cannot write
he will explode.
stupid america, remember that chicanito
flunking math and english
he is the picasso
of your western states
but he will die
with one thousand masterpieces
hanging only from his mind.

WALLACE STEGNER

THE WILDERNESS IDEA

Something will have gone out of us as a people if we ever let the remaining wilderness be destroyed.

Wallace Stegner (1909–) was born in Iowa, and he graduated from the University of Utah. Stegner is a prolific author who has written many novels and diverse nonfiction; his novels have been honored with the Pulitzer Prize and the National Book Award. His nonfiction works include several books *(This is Dinosaur, Wolf Willow,* and *The Sound of Mountain Water)* that reflect his love of nature and the West. "The Wilderness Idea" is from *The Sound of Mountain Water* (1969).

. . . What I want to speak for is . . . the wilderness idea, which is a resource in itself. Being an intangible and spiritual resource, it will seem mystical to the practical-minded—but then anything that cannot be moved by a bulldozer is likely to seem mystical to them.

I want to speak for the wilderness idea as something that has helped form our character and that has certainly shaped our history as a people. . . .

Something will have gone out of us as a people if we ever let the remaining wilderness be destroyed; if we permit the last virgin forests to be turned into comic books and plastic cigarette cases; if we drive the few remaining members of the wild species into zoos or to extinction; if we pollute the last clear air and dirty the last clean streams and push our paved roads through the last of the silence, so that never again will Americans be free in their own country from the noise, the exhausts, the stink of human and automotive waste. And so that never again can we have the chance to see ourselves single, separate, vertical and individual in the world, part of the environment of trees and rocks and soil, brother to the other animals, part of the natural world and competent to belong in it. Without any remaining wilderness we are committed wholly, without chance for even momentary reflection and rest, to a headlong drive into our technological termite-life, the Brave New World of a completely man-controlled environment.

We need wilderness preserved—as much of it as is still left, and as many kinds—because it was the challenge against which our character as a

Earth Day poster by artist Robert Rauschenberg, 1970. The first Earth Day signified the arrival of environmentalism as a major political issue.

people was formed. The reminder and the reassurance that it is still there is good for our spiritual health even if we never once in ten years set foot in it. It is good for us when we are young, because of the incomparable sanity it can bring briefly, as vacation and rest, into our insane lives. It is important to us when we are old simply because it is there—important, that is, simply as idea.

LORNA DEE CERVANTES

REFUGEE SHIP

Lorna Dee Cervantes (1954–   ) was born in the Mission District of San Francisco. She grew up in San Jose, California. As an adolescent, she loved the English romantic poets, particularly Byron, Keats, and Shelley. She first published poetry in her high school newspaper. In 1974, at the age of twenty, she read "Refugee Ship" at a theatrical performance in Mexico City, and it was published by a newspaper there. The poem speaks of the dilemma of immigrants who have lost their original culture, yet do not feel themselves part of American culture. In 1974, Cervantes launched a literary review called *Mango* to publish the work of Chicano writers.

"Refugee Ship" appeared in Cervantes's collection *Emplumada*, which was published in 1981.

like wet cornstarch
I slide past *mi abuelita's* eyes
bible placed by her side
she removes her glasses
the pudding thickens

mamá raised me with no language
I am an orphan to my spanish name
the words are foreign, stumbling on my tongue

I stare at my reflection in the mirror
brown skin, black hair

I feel I am a captive
aboard the refugee ship
a ship that will never dock
a ship that will never dock

CONTEMPORARY TIMES

The United States celebrated the bicentennial of its Declaration of Independence with a national party and fireworks on July 4, 1976. Shown here is the sailing ship Gorch Foch *in the New York harbor, which paraded with other tall ships up the Hudson River. A fireboat adds its spray to the festivities.*

JUDY GRAHN

NADINE, RESTING ON HER NEIGHBOR'S STOOP

Judy Grahn (1940–   ) was born in Chicago. She grew up in New Mexico and graduated from San Francisco State University. In 1970, she co-founded the first women's press. She has written several volumes of poetry and edited collections of short stories. The following poem appears in *The Work of a Common Woman* (1978).

She holds things together, collects bail,
makes the landlord patch the largest holes.
At the Sunday social she would spike
every drink, and offer you half of what she
   knows,
which is plenty. She pokes at the ruins of the
   city
like an armored tank; but she thinks
of herself as a ripsaw cutting through
knots in wood. Her sentences come out
like thick pine shanks

and her big hands fill the air like smoke.
She's a mud-chinked cabin in the slums,
sitting on the doorstep counting
rats and raising 15 children,
half of them her own. The neighborhood
would burn itself out without her;
one of these days she'll strike the spark herself.
She's made of grease
and metal, with a hard head
that makes the men around her seem frail.
The common woman is as common as a nail.

ALICE WALKER

GOOD NIGHT, WILLIE LEE, I'LL SEE YOU IN THE MORNING

Alice Walker (1944–   ) was born in Georgia and educated at Sarah Lawrence College. She has been a prolific writer of fiction, essays, and poetry. Among her novels are *Meridian* and *The Color Purple*. Her collected essays about women have been published as *In Search of Our Mothers' Gardens*. She has also written a biography of Langston Hughes and edited an anthology of the works of Zora Neale Hurston. Her poem "Good Night, Willie Lee, I'll See You in the Morning" first appeared in the *Iowa Review* in 1975 and was the title poem of a collection published in 1979.

Looking down into my father's
dead face
for the last time
my mother said without
tears, without smiles
without regrets
but with *civility*
"Good night, Willie Lee, I'll see you

in the morning."
And it was then I knew that the healing
of all our wounds
is forgiveness
that permits a promise
of our return
at the end.

A CITY OF NEIGHBORHOODS

The American Dream starts with the neighborhoods.

Harvey Milk (1930–1978) was the first openly homosexual candidate to win election to San Francisco's Board of Supervisors. Elected in 1977 after three unsuccessful campaigns, Milk represented the Castro, an ethnically and racially diverse district. For many of its residents, the district was like a small town. They did not welcome urban redevelopment, particularly not the kind that had bulldozed other neighborhoods and replaced them with high-rise buildings. Milk's constituents worried about maintaining their quality of life and preventing the decay that had destroyed communities in other major American cities. Milk intended to be a spokesman not only for gay issues but for the revitalization of the neighborhoods of urban America. However, on November 27, 1978, Harvey Milk and Mayor George Moscone were assassinated by an embittered former supervisor.

Harvey Milk delivered the following speech to a fund-raising dinner shortly after he was inaugurated as a member of the Board of Supervisors.

. . . Let's make no mistake about this: The American Dream starts with the neighborhoods. If we wish to rebuild our cities, we must first rebuild our neighborhoods. And to do that, we must understand that the quality of life is more important than the standard of living. To sit on the front steps—whether it's a veranda in a small town or a concrete stoop in a big city— and talk to our neighborhoods is infinitely more important than to huddle on the living-room lounger and watch a make-believe world in not-quite living color.

Progress is not America's only business— and certainly not its most important. Isn't it strange that as technology advances, the quality of life so frequently declines? Oh, washing the dishes is easier. Dinner itself is easier—just heat and serve, though it might be more nourishing if we ate the ads and threw the food away. And we no longer fear spots on our glassware when guests come over. But then, of course, the guests don't come, because our friends are too afraid to come to our house and it's not safe to go to theirs.

And I hardly need to tell you that in that 19- or 24-inch view of the world, cleanliness has long since eclipsed godliness. So we'll all smell, look, and actually be laboratory clean, as sterile on the inside as on the out. The perfect consumer, surrounded by the latest appliances. The perfect audience, with a ringside seat to almost any event in the world, without smell, without taste, without feel—alone and unhappy in the vast wasteland of our living rooms. I think that what we actually need, of course, is a little more dirt on the seat of our pants as we sit on the front stoop and talk to our neighbors once again, enjoying the type of summer day where the smell of garlic travels slightly faster than the speed of sound.

There's something missing in the sanitized life we lead. Something that our leaders in Washington can never supply by simple edict, something that the commercials on television never advertise because nobody's yet found a way to bottle it or box it or can it. What's missing is the touch, the warmth, the meaning of life. A four-color spread in *Time* is no substitute for it. Neither is a 30-second commercial or a reassuring Washington press conference.

I spent many years on both Wall Street and Montgomery Street and I fully understand the debt and responsibility that major corporations owe their shareholders. I also fully understand the urban battlefields of New York and Cleveland and Detroit. I see the faces of the unemployed—and the unemployable—of the city. I've seen the faces in Chinatown, Hunters Point, the Mission, and the Tenderloin . . . and I don't like what I see.

Oddly, I'm also reminded of the most successful slogan a business ever coined: The customer is always right.

What's been forgotten is that those people of the Tenderloin and Hunters Point, those people in the streets, are the customers, certainly potential ones, and they must be treated as such. Government cannot ignore them and neither can business ignore them. What sense is there in making products if the would-be customer can't afford them? It's not alone a question of price, it's a question of ability to pay. For a man with no money, 99¢ reduced from $1.29 is still a fortune.

American business must realize that while the shareholders always come first, the care and feeding of their customer is a close second. They have a debt and a responsibility to that customer and the city in which he or she lives, the cities in which the business itself lives or in which it grew up. To throw away a senior citizen after they've nursed you through childhood is wrong. To treat a city as disposable once your business has prospered is equally wrong and even more short-sighted.

Unfortunately for those who would like to flee them, the problems of the cities don't stop at the city limits. There are no moats around our

The "Names Project," also known as the AIDS quilt, was displayed at the foot of the Lincoln Memorial during the Gay Rights March in 1987. Each panel of the quilt was designed by friends and relatives in tribute to a person who had died of AIDS.

cities that keep the problems in. What happens in New York or San Francisco will eventually happen in San Jose. It's just a matter of time. And like the flu, it usually gets worse the further it travels. Our cities must not be abandoned. They're worth fighting for, not just by those who live in them, but by industry, commerce, unions, everyone. Not alone because they represent the past, but because they also represent the future. Your children will live there and hopefully, so will your grandchildren. For all practical purposes, the eastern corridor from Boston to Newark will be one vast strip city. So will the area from Milwaukee to Gary, Indiana. In California, it will be that fertile crescent of asphalt and neon that stretches from Santa Barbara to San Diego. Will urban blight travel the arteries of the freeways? Of course it will—unless we stop it.

So the challenge of the 80s will be to awaken the consciousness of industry and commerce to the part they must play in saving the cities which nourished them. Every company realizes it must constantly invest in its own physical plant to remain healthy and grow. Well, the cities are a part of that plant and the people who live in them are part of the cities. They're all connected; what affects one affects the others.

In short, the cheapest place to manufacture a product may not be the cheapest at all if it results in throwing your customers out of work. There's no sense in making television sets in Japan if the customers in the United States haven't the money to buy them. Industry must actively seek to employ those without work, to train those who have no skills. "Labor intensive" is not a dirty word, not every job is done better by machine. It has become the job of industry not only to create the product, but also to create the customer.

Costly? I don't think so. It's far less expensive than the problem of fully loaded docks and no customers. And there are additional returns: lower rates of crime, smaller welfare loads. And having your friends and neighbors sitting on that well-polished front stoop. . . .

Many companies feel that helping the city is a form of charity. I think it is more accurate to consider it a part of the cost of doing business, that it should be entered on the books as amortizing the future. I would like to see business and industry consider it as such, because I think there's more creativity, more competence perhaps, in business than there is in government. I think that business could turn the south of Market Area not only into an industrial park but a neighborhood as well. To coin a pun, too many of our cities have a complex, in fact, too many complexes. We don't need another concrete jungle that dies the moment you turn off the lights in the evening. What we need is a neighborhood where people can walk to work, raise their kids, enjoy life. . . .

The cities will be saved. The cities will be governed. But they won't be run from three thousand miles away in Washington, they won't be run from the statehouse, and most of all, they won't be run by the carpetbaggers who have fled to the suburbs. You can't run a city by people who don't live there, any more than you can have an effective police force made up of people who don't live there. In either case, what you've got is an occupying army. . . .

The cities will not be saved by the people who feel condemned to live in them, who can hardly wait to move to Marin or San Jose—or Evanston or Westchester. The cities will be saved by the people who like it here. The people who prefer the neighborhood stores to the shopping mall, who go to the plays and eat in the restaurants and go to the discos and worry about the education the kids are getting even if they have no kids of their own.

That's not just the city of the future; it's the city of today. It means new directions, new alliances, new solutions for ancient problems. The typical American family with two cars and 2.2 kids doesn't live here anymore. It hasn't for years. The demographics are different now and we all know it. The city is a city of singles and young marrieds, the city of the retired and the poor, a city of many colors who speak in many tongues.

The city will run itself, it will create its own

solutions. District elections was not the end. It was just the beginning. We'll solve our problems —with your help, if we can, without it if we must. We need your help. I don't deny that. But you also need us. We're your customers. We're your future.

I'm riding into that future and frankly I don't know if I'm wearing the fabled helm of Mambrino on my head or if I'm wearing a barber's basin. I guess we wear what we want to wear and we fight what we want to fight. Maybe I see dragons where there are only windmills. But something tells me the dragons are for real and if I shatter a lance or two on a whirling blade, maybe I'll catch a dragon in the bargain....

Yesterday, my esteemed colleague on the Board said we cannot live on hope alone. I know that, but I strongly feel the important thing is not that we cannot live on hope alone, but that life is not worth living without it. If the story of Don Quixote means anything, it means that the spirit of life is just as important as its substance. What others may see as a barber's basin, you and I know is that glittering, legendary helmet.

MILTON AND ROSE FRIEDMAN
FREE TO CHOOSE

Economic freedom is an essential requisite for political freedom.

Few economists are as well known to the public as Milton and Rose Friedman, whose books, articles, and television programs have popularized free-market economics. Born in New York City, Milton Friedman (1912–) was educated at Rutgers University, the University of Chicago, and Columbia University. At the University of Chicago, he was the leading theorist of the Chicago school of economics, which criticized government intervention in the economy. Milton Friedman was awarded the Nobel Prize for Economic Science in 1976. His economic theories directly influenced the policies of President Ronald Reagan and British Prime Minister Margaret Thatcher.

Rose Director and Milton Friedman were married in 1938. Born in Poland, she attended Reed College and earned a degree at the University of Chicago. As a writer and economist, she collaborated with her husband in writing three best-selling explications of free-market economics, *Capitalism and Freedom* (1962), *Free to Choose* (1980), and *Tyranny of the Status Quo* (1984). The latter two were presented as television series of the same name on public television.

Free to Choose is excerpted here.

Ever since the first settlement of Europeans in the New World—at Jamestown in 1607 and at Plymouth in 1620—America has been a magnet for people seeking adventure, fleeing from tyranny, or simply trying to make a better life for themselves and their children.

An initial trickle swelled after the American Revolution and the establishment of the United States of America and became a flood in the nineteenth century, when millions of people streamed across the Atlantic, and a smaller number across the Pacific, driven by misery and tyranny, and attracted by the promise of freedom and affluence.

When they arrived, they did not find streets paved with gold; they did not find an easy life. They did find freedom and an opportunity to make the most of their talents. Through hard work, ingenuity, thrift, and luck, most of them succeeded in realizing enough of their hopes and dreams to encourage friends and relatives to join them.

The story of the United States is the story of an economic miracle and a political miracle that was made possible by the translation into practice of two sets of ideas—both, by a curious coincidence, formulated in documents published in the same year, 1776.

One set of ideas was embodied in *The Wealth of Nations,* the masterpiece that established the Scotsman Adam Smith as the father of modern economics. It analyzed the way in which a market system could combine the freedom of individuals to pursue their own objectives with the extensive cooperation and collaboration needed in the economic field to produce our food, our clothing, our housing. Adam Smith's key insight was that both parties to an exchange can benefit and that, *so long as cooperation is strictly voluntary,* no exchange will take place unless both parties do benefit. No external force, no coercion, no violation of freedom is necessary to produce cooperation among individuals all of whom can benefit. That is why, as Adam Smith put it, an individual who "intends only his own gain" is led by an invisible hand to promote an end which was no part of his intention. Nor is it always the worse for the society that it was no part of it. By pursuing his own interest he frequently promotes that of the society more effectually than when he really intends to promote it. "I have never known much good done by those who affected to trade for the public good."

The second set of ideas was embodied in the Declaration of Independence, drafted by Thomas Jefferson to express the general sense of his fellow countrymen. It proclaimed a new nation, the first in history established on the principle that every person is entitled to pursue his own values: "We hold these truths to be self-evident, that all men are created equal, that they are endowed by their Creator with certain unalienable Rights; that among these are Life, Liberty, and the pursuit of Happiness." . . .

Much of the history of the United States revolves about the attempt to translate the principles of the Declaration of Independence into practice—from the struggle over slavery, finally settled by a bloody civil war, to the subsequent attempt to promote equality of opportunity, to the more recent attempt to achieve equality of results.

Economic freedom is an essential requisite for political freedom. By enabling people to cooperate with one another without coercion or central direction, it reduces the area over which political power is exercised. In addition, by dispersing power, the free market provides an offset to whatever concentration of political power may arise. The combination of economic and political *power* in the same hands is a sure recipe for tyranny.

The combination of economic and political *freedom* produced a golden age in both Great Britain and the United States in the nineteenth century. The United States prospered even more than Britain. It started with a clean slate: fewer vestiges of class and status; fewer government restraints; a more fertile field for energy, drive, and innovation; and an empty continent to conquer.

The fecundity of freedom is demonstrated most dramatically and clearly in agriculture. When the Declaration of Independence was enacted, fewer than 3 million persons of European and African origin (i.e., omitting the native Indians) occupied a narrow fringe along the eastern coast. Agriculture was the main economic activity. It took nineteen out of twenty workers to feed the country's inhabitants and provide a surplus for export in exchange for foreign goods. Today it takes fewer than one out of twenty workers to feed the 220 million inhabitants and provide a surplus that makes the United States the largest single exporter of food in the world.

What produced this miracle? Clearly not central direction by government—nations like Russia and its satellites, mainland China, Yugoslavia, and India that today rely on central direction employ from one-quarter to one-half of

In October 1989, pro-abortion and anti-abortion demonstrators clashed in Tallahassee, Florida. The Supreme Court invalidated state abortion laws in 1973; however, in 1989, the Court ruled that some state restrictions were permissible, and the political fight moved to the state legislatures. The battle over abortion became one of the most contentious issues of the late twentieth century.

their workers in agriculture, yet frequently rely on U.S. agriculture to avoid mass starvation. During most of the period of rapid agricultural expansion in the United States the government played a negligible role. Land was made available—but it was land that had been unproductive before. After the middle of the nineteenth century land-grant colleges were established, and they disseminated information and technology through governmentally financed extension services. Unquestionably, however, the main source of the agricultural revolution was private initiative operating in a free market open to all —the shame of slavery only excepted. And the most rapid growth came after slavery was abolished. The millions of immigrants from all over

the world were free to work for themselves, as independent farmers or businessmen, or to work for others, at terms mutually agreed. They were free to experiment with new techniques —at their risk if the experiment failed, and to their profit if it succeeded. They got little assistance from government. Even more important, they encountered little interference from government. . . .

Ironically, the very success of economic and political freedom reduced its appeal to later thinkers. The narrowly limited government of the late nineteenth century possessed little concentrated power that endangered the ordinary man. The other side of that coin was that it possessed little power that would enable good people to do good. And in an imperfect world there were still many evils. Indeed, the very progress of society made the residual evils seem all the more objectionable. As always, people took the favorable developments for granted. They forgot the danger to freedom from a strong government. Instead, they were attracted by the good that a stronger government could achieve—if only government power were in the "right" hands.

These ideas began to influence government policy in Great Britain by the beginning of the twentieth century. They gained increasing acceptance among intellectuals in the United States but had little effect on government policy until the Great Depression of the early 1930s. . . . Government's responsibility for the depression was not recognized—either then or now. Instead, the depression was widely interpreted as a failure of free market capitalism. That myth led the public to join the intellectuals in a changed view of the relative responsibilities of individuals and government. Emphasis on the responsibility of the individual for his own fate was replaced by emphasis on the individual as a pawn buffeted by forces beyond his control. The view that government's role is to serve as an umpire to prevent individuals from coercing one another was replaced by the view that government's role is to serve as a parent charged with the duty of coercing some to aid others.

These views have dominated developments in the United States during the past half-century. They have led to a growth in government at all levels, as well as to a transfer of power from local government and local control to central government and central control. The government has increasingly undertaken the task of taking from some to give to others in the name of security and equality. . . .

The experience of recent years—slowing growth and declining productivity—raises a doubt whether private ingenuity can continue to overcome the deadening effects of government control if we continue to grant ever more power to government, to authorize a "new class" of civil servants to spend ever larger fractions of our income supposedly on our behalf. Sooner or later—and perhaps sooner than many of us expect—an ever bigger government would destroy both the prosperity that we owe to the free market and the human freedom proclaimed so eloquently in the Declaration of Independence.

We have not yet reached the point of no return. We are still free as a people to choose whether we shall continue speeding down the "road of serfdom," as Friedrich Hayek entitled his profound and influential book, or whether we shall set tighter limits on government and rely more heavily on voluntary cooperation among free individuals to achieve our several objectives. Will our golden age come to an end in a relapse into the tyranny and misery that has always been, and remains today, the state of most of mankind? Or shall we have the wisdom, the foresight, and the courage to change our course, to learn from experience, and to benefit from a "rebirth of freedom"? . . .

 ## A NATION AT RISK

The educational foundations of our society are presently being eroded by a rising tide of mediocrity that threatens our very future as a Nation and a people.

In the late 1970s and early 1980s, study after study described the lamentable performance of American students on tests of mathematics, science, and other academic areas. But nothing captured the public's attention like *A Nation at Risk*, the 1983 report of the National Commission on Excellence in Education. Sponsored by President Ronald

Reagan and appointed by Secretary of Education Terrell Bell, the commission documented the fall of academic standards and the need to improve the quality of teaching and learning. Its findings were featured on national television, in the daily press, and in the newsmagazines. The commission's report encouraged many state legislatures and local school boards to take action to improve their schools.

Our nation is at risk. Our once unchallenged preeminence in commerce, industry, science, and technological innovation is being overtaken by competitors throughout the world. This report is concerned with only one of the many causes and dimensions of the problem, but it is the one that undergirds American prosperity, security, and civility. We report to the American people that while we can take justifiable pride in what our schools and colleges have historically accomplished and contributed to the United States and the well-being of its people, the educational foundations of our society are presently being eroded by a rising tide of mediocrity that threatens our very future as a Nation and a people. What was unimaginable a generation ago has begun to occur—others are matching and surpassing our educational attainments.

If an unfriendly foreign power had attempted to impose on America the mediocre educational performance that exists today, we might well have viewed it as an act of war. As it stands, we have allowed this to happen to ourselves. We have even squandered the gains in student achievement made in the wake of the Sputnik challenge. Moreover, we have dismantled essential support systems which helped make those gains possible. We have, in effect, been committing an act of unthinking, unilateral educational disarmament.

Our society and its educational institutions seem to have lost sight of the basic purposes of schooling, and of the high expectations and disciplined effort needed to attain them. This report, the result of 18 months of study, seeks to generate reform of our educational system in fundamental ways and to renew the Nation's commitment to schools and colleges of high quality throughout the length and breadth of our land.

That we have compromised this commitment is, upon reflection, hardly surprising, given the multitude of often conflicting demands we have placed on our Nation's schools and colleges. They are routinely called on to provide solutions to personal, social, and political problems that the home and other institutions either will not or cannot resolve. We must understand that these demands on our schools and colleges often exact an educational cost as well as a financial one. . . .

History is not kind to idlers. The time is long past when America's destiny was assured simply by an abundance of national resources and inexhaustible human enthusiasm, and by our relative isolation from the malignant problems of older civilizations. The world is indeed one global village. We live among determined, well-educated, and strongly motivated competitors. We compete with them for international standing and markets, not only with products but also with the ideas of our laboratories and neighborhood workshops. America's position in the world may once have been reasonably secure with only a few exceptionally well-trained men and women. It is no longer.

The risk is not only that the Japanese make automobiles more efficiently than Americans and have government subsidies for development and export. It is not just that the South Koreans recently built the world's most efficient steel mill, or that American machine tools, once the pride of the world, are being displaced by German products. It is also that these developments signify a redistribution of trained capability throughout the globe. Knowledge, learning, information, and skilled intelligence are the new raw materials of international commerce and are today spreading throughout the world as vigorously as miracle drugs, synthetic fertilizers, and blue jeans did earlier. If only to keep and improve on the slim competitive edge we still retain in world markets, we must dedicate ourselves to the reform of our educational system for the benefit of all—old and young alike, affluent and poor, majority and minority. Learning is the indispensable investment required for success in the "information age" we are entering.

Our concern, however, goes well beyond matters such as industry and commerce. It also includes the intellectual, moral, and spiritual strengths of our people which knit together the very fabric of our society. The people of the United States need to know that individuals in our society who do not possess the levels of skill, literacy, and training essential to this new era will be effectively disenfranchised, not simply from the material rewards that accompany competent performance, but also from the chance to participate fully in our national life. A high level of shared education is essential to a free, democratic society and to the fostering of a common culture, especially in a country that prides itself on pluralism and individual freedom.

For our country to function, citizens must be able to reach some common understandings on complex issues, often on short notice and on the basis of conflicting or incomplete evidence. Education helps form these common understandings, a point Thomas Jefferson made long ago in his justly famous dictum:

> I know no safe depository of the ultimate powers of the society but the people themselves; and if we think them not enlightened enough to exercise their control with a wholesome discretion, the remedy is not to take it from them but to inform their discretion.

Part of what is at risk is the promise first made on this continent: All, regardless of race or class or economic status, are entitled to a fair chance and to the tools for developing their individual powers of mind and spirit to the utmost. This promise means that all children by virtue of their own efforts, competently guided, can hope to attain the mature and informed judgment needed to secure gainful employment and to manage their own lives, thereby serving not only their own interests but also the progress of society itself. . . .

GEORGE J. MITCHELL

THE IRAN-CONTRA HEARINGS

Although He is regularly asked to do so, God does not take sides in American politics.

Two foreign policy issues frustrated the Reagan administration. First, the administration was unable to gain the release of American hostages in the Middle East; second, it wanted to help the contras, the opponents of the leftist Sandinista regime in Nicaragua. The administration could not pay ransom for the hostages, since it had publicly foresworn negotiations with terrorists; and it could not openly support the contras, since Congress had halted funding for them in 1984. So a covert scheme was developed to sell arms to Iran, in the hopes that Iran would use its leverage to release American hostages, and to direct the proceeds from the arms sales to aid the contras.

The person who symbolized the Iran-contra affair was Lieutenant-Colonel Oliver North, who administered the operation at the National Security Council. When he testified at congressional hearings in 1987, he defended his actions as those of a soldier who acted from patriotic motives.

On July 13, 1987, Senator George J. Mitchell (1933—   ) took issue with Colonel North. With the mass media and national attention focused on the hearings, Senator Mitchell gave the American people a civics lecture.

Colonel North, you talked here often and eloquently about the need for a democratic outcome in Nicaragua. There is no disagreement on that. There is disagreement over how best to achieve that objective.

Many Americans agree with the President's policy. Many do not.

Many patriotic Americans, strongly anti-Communist, believe there's a better way to contain the Sandinistas, to bring about a democratic outcome in Nicaragua, and to bring peace to Central America.

And many patriotic Americans are concerned that in the pursuit of democracy abroad, we not compromise it in any way here at home.

You and others have urged consistency in our policies. You said that if we are not consistent, our allies and other nations will question our reliability.

That's a real concern. But, if it's bad to change policies, it's worse to have two different policies at the same time, one public policy and an opposite policy in private.

It's difficult to conceive of a greater inconsistency than that. It's hard to imagine anything that would give our allies more cause to consider us unreliable than that we say one thing in public and secretly do another.

And that's exactly what was done when arms were sold to Iran, and those arms were swapped for hostages.

Now, you've talked a lot about patriotism and the love of our country.

Most nations derive from a single tribe or a single race. They practice a single religion. Common racial, ethnic, and religious heritages are the glue of nationhood for many.

The United States is different. We have all races, all religions, a limited common heritage. The glue of nationhood for us is the American ideal of individual liberty and equal justice.

The rule of law is critical in our society. The law is the great equalizer, because in America everybody is equal before the law.

We must never allow the end to justify the means where the law is concerned. However important and noble an objective—and surely democracy abroad is important and noble—it cannot be achieved at the expense of the rule of law in our country.

You talked about your background and it was really very compelling. It's obviously one of the reasons why the American people are attracted to you.

Let me tell you a story from my background.

Before I entered the Senate I had the great honor of serving as a Federal Judge. In that position I had great power. The one I most enjoyed exercising was the power to make people American citizens.

From time to time I presided at what we call naturalization ceremonies. They are citizenship ceremonies.

People came from all over the world, risked their lives, sometimes left their families and fortunes behind to come here. They had gone through the required procedures and I, in the final act, administered to them the oath of allegiance to the United States and I made them American citizens.

To this moment—to this moment it was the most exciting thing I have ever done in my life.

The ceremonies were always moving for me because my mother was an immigrant and my father was the orphan son of immigrants. Neither of them had any education and they worked at very menial tasks in our society. But because of opportunity and equal justice under law in America, I sit here today a United States senator.

After every one of these ceremonies, I made it a point to speak to these new Americans. I asked them why they came, how they came to this country. Their stories, each of them, were inspiring. I think you would be interested and moved by them, given the views you have expressed on this country.

When I asked them why they came they said several things, mostly two. The first is that "We came because here in America everyone has a chance, an opportunity." They also said over and over again, particularly those from totalitarian societies, "We came here because in America you can criticize the government without looking over your shoulder." Here we have freedom to disagree with our government.

You have addressed several pleas to this Committee, none more forceful than when you asked that the Congress not cut off aid to the Contras, for the love of God and for the love of country.

Now I address a plea to you.

Of your qualities which the American people find compelling, none is more compelling than your obvious devotion to our country. Please remember that others share that devotion. And recognize that it is possible for an American to disagree with you on aid to the Contras, and still love God and still love this country as much as you do.

Although He is regularly asked to do so, God does not take sides in American politics.

And, in America, disagreement with the policies of the government is not evidence of a lack of patriotism. I want to repeat that. In America, disagreement with policies of the government is not evidence of a lack of patriotism. Indeed, it's the very fact that we can openly disagree with the government without fear of reprisal that is the essence of our freedom, and will keep us free.

I have one final plea. Debate this issue forcefully and vigorously, as you have and as you surely will. But, please, do it in a way that respects the patriotism and the motives of those who disagree with you, as you would have them respect yours.

RONALD REAGAN
SPEECH AT MOSCOW STATE UNIVERSITY

Progress is not foreordained. The key is freedom—freedom of thought, freedom of information, freedom of communication.

Ronald Reagan (1911–   ) was elected President of the United States in 1980. His election signaled the triumph of a strongly conservative tide in the 1980s. Born in Illinois, Reagan was a movie star before he entered politics and was elected governor of California.

Throughout his political career, Ronald Reagan expressed his repugnance for Communism as a system that was politically repressive and economically stagnant. Soviet-American relations changed abruptly for the better after Mikhail Gorbachev's ascension to power. Gorbachev initiated sweeping political and economic changes in Soviet life, which contributed to the collapse of Communist domination of the nations of Eastern Europe in 1989.

In this time of historic change, Gorbachev invited Reagan to visit the Soviet Union. One of the high points of Reagan's trip occurred when he addressed the students at Moscow State University on May 31, 1988. There, standing in front of a portrait of Lenin, Reagan described the spread of the global democratic revolution and the power of the idea of freedom in an age of instant communication.

. . . Standing here before a mural of your revolution, I want to talk about a very different revolution that is taking place right now, quietly sweeping the globe, without bloodshed or conflict. Its effects are peaceful, but they will fundamentally alter our world, shatter old assumptions, and reshape our lives.

It's easy to underestimate because it's not accompanied by banners or fanfare. It has been called the technological or information revolution, and as its emblem, one might take the tiny silicon chip—no bigger than a fingerprint. One of these chips has more computing power than a roomful of old-style computers.

As part of an exchange program, we now have an exhibition touring your country that shows how information technology is transforming our lives—replacing manual labor with robots, forecasting weather for farmers, or mapping the genetic code of DNA for medical researchers. These microcomputers today aid the design of everything from houses to cars to spacecraft—they even design better and faster computers. They can translate English into Russian or enable the blind to read—or help Michael Jackson produce on one synthesizer the sounds of a whole orchestra. Linked by a network of satellites and fiber-optic cables, one individual with a desktop computer and a telephone commands resources unavailable to the largest governments just a few years ago.

Like a chrysalis, we're emerging from the economy of the Industrial Revolution—an economy confined to and limited by the Earth's physical resources—into . . . an era in which there are no bounds on human imagination and the freedom to create is the most precious natural resource.

Think of that little computer chip. Its value isn't in the sand from which it is made, but in the microscopic architecture designed into it by ingenious human minds. Or take the example of the satellite relaying this broadcast around the world, which replaces thousands of tons of copper mined from the Earth and molded into wire.

In the new economy, human invention increasingly makes physical resources obsolete. We're breaking through the material conditions of existence to a world where man creates his own destiny. Even as we explore the most advanced reaches of science, we're returning to the age-old wisdom of our culture, a wisdom contained in the book of Genesis in the Bible: In the beginning was the spirit, and it was from this spirit that the material abundance of creation issued forth.

But progress is not foreordained. The key is freedom—freedom of thought, freedom of information, freedom of communication. The renowned scientist, scholar, and founding father of this University, Mikhail Lomonosov, knew that. "It is common knowledge," he said, "that the achievements of science are considerable and rapid, particularly once the yoke of slavery is cast off and replaced by the freedom of philosophy." . . .

The explorers of the modern era are the entrepreneurs, men with vision, with the courage to take risks and faith enough to brave the unknown. These entrepreneurs and their small enterprises are responsible for almost all the economic growth in the United States. They are the prime movers of the technological revolution. In fact, one of the largest personal computer firms in the United States was started by two college students, no older than you, in the garage behind their home.

Some people, even in my own country, look at the riot of experiment that is the free market and see only waste. What of all the entrepreneurs that fail? Well, many do, particularly the successful ones. Often several times. And if you ask them the secret of their success, they'll tell you, it's all that they learned in their struggles along the way—yes, it's what they learned from failing. Like an athlete in competition, or a scholar in pursuit of the truth, experience is the greatest teacher.

And that's why it's so hard for government planners, no matter how sophisticated, to ever substitute for millions of individuals working night and day to make their dreams come true....

We Americans make no secret of our belief in freedom. In fact, it's something of a national pastime. Every four years the American people choose a new president, and 1988 is one of those years. At one point there were 13 major candidates running in the two major parties, not to mention all the others, including the Socialist and Libertarian candidates—all trying to get my job.

About 1,000 local television stations, 8,500 radio stations, and 1,700 daily newspapers, each one an independent, private enterprise, fiercely independent of the government, report on the candidates, grill them in interviews, and bring them together for debates. In the end, the people vote—they decide who will be the next president.

But freedom doesn't begin or end with elections. Go to any American town, to take just an example, and you'll see dozens of churches, representing many different beliefs—in many places synagogues and mosques—and you'll see families of every conceivable nationality, worshipping together.

Go into any schoolroom, and there you will see children being taught the Declaration of Independence, that they are endowed by their Creator with certain inalienable rights—among them life, liberty, and the pursuit of happiness —that no government can justly deny—the guarantees in their Constitution for freedom of speech, freedom of assembly, and freedom of religion.

Go into any courtroom and there will preside an independent judge, beholden to no government power. There every defendant has the right to a trial by a jury of his peers, usually 12 men and women—common citizens, they are the ones, the only ones, who weigh the evidence and decide on guilt or innocence. In that court, the accused is innocent until proven guilty, and the word of a policeman, or any official, has no greater legal standing than the word of the accused.

Go to any university campus, and there you'll find an open, sometimes heated discussion of the problems in American society and what can be done to correct them. Turn on the television, and you'll see the legislature conducting the business of government right there before the camera, debating and voting on the legislation that will become the law of the land. March in any demonstration, and there are many of them—the people's right of assembly is guaranteed in the Constitution and protected by the police. Go into any union hall, where the members know their right to strike is protected by law....

But freedom is even more than this: Freedom is the right to question, and change the established way of doing things. It is the continuing revolution of the marketplace. It is the understanding that allows us to recognize shortcomings and seek solutions. It is the right to put forth an idea, scoffed at by the experts, and watch it catch fire among the people. It is the right to follow your dream, to stick to your conscience, even if you're the only one in a sea of doubters.

Freedom is the recognition that no single person, no single authority or government has a monopoly on the truth, but that every individual life is infinitely precious, that every one of us put on this earth has been put here for a reason and has something to offer....

Democracy is less a system of government than it is a system to keep government limited, unintrusive: A system of constraints on power to keep politics and government secondary to the important things in life, the true sources of value found only in family and faith.

But I hope you know I go on about these things not simply to extol the virtues of my own country, but to speak to the true greatness of the heart and soul of your land. Who, after all, needs to tell the land of Dostoevsky about the quest for truth, the home of Kandinsky and Scriabin about imagination, the rich and noble culture of the Uzbek man of letters, Alisher Navio, about beauty and heart?

The great culture of your diverse land speaks

with a glowing passion to all humanity. Let me cite one of the most eloquent contemporary passages on human freedom. It comes, not from the literature of America, but from this country, from one of the greatest writers of the twentieth century, Boris Pasternak, in the novel *Dr. Zhivago*. He writes, "I think that if the beast who sleeps in man could be held down by threats—any kind of threat, whether of jail or of retribution after death—then the highest emblem of humanity would be the lion tamer in the circus with his whip, not the prophet who sacrificed himself. But this is just the point—what has for centuries raised man above the beast is not the cudgel, but an inward music—the irresistible power of unarmed truth."

The irresistible power of unarmed truth. Today the world looks expectantly to signs of change, steps toward greater freedom in the Soviet Union. . . .

Your generation is living in one of the most exciting, hopeful times in Soviet history. It is a time when the first breath of freedom stirs the air and the heart beats to the accelerated rhythm of hope, when the accumulated spiritual energies of a long silence yearn to break free.

I am reminded of the famous passage near the end of Gogol's *Dead Souls.* Comparing his nation to a speeding troika, Gogol asks what will be its destination. But he writes, "There was no answer save the bell pouring forth marvelous sound."

We do not know what the conclusion of this journey will be, but we're hopeful that the promise of reform will be fulfilled. In this Moscow spring, this May 1988, we may be allowed that hope—that freedom, like the fresh green sapling planted over Tolstoi's grave, will blossom forth at last in the rich fertile soil of your people and culture. We may be allowed to hope that the marvelous sound of a new openness will keep rising through, ringing through, leading to a new world of reconciliation, friendship, and peace. . . .

JESSE JACKSON

SPEECH TO THE DEMOCRATIC NATIONAL CONVENTION

Common ground!

Jesse Jackson (1941–   ) was born in Greenville, South Carolina, and he grew up in poverty. He attended the University of Illinois, then transferred to the historically black Agricultural and Technical College of North Carolina. He studied next at the Chicago Theological Seminary, and was ordained a Baptist minister in 1968.

During his undergraduate years, Jackson marched with Martin Luther King, Jr., in Selma, Alabama, and became associated with the Southern Christian Leadership Conference. A charismatic speaker, Jackson often urged teenagers to study and work hard and believe in themselves.

Jackson became active in electoral politics in the 1980s. He directed a voter registration drive in Chicago that helped to elect the city's first black mayor. Jackson ran for the Democratic presidential nomination in 1984, the first black candidate to launch a serious bid for the presidency. He campaigned again for the Democratic nomination in 1988, finishing second to Massachusetts governor Michael Dukakis. Jackson's speech to the Democratic National Convention in Atlanta, Georgia, on July 20, 1988, was the emotional high point of the campaign, for it signaled the coming-of-age of blacks as a major force in American politics.

. . . We meet tonight at a crossroads, a point of decision.

Shall we expand, be inclusive, find unity and power; or suffer division and impotence?

We come to Atlanta, the cradle of the old south, the crucible of the new South.

Tonight there is a sense of celebration because we are moved, fundamentally moved, from racial battlegrounds by law, to economic common ground, tomorrow we will challenge to move to higher ground.

Common ground!

Think of Jerusalem—the intersection where many trails met. A small village that became the birthplace for three great religions—Judaism, Christianity and Islam.

Why was this village so blessed? Because it provided a crossroads where different people met, different cultures, and different civilizations could meet and find common ground.

When people come together, flowers always flourish and the air is rich with the aroma of a new spring.

Take New York, the dynamic metropolis. What makes New York so special?

It is the invitation of the Statue of Liberty—give me your tired, your poor, your huddled masses who yearn to breathe free.

Not restricted to English only.

Many people, many cultures, many languages—with one thing in common, they yearn to breathe free. . . .

Common ground!

That is the challenge to our party tonight.

Left wing. Right wing. Progress will not come through boundless liberalism nor static conservatism, but at the critical mass of mutual survival. It takes two wings to fly.

Whether you're a hawk or a dove, you're just a bird living in the same environment, in the same world.

The Bible teaches that when lions and lambs lie down together, none will be afraid and there will be peace in the valley. It sounds impossible. Lions eat lambs. Lambs sensibly flee from lions. But even lions and lambs find common ground. Why?

Because neither lions nor lambs want the forest to catch on fire. Neither lions nor lambs want acid rain to fall. Neither lions nor lambs can survive nuclear war. If lions and lambs can find common ground, surely we can as well, as civilized people.

The only time that we win is when we come together. . . .

Common ground.

America's not a blanket woven from one thread, one color, one cloth. When I was a child growing up in Greenville, S.C., and grandmother could not afford a blanket, she didn't complain and we did not freeze. Instead, she took pieces of old cloth—patches, wool, silk, gabardine, crockersack on the patches—barely good enough to wipe off your shoes with.

But they didn't stay that way very long. With sturdy hands and a strong cord, she sewed them together into a quilt, a thing of beauty and power and culture.

Now, Democrats, we must build such a quilt. Farmers, you seek fair prices and you are right, but you cannot stand alone. Your patch is not big enough. Workers, you fight for fair wages. You are right. But your patch is not big enough. Women, you seek comparable worth and pay equity. You are right. But your patch is not big enough. Women, mothers, who seek Head Start and day care and pre-natal care on the front side of life, rather than jail care and welfare on the back side of life, you're right, but your patch is not big enough.

Students, you seek scholarships. You are right. But your patch is not big enough. Blacks and Hispanics, when we fight for civil rights, we are right, but our patch is not big enough. Gays and lesbians, when you fight against discrimination and a cure for AIDS, you are right, but your patch is not big enough. Conservatives and progressives, when you fight for what you believe, right-wing, left-wing, hawk, dove—you are right, from your point of view, but your point of view is not enough.

But don't despair. Be as wise as my grandmama. Pool the patches and the pieces together, bound by a common thread. When we form a great quilt of unity and common ground we'll have the power to bring about health care and housing and jobs and education and hope to our nation.

We the people can win. We stand at the end of a long dark night of reaction. We stand tonight united in a commitment to a new direction. For almost eight years, we've been led by those who view social good coming from private interest, who viewed public life as a means to increase private wealth. They have been prepared to sacrifice the common good of the many to satisfy the private interest and the wealth of a few. We believe in a government that's a tool of our democracy in service to the public, not an instrument of the aristocracy in search of private wealth. . . .

I just want to take common sense to high

A Hispanic community gathering in Miami. The number of Hispanic Americans grew substantially during the 1970s and 1980s because of increased immigration from Latin America, especially from Cuba, Puerto Rico, and Mexico.

places. We're spending $150 billion a year defending Europe and Japan 43 years after the war is over. We have more troops in Europe tonight than we had seven years ago, yet the threat of war is ever more remote. Germany and Japan are now creditor nations—that means they've got a surplus. We are a debtor nation—it means we are in debt.

Let them share more of the burden of their own defense—use some of that money to build decent housing!

Use some of that money to educate our children!

Use some of that money for long-term health care!

Use some of that money to wipe out these slums and put America back to work! . . .

Whether white, black or brown, the hungry baby's belly turned inside out is the same color. Call it pain. Call it hurt. Call it agony. Most poor people are not on welfare.

Some of them are illiterate and can't read the want-ad sections. And when they can, they can't find a job that matches their address. They work hard every day, I know. I lived amongst them. I'm one of them.

I know they work. I'm a witness. They catch the early bus. They work every day. They raise other people's children. They work every day. They clean the streets. They work every day. They drive vans with cabs. They work every day. They change the beds you slept in these hotels last night and can't get a union contract. They work every day.

No more. They're not lazy. Someone must defend them because it's right, and they cannot speak for themselves. They work in hospitals. I know they do. They wipe the bodies of those who are sick with fever and pain. They empty their bedpans. They clean out their commode. No job is beneath them, and yet when they get sick, they cannot lie in the bed they made up every day. America, that is not right. We are a better nation than that. . . .

And then, for our children, young America, hold your head high now. We can win. We must not lose you to drugs and violence, premature pregnancy, suicide, cynicism, pessimism and despair. We can win.

Wherever you are tonight, I challenge you to hope and to dream. Don't submerge your dreams. Exercise above all else, even on drugs, dream of the day you're drug-free. Even in the gutter, dream of the day that you'll be up on your feet again. You must never stop dreaming. Face reality, yes. But don't stop with the way things are; dream of things as they ought to be. Dream. Face pain, but love, hope, faith, and dreams will help you rise above the pain.

Use hope and imagination as weapons of survival and progress, but you keep on dreaming, young America. Dream of peace. Peace is rational and reasonable. War is irrational in this age and unwinnable.

Dream of teachers who teach for life and not for a living. Dream of doctors who are concerned more about public health than private wealth. Dream of lawyers more concerned about justice than a judgeship. Dream of preachers who are concerned more about prophecy than profiteering. Dream on the high road of sound values. . . .

Don't surrender and don't give up. Why can I challenge you this way? Jesse Jackson, you don't understand my situation. You be on television. You don't understand. I see you with the big people. You don't understand my situation. I understand. You're seeing me on TV but you don't know the me that makes me, me. They wonder why does Jesse run, because they see me running for the White House. They don't see the house I'm running from.

I have a story. I wasn't always on television. Writers were not always outside my door. When I was born late one afternoon, October 8th, in Greenville, S.C., no writers asked my mother her name. Nobody chose to write down our address. My mama was not supposed to make it. And I was not supposed to make it. You see, I was born to a teen-age mother who was born to a teen-age mother.

I understand. I know abandonment and people being mean to you, and saying you're nothing and nobody, and can never be anything. I understand. Jesse Jackson is my third name. I'm adopted. When I had no name, my grandmother gave me her name. My name was Jesse Burns until I was 12. So I wouldn't have a blank space, she gave me a name to hold me over. I understand when nobody knows your name. I understand when you have no name. I understand.

I wasn't born in the hospital. Mama didn't have insurance. I was born in the bed at home. I really do understand. Born in a three-room-house, bathroom in the backyard, slop jar by the bed, no hot and cold running water. I understand. Wallpaper used for decoration? No. For a windbreaker. I understand. I'm a working person's person, that's why I understand you whether you're black or white.

I understand work. I was not born with a silver spoon in my mouth. I had a shovel programmed for my hand. My mother, a working woman. So many days she went to work early with runs in her stockings. She knew better, but she wore runs in her stockings so that my brother and I could have matching socks and not be laughed at at school.

I understand. At 3 o'clock on Thanksgiving Day we couldn't eat turkey because mama was preparing someone else's turkey at 3 o'clock. We had to play football to entertain ourselves and then around 6 o'clock she would get off the Alta Vista bus; then we would bring up the leftovers and eat our turkey—leftovers, the carcass, the cranberries around 8 o'clock at night. I really do understand.

Every one of these funny labels they put on you, those of you who are watching this broadcast tonight in the projects, on the corners, I understand. Call you outcast, low down, you can't make it, you're nothing, you're from nobody, subclass, underclass—when you see Jesse Jackson, when my name goes in nomination, your name goes in nomination.

I was born in the slum, but the slum was not born in me. And it wasn't born in you, and you can make it. Wherever you are tonight you can make it. Hold your head high, stick your chest out. You can make it. It gets dark sometimes, but the morning comes. Don't you surrender. Suffering breeds character. Character breeds faith. In the end faith will not disappoint.

You must not surrender. You may or may not get there, but just know that you're qualified and you hold on and hold out. We must never surrender. America will get better and better. Keep hope alive. Keep hope alive. Keep hope alive. On tomorrow night and beyond, keep hope alive.

I love you very much. I love you very much.

TATO LAVIERA
AmeRícan

Tato Laviera (1950–   ), a poet and playwright, was born in Puerto Rico. He arrived in New York City in 1960 and spent his formative years in the urban barrio. His first book of poetry, *La Carreta Made a U-Turn,* was published in 1979, and he quickly emerged as an accomplished poet of the Nuyorican school, with a distinctive voice. He has published several other collections of poetry.

"AmeRícan" is the title poem of a collection by the same name, published in 1985. In the title poem, Laviera affirms a vision of "a new generation," a generation for whom the possibilities of reconciliation and pluralism within the American context are real.

Laviera first read "AmeRícan" at Hunter College in New York City in March 1984.

We gave birth to a new generation,
AmeRícan, broader than lost gold
never touched, hidden inside the
puerto rican mountains.

we gave birth to a new generation,
AmeRícan, it includes everything
imaginable you-name-it-we-got-it
society.

we gave birth to a new generation,
AmeRícan salutes all folklores,
european, indian, black, spanish,
and anything else compatible:

AmeRícan singing to composer pedro flores'
          palm trees high up in the universal
          sky!

AmeRícan, sweet soft spanish danzas gypsies
           moving lyrics la española
           cascabelling presence always
           singing at our side!

AmeRícan, beating jíbaro modern troubadours
           crying guitars romantic continental
           bolero love songs!

AmeRícan, across forth and across back back
           across and forth back forth across
           and back and forth our trips are
           walking bridges! it all dissolved
           into itself, the attempt was truly
           made, the attempt was truly
           absorbed, digested, we spit out the
           poison, we spit out the malice, we
           stand, affirmative in action, to
           reproduce a broader answer to the
           marginality that gobbled us up
           abruptly!

AmeRícan, walking plena-rhythms in new york,
           strutting beautifully alert, alive,
           many turning eyes wondering,
           admiring!

AmeRícan, defining myself my own way any
           way many ways Am e Rícan, with
           the big R and the accent on the í!

AmeRícan, like the soul gliding talk of gospel
           boogie music!

AmeRícan, speaking new words in spanglish
           tenements, fast tongue moving
           street corner "que corta" talk being
           invented at the insistence of a
           smile!

AmeRícan, abounding inside so many ethnic
           english people, and out of
           humanity, we blend and mix all
           that is good!

AmeRícan, integrating in new york and
           defining our own destino, our own
           way of life,

AmeRícan, defining the new america, humane
           america, admired america, loved
           america, harmonious america, the
           world in peace, our energies
           collectively invested to find other
           civilizations, to touch God, further
           and further, to dwell in the spirit of
           divinity!

AmeRícan, yes, for now, for i love this, my
           second land, and i dream to take
           the accent from the altercation, and
           be proud to call myself american,
           in the u.s. sense of the word,
           AmeRícan, America!

THEODORE H. WHITE

THE AMERICAN IDEA

Americans are a nation born of an idea; not the place, but the idea, created the United States Government.

Theodore H. White (1915–1986) was one of the most accomplished writers of his generation. Journalist, essayist, and historian, White excelled as a storyteller. Born in Boston, he grew up in poverty during the Depression. He attended Harvard College on a scholarship, then began his career in China as a journalist for *Time* magazine. After writing two novels, he turned to writing about presidential campaigns in a novelistic fashion. White's *The Making of the President, 1960* won the Pulitzer Prize and launched him on a series of similarly titled books about the presidential elections of 1964, 1968, and 1972.

White had a passionate love for his country and for the people who labored to make the democratic process work. When he died in May 1986, he was writing an article for the *New York Times Magazine* to commemorate the two-hundred-tenth birthday of the nation. What follows is an excerpt from his last article.

The idea was there at the very beginning, well before Thomas Jefferson put it into words—and the idea rang the call.

Jefferson himself could not have imagined the reach of his call across the world in time to come when he wrote:

"We hold these truths to be self-evident, that all men are created equal, that they are endowed by their Creator with certain unalienable rights, that among these are life, liberty and the pursuit of happiness."

But over the next two centuries the call would reach the potato patches of Ireland, the ghettoes of Europe, the paddyfields of China, stirring farmers to leave their lands and townsmen their trades and thus unsettling all traditional civilizations.

It is the call from Thomas Jefferson, embodied in the great statue that looks down the Narrows of New York Harbor, and in the immigrants who answered the call, that we now celebrate.

Some of the first European Americans had come to the new continent to worship God in their own way, others to seek their fortunes. But over a century-and-a-half, the new world changed those Europeans, above all the Englishmen who had come to North America. Neither King nor Court nor church could stretch over the ocean to the wild continent. To survive, the first emigrants had to learn to govern themselves. But the freedom of the wilderness whetted their appetites for more freedoms. By the time Jefferson drafted his call, men were in the field fighting for those new-learned freedoms, killing and being killed by English soldiers, the best-trained troops in the world, supplied by the world's greatest navy. Only something worth dying for could unite American volunteers and keep them in the field—a stated cause, a flag, a nation they could call their own .

When, on the Fourth of July, 1776, the colonial leaders who had been meeting as a Continental Congress in Philadelphia voted to approve Jefferson's Declaration of Independence, it was not puffed-up rhetoric for them to pledge to each other "our lives, our fortunes and our sacred honor." Unless their new "United States of America" won the war, the Congressmen would be judged traitors as relentlessly as would the irregulars-under-arms in the field. And all knew what English law allowed in the case of a traitor. The victim could be partly strangled; drawn, or disemboweled, while still alive, his entrails then burned and his body quartered.

The new Americans were tough men fighting for a very tough idea. How they won their battles is a story for the schoolbooks, studied by scholars, wrapped in myths by historians and poets.

But what is most important is the story of the idea that made them into a nation, the idea that had an explosive power undreamed of in 1776.

All other nations had come into being among people whose families had lived for time out of mind on the same land where they were born. Englishmen are English, Frenchmen are French, Chinese are Chinese, while their governments come and go; their national states can be torn apart and remade without losing their nationhood. But Americans are a nation born of an idea; not the place, but the idea, created the United States Government.

A first-grade class in an American school—the citizens, scientists, entrepreneurs, artists, executives, lawyers, teachers, journalists, engineers, doctors, workers, and leaders of the twenty-first century.

★ BIBLIOGRAPHY

Abraham Lincoln: Selected Speeches, Messages, and Letters, ed. T. Harry Williams (New York: Holt, Rinehart and Winston, 1957).

AFL-CIO Song Book (Washington, D.C.: AFL-CIO, 1974).

The American Intellectual Tradition, ed. David A. Hollinger and Charles Capper (New York: Oxford University Press, 1989).

American Poetry and Prose, ed. Norman Foerster (Boston: Houghton Mifflin, 1925).

An American Primer, ed. Daniel Boorstin (Chicago: University of Chicago Press, 1968).

American Public Addresses: 1740–1952, ed. A. Craig Baird (New York: McGraw-Hill, 1952).

American Writers: A Collection of Literary Biographies, ed. Leonard Unger (New York: Scribner's, 1974).

American Writers to 1900, ed. James Vinson (Chicago: St. James Press, 1983).

The Annals of America, 22 vols. (Chicago: Encyclopaedia Britannica, 1976).

The ASCAP Biographical Dictionary of Composers, Authors and Publishers, ed. Lynn Farnol Group, Inc. (ASCAP, 1966).

Benét's Reader's Encyclopedia, third ed. (New York: Harper & Row, 1987).

The Best Loved Poems of the American People, selected by Hazel Fellman (Garden City, N.Y.: Doubleday, 1936).

Black Leaders of the Twentieth Century, ed. John Hope Franklin and August Meier (Urbana: University of Illinois Press, 1982).

The Black Poets, ed. Dudley Randall (New York: Bantam, 1971).

Black Protest: History, Documents and Analyses, ed. Joanne Grant (New York: Fawcett, 1968).

The Book of Abigail and John ed. L. H. Butterfield, Marc Friedlaender, and Mary-Jo Kline (Cambridge, Mass.: Harvard University Press, 1975).

The Book of Negro Folklore, ed. Langston Hughes and Arna Bontemps (New York: Dodd, Mead, 1983).

Booth, Mark W., *American Popular Music: A Reference Guide* (Westport, Conn.: Greenwood Press, 1983).

Borinquen: An Anthology of Puerto Rican Literature, ed. María Teres Babín and Stan Steiner (New York: Knopf, 1974).

The Burden and the Glory, ed. Allan Nevins (New York: Harper & Row, 1964).

Calafia: The California Poetry, Ishmael Reed, project director (Berkeley, Calif.: Y'Bird Books, 1979).

The Cambridge Handbook of American Literature, ed. Jack Salzman (New York: Cambridge University Press, 1986).

Carson, Rachel, *Silent Spring* (Boston: Houghton Mifflin, 1962).

Cervantes, Lorna Dee, *Emplumada* (Pittsburgh: University of Pittsburgh Press, 1981).

Columbia Literary History of the United States, ed. Emory Elliott (New York: Columbia University Press, 1988).

The Complete Poetical Works of James Whitcomb Riley (New York: Grosset and Dunlap, 1937).

Cullen, Countee, *On These I Stand* (New York: Harper & Bros., 1947).

The Democratic Spirit, ed. Bernard Smith (New York: Knopf, 1941).

Dictionary of American Negro Biography, ed. Rayford W. Logan and Michael R. Winston (New York: Norton, 1982).

A Documentary History of the Negro People in the United States, ed. Herbert Aptheker (New York: Citadel Press, 1968).

Documents of American History, ed. Henry Steele Commager (Englewood Cliffs, N.J.: Prentice-Hall, 1973).

Dylan, Bob, *Lyrics, 1962–1985* (New York: Knopf, 1985).

Early Negro American Writers, ed. Benjamin Brawley (New York: Dover, 1970).

The Educated Woman in America, ed. Barbara M. Cross (New York: Teachers College Press, 1965).

Emerson's Essays, introduction by Irwin Edman (New York: Thomas Y. Crowell, 1951.)

Emurian, Ernest K., *Living Stories of Favorite Songs* (Boston: Wilde Col., 1958).

Encyclopaedia Britannica, fifteenth ed. (Chicago: Encyclopaedia Britannica, 1985).

Ewen, David, *Complete Book of the American Musical Theater* (New York: Holt, Rinehart and Winston, 1965).

The Folk Song Abecedary, ed. James F. Leisy (New York: Hawthorn Books, 1966).

Fowke, Edith, and Joe Glazer, *Songs of Work and Freedom* (New York: Doubleday, 1960).

Franklin, Benjamin. *Poor Richard's Almanacks,* introduction by Van Wyck Brooks (New York: Paddington Press, 1976).

Fuld, James J., *The Book of World-Famous Music,* third ed. (New York: Dover, 1985).

Glazer, Tom, *Songs of Peace, Freedom and Protest* (New York: David McKay Co., 1971).

Gonzales, Rodolfo, *I Am Joaquin (New York: Bantam Books, 1972).*

Green, Stanley, The World of Musical Comedy (New York: Ziff-Davis Co., 1960).

Hand, Learned, *The Spirit of Liberty* (Chicago: University of Chicago Press, 1977).

Hard Hitting Songs for Hard-Hit People, compiled by Alan Lomax, notes by Woody Guthrie (New York: Oak Publications, 1967).

Heaps, Willard A., and Porter W. Heaps, *The Singing Sixties: The Spirit of Civil War Days Drawn from the Music of the Times* (Norman: University of Oklahoma Press, 1960).

Hofstadter, Richard, and Beatrice K. Hofstadter, *Great Issues in American History* (New York: Vintage Books, 1982).

Hom, Marlon K., *Songs of Gold Mountain: Cantonese Rhymes from San Francisco Chinatown* (Berkeley: University of California Press, 1987).

Island: Poetry and History of Chinese Immigrants on Angel Island, 1910–1940, translated by Him Mark Lai (San Francisco: San Francisco Study Center, 1980).

Jacob Riis Revisited, ed. Francis Cordasco (Garden City, N.Y.: Doubleday, 1968).

Johnson, James Weldon, *The Book of American Negro Spirituals* (New York: Viking Press, 1925).

Kang, Younghill, *East Goes West* (New York: Charles Scribner's Sons, 1937).

Klein, Joe, *Woody Guthrie: A Life* (New York: Random House, 1980).

Kobbe, Gustav, *Famous American Songs* (New York: Y. Crowell, 1906).

The Langston Hughes Reader (New York: George Braziller, 1958).

Laviera, Tato, *AmeRícan* (Houston: Arte Público Press, 1985).

Lawrence, Vera Brodsky, *Music for Patriots, Politicians, and Presidents: Harmonies and Discords of the First Hundred Years* (New York: Macmillan, 1975).

Longfellow, Henry Wadsworth, *Poems* (New York: Dutton, 1970).

Lowell, James Russell, *The Poetical Works of James Russell Lowell* (Boston: Houghton Mifflin, 1890).

McKay, Claude, *Selected Poems of Claude McKay* (New York: Bookman Associates, 1953).

Martin, Deac (C.T.), *Deac Martin's Book of Musical Americana* (Englewood Cliffs, N.J.: Prentice-Hall, 1970).

Miller, Alice Duer, *Selected Poems* (New York: Coward-McCann, 1949).

Millstein, Beth, and Jeanne Bodin, *We, the American Women: A Documentary History* (Chicago: Science Research Associates, 1977).

Modern Eloquence, ed. Ashley H. Thorndike, 10 vols. (New York: 1923).

Muir, John, *The Mountains of California* (New York: Century Co., 1894).

The Negro in Twentieth-Century America, ed. John Hope Franklin and Isidore Starr (New York: Random House, 1967).

The New Grove Dictionary of American Music, ed. H. Wiley Hitchcock and Stanley Sadie (New York: Macmillan, 1986).

No More Masks! An Anthology of Poems by Women, ed. Florence Howe and Ellen Bass (New York: Doubleday, 1973).

The Norton Anthology of Literature by Women, ed. Sandra M. Gilbert and Susan Gubar (New York: Norton, 1985).

Notable American Women, 1907–1950, ed. Edward T. James (Cambridge, Mass.: Harvard University Press, 1971).

The Oxford Companion to American Literature, ed. James D. Hart (New York: Oxford University Press, 1983).

The Papers of Woodrow Wilson, ed. Arthur S. Link (Princeton, N.J.: Princeton University Press, 1982).

The Penguin Book of American Folk Songs, ed. Alan Lomax (Baltimore: Penguin, 1964).

The Poetry of the Negro, 1746–1970, ed. Langston

Hughes and Arna Bontemps (Garden City. N.Y.: Doubleday, 1970).

The Presidents Speak: The Inaugural Addresses of the American Presidents from Washington to Nixon, annotated by Davis Newton Lott (New York: Holt, Rinehart and Winston, 1969).

The Reader's Encyclopedia of American Literature, ed. Max J. Herzberg (New York: Thomas Y. Crowell, 1962).

The Republic and the School: Horace Mann on the Education of Free Men, ed. Lawrence A. Cremin (New York: Teachers College Press, 1957).

The Rolling Stone Encyclopedia of Rock & Roll, ed. Jon Pareles and Patricia Romanowski (New York: Rolling Stone Press/Summit Books, 1983).

The Samuel Gompers Papers, ed. Stuart B. Kaufman (Urbana: University of Illinois Press, 1987).

Sanchez, Marta Ester, *Contemporary Chicana Poetry: A Critical Approach to an Emerging Literature* (Berkeley, Calif.: University of California Press, 1985).

Schlesinger, Arthur M., Jr., *Robert Kennedy and His Times* (Boston: Houghton Mifflin, 1978).

Seeger, Pete, and Bob Reiser, *Carry It On: A History in Song and Picture of the Working Men and Women of America* (New York: Simon & Schuster, 1985).

Shapiro, Karl, *Collected Poems: 1940–1978* (New York: Random House, 1978).

Shilts, Randy, *The Mayor of Castro Street* (New York: St. Martin's Press, 1982).

Songs of the Gilded Age, selected and arranged by Margaret Bradford Boni (New York: Golden Press, 1960).

The Songs We Sang: A Treasury of American Popular Music, ed. Theodore Raph (New York: Castle Books, 1964).

Sonneck, Oscar George Theodore, *Report on "The Star-Spangled Banner," "Hail, Columbia," "America," and "Yankee Doodle"* (New York: Dover, 1972; first ed., 1909).

Spaeth, Sigmund, *A History of Popular Music in America* (New York: Random House, 1948).

The Speeches of Daniel Webster and His Masterpieces, ed. B. F. Tefft (Philadelphia, 1854).

Stanton, Elizabeth Cady, Susan B. Anthony, and Matilda Joslyn Gage, *History of Woman Suffrage (1881–1922)* (New York: National American Women Suffrage Association, 1889–1922, 6 vols.).

Star-Spangled Books: Books, Sheet Music, News-papers, Manuscripts, and Persons Associated with "The Star-Spangled Banner," compiled by P. W. Filby and Edward G. Howard (Baltimore: Maryland Historical Society, 1972).

Stegner, Wallace, *The Sound of Mountain Water* (New York: Doubleday, 1969).

A Testament of Hope: The Essential Writings of Martin Luther King, Jr., ed. James Melvin Washington (New York: Harper & Row, 1986).

This Land Is Mine: An Anthology of American Verse, ed. Al Hine (New York: Lippincott, 1965).

Thoreau, Henry David, *Walden and Other Writings,* ed. Brooks Atkinson (New York: Random House, 1950).

A Treasury of Great American Letters: Our Country's Life & History in the Letters of Its Men & Women, selected by Charles and Eleanor Hurd (New York: Hawthorn Books, 1961).

A Treasury of Stephen Foster (New York: Random House, 1946).

A Treasury of the World's Great Speeches, ed. Houston Peterson (New York: Simon and Schuster, 1965).

The Truman Administration: A Documentary History, ed. Barton J. Bernstein and Allen J. Matusow (New York: Harper & Row, 1968).

Up from the Pedestal: Selected Writings in the History of American Feminism, ed. Aileen S. Kraditor (New York: Quadrangle, 1968).

Walker, Alice, *Good Night, Willie Lee, I'll See You in the Morning.* (New York: Dial Press, 1979).

Walt Whitman, selected, and with notes, by Mark Van Doren (New York: Viking Press, 1973).

Webster's New World Companion to English and American Literature, ed. Arthur Pollard (New York: World Publishing, 1973).

White, E. B., *One Man's Meat* (New York: Harper Bros. 1942).

Who's Who in America (New York: R. R. Bowker, 1988). 45th ed.

Who's Who in American Politics, eleventh ed. (New York: R. R. Bowker, 1987).

Woman of Her Word: Hispanic Women Write, ed. Evangelína Vigil (Houston: Arte Público Press, 1987).

Woodson, Carter G., *Negro Orators and Their Orations* (New York: Russell & Russell, 1925).

The World's Famous Orations, ed. William Jennings Bryan (New York: Funk and Wagnalls Co., 1906), Vol. VIII.

⭐ AUTHOR INDEX

The poem "I Am Joaquín" by Rodolfo Gonzales. Reprinted by permission of Nita Gonzales.

The poem "Stupid America" by Abelardo Delgado. Reprinted by permission of Abelardo Delgado.

The poem "Refugee Ship" (*Revista*—now *The Americas Review*—volume III, no. 1, 1975) by Lorna Dee Cervantes. The poem "AmeRícan" from *AmeRícan* (Arte Publico Press, University of Houston, 1985) by Tato Laviera. Both reprinted by permission of Arte Publico Press.

The poem "Nadine, resting on her neighbor's stoop" from *The Work of a Common Woman* by Judy Grahn. Copyright © 1978 by Judy Grahn. Reprinted by permission of The Crossing Press, Freedom, California 95019.

The speech "A City of Neighborhoods" by Harvey Milk. Copyright © 1978 by the Estate of Harvey Milk. All rights reserved. Reprinted by permission of the Estate of Harvey Milk.

Excerpts from an unfinished article here entitled The American Idea by Theodore H. White. Copyright © 1986 by the *New York Times*. Reprinted by permission of the *New York Times*.

PHOTO CREDITS